WALKING
WITH
PRESIDENTS

STORIES FROM INSIDE THE PERIMETER

Written by
Michael A. Endicott
United States Secret Service, Retired

ISBN: 1-4392-1975-3
EAN13: 9781439219751

Visit www.booksurge.com to order additional copies.

To my mother, Flora Endicott, 88, her sister, Yolanda Dunlap, 87, their brothers Guido Giorgetti, 94, and Medio Georgetti, 91, who all passed away during the writing of this book.

PROLOGUE

The Secret Service, founded in July 1865, originally was part of the Treasury Department and is now under Homeland Security. It is a unique law enforcement agency whose duties are not well known by many in the public at large. From its creation in 1865 to suppress rampant counterfeiting through today it has maintained its original charter of protecting the U.S. currency and performing other investigations at the direction of the president.

Over the last 143 years, protection of the currency has been expanded to include treasury notes, government-issued checks, various credit card and debit card frauds, and selected banking schemes. During the 1990s and early 2000s, the Secret Service's responsibilities were expanded to include telemarketing fraud prevention, identity theft, security at national special events, and computer fraud. Under the Patriot Act, the director of the Secret Service has established a nationwide electronic crimes task force to assist the law enforcement community, our public sector, and academia. On March 1, 2003, responsibility for the Secret Service was transferred from the Treasury Department to the Department of Homeland Security.

Presidential protection by the Secret Service began informally on a part-time basis with President Grover Cleveland in 1894 and continued with President William McKinley. In the aftermath of the assassination of President McKinley in September 1901, full-time protection of our presidents began with his replacement, Theodore Roosevelt. Most of the significant changes in the protective responsibilities of the Secret Service have evolved in the aftermath of the assassination of President John F. Kennedy on November 22, 1963.

This book chronicles my journey through life as a special agent of the United States Secret Service. Readers are provided a glimpse of what was going on in our country during the most tumultuous period of time of my life and possibly of the twentieth century. Major changes in the protective responsibilities and the size of the Secret Service in response to the assassination of President John F. Kennedy in 1963 in Dallas, Texas, have continued into the new millennium.

The journey began in Tacoma, Washington, where I was born and raised. My athletic skills were developed at the South End Boys Club under the guidance of Director Don Danielson. As my first mentor during one of the most formative times of my life, Danielson nurtured my leadership skills while demanding a high moral and ethical standard. In 1960 I was selected to receive the "Boy of the Year" award at the boys club. In 1961, my senior year at Lincoln High School, I was elected to the first teams of the Tacoma City League and the Capitol High School Basketball League. That same year the students at Lincoln High School voted me Athlete of the Year. This laid the groundwork for me to receive a basketball scholarship to St. Martin's College in Lacey, Washington, which paid for room, board, and books.

During a basketball trip to Fairbanks, Alaska, in 1963, I met and later married Virginia Nagle. Ginny's father, Fred Nagle, was a resident agent of the Secret Service in Anchorage, Alaska, at the time. In the aftermath of the Kennedy assassination and the Warren Report, and at the urging of my father-in-law, I decided to pursue a career in the United States Secret Service.

I took the Treasury Agents' Entrance Exam, passed a top secret full field background investigation, and instead of teaching biology and coaching basketball, I entered the Secret Service on July 5, 1965. The odyssey of the next twenty years with the Secret Service was absolutely unbelievable. To say it was interesting, exciting, unusual, and unique is an understatement.

Walking with Presidents gives readers a penetrating, inside look at my travels to over one hundred countries around the world and all fifty states. During my life's adventure I not only saw history from a distance but enjoyed watching it close up as I lived it. I served in Washington, D.C., assigned to Secretary of State Henry Kissinger in 1974 for two years. This led to an exposure to an interest in domestic and foreign policy activities, especially the Middle East war and Watergate scandal. The opportunity to observe firsthand the professional relationship between Nixon and Kissinger, two of the United States' great global strategic thinkers, was definitely a bonus.

My position as a member of the Secret Service presented me with a front row seat to world events from 1965–85. In fact, sometimes it was like watching a play from the wings. I was inside the perimeter.

Woven throughout my life's story is a glimpse at history, reasons for the growth of the Secret Service, and interesting and amusing stories about some of the people I protected and the battles I fought. This book is a collection of memories of my twenty years as I worked toward retirement. It gives insight into my retirement in 1985 and discussions with President Nixon as he became the first president in our history to give up his government-provided Secret Service detail. A new world opened up to me when the former president hired me to provide private security, make travel arrangements for him and Mrs. Nixon, work as a staff assistant, and became his friend.

A good portion of my book is about the thirty-seven Th president of the United States, Richard Nixon. He is an enigma to just about everyone. Much has been written about Nixon's life as a leader, politician, foreign policy guru, and, of course, his involvement in the Watergate scandal.

The broad spectrum of the life of Richard Nixon has not been covered by many writers, historians, family, friends, and others. There is very little recorded that deals with Nixon as a person, husband, father, grandfather, and friend. My relationship with President Nixon, Mrs. Nixon, and their daughters, Tricia and Julie, evolved over my years as a member of the Presidential Protective Division of the United States Secret Service in 1969 to agent in charge of the former president's detail in 1979. His close interaction with the few who were nearest to him was jealously protected by them during their lifetime, creating a vacuum of information.

Upon my retirement in August 1985, I became a special assistant on Nixon's staff. I was there when Nixon become president, fell from power, resigned in disgrace, and exiled himself to San Clemente, California. I never dreamed I would join him as he resurrected his public life while he enjoyed his twilight years with his family and friends.

When Nixon gave up his Secret Service detail and hired me privately, he put me on his personal payroll to assume responsibility for his and Mrs. Nixon's safety. For over five years I traveled with him, mostly privately, throughout the United States and around the world. My role as staff assistant, security agent, driver, repairman, cook, confidant, and traveling companion paved the way for us to become close personal friends. The roles of Secret Service agent, staff assistant, and friend offered a unique and unusual opportunity to observe him and his family from both outside and within. Living inside the Nixon family allowed me to see a Richard and Pat Nixon no one outside the family ever has.

During my twenty-year Secret Service career and my private role with President Nixon, I observed and learned a great deal. My assignments and global travels influenced my views of the United

States and the world. These included the 1968 and 1972 presidential campaigns and an eighteen-month assignment with Henry Kissinger.

Workings as operations supervisor for Rockefeller and Mondale offered an opportunity for me use my operations and logistical skills to develop cost-effective procedures for vice presidential travel and budget analysis.

Moving Nixon from California to New York and then to New Jersey presented a close-up look at his coming out and resurrection after Watergate. When I hand delivered his letter declining continued Secret Service protection to the office of Secretary of the Treasury James Baker in January 1985, it marked an historical moment in Secret Service presidential protection. Assuming private responsibility for the protection of Richard Nixon, one of the most controversial presidents of our time, was without question a challenge. Since 1965, when the Secret Service assumed responsibility for the protection of former presidents, no one had ever provided private protection to a former president. Currently all former presidents have Secret Service protection.

Throughout the journey of the past thirty-five-plus years, I have often asked myself, "Why me? Why have I been so fortunate to have lived such an interesting and exciting life?"

It is time to share some answers to these questions so my children and grandchildren know who I am and what I did. I can do this best through my stories and insights into Secret Service operations, presidents, the White House, State Department, and some of the men and women with whom I worked. This opportunity, to preserve and share stories of the personal sides of the historical events and distinguished people I had the good fortune to protect and get to know, is one I knew I must not miss.

WALKING WITH PRESIDENTS

CHAPTER ONE

AMERICA UNDER FIRE
1965 - 1973

AMERICA UNDER FIRE 1965-1973

The assassination of President John F. Kennedy in Dallas, Texas, on November 22, 1963, was the first tragedy in a string of violence that would span more than a decade in the United States. President Lyndon B. Johnson selected Earl Warren, Chief Justice of the Supreme Court, to head the Commission on the Assassination of President Kennedy (commonly known as the Warren Commission). By executive order the investigation began on November 29, 1963. The Warren Commission Report was published on September 27, 1964. The conclusion of the commission in the report was that Lee Harvey Oswald acted alone without accomplices in the assassination of President Kennedy. There were almost a dozen recommendations in the report. Some concerned oversight of the Secret Service, while others called for the overhaul and improvement of intelligence gathering, motorcade security, and coordination between the FBI and other federal agencies.

In the end, the commission's report raised as many questions as it answered. Conspiracy theorists, especially, would question the results of the comprehensive investigation. Some felt the investigation was flawed from the beginning. Was the purpose of the investigation to prove Oswald shot President Kennedy or to find out who shot the president?

Over the next twenty to twenty-five years, numerous books and articles would be written questioning the findings of the report. Movies and television specials presented other views of the tragic event. The print media has written thousands of stories about the assassination. However, all the stories, reviews, and perspectives would resolve nothing. All the reporting and theories frankly added to the confusion, simply throwing more gas on the fire. In the aftermath of Kennedy's death, a new genre of media members, the investigative reporters, was born.

In the end, the Warren Commission Report probably created as much controversy as any commission report in my lifetime. In fact, today, over forty years after the assassination of President Kennedy, there seem to be so many unanswered questions. Who actually assassinated Kennedy? Was it Lee Harvey Oswald or the Russian KGB? Perhaps Cuban security or the Mafia was responsible? Or did the CIA or the FBI cause his death? The Warren Commission said Oswald acted alone, and since the report was issued in 1964 no one has proved otherwise.

❖ ❖ ❖

The Civil Rights Act, which Congress had been encouraged to pass by President Kennedy, was enacted in 1964. It would become the cornerstone of President Johnson's Great Society. Johnson would pursue other legislation to improve the quality of our lives. Aid to education, fighting disease, new medicines, roadside beautification, conservation and urban renewal, crime and delinquency control, and removing obstacles to the right to vote were among the components of Johnson's new Great Society.

Some states, however, began passing acts to try to circumvent the new laws. California enacted Proposition 14 as a move to block the fair housing components of the Civil Rights Act. That enactment, along with others, created anguish in the inner cities. Race relations were undergoing dramatic changes in dividing our country. Feelings of injustice and despair were eroding our black communities in the large inner cities. Malcolm X, a black activist, Muslim minister, ex-convict, and community leader, was assassinated in New York City at the Audubon Ballroom on February 21, 1965, as he was beginning a speech. America was being torn apart by divergent views of race relations, and the violence associated with it was beginning to be a part of the political process.

Blacks in the Los Angeles area were especially frustrated by the inability to find relief from their lives of poverty with the passage of the 1964 Civil Rights Act. On August 11, 1965, a routine traffic stop in South Central Los Angeles turned out to be the match that lit the fuse starting the "Watts riots." Six days of rioting left thirty-four dead, over a thousand people injured, nearly four thousand arrested, and hundreds of buildings destroyed. A commission appointed by California Governor Pat Brown concluded that the riots weren't random acts of violence. The commission identified the cause as much deeper social problems: the high jobless rate in the inner city, poor housing, and bad schools.

The 1964 Civil Rights Act weighed heavily on our citizens, splitting and polarizing our great country. Governors from the South such as Lester Maddox and George Wallace built their careers on hate and fear of blacks. Two black Americans, Rosa Parks, who in 1955 refused to ride in the back of the bus, and civil rights activist Medgar Evers, who was denied admittance to the University of Mississippi's Law School in 1954, led the initial fight for black Americans. Evers was killed in June 1963 at age thirty-eight by white Supremacist Byron De La Beckwith, who after his third trial in 1994 was convicted and sentenced to prison for life.

Because of her courage in standing up to racism, Rosa Parks was dubbed by Congress the "Mother of the Modern-Day Civil Rights Movement." As a result of her civil disobedience, arrest, and trial she became a living icon of the movement. Rosa Parks died in 2006 at 93. Both Evers and Parks stood up to the racial hatred and violence of the 1950s and '60s. Great leaders, black and white, rose to the top of their causes and helped our country through the turbulent, uncharted waters of the early civil rights movement. John F. Kennedy and Martin Luther King Jr. were among the many that greatly impacted American lives by negotiating the hate and anger of their times. Though neither is here today due to their separate assassinations, their presence still has a profound effect on many of our citizens.

Overseas the United States was routinely portrayed as the "Ugly American." In response to two allegedly unprovoked attacks by a North Vietnamese torpedo boat against the USS Maddox and the USS C. Turner Joy on August 4, 1964, the Gulf of Tonkin Resolution was passed by our Congress on August 7, 1964. It turned out only one attack occurred as the USS Maddox was conducting intelligence operations that were shared with the South Vietnamese military. President Johnson and later President Richard Nixon would use the resolution to pursue military action against the North Vietnamese in Southeast Asia.

Many of our youth eagerly volunteered to join the military service, while others were drafted. Some received deferments by going to college or getting married and having children. The Vietnam War was beginning to take larger and larger numbers of our young men. College campuses were beginning to react; Mario Savio, a member of the Student Nonviolent Coordinating Committee, began the "free speech" movement on the University of California campus in Berkeley, California, during a speech at Sproul Plaza on December 2, 1964.

In the mid-1960s our country was in the early days of the transition from supporting the war in Vietnam to the anti-war rhetoric and violence of the late 1960s and early '70s. Flower Children were sprouting up all over, drugs were becoming an everyday part of the lives of our younger generation, and "baby boomers" were marching through our schools. Anti-war sentiment in our colleges and universities manifested itself in marches, rioting, and other forms of unrest. "Draft dodgers" fleeing to Canada were assisted by anti-war support groups.

Six months after Savio's speech, I graduated from St. Martin's College in Lacey, Washington, and in July I found myself settling in Sacramento, California, to go to work for our government.

❖ ❖ ❖

Meanwhile, growing frustration over the war in Vietnam and the 1964 Civil Rights Act was spreading rapidly across our country. The anti-war movement and the hate segment of our country spawned many radical fringe groups. These included Students for a Democratic Society (SDS), in 1960, the Black Panthers and the Student Nonviolent Coordinating Committee (SNCC) in 1967. The Weatherman faction of the SDS became the ultra-radical Weather Underground in 1968. The Symbionese Liberation Army (SLA) came on the scene in 1973. The Weather Underground advocated the violent overthrow of our government and was responsible for several bombings and deaths.

The Ku Klux Klan, the John Birch Society, and other anti-Communist and anti-tax groups' activities during the 1960s and '70s added to the government's woes. The FBI was busy in the late '60s with surveillance and the penetration of many radical and subversive groups. Informants were extensively used by the government to try to keep track of these growing factions in our rapidly changing country.

On the international scene, the Middle East was becoming a pressure cooker as terrorist groups such as the Palestinian Liberation Organization (PLO) and the Popular Front for the Liberation of Palestine (PFLP) were turning their guns and bombs on Israeli citizens. Their leaders, Yassar Arafat and Dr. George Habash, had become household names in the intelligence community. Israel, Syria, and Egypt were beginning a new journey of bloodshed with a war that started in the 1940s and continues today. Libya, Iran, Iraq, and Saudi Arabia, along with other radical Arab states in the region, would join together to control the flow of oil from the region and finance the support of the growing terrorist groups. After taking over Libya in September 1969 through a military coup, Col. Moammor Kadahfi raised terrorism to a new level. He introduced state-sponsored global terrorism. I want to welcome readers to the violent world in which I began serving as a special agent with the United States Secret Service in 1965.

❖ ❖ ❖

When I grew up in Tacoma, Washington, my first job in 1956 at age twelve was at the front desk of the South End Boys Club checking out ping-pong equipment, pool cues, and board games, making twenty-five cents per hour. Director Don Danielson was my first mentor. He had a unique way of getting club members to take advantage of the facility. He challenged everyone to work hard whether they were playing on a team, working in the shop, or playing games. In the fall of 1960, during my senior year at Lincoln High School, I was truly surprised when I was unexpectedly named "Boy of the Year" at the South End Boys Club. At the end of the basketball season at Lincoln, in the spring of 1961, I was selected to the Tacoma All-City Basketball first team and the Capitol League first team.

In April, my friend from South Tacoma, Jim Sims, recruited me to attend St. Martin's College, a small Benedictine liberal arts institution in nearby Lacey, Washington. Sims was on the basketball team and introduced me to athletic director and basketball coach Art Acuff. I was awarded a full scholarship to play basketball. At the time, St. Martin's had an old dilapidated building on the lower campus with a gym not suitable for college basketball practice. We practiced daily at the Olympia Armory and played our home games at the North Thurston High School gym.

In the spring of 1962, when baseball season began at St. Martin's, I decided to join the team and played third base. During this time I ran for student body president, urging the administration to build a field house for basketball and other activities. Even though I lost, a lot of interest in a new athletic facility was generated by my candidacy. Over the next two years a plan was put together by the college to erect a new field house/convention center.

I arrived at St. Martin's for my sophomore year to find I was listed in *Who's Who in American Colleges and Universities*. During the summer a new basketball coach was hired, Jerry Vermillion. He was one of the greatest players to attend Gonzaga University in Spokane, Washington. Fifty-five years later Vermillion still holds the season record for the most rebounds in a career of 1,670. Playing point guard on the basketball team for Coach Vermillion, I enjoyed a leadership role and developed my overall skills. In the spring I again played baseball, and playing centerfield, stealing bases, and hitting over .300 put me in a leadership role on the team.

In December 1963 I married Virginia Nagle whom I had met on a basketball trip to Fairbanks, Alaska, while play the University of Alaska. In the spring of 1964 Athletic Director Art Acuff asked me if I would manage the baseball team as well as play. He told me since I was on a full scholarship for basketball he could not give me anything additional. I agreed to the new role, but wondered "Why me?" as we had a number of players on the team who were seniors. This was the first of many times over the next thirty years I would ask that question, "Why me?"

❖ ❖ ❖

My life began to change in the spring of 1964 when my father-in-law, Fred Nagle, who was the Secret Service resident in charge of their office in Anchorage, Alaska, suggested I might want to look into the Secret Service as a career. He mentioned that the Secret Service was going to be hiring a large number of agents in response to recommendations made by the Warren Commission. At his urging, I took the United States Treasury Agents Law Enforcement Examination the summer of 1964.

My senior year at St. Martin's began with me student teaching a biology class at Olympia High School in Olympia, Washington. Teaching biology and coaching basketball had for a long time been my goal in life. However, after passing the Secret Service exam, I was invited to the Seattle field office in the fall for an interview. A full background investigation followed that cleared me for employment with the Secret Service by the spring of 1965. I was excited about the opportunity to join the most elite law enforcement group in the world.

Right after my graduation from St. Martin's in late May, my wife and I and our five-month-old son, Michael, moved to Tacoma, thirty miles north. Less than two weeks after the relocation I received notice from the United States Secret Service to report to Sacramento, California, on July 5 for duty. To say I was elated is an understatement. During the last week of June my wife Ginny and I loaded all our possessions into our car and a rental U-Haul trailer. We departed with Michael to make the 850-mile drive from Tacoma, Washington, to Sacramento, California. Fortunately, we quickly found a completely furnished three-bedroom apartment with a swimming pool located in West Sacramento. It was only three miles from the downtown Sacramento Federal Court House, where I would be working.

❧ ❧ ❧

Little did I realize the unique journey that had started as I drove to Sacramento. Because Monday, July 5th was a federal holiday, agent

Larry Sheafe and I were sworn in before Federal Judge Sherrill Halbert in his federal court office on Tuesday the 6th. With the official swearing-in ceremony at the court house over my on-the-job training began. Special Agent-in-Charge Steve Byrne provided guidance and coordinated the training. The first few weeks were spent in the office reading the Secret Service manual, the Warren Commission Report on the assassination of President John F. Kennedy, and getting to know other federal and local law enforcement officers. Trips to the firing range allowed me to handle a gun for the first time in my life and to qualify with my government issued .38 caliber Colt revolver. Agents Gary Miller and Hugh Pettit, hired only months before agent Larry Sheafe and me, were a great help to me during the training period. Miller, Pettit, and Sheafe were graduates of the Law Enforcement School at Sacramento State College. Agents Miller and Pettit had already spent twelve weeks at the Treasury Law Enforcement Training School in Washington, D.C., and would soon attend United States Secret Service Training School, also in Washington, D.C.

Formal training for me began in the fall of 1965 with twelve weeks in Washington at Treasury School. The courses included criminal law, arrest procedures, interrogations, finger printing, photography, shooting, and physical training. I returned to the office and worked with Sheafe, Miller, and Pettit, developing techniques taught in school.

My eight-week Secret Service Training School in the spring of 1966 focused on protection-related activities and also included specific courses on check forgery, counterfeiting, and threats against people protected by the Secret Service. The physical training and weapons training were much more comprehensive than at the treasury training school. They were completed by the summer of 1966.

❧ ❧ ❧

Armed with my Secret Service issue .38 Colt, handcuffs, Secret Service five-star marshal's badge, official identification, and government-issued briefcase, I headed out alone to protect our currency and support the various protective responsibilities of the U.S. Secret Service. The next two years were spent mainly working criminal cases involving counterfeiting of our currency as well as forgery of U.S. government checks and U.S. Savings Bonds.

Most of my weekends were free the first two and a half years. I generally was able to spend time relaxing with my family, which had grown with the birth of our daughters, Robin and Leslie. The swimming pool at our apartment complex was our favorite pastime activity. Michael loved the pool, first jumping off the diving board with a small float around his waist when he was only eighteen months old. He especially enjoyed the wading pool, where he would hold his breath to see how long he could stay on the bottom. Ginny and I would sit nearby in lounge chairs surveying the scene. Once, a new neighbor came walking by the wading pool. She saw Michael on the bottom. Looking around, she did not realize that Ginny and I were tending to our son on the bottom of the pool and jumped into the pool fully clothed. As she lifted Michael off the bottom and out of the pool she realized we were watching him. The concern on her face was replaced with a big smile, as she said, "He can swim, can't he?"

Sacramento had wonderful parks with playground equipment, rides, walking trails, and ducks and geese to feed. Ginny and I also made several trips a year to the Seattle/Tacoma area of Washington State to visit family and friends. Before departing we would put one of our crib mattresses on the back seat of our car, forming a playpen/bed. Seat belts were not required back in the late 1960s and most cars did not have them. By departing after work between 4 and 5 p.m., the children slept for much of the trip. We usually drove straight through to the Northwest, making the trip in fourteen to sixteen hours.

❖ ❖ ❖

The late summer of 1967 found me working a protective assignment at Hearst Castle in San Simeon, California, which had been built by newspaper mogul William Randolph Hearst in 1945. The 165-room castle was built atop 127 acres near Highway One overlooking the Pacific Ocean halfway between San Francisco and Los Angeles. The first lady, Lady Bird Johnson, was attending a dedication ceremony celebrating the transfer of part of the Hearst Castle facility to the State of California. During the visit I was assigned to assist San Francisco Field Office agent Larry Newman, who was the Intelligence (ID) agent for the visit. After parking my car in an assigned area, I approached the gate at the bottom of the hill leading to the castle to report to Newman. He was engaged in a pissing contest with the local FBI liaison agent assigned to assist San Francisco Field Office agent Larry Newman, who was the Intelligence (ID) agent for the visit.

The FBI, on the other hand, was responsible by statute for investigating attacks on all government officials, including people protected by the Secret Service. The FBI liaison agent wanted to be positioned atop the hill at the castle, near where the event was taking place. Newman knew he had the final say and knew it was very unlikely there would be an incident involving the first lady. After several minutes of arguing with each other, Newman ended the confrontation by announcing to the FBI agent, "Stay here at the gate." Turning away from the agent, Newman motioned for me to get in his official car and we drove up the hill to the castle. On the ride he briefed me on the evening's activities. When we parked the car, Newman gave me a quick tour of the facility while we waited for the first lady to arrive.

The problem of overlapping jurisdiction with the FBI was later corrected when the statutory authority of the Secret Service was revised, giving the Secret Service sole responsibility for investigating attacks on the people they protected.

After the arrival of Mrs. Johnson the gala ceremony began with a woman's synchronized swimming group performing in a large outdoor pool with a waterfall at one end. While the swimmers performed, the first lady and guests sipped their California champagne with an oversized fresh California strawberry in each glass. Later, after a lavish dinner, the first lady spoke eloquently about the need for support of our natural resources and about her national beautification program. My evening ended as the limousine carrying Lady Bird Johnson departed the castle grounds for her government aircraft a short drive away. Due to the lateness of the evening and the remote location, Newman had arranged for us to stay overnight at the Hearst Castle. I was assigned to sleep in a four-poster bed in one of the small bedrooms inside the castle.

My first protective assignment in support of President Johnson was at El Toro Marine Air Station in Southern California on Veteran's Day, 1967. President Johnson was visiting El Toro to greet returning Vietnam veterans. Today, over thirty-seven years later, that November day is still etched in my mind. Along with several of my colleagues from the Sacramento office, I reported to El Toro the afternoon before the visit of President Johnson for briefing and post assignments. The next morning over thirty agents reported to their security post on the El Toro ramp several hours prior to the scheduled arrival of the commander-in-chief. It was my responsibility to secure the immediate area, where the president would review and greet the troops returning from Vietnam.

The Southern California sky was typically clear that Monday morning. The bright sun began to cast a warm glow as we reported for assignment; there was no question it was going to be a beautiful, warm afternoon on the ramp for our returning Marines.

As I stood on that hard, noisy, sun-baked ramp, not knowing what to expect, the first of many planes full of returning combat-hardened veterans landed. Many of those disembarking were probably twenty or older, but so many appeared to be younger. Seeing these young warriors, veterans of the jungles of Vietnam, walking on the ramp area, I was stunned, really taken aback by their youthful appearance. These were the young men fighting in Vietnam that were the main focus of nightly news broadcasts. Each evening in living color, scenes of the Vietnam War were repeated. ABC, CBS, and NBC brought to all of us vivid, real pictures of death and destruction. Sadly, prime time news programs brought into our living rooms pictures of "body bags" with our friends, loved ones and neighbors, all heroes, being evacuated. The media announced not only the numbers of deaths we suffered that day but also the numbers of the enemy killed. The media had somehow developed the enemy body count as their barometer of how the war was going.

In addition to the war scenes, we were being inundated by TV reports and pictures of growing anti-war sentiments here at home. In living color on ABC, CBS, and NBC extreme radical demonstrators were shown burning our flag while they waved the flag of the North Vietnamese. They were waving the flag of our enemy, who were killing our sons, brothers, fathers, friends, and neighbors. These radical activists proudly parading under the Viet Cong flag carrying posters of Hollywood actress "Hanoi Jane" Fonda sitting on an anti-aircraft artillery gun used to shoot down our aircraft in North Vietnam, all the time chanting, screaming, "One, two, three, four, we don't want your f—ing war."

On this day at El Toro Marine Air Station there would be no anti-war demonstrators, no flag burnings, no enemy flags waved in front of our Marines and their loved ones. The public at the reception for our returning hero warriors would be comprised mainly of families, friends, loved ones, and supporters of our military. Demonstrators were only allowed to mass far away near one of the entrances to the base, out of sight of our returning troops.

Surveying the returning Marines relaxing in the warm sun on the ramp at the El Toro Marine Air Station waiting for the president was a very emotional time for me. It was a great honor for our returning fighting men to be greeted by their Commander-in-Chief. It was difficult to believe these young men had spent a year in combat in the jungles of Southeast Asia. These hard warriors knew it would be a two hour wait for their President. Many of the veterans moved into a comfortable, relaxing squat that they had perfected while resting and waiting in the jungles of Vietnam. Smiling and joking, they spoke quietly with each other, while cigarette smoke curled over their heads and vanished. My mouth became dry and my eyes welled up as I realizing during their tour of duty they had attacked and been under attack. While under fire, they saw their comrades fall, making the ultimate sacrifice.

Looking out at the scene of our troops awaiting the arrival of their president, I thought over and over, "So young, so brave." Standing there, my college years flashed before my eyes. While I was attending classes, serving as captain of the basketball team and player/manager of the baseball team, raising Michael, and working a part-time job, men like these had been in the jungles of Vietnam fighting for their lives, fighting for our freedom. They were fighting to prevent the "Domino Theory," the predicted fall of Southeast Asia to Communism (one country at a time). I thought about those that came home in the long, black, zippered body bags.

If not for a quirk of fate whereby the Secret Service had become my chosen profession, after my graduation from St. Martin's College in 1965, I could very well be wearing a uniform, crouched on that ramp. Or I could have been one of 58,159 names on the Vietnam War Memorial in Washington, D.C., when it was dedicated in 1982. However, Sacramento, California, was now my home. Unlike the young men now standing erect near me preparing for their commander to deplane, I had not served in the military. First there had been the deferment for college and later the Secret Service was placed on the Department of Labor's exempted list. As I stood my post on that hot Memorial Day I had just turned twenty-four years old. I was so proud of those young men, waiting for their commander-in-chief to greet them, to recognize them.

Upon the arrival of Air Force One, President Johnson paused at the top of the stairs looking out at his troops. He walked down the stairs with his eyes fixed on the battle-hardened warriors. The young men, aged beyond their years, stood erect, as rigid as steel beams, chins tucked in tight and heads held high. The electricity of the moment could be felt in the air by everyone. Though I have no recollection of what the president said or how long he spoke, I am sure he thanked and comforted our returning heroes.

As Air Force One disappeared into the sky the event came to an end. Few if any of us on the ramp that day really understood the turmoil that would grip our military, our government, and our people over the next five years. Unfortunately these young men and those that followed would find a public increasingly questioning our country's involvement in the war. They would see a public becoming divided. Our heroes would feel the sting of a country that would no longer continue to support them or receive them proudly. The growing anti-war movement, emboldened by larger citizen turnouts, not only turned against our government, but sadly against those serving so nobly, so bravely. At day's end I better understood and respected the invincibility projected by the youth of our great nation. Unfortunately, I began to resent those that had dishonored our young men with their unpatriotic acts. They dishonored men whose only sin was to fight and in some cases to die in service of their country. They died for the freedom that allowed others to disrespect them.

❊ ❊ ❊

It was truly saddening for me to see the split embroiling our great country. One of my younger brothers, Jim, was an outspoken peace activist at the time. Though he opposed the Vietnam War, he would not go to Canada as so many of his generation did. Instead, Jim bravely served a tour in Vietnam in 1970. Today, my brother Jim is retired and was an outstanding educator. He is continually recognized in his profession by his students, peers, and parents as a superbly accomplished educator of gifted children. My brother taught at Clarkmoor Elementary School on Fort Lewis army base just outside of our home town of Tacoma, Washington. He continues to be an outspoken peace activist, opposed to the conflicts and wars our government embarks upon. It is his right. He fought for it. He earned it and I love him for it. Jim and I have maintained a very close relationship in spite of our divergent views on politics and foreign policy. On occasions we continue to have heated discussions, always ending with a hug, understanding a free and open society is a great place to live.

❊ ❊ ❊

Shortly after the trip to El Toro I headed for a two-week assignment in Washington, D.C, at Protective Intelligence Division. A group of us were brought in to review some files and help prepare them for entry into a new database developed by the Secret Service. I flew back to Sacramento on Thanksgiving Day. In those days when an agent flew commercial, he or she was required to tell the airline agent at the gate that he/she was carrying a weapon and notify the pilot personally upon entering the aircraft. Shortly after takeoff one of the stewardesses came to my seat in coach class and said I was being upgraded to first class. Entering the front section of the plane, I noticed there was no one in any of the seats. The stewardess showed me to a seat and said they needed someone in their section and hoped I would not mind. Talk about a first class flight; the stewardess kept changing, but one sat with me almost the entire flight. We chatted, played cards, and I had a wonderful meal. Since I was armed, I was not served any liquor. However, upon landing in San Francisco, where I changed planes for the flight to Sacramento, I was given an unopened bottle of scotch and a bag full of macadamia nuts for my Thanksgiving dinner by the cabin crew.

I was fortunate to remain in Sacramento for the remainder of the year. A quick trip home allowed me to have Christmas in the Northwest. The New Year would bring dramatic changes to the Secret Service and my calm life in the Sacramento Field Office.

❖ ❖ ❖

In 1961, when John F. Kennedy replaced Dwight Eisenhower as president, some on Kennedy's senior staff expressed concern to him about former President Eisenhower's adjustment to private life. It seems that when Eisenhower left office there was little official government support for former presidents. Former President Harry Truman, upon leaving office, worked out of his presidential library in Independence, Missouri, on a daily basis.

The rumor in the Secret Service was that Eisenhower had a full staff for such a prolonged period of time that there was concern he would not be able to run his office. Among other things, Eisenhower had not placed a phone call on his own for years and did not know about area codes. Kennedy's staff began working on legislation to provide some type of governmental support for former presidents. The legislation had not been completed when he was assassinated.

After the tragic death of Kennedy, President Johnson directed his presidential staff to continue the project begun under Kennedy. Working with Congress, the White House drafted legislation that would provide both administrative and security support to former presidents. In December 1965 this legislation was enacted. Among other things, the Secret Service was directed to protect former presidents and their spouses during their lifetimes and minor children until age sixteen. Former Presidents Truman and Eisenhower immediately received full Secret Service details for themselves and their spouses.

❖ ❖ ❖

In January 1968, I began a four-month temporary assignment to Palm Desert, California, in support of former President Eisenhower's detail. Ike and Mamie Eisenhower would annually travel to a friend's home in Palm Desert at the Palm Desert Country Club in January and return to their Gettysburg, Pennsylvania, farm in May. The Eisenhower detail routinely requested field support for the four-to-five-month stay in the desert. For me the assignment was like winning the lotto, as I was allowed to take my family with me. Three years after the enactment of the legislation, Ginny and I loaded up our car with our three children, Michael, Robin, and Leslie, and drove to Palm Desert, California, for an extended stay. Before departing Sacramento I was given the name of a realtor, provided by the Eisenhower detail, to assist us in finding a furnished, temporary residence. We were able to move into our temporary quarters the day we arrived in Palm Desert.

Former President Eisenhower had an office at the Palm Desert Country Club, where they were staying. He normally visited his office Monday through Friday. One agent (usually agent Jerry Terry) drove him to his office at 8 a.m. Not the least bit pretentious, President Eisenhower participated occasionally in local events. I did the security advance when he made an appearance at the new Canyon Country Club in Palm Springs at a fund-raiser sponsored by television actor Chuck Connors.

President Eisenhower also enjoyed very much getting together with some of his old friends to play cards. The favorite site for the card game was at billionaire publisher Walter Annenberg's winter estate, Sunnylands, in nearby Rancho Mirage. The Sunnylands mansion, 36,000 square feet, was built on Annenberg's private eighteen-hole golf course. There were ponds, many stocked with fish.

Eisenhower, who liked occasional pool parties at his residence on the golf course with some of his card-playing friends, was known for his cooking skills, especially barbecuing. In fact, there is reported to be a picture of him in the National Archives cooking a steak on the roof of the White House. Though I did not see it firsthand, I was told that sometimes when he entertained in Palm Desert he cooked the steaks on charcoal right on the concrete patio near the pool.

Mrs. Eisenhower did a lot of reading and relaxing at the desert retreat. She occasionally went out for hair appointments and shopping. Unlike her husband, Mrs. Eisenhower enjoyed being accompanied by a small cadre of Secret Service agents. Normally this meant four agents accompanied her, a limousine with a driver and supervisor and a follow-up car with a driver and accompanying agent.

❖ ❖ ❖

Both President and Mrs. Eisenhower took time to personally meet all the agents and their families. They hosted a special get-together where all agents and their families were present. Ginny, the kids, and I had the good fortune to attend one such gathering before former President Eisenhower had his heart attack in March 1968.

The temporary assignment to Palm Desert was really a great assignment for the Endicott family. My per diem covered most of our normal living expenses in Palm Desert. This allowed us to pay our normal bills and save a little money from my regular paycheck. The manager of my apartment complex in Sacramento agreed to give me a substantial reduction in rent for the time I was away. Work with the Eisenhower detail was normally forty hours a week with two days off. Ginny, Michael, Robin, Leslie, and I had many sightseeing adventures in the area.

Palm Springs, which was a small blip on the map at the time, had not been "discovered" yet and tourism had not become the life blood of this community. Usually when we made excursions into the desert we saw very few people. The countryside was arid but pristine with much to see. Joshua Tree National Park, part of the Mojave Desert northeast of Palm Desert, was visited on several occasions. We entered the park through Cottonwood Springs Oasis, which for centuries had been inhabited by the Cahuilla Indians. Cottonwood Springs Oasis had been an important stopover for prospectors and others on their way to and from the mines in the north as was the nearby Lost Oasis. Seven miles up the road from the Cottonwood Springs Oasis was the southern entrance to the national park. A car tour through the park provided many opportunities for stops where our family could get out and see the trees, cacti, and other desert life. When walking on foot it was important to be very careful to stay on the trails. Some cactuses dropped long, thin spikes that could penetrate the soles of tennis shoes.

Our family visited other parks and some recreational sites in the area, including the largest lake in California, the Salton Sea. The salty lake was only a short drive from Palm Desert. Though the Salton Sea does not have as high a concentration of salt as the Dead Sea in Israel or the Great Salt Lake in Utah, the salinity made it much easier to float on top of the water.

❖ ❖ ❖

The news of a pending sandstorm was soon buzzing through the detail. It would be the first sandstorm of the season since we arrived in Palm Desert and was predicted to hit the area during my days off. Agents from the Eisenhower detail familiar with past sandstorms warned those of us that were new to the detail to keep doors and windows tightly shut during the storm. We were told rooms or cars could rapidly fill with sand through even a tiny opening if the windows and doors were not tightly closed. We were also advised that on some occasions sandstorms could damage the windshields of cars. My wife and I decided to leave before the storm arrived and go sightseeing for two days. When we got back we found I had inadvertently left a window in the bathroom open about half an inch. There must have been three buckets of sand on the floor, counter, and in the bathtub. So much for paying attention to detail; I was embarrassed as I cleaned up the mess.

❖ ❖ ❖

Ginny nervously recalls the time when we returned from a weekend excursion and she spied a large hairy tarantula on the ceiling in our living room. I was busy unpacking the car and had not noticed the big, venomous spider. Being a strongly independent woman, Ginny managed to get the spider down onto the rug with the broom and squashed it with a towel before telling me about it. When she showed me the dead spider I was relieved she had disposed of it before it had a chance to bite anyone. Although a tarantula bite is very painful, it is not deadly; however, I was sure a visit to the emergency room at the local hospital would be required if one of the children were bitten. Throughout the rest of our stay in the rental house we kept our eyes open for spiders, but fortunately never saw another one.

❖ ❖ ❖

When President Eisenhower suffered his second heart attack in March 1968 (his first heart attack was in 1955 while president), he was transported to the hospital at March Air Force Base for treatment. The drive to the Air Force base hospital was about one hour. Once there I found myself working alone on the midnight shift, which I enjoyed. Everything was fairly routine and consisted of sitting, listening, watching, and talking. I sat next to the monitoring equipment hooked up to President Eisenhower, listened for an alarm to signal a problem, watched the monitor registering his heart beat, and talked with the nurse, learning about heart attacks and how to read the monitor.

The regular Eisenhower detail agents worked the day shift at the hospital and continued the normal twenty-four-hour coverage of Mrs. Eisenhower. The former first lady made daily visits to see her husband. Due to the requirement for the detail to establish a second base of operations at March Air Force Base, all days off were cancelled.

I felt I was lucky because I had the morning and afternoon to do things with my family and could get my normal four or five hours sleep before driving to the air base for duty.

❖ ❖ ❖

Leslie was only seven months old and of course has no memories of the desert; however, Michael, who was three-and-a-half and Robin, who was a year younger, had an especially wonderful time during the almost five months we lived in Palm Desert. Because of pictures we took and stories we told, to this day both of them remember the two ducks we bought for them during the Easter season. Gomer and Sally were the names we helped them select for their pets. They both enjoyed holding, chasing, and feeding their ducks. While I traveled daily to March Air Force Base, the ducks became the focus of Michael and Robin's lives. We continued to take short day trips to parks in the area and sightseeing drives. Sometimes Gomer and Sally accompanied us on our short day trips.

❖ ❖ ❖

A tragedy of enormous impact on our country occurred on April 4, 1968. Reverend Martin Luther King Jr., a Baptist minister and founder of the Southern Christian Leadership Conference (SCLC), was assassinated by James Earl Ray at the Motel Lorraine in Atlanta, Georgia. Reverend King had been globally recognized at the time of his death for his vocal leadership of the Civil Rights Movement. He had received both the Nobel Peace Prize and the Presidential Medal of Freedom prior to his violent death. At the time, King's assassin, James Earl Ray, was described in the press as a racist petty criminal. He fled after the assassination of King, leaving behind his gun with prints on it and a radio that was engraved with his prison ID number. As anger over the assassination of Reverend King consumed our nation, race riots broke out all across the country. It has been reported that over 120 cities experienced rioting after King's slaying. The worst rioting in the country was reported to be in Baltimore, Maryland, and Washington, D.C.

In the aftermath of the assassination of King the media, conspiracy theorists, and others had a field day. Rev. Jesse Jackson, a young activist, and Atlanta mayor Andrew Young both pointed fingers at our government. Others suggested the KKK was responsible. Ray initially made a clean get-away. However, two months later as he entered England at Heathrow Airport he was arrested by Scotland Yard. Even though many suspected more sinister motives it was never proven that anyone hired, helped, or supported Ray. When he died in prison in 1998, a review of his case was being conducted by President Bill Clinton's Attorney General Janet Reno. The review ended in 2000 with a finding that no credible evidence existed to support claims of conspiracy theorists.

❖ ❖ ❖

It was two months after Eisenhower's heart attack in May before the former president had recovered enough for him and Mamie to return to their residence in Gettysburg, Pennsylvania. Ginny and I reminisced about the wonderful trips to the Joshua Tree National Park, Salton Sea, the San Diego Zoo, and so many other places as we packed up our things at our temporary home. We knew the kids were going to really miss Gomer and Sally, but we convinced them they should remain in the area with our neighbors when we departed for Sacramento. As we headed out of Palm Springs, Ginny and I were well aware of the great opportunity we had just experienced to be together as a family during the assignment with former President Eisenhower.

❈ ❈ ❈

While we were in Palm Desert, we had managed to avoid television and the constant stream of news on the Vietnam War. However, our president was not so lucky. With the Vietnam War weighing heavily on him and his popularity falling, President Johnson had announced on March 31, 1968, he would not seek re-election. Anti-war candidate Senator Eugene McCarthy (D-MN), had earlier challenged President Johnson in the New Hampshire primary, finishing a strong second. After Johnson's announcement both Senator Robert Kennedy (D-N.Y.), brother of assassinated President John F. Kennedy, and Vice President Hubert Humphrey announced their candidacies as well.

Humphrey did not run in the important California primary in early June. He had previously decided to rely on the institutional structure (caucuses), which was controlled by the party bosses, to get the nomination. Vice President Humphrey believed with the support of the unions he could win the Democratic Party nomination without competing in the primaries. Senator Kennedy and Senator McCarthy, meanwhile, ran in the primaries hoping to secure the party nomination at the convention. In the last and the most important primary, Kennedy and McCarthy went head to head on June 4th in California.

While he waited for the polls to close and the votes to be counted, Kennedy rested in his suite at his campaign headquarters at the Ambassador Hotel in Los Angeles. Downstairs in the Embassy Ballroom there was a very festive mood among the Kennedy supporters waiting for the winner to be announced. They seemed sure it would be Kennedy.

STORIES FROM INSIDE THE PERIMETER

Senator Kennedy rode the elevator to the Embassy Ballroom to address his supporters shortly after his victory was announced on the evening news. In the elevator with him were retired Los Angeles Rams football great Roosevelt (Rosie) Grier and 1960 Olympic gold medal decathlon champion Rafer Johnson. Security for Kennedy in the ballroom had been limited to a hotel security person and a couple of guards from Ace Security. Later it would be reported there were no Los Angles Police personnel in the ballroom during the evening's celebration.

After addressing his supporters, Kennedy was escorted from the Embassy Ballroom through a kitchen pantry by Grier, Johnson, and an Ace Security guard. They were accompanying Senator Kennedy along a pre-arranged route through the pantry to another location, where Kennedy would conduct a press conference. Sirhan Sirhan, a Palestinian born on March 19, 1944 in Jerusalem, was loitering in the kitchen area. Sirhan had migrated to the United States in the late 1950s and had become obsessed with Robert Kennedy after the Middle East "Six-Day War," in the fall of 1967 between Israel, Egypt, and Syria.

Sirhan, who is reported to have despised Kennedy for his support of Israel, had a gun in his waistband and was waiting for him near the pantry. A little after midnight on June 5, Sirhan rushed toward Kennedy after the senator and his group had entered the pantry area. Firing all eight rounds from his .22 caliber Iver Johnson eight-shot revolver, he mortally wounded Kennedy. One shot hit Kennedy in the head, two rounds hit him in the body, and another shot grazed his coat sleeve. Several other people were hit in the gunfire of Sirhan and the return of fire from Ace Security guard Thane Cesar.

Sirhan was immediately arrested, quickly tried, and convicted of the assassination of Kennedy and condemned to death. The death sentence was later commuted to life in prison. He was sent to Corcoran

State Prison, Corcoran, California, where all requests for parole by him were turned down. Sirhan was released near the end of his prison term and sent to Turkey where he is in jail finishing a previous ten-year sentence for an earlier murder.

✤ ✤ ✤

The assassination of Robert Kennedy should have made Humphrey a huge favorite to win the Democratic presidential nomination. However, the vice president had been tainted by the war policies of President Johnson. Humphrey had become an unpopular candidate with the vocal and growing anti-war element in the Democratic Party. President Johnson, in the aftermath of Kennedy's assassination, had signed an executive order directing the Secret Service to provide protection of all major presidential and vice presidential candidates and nominees. The Secret Service found itself in a hectic scramble, putting together multiple security details and coordinating plans for the national conventions of both the Republican and Democratic parties.

✤ ✤ ✤

The 1968 presidential campaign was to become my life for the better part of five months. I would leave on June 8th and return home only three times (for a week each) until the election was over in November. My 1968 campaign introduction began with an assignment to Harold Stassen, a relative unknown Republican politician and former governor of Minnesota (1938-1943). The former Minnesota "Wonder Boy" had unsuccessfully tried to unseat Richard Nixon in 1956 as the vice presidential candidate to run on the Republican ticket with President Eisenhower. Frankly, I had never heard of Stassen, a perennial presidential candidate, residing in Bucks County, Pennsylvania. He was a corporate lawyer for consumer care products manufacturer S. C. Johnson. During my short assignment with Stassen, he made a business trip to Johnson's corporate headquarters in Racine, Wisconsin. As we boarded our commercial flight to Racine, the stewardesses on our flight asked us who we were protecting. Since most of the airline attendants were in their twenties, their usual response to our answer was, "Who is he?" Stassen kept a very low profile and was rarely recognized by the public at large.

About ten days into the Stassen assignment my shift leader, agent Doug Duncan of our San Francisco Field Office, advised me he was going to "get us off this detail." He told me he was going to make a call to Washington. The next day he told me to pack my bags, as we were going to Washington, D. C., to "hook up" with California Governor Ronald Reagan. Duncan said that Governor Reagan had just announced he was running for president. Duncan said he and I were being assigned to the Reagan detail. According to him, Reagan was in Washington, D.C., giving a speech and we would meet the detail at the hotel. Needless to say, we were delighted to be going back to California, especially Sacramento for me.

Duncan and I arrived in Washington on Friday evening, June 22nd. We immediately went to the Marriott Hotel, where Reagan was speaking, to join detail leader John Simpson. Agent Simpson advised Duncan and me that we would be joining him and agent Ed Hickey on a private plane with Governor Reagan for a quick campaign stop in Kentucky on the way to Los Angeles. The remainder of the detail, we were told, would go directly to Sacramento to familiarize themselves with Governor Reagan's residence and his office at the state capitol. They would prepare for the governor's arrival Monday morning. We were instructed to go ahead to Washington National Airport and wait at the private plane.

When Reagan arrived, we boarded the private aircraft. The atmosphere was cordial and somewhat festive. Duncan and I were introduced to the governor and his traveling aide, Art Van Court. Reagan, after saying hello to everyone, relaxed and shared a few jokes before preparing himself to speak at the airport rally in Kentucky.

The Kentucky airport stop was my first exposure to the charisma of Reagan. As he slowly came down the steps to deplane, Reagan, smiling, paused and waved as the crowd went wild. Even though the crowd was separated from Governor Reagan by a buffer area and a raised podium, women, old and young, were yelling, screaming his name, and reaching out to him. He was greeted on the ramp by the normal line-up of local politicos, and after shaking hands with them, he gave a short, stirring speech to the crowd. With his remarks over, Governor Reagan walked toward the crowd line. I was watching the crowd pressing against the barriers trying to touch him. With people pushing, yelling, screaming, and trying to touch Reagan, the scene reminded me of an Elvis Presley visit to Tacoma, Washington, in the early 1960s.

Reagan seemed to enjoy all the chaos as he worked the crowd, smiling, shaking hands, touching well-wishers, and signing a few autographs for five minutes. Stopping, Reagan backed up a few steps and then waved to the crowd. Before boarding the plane he shook hands and thanked his hosts. We were seated waiting for the police and campaign staff to clear the ramp area around the plane when one of the Kentucky State Police officers came on board. He gave Governor Reagan a small glass vial with several lightning bugs inside. I craned my neck to see the insects, since we did not have lightning bugs in the Pacific Northwest. Until the 1968 campaign I knew these glowing, flying insects only as a creation of Walt Disney, presented by Jiminy Cricket.

The departure from Kentucky provided another opportunity for small talk among Reagan and the agents. Agent Hickey, a crusty

Irishman, regaled Reagan with a few of his jokes. The governor, who loved exchanging jokes, bonded immediately with Hickey. Soon, however, it was decided the lights would go out and we would all try to get a little sleep. Reagan was reclining on the couch; Simpson was in one of the captain's chairs, while Duncan and Van Court were in the other two chairs. Hickey and I were on the floor. I was fascinated when Reagan released the lightning bugs once the cabin lights were turned off. During the next thirty minutes before I fell asleep, the blinking fireflies floated throughout the cabin, landing here and there.

When the plane arrived in Los Angeles early Saturday morning it was met by agents from the Los Angeles Field Office. They quietly and efficiently spirited Governor Reagan off the airplane to his Pacific Palisades residence for the weekend. Duncan, Hickey, and I were taken to a hotel to rest. On Sunday Simpson briefed me that when we got to Sacramento I would be the person responsible for setting up and implementing a security plan at the Reagan residence. I would be coordinating this with the White House Communication Agency (WHCA) and working with our Secret Service technical support people on the installation of security alarms. The whole project figured to take a week to ten days. I was surprised to be given the assignment but relished the opportunity to contribute. From my perspective this was another "Why me?" moment.

❖ ❖ ❖

Summers in Sacramento were usually hot and humid, and this one was no exception. When Reagan's jet arrived in Sacramento Monday morning he was taken directly to his capitol office. I was taken to Reagan's residence at 1341 Forty-fifth Street, which was situated on a beautiful, tree-lined street in an older, exclusive part of the downtown area. Many of the homes, including the Reagan house, were large two-story structures, probably over seventy-five years old. Along the north side of the house near the property line was a macadam driveway leading to the garage at the rear of the house. Near the garage was a fairly large greenhouse with plants and shrubs, used by the gardener to fill the beds around the property. Directly behind the house in the slightly elevated rear yard was a swimming pool that was protected from prying eyes on three sides by a fence and foliage. The property was fenced not just in the back but along the north and south property lines to the rear of the house. Strategically placed trees, shrubs, and other foliage along the side property lines added to the privacy of the residence. On the north side of the property near the front of the house but across the driveway was a small guard booth normally used by the California State Police.

Governor Reagan's routine was to leave for the five-minute drive to his office each morning around eight by armored limousine accompanied by his cadre of Secret Service agents. Arriving in the basement of the state capitol building near his private elevator provided Governor Reagan the safest and most direct route to his office. While he was at the office there was minimal support at the residence. Daughter Patti (sixteen years old) and son Ron Jr., usually called "Skip" (ten years old), did not have specific Secret Service coverage. They would usually spend time in the backyard at the pool. Agents were available to accompany California First Lady Nancy Reagan in the event she left the residence. While working on the residence security project I often hung out in the backyard to keep an eye the two Reagan children while they swam.

On one particular day the calm and quiet of the afternoon was interrupted by a loud "boom" coming from the north side of the house. Standing in the back yard I immediately instructed Patti and Skip to get out of the pool and go inside the house. Following them to the back door I met Mrs. Reagan, who had a concerned look, as she was coming outside responding to the loud noise. I urgently directed her to get back in the house. At first she balked and started to follow me, asking questions. Pivoting quickly, I looked her in the eye and forcefully insisted she return to the house immediately. As she left, I turned and saw the WHCA technician coming around the greenhouse holding his arm. It was bleeding profusely, and an agent and the other technician were attending to him. By the time I got there the command post agent had already started to call an ambulance and a tourniquet had been applied.

One of the WHCA technicians had been installing a radio antenna on the roof of the greenhouse when he lost his balance, slipped, and fell, according to the men assisting him. In trying to break his fall, his arm went through one of the glass panes, putting a gash in his arm. The men were giving first aid as they waited for the ambulance. In a few minutes the technician was treated by the ambulance crew and transported to the hospital. Though there was a lot of blood, the injury was not severe and later that day the technician returned to work.

After the medical help stabilized the injury I returned to the rear of the residence to speak with Mrs. Reagan. Coming outside she asked what had happened and if anyone had been hurt. When she learned of the accident she asked about the condition of the technician and if he had gone to the hospital. While I was answering her questions, Mrs. Reagan invited me to finish our conversation in the kitchen. It was explained to her that the ambulance had left and she would be briefed as soon as we got a report from the hospital. After fully discussing the accident and answering all her questions, I told her that I wanted to speak to her about emergency situations. First I mentioned that she should have gone into the house immediately when directed to do so. Then I explained to Mrs. Reagan that in a real or perceived emergency situation she, the governor, and other members of the family must respond at once to what any agent told them. There would always be time to discuss the appropriateness of the instruction after the crisis, she was advised. We chatted a few minutes and Mrs. Reagan apologized, saying she realized she should have immediately gone in the house when instructed to do so. Throughout the discussion a calm Mrs. Reagan was attentive and relaxed, asking probing questions. When she indicated she was comfortable with everything, I pointed out that Patti and Skip should be commended for quickly following instructions to "get into the house."

❈ ❈ ❈

Governor and Mrs. Reagan traveled during the time I was working on the residence project. He attended meetings in Southern California and made a few political trips in pursuit of the nomination for president. Mrs. Reagan took Patti and Skip to their Pacific Palisades residence in Los Angeles on the weekends or longer, in one case. If the governor was out of town he would usually meet them there when he came back. On a couple of occasions they went to his ranch in the Santa Barbara area. The Reagan family went to the ranch and to Pacific Palisades for the Fourth of July holidays. Governor Reagan liked to shoot his gun at a safe place on his ranch. During one trip to the ranch, Governor Reagan was given a chance to shoot the Uzi machine gun and the Remington shotgun normally carried on protective details. According to the day shift at the ranch, Reagan was impressed and enjoyed the opportunity to shoot very much.

Once my project was over I returned to my shift, supervised by agent Duncan. We traveled to the Reagan's Pacific Palisades residence. While there, detail leader Simpson asked me to take daughter Patti for a driving lesson. She drove me around the area for over forty-five minutes practicing parking and other driving skills. When we returned to the residence I jumped out of the front passenger seat of the car to open the garage without first notifying the command post. As I rushed toward the garage I was intercepted by agent John O'Toole, who had his weapon drawn. He yelled for me to identify myself. That was the last time I ever approached a protected compound without first radioing ahead.

❖ ❖ ❖

After the long Fourth of July weekend, Governor Reagan returned to Sacramento with Mrs. Reagan and the children. Meanwhile, our great country continued to be wracked with more race riots in Washington, D.C., Baltimore, and other cities during the summer. Sacramento was not to be exempt. With the oppressive summer heat and no air conditioning, many people in downtown Sacramento often hung out outside their homes in their neighborhoods. Near the governor's residence was the Oak Park section, a predominately black area, where periodically there had been problems with frustrated residents and others hanging around outside on hot, humid evenings.

On July 9, detail leader Duncan, agents Bob Horan, Bob Barker, and I were working the four to midnight shift. Mrs. Reagan and her husband were relaxing upstairs in the house. Earlier in the evening Duncan had advised the shift that he had been notified by our intelligence agent that there was some racial unrest in the Oak Park section of Sacramento. He said it was understood the Sacramento Police had responded and the situation was stable but still tense. Everyone knew we needed to be extra vigilant in light of the close proximity of the unrest to Governor Reagan's residence.

Our four-man shift was maintaining three exterior security posts plus the command post at the Reagan residence. Post one was at the California State Police guard booth alongside the house. Post two was in the backyard near the rear door to the house. Post three was in one of our shift cars on the street at the far end of the property opposite the guard booth. A large tree near the sidewalk in the front yard between the guard booth and the car did not block the view between the two posts. The fourth person sat in the command post answering the phones and monitoring the alarm system. We rotated the posts every thirty minutes.

At about 10:30 p.m. a shift rotation had just been completed. Shift leader Duncan was at the guard booth, agent Baker was in the backyard with a shotgun, and I had just relieved Horan in the car. Horan moved to the back seat (curb side) to talk with me before heading to the command post. I was in the front seat sitting behind the steering wheel on the street side with the window down. I had my Secret Service issue, six-shot Colt revolver firmly in my grip, resting in my lap. On the bench seat next to me was an Uzi submachine gun loaded with a thirty-round clip. A spare clip, full of ammunition, was next to the automatic weapon.

At the far end of the property thirty feet from the guard booth was a dimly lit light post next to the sidewalk. As Horan and I talked we noticed two individuals walking up the sidewalk toward the Reagan residence. Duncan radioed us advising of the approaching individuals, cautioning everyone to keep alert. He said something did not seem right. His comments confirmed the feelings that Horan and I had. The two individuals passed under the dim light and proceeded ahead on the sidewalk, crossing the driveway. The pair continued walking until they got to the big tree between them and the guard booth. This prevented Duncan, who had stepped out of the booth, from seeing them. Now stopped, the would-be lawbreakers faced each other, not realizing two Secret Service agents were no more than forty feet away observing them. Together they brought bottles with rags sticking out of the top (known as Molotov cocktails) from alongside their legs. During the walk the Molotov cocktails had been hidden next to their legs and were not visible to any of us. Simultaneously the one nearest to us was taking what looked like a lighter out of his pocket.

Horan and I were completely taken by surprise. Recovering quickly, I tossed the Uzi to Horan in the back seat, who jumped out of the driver's side of the car and ran to the front door. While radioing Duncan, "They have gas bombs," I was getting out of the car with my weapon in my hand yelling to the two of them to "halt." Surprised and caught unaware by the additional security, the two perpetrators panicked, freezing for an instant, thus losing their advantage. They did not get the gasoline bombs lit; instead, flight became their priority. Both turned and began running away, jettisoning the Molotov cocktails. One tossed his unlit bottle on the grass in the Reagan front yard before fleeing down the sidewalk away from us. The other criminal headed diagonally across the street toward the corner. He tossed his gas bomb onto the street, where it broke. Duncan yelled at the individual going by him to halt and ran after him.

Near the sidewalk Duncan managed to fire a shot at the fleeing lawbreaker and then raced back to the guard booth. Horan, while sprinting to the front door to take up a defensive position with the Uzi, yelled over the fence to agent Barker to get inside the house at once. Back at the guard booth Duncan radioed Barker also, telling him to get inside the house while he was picking up the direct line to the Sacramento Police Department. He notified them of the attempted firebombing of the

Reagan residence and asked for an emergency response unit. Quickly agent Duncan made additional calls to detail leader Simpson, our detail ID agent, the Secret Service Intelligence Division, and protective operations about the incident. Finally, he called the midnight shift directing them to report to the residence at once.

While Duncan was heading for the phone, I chased after the individual crossing the street, who had a good fifty-foot lead on me. When both of the bad guys fled around the corner, I spun around to return to the residence, concerned there could be more people intent on harming Governor Reagan. However, hearing a nearby car door slam, I rushed to the corner to see if I could get a description or license plate number of the departing vehicle. It was too dark to get any useful information as the vehicle, already half a block away, sped off down the street, so I returned to the residence at once. Proceeding to the guard booth I was debriefed by Duncan, who took notes on the incident. After my debriefing I took an observation post across the driveway in front of the house between the corner of the house and the front door.

The Sacramento Police Department, upon getting the call from Duncan, immediately dispatched a marked car and an ambulance to Governor Reagan's residence. They also sent over two detectives to investigate the incident and take statements. The first car to arrive at the Reagan residence was neither of the dispatched emergency vehicles, but a local news media car with a reporter and cameraman. The media had been in the area covering the Oak Park disturbances when they heard the emergency vehicles dispatched to the governor's residence. Duncan directed the reporter and cameraman to remain on the sidewalk near where the marked Sacramento Police car and the ambulance parked when they arrived.

The Sacramento detectives, who I recognized, arrived, and I had them join me at my new post. Going over the activities of the two individuals with the fire bombs, I responded to their questions concerning the event. I was not sure how good a look I had gotten as they walked under the dim street light at the end of the driveway, but I knew I had caught a quick glimpse of their faces. During the conversation with the detectives I noticed someone dressed in white standing behind a shrub at the corner of the house listening to my conversation with the detectives. I thought it was one of the ambulance crew. The discussion took about ten minutes, and when it was over I agreed to look at some pictures at the police station the next day. Heading for the command post I neared the individual by the shrub. What a surprise when I realized it was not an ambulance person but Governor Reagan. The governor was standing there in a white bathrobe, hidden from the street by one of the shrubs, listening to the conversation between the detectives and me. He had a wide grin on his face as I walked over to him, but before he could say anything, I quietly whispered, "Governor, the press is out there. I am sure they would love to get a picture of you in your robe."

With the grin getting bigger, the visibly excited Governor said, "Well, this is certainly much more exciting than watching *The Invaders.*" (*The Invaders* was a sci-fi television series starring Roy Thinnes.) Reagan had been watching it when he heard a shot. We walked together to the rear of the house and I watched him enter the residence before continuing the short walk to the command post.

The midnight shift had arrived while I was meeting with the detectives. Once they took over the normal security posts, agent Baker was debriefed by Duncan. Later I was told that, upon entering the house, Baker positioned himself at the bottom of the grand staircase with the shotgun in his arms. He reported to Duncan that shortly after he took his post, Governor Reagan came rushing to the top of the grand staircase. According to Barker, Reagan commented about the shot he heard fired outside. The governor then asked Barker if it was okay for him to get his gun. Barker advised Duncan that he told Governor Reagan he could get his gun but to stay away from the windows. We all had a hearty laugh about Reagan's comment concerning his gun.

The next day I met with the two detectives at their office and looked at a number of pictures. A couple of them looked like the guys from the night before, but I could not be absolutely sure. The Sacramento PD conducted a full investigation over the next several weeks. They received information from several persons that there were a couple of people outside the fence in back. According to the information gathered they were supposed to come over the back fence but decided not to when they "saw the agent with the shotgun at the back door." No one interviewed by the police was willing to positively identify the suspects.

❖ ❖ ❖

Several days after the incident Reagan was hosting a dinner at his residence for perennial presidential candidate Harold Stassen, who was making a tour visiting some of the Republican presidential candidates. Agents on the detail were invited by Governor and Mrs. Reagan to attend the dinner as guests. Duncan and I contacted our colleagues on the Stassen detail asking to make a swap of some Reagan campaign buttons for Stassen buttons. We had the Stassen detail bring them with their candidate and made the swap at the Sacramento airport during their arrival. Our shift decided to wear the Stassen buttons on the back of our lapels in silent support of our first "protectee" of the 1968 campaign. We gave a couple of buttons to Reagan when he returned home from the office, advising him that some of us were going to wear them on the back of our lapels that night at the dinner.

When my wife and I went through the receiving line as the governor and Mrs. Reagan greeted their arriving guests. Carefully, so no one else could see me, I flashed my Stassen button to the governor. He smiled while showing his hidden Stassen button. Governor Reagan seemed to enjoy his show of support for Duncan and the rest of the shift.

❖ ❖ ❖

Detail leader Simpson asked me to travel in advance of Reagan to Baltimore Airport to arrange a meeting between Governor Reagan and Secret Service Director James J. Rowley. He asked me to brief the director on the attempted firebombing of the Reagan residence and the preliminary results of the Sacramento Police Department investigation. I rented a room for the two of them to have a short meeting at one of the hotels on the grounds of the airport.

After briefing the director I had the pleasure of spending some additional time with him before Reagan's arrival. Director Rowley a true professional had a distinguished career as an agent and the head of the white house detail. He had been director of the Secret Service for twelve years. When the governor arrived, I introduced the two of them to each other and left so they could speak alone.

Returning to California, Horan and I were selected by Simpson to travel in advance to Miami to coordinate Governor Reagan's presence at the Republican National Convention scheduled for August 5-8, 1968. Horan and I arrived in Miami five days ahead of Reagan and the detail. Paul Rundle was the Secret Service agent in charge of security for the convention. He provided rooms, cars, and logistical support to all the details; he was also responsible for advance agents and support personnel coming to Miami. Due to the late entry of the Secret Service in the convention, rooms in the Miami Beach area were at a premium.

Rundle had a ship brought into Miami that could sleep five hundred people. Almost all the support Secret Service agents, other supporting federal agents, technical support, and military support stayed on the ship. Horan and I knew we probably had one of the smallest groups, while Nixon had the largest entourage. The two of us stayed in a small motel a block away from the Deauville Hotel where Governor and Mrs. Reagan stayed. A small number of our detail agents stayed in the Deauville. The remainder of the detail was staying in nearby hotels.

Rundle and his team had designed a great security plan for the convention hall and the candidates. The logistical challenges must have been a nightmare considering the limited time they had to design the plan and put everything into motion. Collins Avenue was the main motorcade route used for north and south traffic up and down Miami Beach. Helicopters patrolled the main routes and accompanied motorcades whenever possible. All of the candidates' Secret Service motorcades included a Miami marked police vehicle, a Secret Service lead car, a limousine, follow-up car, and a staff car. Police and Secret Service vehicles had red lights and sirens. The lead police car had a large two digit number painted on top for ease of identification by the security helicopters patrolling the main motorcade routes. Also, all motorcades had strobe lights in the follow-up cars that were used after dusk to ensure the motorcade route security helicopters were able to identify each motorcade. Pools of agents, staying on the ship, were used for advance posting in support of the activities of the candidates outside the convention center.

Inside the center, the general security posts were manned by Secret Service agents, Miami Police, and personnel from other federal and local law enforcement agencies. Flexible security teams were available to assist in creating security zones around people we were responsible for when they were on the floor of the convention center.

Everyone knew Governor Reagan and Governor Rockefeller were long shots to wrestle the presidential nomination from Richard Nixon. The other candidates in Miami—George Romney, Governor of Michigan; James Rhodes, Governor of Ohio; John Volpe, Governor of Massachusetts, and Harold Stassen, former Governor of Minnesota—really didn't have a chance.

While waiting at the airport for Reagan to arrive, the motorcade was pre-positioned to be driven directly to the chartered aircraft to pick up the governor and Mrs. Reagan. Barriers were put in place to restrict the access of other vehicles and unauthorized people. The agent driving the limo opened the trunk of the convertible being used as the limo and put his shoulder bag and the emergency kit inside. A half hour later, when we got word the aircraft was on final approach, the keys to the limo could not be found. We managed to push the convertible out of the way and replace it with a sedan just moments before the aircraft taxied to our location. It was especially embarrassing since a large crowd had gathered and watched as several of us helped the driver push the car out of the area. It turned out the keys were in the trunk (there was no trunk release in the glove box in those days).

Though the Republican National Convention in Miami was a challenge for the Secret Service, it did not evolve into the chaotic situation our agents faced in Chicago with the Democrats. The Miami demonstrators were not a major disruption to any of the candidates or the convention. Most radical groups, it seemed, had decided to keep their powder dry for the Chicago convention.

Reagan and the other candidates made multiple trips up and down Miami Beach visiting various state delegations trying to woo their support. Reagan and Rockefeller were both unsuccessful in trying to win the nomination. They were hoping to keep Nixon from getting the nomination on the first ballot so that state delegations would be allowed to vote for anyone they wanted on the succeeding ballots. Nixon denied them their dreams as he won on the first ballot with 692 votes to 277 for Rockefeller and 182 for Reagan.

There were a number of people in the running for the vice president position on the ticket, including Reagan and Rockefeller; however, neither of those governors wanted the post. Nixon surprised everyone when he chose the little-known governor of Maryland, Spiro T. Agnew, to be his running mate.

With the convention winding down to its last day there wasn't any talk of the agents on Reagan's detail going home. I didn't know where I would be going until the next day.

❖ ❖ ❖

Simpson was designated to head the Agnew detail and told me to help agent Horan pick up Agnew and bring him to Nixon's hotel in the afternoon. When we got to the hotel, Simpson mentioned to me that I would be leaving with Agnew the next day. That night Agnew was nominated and the delegates voted him the vice presidential nominee of the party. I left Miami the next day with Agnew and his family on his new chartered campaign airplane. We flew cross-country to San Diego, where Agnew and his staff met with Nixon and his staff to lay out strategy and contact points for the campaign for the White House. The campaign strategy session lasted almost a week. When Agnew departed San Diego, J. Roy Goodearle was aboard the vice president's charter campaign airplane. Goodearle was a Texas oilman who was responsible for coordinating Agnew's travel schedule with the senior Nixon campaign staff.

❖ ❖ ❖

Vice presidential nominee Agnew, accompanied by his family, made a quick campaign stop in Honolulu, Hawaii, where detail leader Simpson assigned me to take Agnew's daughter Susan to the beach. He asked that I contact Honolulu PD to provide two officers to assist at the beach. He indicated it would be nice if the officers could teach her to surf. The officers came by our hotel and accompanied us to the beach. We all spent the afternoon in the ocean as they taught her how to surf. By the end of the day Susan Agnew and I were both able to get up on the surfboard alone. It was quite a day for my first time in Hawaii.

❖ ❖ ❖

The next day Agnew returned to the mainland. He made a number of campaign appearances before returning to Annapolis for a rest during the Democratic National Convention August 26th to 28th. My college mentor from South Tacoma, Jim Sims, who had recruited me to play basketball at St. Martin's College, was in the Marine Corps and stationed at the Naval Academy in Annapolis. Sims, who was four years my senior, and I had gone to Visitation Grade School in South Tacoma and grown up together at the South End Boys Club. I called him when I got to Annapolis the first time and he was pleased to hear from me. Sims invited my shift to his home for drinks and dinner. It was a very enjoyable break from the campaign routine of bars and restaurants. Sims said to notify him ahead of time the next time we came to Annapolis.

❖ ❖ ❖

It is a tradition that candidates do not campaign when the other party has its convention. With the Democrats holding the White House, their convention was held second, also as tradition dictated. Chicago,

Illinois, site of the 1968 Democratic National Convention, had Richard Daly, the last of the "Big-City Bosses," as mayor. On August 26, Chicago became the site of the ultimate confrontation between demonstrators and police. All of the pent-up anger and frustration of the 1964 Civil Rights Act, the Vietnam War, the race riots of Watts, Washington, D.C., Baltimore, and other cities boiled over and played out in the streets and parks of Chicago.

A number of leading political activists had met several months prior to the Chicago convention to map out a strategy of demonstrations and civil disobedience. They wanted to march on the Conrad Hilton Hotel, where the delegates were staying, and the amphitheatre, where the convention was being held. They wanted to tie up the city. Mayor Daley was determined to keep the hotel and convention center free of demonstrators. Security for the convention and visitors was reported to be provided by almost 12,000 Chicago police officers, 7,500 Illinois National Guardsmen, 7,500 Army troops, and 1,000 FBI, Secret Service, and other federal law enforcement officers.

During the first day of the convention, demonstrators and activists gathered in Lincoln Park. There was a festive mood that evening with bands scheduled to play, people singing and enjoying themselves. The Yippies (Youth International Party) had nominated a pig, Pegasus the Immortal, as their candidate. They were a radical, counterculture alternative to the free speech movement. That first night in Lincoln Park the Yippies were looking for a confrontation. Mayor Daley had decided ahead of time not to issue any permits for gatherings, protests, or marches. The police confronted those in Lincoln Square, using nightsticks, teargas, and mace, and in the ensuing chaotic confrontation many people and police were injured. The activists knew the tone was being set for the remainder of the convention and continued their confrontations with the police.

Daily, blow-by-blow coverage of anti-war activists, anarchists, and the thousands of protesters confronting the Chicago police and other law enforcement groups gripped television viewing audiences everywhere. Teargas, shields, and night sticks were the equipment of the day for the police as they confronted the anti-war supporters of Senator Eugene McCarthy. Demonstrator fought back with fists and feet and threw anything they could get their hands on at the police. Much of the rest of the world must have thought that we were all crazy.

Instead of the confrontations abating as the day for nominating speeches approached, violence by the police during encounters with the more extreme groups increased. Each time riot police fought with the demonstrators, television cameras captured the violent, gory scenes: cracked heads, teargas drifting through neighborhoods around the amphitheatre, and injured police and demonstrators being carried away. All of this was being beamed across our country to a confused electorate and across the world.

It seemed to some as if Vice President Hubert Humphrey would be doomed. The country had dramatically changed since Johnson and Humphrey took office in 1964. The vice president, like it or not, was saddled with the Vietnam War. Once Johnson dropped out of the campaign, Humphrey was viewed as the person responsible for the war in Southeast Asia. When he arrived at the convention, however, Humphrey knew he had more than enough delegates to win the nomination. His caucus strategy was certain to make him the party's presidential nominee. Since many of the core support groups of the Democratic Party supported the anti-war movement, loyal and unquestioning support of the White House and the Democratic Party was fading.

The scenes playing out on the convention floor were almost as chaotic as the ones being filmed in the streets around the convention center. Inside it took two days and much maneuvering to get the Vietnam War settled in the platform and the delegates seated. A strategy of challenging delegates committed to Humphrey from the very beginning was intended to keep Humphrey from getting the nomination. The strategy failed when at the end of the first round Humphrey had 1759.5 votes, more than enough to secure the nomination.

Humphrey and his VP candidate, Senator Edmund Muskie of Maine, were caught right in the middle of the reform waves that were flooding the Democratic Party. After the Democratic Convention, the anti-war movement continued to grow and had a dramatic effect on the remainder of the 1968 presidential campaign. As the anti-war sentiment and demonstrations swept across our country, the campaign became increasingly ugly. College students, who used the summer to warm up, officially joined the fray when classes began in September. It seemed as if the evening news reports were constant anti-war, anti-Nixon, anti-Agnew, anti-Johnson, and anti-Humphrey. Sit-ins, peaceful and not so peaceful, challenged our civil and law enforcement officials.

Once the Chicago convention was over, Agnew crisscrossed the country campaigning for most of the next three months, returning to his governor's office periodically in Annapolis, Maryland, to tend to state business. There were also several short rest stops at Maryland's Eastern Shore. Agnew drew large crowds nearly everywhere he campaigned. He and Nixon were constant targets of the widening anti-war demonstrations. I spent much of the campaign on the road making advance security arrangements for Agnew stops. The rest of the time I was on the campaign charter airplane with the working shift. I called Sims to let him know the date of Agnew's scheduled arrival in Annapolis for state business.

❖ ❖ ❖

The next time we went to Annapolis, when I got to my room, I could tell Sims had been there. First, my room adjoined another shift member's room and the connecting door was open. Going into the bathroom I found in my bathtub two cases of Rolling Rock beer covered with ice. On the table was a note inviting our shift to have a good home-cooked meal at the Sims' quarters that evening. It turned out it was not an inconvenience to shower in the adjoining room until the bathtub was emptied. The home-cooked dinner at the Sims' residence, prepared, by his wife Pat, was excellent. There was at least one more occasion when my bathtub became a cooler, where an ample amount of green bottles covered with ice awaited us. Sims and I would cross paths in Washington, D.C., a number of times over the next fifteen years as our careers advanced.

❖ ❖ ❖

There were many memorable stops along the campaign trail. I would like to share two in particular of off-duty activities that are of interest. Agent Joe Worthington and I were in Milwaukee waiting for a third agent to arrive to assist him with advance security arrangements for a campaign visit by Agnew. We had checked into a downtown hotel and decided to have a beer at a nearby tavern while we waited for our colleague. We left our guns unloaded in the hotel safe and placed a note for him at the front desk to meet us around the corner. When agent Worthington and I entered the neighborhood establishment there were several people sitting on stools at the long bar, but we headed for the pool table in an open back room area. The cute, friendly barmaid smiled, chatted, and took our order while we enjoyed a game of pool. A short time later she brought us a refill and flirted with Worthington and me. When she left, Worthington said he had seen track marks from drug use on her arm.

At some point the barmaid left and the bartender was replaced by the late night man. While Worthington was at the bar ordering two more beers the off-duty bartender, sitting on a stool, made a snide comment about the barmaid to Worthington and tried to kick him in the groin. Worthington dropped his cue stick and prepared to defend himself; however, a couple of customers intervened, convincing the bartender to sit down. With a smile Worthington walked away with our two beers as the angry bartender made a comment about getting a gun and shooting him. A few minutes later I was at the far end of the pool table setting up a shot when I heard a pool cue crash to the floor. Looking up I saw agent Worthington with both of his hands in the air saying, "Don't shoot, don't shoot."

Turning my head and laying my cue on the table, I saw the bartender with a revolver in his hand, the hammer cocked, waving it threateningly at Worthington. When he swung the gun toward me, I could see the bullets in the cylinder and his finger on the trigger. The off-duty bartender, waving the cocked gun at me, said he was going to shoot me too. Worthington, in a calm, controlled voice, kept telling the drunken bartender he did not want him to shoot us and to think about what he was doing.

My heart was pounding as we slowly began backing up across the room toward the exit. Worthington continued to caution the man wielding the gun not to shoot. Turning, the bartender followed us with his finger still on the trigger, weaving back and forth, cursing and continuing to make threats against us. Nearing the door I rushed out followed a seconds later by Worthington. Walking back to the hotel we talked about how lucky we were not to have been shot. The next day we told the story to two of the Milwaukee police detectives working with us. They said that as soon as we left town they would have ABC (Alcohol Beverage Control) close down the bar. Later to rib me Worthington would spread the story that I had run out on him. We continued to have a good laugh for years about the tavern in Milwaukee.

❖ ❖ ❖

The campaign was long and challenging. I had two quick visits to Sacramento to see my family and then it was back to traveling. Everyone knew we had to suck it up until the November elections. If anyone had a personal problem it was dealt with immediately and they were allowed to return to their office. There were no days off while on the campaign trail. Schedules did allow for working. We were on our own trying to maintain some semblance of physical fitness on an irregular basis.

Agents traveling with Agnew heard the campaign stump speech at every stop for days in a row before a new speech was introduced. Doing advances usually meant seeing Agnew every four or five days and not hearing the same stump speech as often.

❖ ❖ ❖

The race for the presidency was close between Nixon and Humphrey, especially due to the candidacy of Governor George Wallace of Alabama. Wallace's American Independent Party played a spoiler role in the 1968 campaign even though Wallace did not develop a lot of support outside the Deep South. On Election Day the polls showed the race too close to call. When the votes were counted, Nixon ended up with 43.2 percent of the vote and 301 electoral votes. Humphrey had 42.6 percent but only 191 electoral votes. Wallace, with 12.9 percent and 45 electoral votes, had almost 10 million votes in a race Nixon won with a little over 500,000 votes more than Humphrey.

❧ ❧ ❧

Two days after the election I was released to return to Sacramento, thinking my travel was over for the year. Well, I was wrong. The first week of December I was assigned to travel to Palm Springs, California, to assist with advance arrangements for President-Elect Nixon to attend the National Governors' Conference, hosted by Governor Reagan. The governors, dressed in western garb, rode on horseback into the desert for an old-time western barbecue. Watching the group of cowboy and chuck wagon chefs cooking the steaks over the huge open grill stirred the cook in me. The Palm Springs assignment gave me an opportunity to say hello to Governor and Mrs. Reagan one last time. Mrs. Reagan asked me to please drop by the governor's house saying she had something for me. I told her I would even though I had no intention of doing so. It just didn't seem appropriate for me to go to their house.

❧ ❧ ❧

Back in the office in Sacramento things were busy. I had a feeling I would be going to a new assignment in Washington, D.C., in the spring. My focus was trying to get back in the normal routine. I received an expected assignment to Washington for the inauguration. I arrived a week in advance of the swearing-in ceremony. There were various pre-inaugural events attended by President-Elect Nixon and/or Vice President-Elect Agnew that required large numbers of out-of-town post standers. An unprecedented number of Secret Service agents and other law enforcement personnel began pouring into Washington the week of January 12, 1969, to support the activities.

My early arrival found me assigned to work with the advance team for the inaugural ball at the Pension Building. I was also used in the evenings for post assignments at sites of other activities. I ran into a number of Reagan and Agnew staff members I had met during the campaign.

The Pension Building, which covered an entire city block between F and G streets and Fourth and Fifth streets N.W., had a very rich and distinguished history. It was built between 1882 and 1887 to be the distribution point for pension checks to Civil War veterans. The building had four floors; three were offices, and the top floor was originally used for stabling horses. The well-worn, wide brick stairs at the west end of the building were built with small risers and deep steps to allow easy access for horses. The building had a huge atrium in the center with a glass roof that could be mechanically opened and closed. The open roof allowed the air flow to take the odors from the stables away from the building and cool the building during the hot, muggy summers. The Pension Building was first used for an inaugural ball in 1893 by President Grover Cleveland.

The pre-inaugural events went off without a major hitch. Interestingly, Bob Taylor, the agent in charge of the White House detail, was in serious negotiations with the senior White House Staff concerning the placement of agents alongside the limousine during the inaugural parade. Taylor knew that a significant number of radicals, anti-war protesters, and other agitators would try to disrupt the parade. He understood the desire of the White House staff not to have agents riding the rear bumper of the limo, but Taylor knew he needed to have his agents close enough to respond in the event the situation required it. Taylor agreed to have the agents walk parallel to the limousine near the crowd during the initial phase of the parade. He told Chief of Staff H. R. Halderman he would keep open the option of using agents in their traditional positions on the rear bumper, near the rear doors, and next to the front fenders of the limousine if the situation dictated.

There was much traffic over the radio frequencies between the staff and Taylor during the early part of the parade. As the motorcade neared areas along the route dominated by unsavory and boisterous demonstrators, Taylor directed agents to move to their normal positions. The staff would argue with Taylor, telling him to pull the agents away from the limousine. I gained a lot of respect that day for Taylor when he would not relent to the demands of Halderman. The parade was completed safely and without embarrassment with President and Mrs. Nixon standing on the rear seat waving to the throngs of people along the route. A huge group of anti-war demonstrators waving a Viet Cong flag were contained and did not meet the goal of stopping or interrupting the parade.

During the inaugural parade, I was standing post on the south side of Pennsylvania Avenue in front of the Executive Office Building near the reviewing stand. There were huge crowds all along the parade route. President and Mrs. Nixon, who were leading the parade, got out of their limo in front of the White House and entered the reviewing stand. The presidential and vice presidential motorcades preceded motorcade cars carrying the fifty state governors.

Standing on Pennsylvania Avenue, I was facing the crowd while the limousines transporting the governors began passing behind me and I heard a voice say, "Michael, come here please."

Recognizing the voice, I turned and faced Governor and Mrs. Reagan, who had stopped their convertible in the middle of the street. She motioned toward me with her hand and said, "Please come here for a second." Quickly I walked over to the car and Mrs. Reagan asked, "When are you coming to see me at our residence?" Trying to get my thoughts together, I hesitated and before I could answer, Governor

68

Reagan politely said, "Please call the office and make an appointment to stop by the house to see Nancy."

Returning to my post, I was embarrassed at holding up the parade and felt like everyone was looking at me. The next evening I had a flight back to Sacramento through San Francisco. As I entered the first class section on the way to my seat in coach I saw Mrs. Reagan sitting with Reagan Chief of Staff Ed Meese. (Governor and Mrs. Reagan always flew separately on commercial flights.) Mrs. Reagan asked me to give my ticket to Meese and join her in first class. Meese stepped into the aisle and took my ticket as I sat down next to Mrs. Reagan. He proceeded to my seat in the rear of the plane.

Mrs. Reagan immediately asked me, "What does it take to get you to come by the house? Do I have to call your boss?"

"No, I will come by to see you," I told her.

She took a black leather appointment book out of her purse and said, "Okay, let's pick a date."

After agreeing on a date, Mrs. Reagan insisted I remain in first class with her until we arrived in San Francisco. During the flight she spoke about the campaign and the inauguration. Her positive comments about the Secret Service and the night of the attempted firebombing of the residence reinforced my view of how much the Reagans appreciated the Secret Service. As we prepared to deplane in San Francisco, I waited for Meese and bid the two of them goodbye.

❖ ❖ ❖

The visit to the Governor's House went well. When I arrived Mrs. Reagan was very gracious and gave me a full tour of the upstairs and downstairs. Sitting in a den afterwards having a cup of coffee she told me she had something for me and excused herself. When she returned she gave me a framed picture from the *Sacramento Bee* newspaper of her, the Governor, Patti, and Skip walking their dog. Skip was holding the dog's leash and I was clearly visible next to the family. The bottom of the picture was signed separately by Nancy Reagan and Ronald Reagan. I couldn't believe that two such important people could be so interested in people around them.

❖ ❖ ❖

In February 1969 a reassignment to the Secret Service Protective Support Division (PSD) brought me to Washington, D.C. At PSD the agents were providing a detail for Secretary of the Treasury David Kennedy and support for President Nixon and Vice President Agnew. The assignments could be for less than a day or as long as thirty days. When PSD agents were not involved with a protective support assignment they had the option of using the indoor pistol range in the basement of the Treasury Building or remaining in the office to do paperwork. Sometimes we would go for a run. Shooting became a passion with me and I visited the range several days a week.

Many of the agents assigned to PSD got involved when President Eisenhower died on March 28, 1969. He was afforded a state funeral which included lying in state in the Rotunda at the Capitol. His funeral was at the Washington National Cathedral three days later. Before the public entered the Capitol Rotunda, all Secret Service agents were given an opportunity to walk by the casket. My post assignment at the cathedral allowed me to see much of the ceremony. Eisenhower's body was taken by train to Abilene, Kansas, his boyhood home, for burial. I remained in Washington, D.C.

❖ ❖ ❖

Meanwhile, on the news front, the Vietnam War continued to dominating the nightly television news reports. Footage of returning "body bags" and enemy "body counts" persisted as the measure of how the war was going. One of the unique things about being elected president is that if there is a national or international problem when you take office it becomes yours. President Nixon inherited the Vietnam War. With his swearing in on January 20 he could no longer travel without the presence of a constantly growing, vocal anti-war movement.

❖ ❖ ❖

During my first few months in the Support Division I worked with various details and formed a personal relationship with agent John Novak from our Pittsburgh office. After we received a number of assignments working together our families began to spend time together. Novak was a truly unique person. His hobby was playing the accordion. He had his own radio program when he lived in Sharon, Pennsylvania. Novak loved to tell stories and jokes, keeping a file of 3x5 cards, which were used to keep track of many of them. We reported to the Support Division on the same day and traveled the world together over the next six months. Novak always had enough new cards in his shirt pocket to entertain many of the people we met during our travels.

We first bonded while traveling together to Sydney, Australia, to work two midnight shifts for Treasury Secretary David M. Kennedy. This was one of those few assignments where you sit back and say "Wow!" when it is over. Our journey began with a twenty-four-hour first class flight from New York to Australia via Honolulu and Tahiti. The first two legs of the flight to Los Angeles and Honolulu were promotional for Pan Am and in the first class section were Novak and I and the traveling press. Needless to say, the airline had pulled out all the stops for the press. The food, wine, and drinks had all been upgraded and gift menus with etchings of clipper ships on the cover were distributed to everyone. While the traveling guests remained in Hawaii, we had a three-hour layover before leaving for Sydney via Tahiti. It was our first visit to the land Down Under.

We had nice accommodations in a hotel not far from where Secretary Kennedy was staying. The morning after our first midnight shift we were strolling back to the hotel enjoying the sights. Sydney was not a world-class city at the time. It reminded me of Tacoma, Washington, where I grew up. The shops were small, the buildings not huge, and it was easy to get around. As we passed a pastry shop Novak decided to get some donuts to take back to the hotel. With the brown paper bag of donuts in hand we continued down the street toward our hotel. Passing an open air bar on the street we stopped to survey the scene. Since we had just gotten off work we decided a beer was in order. Standing at our high table next to the sidewalk, Novak tore open the bag with our breakfast. The donuts were covered with granulated sugar and were still warm. Our enjoyment of the donuts was interrupted when an elderly Aussie man walked up to our table. Looking at Novak, then at me, he stared at the beer then the donuts. He glared at us incredulously. Shaking his head he snickered, "Americans" and walked away. Novak and I smiled and kept on eating and drinking.

❖ ❖ ❖

We returned to Washington after our assignment in Australia was completed and continued helping with local assignments and going to the pistol range. I had become an expert with my right hand and was improving rapidly with my left. My father-in-law, Fred Nagle, had made a suggestion to help me improve my accuracy. He taught me to cock the weapon using my trigger finger instead of my thumb. The trick was to make a quick, short tug on the trigger sending the hammer to the cocked position before squeezing off the round. My scores right- and left-handed continued to go up. Eventually I was given a certificate recognizing me for being a distinguished expert with my right hand and an expert with my left.

❖ ❖ ❖

The highlight of my six months in the Support Division was when I was selected to accompany New York Governor Nelson Rockefeller on a presidential mission. President Nixon announced on February 17, 1969 that he had selected Governor Rockefeller of New York to go on a presidential mission to Latin America, saying, "The purpose of this mission is to listen to the leaders and to consult with them concerning the development of common goals and joint programs of action, which will strengthen Western Hemisphere unity and accelerate the pace of economic and social development." (Presidential Archives)

Nixon indicated that the mission would begin in April with stops in all the countries south of our border, visiting four to six countries a week.

The Rockefeller study group included various Latin and South American experts, economists, and State Department specialists. Dr. Kenneth Riland, Rockefeller's personal physician, was also a member of the group. Dr. Riland was an osteopath and former physician for U.S. Steel. In addition to Rockefeller, he was known for treating the Shah of Iran and often visiting the White House to treat President Nixon. A close personal friend and confident of Rockefeller, Dr. Riland, known as a practical joker, was jovial and fun to be around.

The mission ended up encompassing four trips, each a week to ten days with around a week off between trips. The Rockefeller family had large holdings in several South American countries, including a large farm in Venezuela. In some of the countries Rockefeller would visit, there would be very aggressive opposition to him personally in addition to the anti-U.S. demonstrations. As a result of the demonstrations, visits to Peru, Chile, and Venezuela were cancelled. The leaders of those countries were worried about the safety of Governor Rockefeller and the ability of their governments to survive the visit.

Governor Rockefeller still visited twenty-four countries south of our border. During the trips there were extensive demonstrations in many of the countries visited; sometimes people were injured and there were several occasions when demonstrators were killed. An Associated Press photographer and an ABC soundman were both wounded during one of the stops.

The initial trip found Novak and me along with our shift leader, agent Jim Goodenough, working the midnight shift. Rockefeller and his group went to Mexico City but our first stop was an overnight in Tegucigalpa, Honduras. We arrived commercially and then took a taxi downtown to the Grand Hotel. We were moving slowly through traffic in downtown Tegucigalpa when we passed an elderly woman wearing a well-worn black top hat with a corncob pipe jutting out of her mouth. In her hand was a thin rope that led to a ring in the nose of a pig she was walking down the street. She was quite a sight as she plodded down the sidewalk with head down. I knew immediately this was a sight that a young man from Tacoma, Washington, would never forget.

The three of us checked into the Grand Hotel and got settled. After some brief sightseeing and lunch we returned to our rooms on the second floor. Novak and I were rooming together and decided to get some sleep and then eat before going to work on the midnight shift.

Around 6 p.m. we were awakened by sounds of booms, crashes, people running down the hall, and loud voices. We could hear yelling and screaming as we quickly got out of bed to get dressed. Grabbing my gun I opened the door even though I was only half dressed. People in a fit of panic were running by our room yelling and screaming. Looking at the chaotic scene in the hallway I saw one of the traveling TV film crews coming my way with their camera. They were wearing flak jackets and gas masks. Jumping into the hallway I stopped them and asked what was all the noise. They said there had been a confrontation between demonstrators and police in front of our hotel. They told us the demonstrators overwhelmed the security forces and had trashed the lobby of the hotel. One of them mentioned he believed the troublemakers had been pushed out of the hotel by the police.

Novak and I decided that it was time to get cleaned up, get our valuables, and head up the street to the compound where Rockefeller was staying. We let Goodenough know we would treat the 4 p.m. to midnight shift with an early relief. By the time the three of us were ready things seemed to have calmed down. As we left the room, a still photographer traveling with us asked where we were going. He was extremely anxious and disturbed over the situation in the lobby. He asked if he could accompany us to the compound. We told him to fall in behind us.

We quietly walked down the side stairwell and entered the lobby from the rear. What a sight. The floor-to-ceiling picture windows in the front of the hotel were broken out. Curtains and drapes were strewn about the room and pictures were on the floor, many broken. The chairs, sofas, tables, and cabinets were overturned and/or broken. It looked as if a tornado had gone through the lobby. There were no demonstrators or security people present. We quickly moved through the wreckage out to the narrow one-way cobblestone street. There was an eerie calmness outside. Turning to the right we were moving against the traffic on the one-way street in front of the hotel. We had to travel about a long city block to get to the corner. The entrance to the heavily protected compound where Governor Rockefeller was staying was directly across the street from the corner.

We heard when we got to the command post that earlier in the day before Rockefeller arrived one of the police officers working crowd control had slipped and fallen. According to one of the agents, the police officer had his finger on the trigger and his shotgun discharged, killing the leader of the demonstrators. The demonstrators were skeptical of the claim the shooting was an accident.

The next morning the three of us caught a flight to San Salvador, El Salvador. Rockefeller went to Guatemala City, Guatemala, before coming to San Salvador. The taxi ride to our hotel in downtown San Salvador was uneventful. While checking into the hotel we asked about shopping and souvenirs. To our delight we were told an open air market was less than half a mile away. Once we got settled Novak and I walked to the market. The stalls, carts, and tables stacked with local goods and souvenirs were enticing. Women dressed in brightly colored dresses, skirts, and blouses loudly announced prices of their goods. Children roamed near some of the stands, staying close to their mothers. Some of the sales forces along the streets were men in their twenties. The men were more aggressive in approaching customers to make sales. Carved goods, leather goods, apparel, sandals, ceramic bowls, platters, bottles, and cups were stacked in every nook and cranny. The brightly colored serapes, shirts, and other clothing displayed on hangers added a festive aura to the day. After some hard negotiations we purchased a couple of souvenirs to remember the visit to El Salvador.

Novak and I continued strolling down the narrow, crowded street where people were going about their chores and selling goods and food. After about thirty minutes the calm was broken by the blare of a loudspeaker in the distance. As we got closer to the speaker we could hear a male voice extolling the shoppers. He was interjecting the words "Gringo" and "Americano" in sentences and using a general tone that certainly was not complimentary. Suddenly we could sense a change in the shoppers and merchants. People were beginning to stare at us. Others were pointing us out to companions and merchants. The local shoppers and merchants began moving away from us as we entered the area of the central market. It was here where a small pickup truck was mounted with the speaker system. We found ourselves in the center of a large circle where people were staring at us, but no one spoke. The rhetoric over the speaker became more aggressive, angry, and anti-American. Very slowly Novak and I simultaneously unzipped our shoulder bags and put our hands on our weapons as we nervously moved toward the crowd line. We tried not to show any reaction to the loud ranting coming from the pickup truck.

Knowing there was no way to defuse the situation, we quickened our pace moving through the crowd to get away from the agitating sound system, hoping no one would follow us. It took several minutes of rapid walking for us to escape from our threatening location. Once we were a few blocks from the market we breathed a sigh of relief. Returning to our hotel we chuckled about how thankful we were to have avoided a potentially threatening situation while buying our souvenirs.

Entering our hotel a few minutes later we joined our colleague Goodenough, who was sitting at a lobby table sipping a beer. We described to him our anti-American adventure in the market area while ordering a beer to help us relax. Shortly after our beers had been delivered a loud boom shook the lobby. The floor-to-ceiling lobby picture window came crashing down. The rock thrown through the window was almost twice the size of a softball. It rolled across the sitting area and stopped a few feet from our table. It was a unanimous decision to retire to the safety of our rooms without finishing our drinks.

The remainder of the first trip was relatively uneventful. After returning to Washington, we spoke with Special Agent-in-Charge and Detail leader Ernie Olsen about working the midnight shift on the remaining trips. Goodenough, Novak, and I enjoyed the calmness of the late shift. We also knew we would be flying on a military support aircraft on at least the next two trips. Meanwhile, visits to the range allowed me to continue my proficiency with my .357 magnum.

❖ ❖ ❖

Our same three man midnight shift flew into Panama, where we were assigned a USAF C-118 to transport us to Quito, Ecuador, to work our shift. During our flight to Quito our crew was buzzing about a business deal they had set up that would return four- or five-fold on their investment. Ecuador was known for unique two-foot-high logs that had scenes carved into the wood. The stewards mentioned they would more than quadruple the investment on their return to Panama, where they would receive $125 per carving. They volunteered to give us the address of the warehouse where we could get good deals of our own if we wanted them.

When we arrived in Quito aboard our VIP military aircraft, security was extremely heavy at the airport. Machine gun-toting soldiers, tanks, and armored personnel carriers surrounded our plane. We were transported by embassy car to a walled compound with a beautiful two-story hotel located just outside the main downtown area.

Security at the hotel was as heavy as at the airport and also highly visible. It included heavily armed militia patrolling both inside and outside the walled compound and fixed posts throughout the hotel. Some of the soldiers outside had two-foot rubber hoses sticking out of their backpacks. This was the first time I had seen these unique interrogation devices.

During our registration at the front desk our advance agent advised that the entire Rockefeller group would be under house arrest during the visit. We were told no one in the party would be allowed to leave the hotel complex. Apparently there was major unrest and large demonstrations in town against the United States and Governor Rockefeller. After our earlier experiences in Honduras and El Salvador, Novak and I understood.

Goodenough, Novak, and I were relaxing in the lobby when one of our crew approached us explaining they were going to lose their business deal because of the ban on leaving the hotel. They told us it was not possible for them to get their order and the money to the warehouse. Asking them for the money, the address of the warehouse, and a list of goods to be purchased, Novak advised we would take care of their merchandise. He said he would also make arrangement for it to be delivered to the aircraft. It looked like we were going to throw caution to the wind.

Novak went out to the hotel arrival area and approached a cab driver dropping off passengers. He made arrangements for the cabbie to meet us outside the compound away from the guards. While Novak was making the arrangements for the cab, Goodenough and I each purchased three dollars in local coins. The three of us took a stroll around the property until we found an area where we could leave the grounds undetected. The cab driver who had agreed to convey us to the warehouse was waiting for us. Upon arrival at the warehouse we found out the crew had been able to place the order over the phone so we paid the bill and arranged for the delivery truck to meet the airplane on the ramp. Walking through the huge building we viewed all the goods for sale and each selected several trinkets to take back home.

Outside the warehouse twenty kids from the neighborhood, who had seen us arrive by taxi, had gathered and were waiting for us to come out. They were all excitedly jumping up and down and yelling at us. Four or five of the youngsters had shoeshine kits and as we came out they surrounded us asking to shine our shoes and begging for money. This was a scene that played out at nearly every stop during our four trips south of the border. We selected three of the children to shine our shoes. When they were through we paid them for the shines. Then each of us distributed about two dollars in local coins to the kids.

When our cab arrived back at the hotel we learned that the Ecuadorian authorities said they had found a "bomb" outside the building where Rockefeller's room was located. The advance team was supported by a United States Army Explosive Ordinance (EOD) team that had been dispatched to the Ecuadorian Army range where the alleged bomb had been transferred to be checked out. We learned later the bomb turned out to be a used oxygen bottle in the shape of a ball that had been discarded outside the rear of Rockefeller's room. Years later when former President Nixon was visiting Dr. Riland for a back manipulation I spoke to him about the "bomb." It turned out the playful Dr. Riland, who was in the suite directly above Governor Rockefeller, admitted to me he had discarded the empty unit out the window to see what would happen. No one on the trip had any idea Dr. Riland was the one responsible for the discarded oxygen bottle.

❖ ❖ ❖

The next morning when we arrived at the airport the crew on our private military aircraft had already loaded their carvings and was waiting for us. As we sat down at the table for breakfast, three green, cold bottles of Heineken beer were waiting for us. In the center of the table was a deck of playing cards. A breakfast of eggs, potatoes, sausage, toast, and coffee was served shortly after takeoff. Once the meal was over, Goodenough, Novak, and I began our ritual card game. We invited the cabin crew to play but they thought the betting was too steep. What they did not know is we were playing for the lowest denomination coin at the next stop. It was nearly impossible to lose more than four or five dollars during the one hour to an hour and a half flights.

The stop in Argentina was memorable for the dinner we had. I had been told before we left the United States that the meat in Argentina was the best. Goodenough, Novak, and I had the largest steaks for dinners I had ever seen. There were very tasty and were less than half the price we paid in the United States.

Rockefeller went to the Dominican Republic for a short stop before going to Haiti for an overnight. We went directly to Haiti on our C-118 and when we arrived at the airport we were met by our advance agent, Brooks Keller. He was dressed in a white linen suit with a Panama hat and had a dark tan. Keller was speaking fluent French and at first I thought he was with our embassy.

I asked Goodenough about agent Keller on the way into town. He said that there is a great story about the flamboyant Brooks Keller when he was assigned to our Secret Service office in the U. S. Embassy in Paris, France. According to Goodenough, Keller had somehow upset headquarters and was sent a telex advising him to take the next available transportation back to the United States. Keller quickly packed a bag and left on the Queen Mary since it was the next available transportation. Keller was one of those people who had become a legend in his own time.

On the drive to downtown Port-au-Prince, Haiti, the country ruled by Francois "Papa Doc" Duvalier, the extreme poverty was readily apparent. There were very few cars or bicycles on the roads. Most people walked, carrying their goods on their heads, backs, or in their arms. The more fortunate ones were the few that had carts or wagons pulled by donkeys. The occasional buses we saw were old and certainly overcrowded. The depth of human suffering was striking. Most children were wearing well-worn clothes and no shoes. There were very few stores and hardly any restaurants.

During the visit we joined the commission in a late afternoon tour of the countryside. Rockefeller and the rest of the panel were driven outside of town to observe a superhighway being built with United States foreign aid. There were only a few people and a couple of machines working on the road project. My interest in why a superhighway was being built in a country with so few automobiles got the best of me, and I asked one of our embassy escort officers, "Where is this road going?"

Without missing a beat he quickly responded, "Until the money runs out." The answer told us all we needed to know about the project.

The average yearly income of a Haitian family at the time was $13. Papa Doc Duvalier, self-proclaimed "President for Life," lived in luxury while his people suffered. He was recognized as one of the most corrupt world leaders at the time. President Duvalier must have gone to bed every evening thanking the gods for his lifestyle that was provided by the United States.

Other visits for Rockefeller on the second trip were to Bogota, Columbia, Bolivia, Port of Spain, Trinidad, and Jamaica.

The third trip to Brazil, Paraguay, Uruguay, and the Dominican Republic went well. Visits to Chile and Peru, however, were cancelled due to the large number of demonstrations and rioting taking place inside those countries. According to the city of Brasilia website, Brasilia was a planned city selected and built to be the capital of Brazil. Their website shows the construction on the streets were completed in 1958, the buildings in 1970, but the city itself was inaugurated as the capitol in 1960.

Asunción, Paraguay, was a beautiful city where we were scheduled for a one-night visit. Our shift was staying in an apartment hotel that rented out rooms when the owners were out of town. Novak and I had a great view of the city. After dinner on the way up to our room the elevator got stuck between floors. Fortunately we had our two-way radios with us and were able to contact help. In less than twenty minutes we were in our room. The next morning we were told the visit to Montevideo, Uruguay had been delayed for security reasons for one day. We spent the next night in Punta del Este and from there went to Montevideo for the official visit.

The fourth and final trip for us began in Georgetown, Guyana, where we stayed in a cabaña that had the biggest paddle fan I had ever seen. It must have been ten feet across from end to end. The cabaña was rustic with wood floors and wood walls that were only three to four feet high. Between the wall and the roof was screen. A chain hung down from the fan allowing us to control the speed with a little tug.

We knew the next couple of stops would be an appropriate end to four interesting and exciting trips to Latin America. However, everyone in the party was talking about Barbados, a new vacation spot off the coast of South America. We were not disappointed. There were no demonstrators, no house arrests, and no large police presence. There were comfortable quarters, island drinks, beautiful white sand beaches with bikini-clad young women, and crystal clear blue water. Rockefeller stayed on a luxury yacht moored at the end of a dock.

❖ ❖ ❖

Relaxing on the commercial flight back to Washington when the last stop was over, little did I realize that in seven years Rockefeller would be vice president and I would be the operations supervisor for his detail. In the short term I was hoping to get an assignment to Vice President Agnew's detail. During my years in the Secret Service it seemed many agents desired to go to the vice president's detail because of the closer interaction with him and the opportunities to travel and conduct advances.

My opportunity to go to the Vice Presidential Protective Division (VPPD) detail had evaporated by the time the Rockefeller trips were over. His detail was full. I was given a thirty-day temporary assignment to the Presidential Protective Division (PPD) in late July.

The Secret Service has a long-recognized history in law enforcement for conducting extremely competent criminal investigations. In the years before the Kennedy assassination, when many agents would never receive a permanent assignment to protect the president or vice president, the service was somewhat divided. Those agents who liked the field and did not want a protective assignment were referred to as "Field Freaks," while some agents who preferred being assigned to the president or the vice president over criminal work were fondly referred to as "Protective Pukes." Not every agent on the presidential or vice presidential details wanted the assignment, however.

Due to the recent growth in Secret Service protective responsibilities, a new career development policy that required agents to have a protective assignment in order to advance beyond the journey-man level was instituted in the late 1960s. Later, in response to the continued growth in the sizes of the details and new protective responsibilities, all Secret Service agents were required to spend one tour of duty (two to four years) assigned to Protective Forces. Agents could voluntarily make a second tour as part of career development or, when openings needed to be filled, agents could be transferred to the president or vice president for a second tour without a choice.

There is a certain swagger or hubris associated with the people working at the center of our government, especially the White House. In fact, some people, including agents, were outright arrogant when assigned there. As I have said, it is not just a Secret Service phenomenon, and people in Washington sometimes refer to it as "Potomac Fever." There are people who believe you get it from the water, while others believe it simply goes with the territory.

I believe strongly that no one should have to apologize for being selected to the "first team." Some agents who really desired to go to the White House detail would never make it and some agents who would rather not go there would be assigned. Looking back, the number of agents selected for permanent assignment to the White House detail, the most respected security detail in the world was small when compared to the total number of agents on other protective assignments. PPD was much more structured and less flexible than VPPD. The president's men and women, as should be the case, had all the best and newest equipment. Much of the work with the president was routine with a lot less travel than with the vice president and other details.

PPD agents routinely spent their work days at the White House, Camp David, Key Biscayne, Florida, and the Western White House, in San Clemente, California. The opportunities to be chosen for cherished special projects or out of town advances were very limited. Selections for advance assignments and special projects were tied to who you knew, who pushed you, and lots of luck.

❖ ❖ ❖

During my temporary assignment to PPD, my shift leader was Ron Pontius, an excellent agent and supervisor. He was a good athlete who coached the Secret Service slow pitch softball team, made up mainly of PPD agents. Pontius was vocal, aggressive, outgoing, and friendly to members of PPD, but he sometimes had a rough exterior. You might think he had drunk from the Potomac. Though he had not, his pride in the Secret Service and his White House assignment could confuse some people. I knew this would be an evaluation period for me. It was clear I was being considered for a permanent transfer to the Nixon White House. I was confident I would pass the test, but sorry I would not be going to VPPD.

We were working the day shift a week or so after I joined the detail when Pontius announced to the shift that we were going across the street the next day to the Treasury pistol range for monthly qualification. On PPD we needed to shoot a monthly score of 270 out of a possible 300 to carry a gun and keep working on the shift. After the shift the next day Pontius told everyone to ante up $5 for the shooting pool (high score wins all the money). When I offered him my money, he announced with certain bluster that I was a "temp" and he could not accept my money. Pontius would not allow me to participate in the shooting pool. Pontius' pride would not allow an outsider to win the pool. He perceived the PPD agents as belonging to a special club and temporary agents could not compete with them. However, temporary agents still had to shoot and qualify. Once you were a permanent member of PPD, Pontius magically elevated you in status. Come to think of it, Pontius may well have drunk from the Potomac. Anyway, at the pistol range in the basement of the Treasury Building, each agent selected a stall to use during the qualification process. I was in a stall shooting next to Charlie McCaffrey, who came to the detail from the New York City Field Office. McCaffrey was a very boisterous, friendly, and outgoing person with a love-of-life personality.

Entering the range each shooter was issued a box of wad cutter ammunition and three paper bulls' eye targets to be used during qualification. Once everyone was set in their stall, the range officer would direct weapons to be unloaded and holstered. Next, everyone was directed to put up one of the paper targets and send it down range. We were then told to un-holster our weapons and load with five rounds of wad cutter.

Qualifying required shooting a set of three targets, ten rounds at each target in five-round segments. The first target was called "slow fire," in which agents shot five rounds in two one-minute segments at the first target. The second target, "time fire," was shooting two five-round segments in twenty seconds each. After slow fire and time fire, I was reloading and preparing to shoot at my "rapid fire" target when I heard McCaffery mumble something. Reloading for the next five-round, ten-second segment, I said, "What did you say?" He did not answer and I asked once again, "Charlie, what do you need?"

He said he needed a ninety-five to win and added he had never shot a ninety-five before. Speaking through the thin-walled partition in a hushed voice I said, "Shoot my target."

McCaffrey replied with a confused, "What?"

"Shoot my target," I quietly repeated. Before either of us could say anything more the range master took control of the shooters. At the buzzer I drew the hammer back with a controlled squeeze of the trigger, instead of using my thumb, smoothly firing a round. The procedure was repeated until all five rounds were fired before the buzzer sounded. As the buzzer sounded for the second time ending the final round I had already squeezed off the fifth round.

Watching my target as it returned to the stall, I got a smile on my face, because I could see McCaffrey had fired at it. He won the pool with my ninety-seven score on his rapid fire target. When all the targets were scored, McCaffrey's New York personality surfaced as he loudly acknowledged he won the pool before he took the money from Pontius. He continued bragging and gleefully smiling after he accepted the pool money from our shift leader.

Walking out of the Treasury Department at the main entrance on Fifteenth Street N.W., we turned left and headed to the corner. Turning left onto Pennsylvania Avenue, we continued to the White House. As we approached the East Wing entrance, McCaffrey and I were far enough ahead of Pontius that he could not hear us talking. Agent McCaffrey quietly offered me half of the pool money we had won. Although he was genuinely surprised when I didn't want any of the money, he understood. My reward was helping him beat the rule maker. He knew I enjoyed beating the person who excluded me because I was not yet part of the team. We shot again before my thirty-day assignment was over, but McCaffrey was not there that day. I had the high score that day but, according to the rules, I could not claim the prize money.

At the end of my thirty-day assignment at the White House I received a permanent transfer to PPD. Initially I was assigned to Wilson Livingood's shift. He was diligent, providing an extensive and comprehensive on-the-job training program. As a people person, Livingood gave every agent assigned to his shift special attention. He was respected by Special Agent-in-Charge Taylor and became my first mentor at the White House detail.

Within thirty days of reporting to my new shift I was assigned a special project to update the White House Pass System. I was sure Livingood had requested the assignment for me, "Why me?" Two weeks after reviewing all the project material, familiarizing myself with the various White House passes, and interviewing a number of pass holders, I told Livingood I needed a meeting with the supervisor in charge of projects. During the meeting I mentioned I had checked all the various categories of passes, spoken to pass holders, and noticed a unique feature that was only on a few of the passes. I was sure the markings were used to restrict or allow access to certain sites. During the briefing the supervisor listened attentively and afterwards told me to keep working on the project without any discussion about my observations. Several days later I was asked to return my project. That was the last I was involved in updating the pass system. I thought at the time I was probably not of a high enough level to get a briefing on the ramifications of the markings.

When Nixon was in town the routine of standing post at the White House was broken on the weekends with regular trips to nearby Camp David. Both President and Mrs. Nixon enjoyed going to Camp David. It was originally called Shangri-La, but later it was renamed Camp David by President Eisenhower in 1953. Eisenhower named it after his grandson David Eisenhower. In the Catoctin Mountains near Frederick, Maryland, Camp David consisted of 125 acres. It was about seventy miles from the White House. All the cabins and lodges at Camp David were named after trees. It was the most famous of the presidential retreats.

President Nixon enjoyed walking the paths that crisscrossed the compound and sitting on the large rear deck of Aspen, the presidential lodge. From the deck there was a spectacular view overlooking the valley. In the fall when the deciduous trees' leaves turned red and orange it was an especially beautiful sight. On occasion Nixon would visit the bowling alley a short walk away to roll a couple of games. He and the family often watched first-run movies in Aspen Lodge shown by the White House Communications Agency. In addition to the bowling alley, Camp David also had tennis courts. Nixon was not a tennis player so the courts were used by his staff and other support people. President and Mrs. Nixon would helicopter directly from the White House to Camp David and the shift agents would drive.

During his first administration, Nixon's staff embarked on an ambitious renovation plan for Camp David that included building new cabins, up-dating existing ones, and putting in new paths. The renovations also included installing a swimming pool near Aspen Lodge. Nixon sometimes held cabinet meetings and other business meetings at Camp David. He also arranged for foreign dignitaries to spend time there.

❖ ❖ ❖

Less than six weeks after learning the shift routine at the White House, I was reassigned to First Lady Pat Nixon's detail. Though I liked working on the shift it was exciting to be assigned a new environment, where I would be traveling, doing advances, and interacting with Mrs. Nixon and her staff. Vern Copeland was in charge of the first lady's group. Agent Copeland had been with Mrs. Nixon during the 1968 campaign, where they developed a close professional and personal relationship. Since the detail was small it gave all her agents an opportunity to interact with her and to accompany her both on her schedule in Washington and out of town. Mrs. Nixon was always pleasant and had a perpetual smile on her face. She often asked agents about their wives, families, and hobbies, making us feel important to her.

Mrs. Nixon was fiercely loyal to her husband and dedicated to her daughters, Tricia and Julie. Much of her general schedule was developed out of the West Wing of the White House by President Nixon's senior staff and sent to the first lady's East Wing office for refinement. The first lady's office coordinated her meetings, local stops, and out-of-town trips with our detail. When appropriate, her staff office would assign an advance person to assist with arrangements for her public schedule. Normally one of the agents from the first lady's detail would precede her visit by three or four days to coordinate security arrangements on domestic travel.

An agent's role with a Nixon family member was much different than with the president. Mrs. Nixon, Tricia, and Julie looked to the agents for some guidance, assistance, and direction. Tricia, who was obsessed with her privacy, was not always comfortable interacting with either the public or many of the Secret Service agents. She was especially nervous when people approached her when she made off the record (unscheduled) journeys out of the White House complex. Her detail leader agent, Chuck Rockner, had his hands full using side doors, basements, and private elevators trying to protect Tricia Nixon's privacy.

Julie and her husband, David Eisenhower, on the other hand, were just the opposite. Julie was outgoing and gregarious and it was not unusual for her and David to seek the advice of detail leader Hal Thomas. They knew the names of all the agents assigned to them. David could sometimes be absentminded but was comfortable with his detail since he grew up in the public spotlight and the Secret Service with his grandfather, President Dwight Eisenhower. The relaxed atmosphere of the Eisenhower detail made it a very enjoyable and highly sought-after assignment.

Mrs. Nixon was the epitome of a lady. Not only was she refined and dignified, she was genuine, the real thing. She always found time to greet people. Her interest and sincerity impressed most who met her. She not only knew every agent on her detail, she knew about their families. She never complained no matter how arduous, routine, or boring her schedule would be. Mrs. Nixon was a real trouper who did not seem to hunger for the limelight.

❖ ❖ ❖

The role with President Nixon for most agents was distant and impersonal. Nixon and his senior staff were detached from the detail agents except for the most senior supervisors. Special Agent-in-Charge Robert "Bob" Taylor, the detail leader, was especially close to and respected by President Nixon. Taylor had accompanied Vice President Nixon to Caracas, Venezuela, in 1958, when his motorcade was besieged by demonstrators as it approached the capital. Rioters with clubs and rocks blocked the motorcade route and tried to overturn Nixon's limousine. The vice president was very appreciative that he was not harmed and also never forgot Taylor. In 1969 most of the agents assigned to PPD would rarely interact personally with the president.

The war President Nixon inherited from President Johnson continued to wrack our country. Even though Nixon was trying to lower the number of troops in Southeast Asia, the disenchanted public wanted him to totally disengage and bring all our men home at once.

October 15, 1969 was declared National Moratorium Day, a time for Americans all across the country to protest against the Vietnam War. It was a success as millions were reported to have turned out. Washington, D.C., had a fairly large number of people turn out. November 15, 1969 was designated for a peace demonstration in Washington. Our national capital was besieged with tourists, protesters, activists, radicals, demonstrators, military personnel, and police officers. Though there had been many demonstrations in Washington, this event was reported afterward to have been the largest single anti-war demonstration ever to hit our nation's capital. Forty thousand demonstrators marched by the White House, each carrying a sign with the name of a soldier killed in Vietnam. Afterwards 250,000–500,000 demonstrators marched down Pennsylvania Avenue with parade marshals hand to hand on both sides of the participants the entire length of the parade route.

Buses, parked bumper to bumper, ringed the White House complex in an effort to keep out the extreme radical elements, which showed up to disrupt the protest against the Vietnam War. Specially-trained Army units were hidden in the basement of the Treasury Department and several other locations as quick reaction forces to be used in the event disruptive radical elements tried to penetrate the security forces outside the White House grounds, the Justice Department, the Capitol, and the Pentagon.

Several hundred of the hard-core radicals roamed around the city in small packs of less than fifty trying to find penetration points to the major government sites. They kept shifting their location trying to avoid a head-on confrontation with security forces. Many were veterans of the rioting in Chicago and were aware the police would use force without hesitation. Helicopters, observation posts, and roving intelligence teams spread out around the city were used to monitor the movement of the Pennsylvania Avenue demonstration and the many small groups of radicals. This helped the security forces to keep one step ahead of the most radical fringe elements trying to cause a major embarrassment to law enforcement and the government.

While the radicals tried to avoid confrontations with the law enforcement forces, they loaded up with rocks and broke lots of windows. Due to a large number of arrests, the Yuppies, SDS, and other radical anti-war elements of the movement failed to make the major statement during the activities of the day as they had hoped. The vast majority of demonstrators involved were peacefully marching to express their anti-war sentiment. A few marchers were arrested, but it was the violent anti-war segment of the movement that failed in the end.

Throughout the day several other agents and I were posted across the street from the White House near Lafayette Park near the ring of buses. We were there to observe the forty thousand demonstrators coming past us with the names of those that had given their lives in the war effort. They passed in a very orderly manner. On one occasion a half-dozen radicals wearing headbands and with their faces painted ran past me chased by agent Paul Rundle and his Secret Service response team. Rundle had damaged his radio during an encounter with the group. I went home that evening knowing we had kept the radicals from achieving their goals.

❖ ❖ ❖

During the eighteen months I was on the first lady's detail, Mrs. Nixon made numerous scheduled trips around the United States, as well as regular visits to New York City for shopping and hair appointments at Elizabeth Arden. President and Mrs. Nixon would normally travel every six weeks to Key Biscayne, Florida, or San Clemente, California. Generally, visits to the Presidential Compound in Key Biscayne were for long weekends, while visits to the Western White House in San Clemente were less frequent but for longer periods of time. The month of August was set aside as vacation time in San Clemente. Holidays would be spent at Camp David, San Clemente, or Key Biscayne.

My assignment with Mrs. Nixon took me to Rome and Vatican City, Belgrade, Madrid, London, and Limerick and Dublin, Ireland. Traveling overseas was always a challenge from a security standpoint. Positioning of agents ahead of the arrival of the president needed to be carefully coordinated with the local police through the embassy. Placement of security cars in the motorcade had to be negotiated with the host government or security forces.

There were occasions when the situation could become strained. Pre-posting of agents might not be allowed in certain government buildings or other sites as was the case here in the United States. One of the biggest overseas problems was traveling to England. The British banned agents from carrying weapons. After negotiations at the highest levels, a limited number of agents (four to six) were allowed to bring handguns into their country. No shoulder weapons were allowed. With Mrs. Nixon this was not a problem since she was not subjected to any threats.

In the summer of 1970, while still assigned to Mrs. Nixon, I was selected to accompany Julie and David Eisenhower on a trip to the World's Fair in Osaka, Japan. President Nixon selected the two of them to represent the United States at the fair. One of the back-up presidential fleet Boeing 707s was used for the trip. Accompanying David and Julie on the USAF Boeing 707 was the normal crew and a small group comprised of an Air Force security detail for the airplane, White House Doctor Walter Tkach, and three of us from the Secret Service. Bill Duncan, assistant special agent in charge of the White House Detail, who was responsible for the family details, led our group. Hal Thomas, agent in charge of the Eisenhower detail, and I were the other lucky ones. In reality, I was the lucky one, having been selected out of a substantial pool of available agents. I wondered why no other agent from the Eisenhower detail went on the trip. It was another one of those times when I asked myself, "Why me?"

On the way to Osaka the plane stopped for two nights in Hawaii. Everyone in the party took advantage of the lay-over and spent time sightseeing, relaxing at the beach, or in their rooms. Julie and David were a very low maintenance couple, neither seeming to yearn for or enjoy the limelight. They preferred quiet, private time together rather than a night on the town. Duncan and Thomas were both very close to the Eisenhowers. I had become acquainted with the two of them through their joint activities with the first lady and at family events at Camp David, Key Biscayne, and San Clemente. Whether the Eisenhowers were out at the beach, swimming, or sightseeing, they interacted with whichever agent was nearby.

One of my main responsibilities during the trip was to make sure all of our bags made it to the hotel and back to the airplane at each stop. The rest of the time I accompanied detail leader agent Thomas augmenting the security. From Honolulu we went to Tokyo for one night and then to Osaka for the fair. Tokyo was just a rest stop with no appointments or meetings. In Osaka the Eisenhowers were greeted by American Embassy personnel and escorted to the fair. There were tours of some of the exhibits, including those of Japan and the Soviet Union. I remember thinking at the time as we entered the Soviet exhibition center that they were filming us. With such a small cadre of agents it went through my mind that the KGB would think I might be someone in the Secret Service who was important. Julie and David Eisenhower spent much of their time at the American exhibit greeting and talking with visitors. I am sure they were tired of shaking hands by the time we left but they never showed it or said so.

When the Osaka visit was over we eventually flew to El Toro Marine Air Station and I brought the luggage by car to the command post at San Clemente. It was brought into the Nixon residence by the on-duty shift. Besides being an interesting week for me, the trip ended up being a refreshing and relaxing break from my normal routine.

❖ ❖ ❖

During my first trip overseas to Rome and Vatican City in late September 1970, I was working with Mrs. Nixon part of the time and on advance assignment at some stops. It was my first visit to the Vatican. Even though most of us were confined to the courtyard while the president and Mrs. Nixon had an audience with Pope Paul VI, it was a very moving event for a Catholic from Visitation Parish in Tacoma, Washington. The agent doing the advance was able to get those of us that wanted one a papal blessing.

While in Rome, President Nixon, accompanied by Mrs. Nixon, went to St. Peter's Square to take a helicopter out to the Seventh Fleet where he was going to spend the night. Just outside the square a large crowd had gathered to see President Nixon depart. He ordered the motorcade to stop and got out of his armored limousine to greet the people. After shaking a few hands, Nixon climbed on top of the rear of the car and began waving to the gathered throng. I took a post at the rear driver's side door while Mrs. Nixon remained inside. When the president got back in the car the motorcade proceeded to the waiting helicopter. Mrs. Nixon got out as her husband boarded the helicopter. She waved as it lifted off for the short flight to the Seventh Fleet and then she returned to the hotel. The next day the Carabinieri police officer assigned to Mrs. Nixon brought me a newspaper that had a picture of Nixon standing on the rear deck of the limousine surrounded by a sea of people. The only face in the crowd that was identifiable was agent Endicott.

❖ ❖ ❖

President and Mrs. Nixon flew to Belgrade, Yugoslavia, on September 30 for a state visit hosted by President Joseph Broz Tito. I had arrived there in advance of the president and Mrs. Nixon. At the airport, while waiting for Air Force One, I watched as the advance team positioned our limo and follow-up car on the ramp. It had been previously negotiated that our follow-up car would be directly behind our presidential limousine. Most of the motorcade cars seemed to be scattered, helter-skelter, across the immediate ramp area. I guessed everyone knew their position in the motorcade. The arrival of Air Force One was closed to the public.

After shaking hands with the greeting government officials and the normal presentation of flowers to the first lady, the president and Mrs. Nixon and the official party were guided to their assigned vehicles. Once the cars were loaded the motorcade began to depart. What followed was like a cartoon of "whacky races" as motorcade vehicles began cutting each other off, completely changing the agreed-upon motorcade alignment. We suddenly had a Yugoslavian security car in front of us. About a half-mile up the road, without any warning, our follow-up driver made a quick maneuver and ended up in a position directly behind the limousine, as had been previously negotiated. We could tell the Yugoslavian security driver and their follow-up agents were furious and embarrassed. During the remainder of the drive to the guest house their government follow-up car repeatedly tried to regain the closer position, but failed. In all of the other presidential motorcades, one of the Yugoslavian agents would stand in front of our follow-up car prior to each departure to make sure they could have the first position.

President and Mrs. Nixon stayed at a guest house during their state visit. There was a dinner hosted by President Tito they both attended and there were separate schedules for the president and first lady. On the second day President Nixon flew to Zagreb with President Tito to visit Tito's birthplace. Mrs. Nixon did not accompany him, having a schedule of her own to visit a local school.

A day earlier I visited the school Mrs. Nixon would visit. While walking the exterior of the school I asked my counterpart why there were no vehicles on the roads around the school. He told me that all motorcade routes for the president and Mrs. Nixon were closed down two days ahead of time. The routes were then patrolled by machine gun-toting militia until the visit was over. I remember at the time wondering what the American public would say about motorcade routes in the United States being closed down two days before a visit instead of less than an hour before. This was so vastly different than our procedures back home it amazed me. I had no idea what their threat was.

Mrs. Nixon made her scheduled visit to the school. Children dressed in local costume sang, danced, and gave her flowers on her arrival. She toured the school, the cafeteria, and the play area before joining one of the classes. When Mrs. Nixon departed she seemed to have genuinely enjoyed meeting the children.

❀ ❀ ❀

After Yugoslavia it was off to Madrid for a festive and regal visit October 2-3. The motorcade into downtown was like a parade and included a large number of police vehicles, motorcycles, and, at one point, horses with riders in formal costumes carrying flags on long poles. President and Mrs. Nixon were state guests of Generalissimo Francisco Franco. President Nixon had an official schedule and Mrs. Nixon a very limited schedule. I had a chance to enjoy the Spanish cuisine at an old Madrid restaurant in the afternoon and in the evening visited a number of tapas bars.

A short trip to England followed the Madrid stop. First President and Mrs. Nixon met informally with Queen Elizabeth II. Then, while President Nixon met informally with Prime Minister Edward Heath, Mrs.

Nixon flew by helicopter to a castle where she toured and had lunch. A very prim and proper woman from the Office of Protocol dressed in a black dress with a white collar and wearing a wide-brimmed black hat with a white band joined Mrs. Nixon on the helicopter. Even though the flight was short, only fifteen minutes or so, the Office of Protocol lady needed to use the air sickness bag. She had never flown before and had been extremely nervous beforehand and was embarrassed afterwards.

❋ ❋ ❋

The most memorable stop on the one-week trip for me was to Ireland October 3-5, which took the Nixon family to Dublin, Ireland, and then to Limerick and County Cork. Tricia and Julie, who had joined the trip in England, accompanied their mother on a visit to a small home where the first lady's Irish ancestors, the Ryans, had lived. The typical small country white home with a thatched roof became quickly crowded with family, relatives, press, and security people. Tricia became agitated and complained to the head of Mrs. Nixon's detail about the number of agents in the small house. This upset some of the agents because most agents did their best to give her as much privacy as possible. There were times, however, when her frustration with agents would boil over. Mrs. Nixon and Julie never mentioned there was an issue with the number of security personnel in the Ryan house. I believe that of the twenty-five people in the house only three were agents.

After the visit to the Ryan home, Mrs. Nixon, Tricia, and Julie drove through the local town where a large crowd had gathered at the main intersection. The motorcade slowed and the first lady requested we stop for a moment. Lowering the rear window, she asked that the people be allowed to approach the car. Mrs. Nixon waved at the cheering throng and urged some to come to the limousine. Several people approached the car and shook hands with Mrs. Nixon. After five minutes the motorcade left so Mrs. Nixon and her daughters could meet the president. They had a one-hour drive to Limerick and County Cork, where they would remain overnight at a friend's estate.

Joining her husband in the limousine, the family began a police-escorted motorcade ride through the beautiful Irish countryside. The drive was right out of a travelogue. If, as Bobby Sherman sang, "The bluest skies you've ever seen are in Seattle," then the greenest green is in Ireland. With the green grass, neatly stacked rock walls along the road and the property lines, small white cottages with thatched roofs, and the narrow roads, there was a quaintness driving through the countryside I had never experienced anywhere else I had been.

Along the way we saw people now and then on the side of the road waving to the presidential motorcade. A half hour or so before arriving in Limerick, a group of at least thirty people were waiting alongside the road waving. As the motorcade slowed approaching the group, President Nixon asked agent Taylor to stop. Everyone in the follow-up car immediately took up defensive positions at the doors of the limousine as directed by shift leader Richard Keiser. The roof window of the limousine was opened and President and Mrs. Nixon stood on the rear seat so he could speak with the crowd. Seeing the bride and groom in their formal dress everyone realized the gathered group was a wedding party. After Nixon had a short exchange with the bride and groom the crowd began chanting, "Kiss the bride! Kiss the bride! Kiss the bride! " President Nixon, not sure what to do, was a little surprised when the bride, who was on the driver's side of the car, was lifted into the air and passed over the heads of the crowd and agents toward the car. President Nixon leaned over next to Mrs. Nixon and gave the new bride a kiss on the cheek. The wedding group went wild, cheering and laughing as the motorcade reformed and slowly pulled away.

Dusk was beginning to turn to dark as the motorcade neared the town of Limerick. People were scattered by the sides of the road waving to the president. Flags, banners, and arms were being waived by people of all ages. The weather was cool and threatening. Most of the people along the route were bundled in winter coats, hats, and gloves. As the crowds became larger the motorcade slowed to less than ten miles per hour.

Agent Keiser, sitting in the right front seat follow-up, barked to the back seat, "One and two up." This meant that the one agent and the first lady's agent should exit the follow-up car and run alongside the rear doors of the president's limousine. I proceeded to sprint to the passenger side of the limousine near Mrs. Nixon and continued to jog, keeping pace with the car. At this point only the two rear positions were directed to move up to the limo. The motorcade continued on the way to the center of town at a speed that was an easy jog for us.

We knew the motorcade would stop and there was going to be a presentation of the key to the city to President Nixon in the center of Limerick a little over a half-mile farther down the road. The roof window had been opened and the president and first lady were standing up on the rear seat waving at the crowd. After several more minutes of jogging, I could see four men with their arms full of flyers or papers step out of the crowd into the street, forty yards ahead. They were not running but were doing a double-time walk. They appeared to be intent on intercepting the limo. As soon as Keiser saw them come out of the crowd he immediately called, "Three and four out," directing the two remaining agents to leave the follow-up car and take positions at the front fenders of the limo. Agent Clarence "Buck" Lyda apparently slipped as he exited the car to take up his position at the front of the limousine on the driver's side. Three of the men were getting closer to the car. I looked back over my shoulder and could see agent Lyda was not going to make it to the front of the limo in time to intercept the interlopers.

Keeping my position near Mrs. Nixon until the three men carrying the flyers were only about ten yards away, I quickly reacted. Sprinting forward I grabbed the driver's door handle. Using the driver's door as a fulcrum, I knew I had gained the edge needed to intercept the three men. Pulling myself forward just as the three were nearing the car I caught the first one at the front bumper with my left forearm, sending him tumbling to the pavement. The second person immediately bore the brunt force of my right forearm, joining his partner rolling on the ground. As both individuals went down onto the pavement, flyers went soaring all over the place. One man left the group while the third culprit jumped over his fallen comrades. He slipped past me before I could react. But as I turned to try a last-second grab, I saw agent Lyda in position next to Mrs. Nixon. He was loading a right-hand roundhouse. When Lyda let the overhand loose, anti war flyers were once again scattered into the air as the last person dropped into a heap on the road.

From his perch on the back seat, President Nixon had moved over to the first lady's side to watch the action. I could see his face right after Lyda had dispatched the last activist. President Nixon had a smile on his face and said to Lyda, "Nice hit, nice hit." Out of the corner of my eye I could see uniformed officers taking control of the men.

Three minutes later we were in the middle of town for the presentation of a key to the city. President Nixon and the first lady got out of the car to join the mayor for the ceremony. Nixon received a key to the city as the crowd struggled with police officers, pushing into the intersection to better see the visiting American president and his wife. After the exchange of remarks and the presentation of the key, it took several minutes for the police to regain control of the intersection so the motorcade could depart.

When we left Limerick heading for the overnight stop, it was a dark, cloudy night, threatening to rain. We took up our positions alongside the limousine as it slowly departed the intersection until our cars had moved safely through and away from the crowd. Shortly afterwards we arrived at a heavily guarded compound where the president, first lady, and their daughters would be staying. The next day the Nixon family returned to Dublin and flew back to the White House.

❖ ❖ ❖

During the Christmas season of 1970, Mrs. Nixon came to me late one afternoon and said that she had seen a Washington, D.C., police officer highlighted on the local news. She mentioned he was directing traffic in one of the busiest intersections in the main shopping area downtown. Mrs. Nixon asked me if I would take her around five in the afternoon to watch the officer. We left the south grounds of the White House at five and the car dropped us five minutes later near the intersection with the officer. We quietly stepped onto the crowded sidewalk and walked twenty feet, where we would have a good view of the intersection. No one seemed to notice the first lady.

All four lights turned red at once, signaling pedestrians could walk through the intersection. A tall, slender officer in his black uniform, wearing a white hat and white gloves, loudly blew his whistle as he moved to the center of the intersection to get everyone's attention. Tooting his whistle to draw attention, he began to signal people through the intersection. He continued a cadence while blowing the whistle and synchronizing his arm movements at the same time. The officer would change the cadence and point at a shopper and blow the whistle loudly.

With the shopper's attention now directed at him he tooted the whistle, directing him to the corner where he was already headed.

The officer's ability to rapidly toot the whistle to get a specific child or adult's attention amazed me. The rhythmic beat of his whistles, coordinated with his hands, the movement of his feet, legs, and body provided enjoyment to those crossing the intersection. People watching and walking had smiles on their faces and seemed awed by his performance.

The tall, handsome officer was able to use his whistle and body to talk with the people. People especially enjoyed being selected for special attention. When the officer cleared the intersection in the grand finale using his whistle with all his theatrics, people standing in stunned silence began clapping and yelling.

The first lady began clapping and had a good laugh, enjoying the entertainment. She turned to me and said, "Let's watch him again." We continued to stand near the corner, comfortable in our winter coats and wearing gloves. I enjoyed seeing her relaxed and especially savored observing her being a regular person. Though the people around us changed, there was still no one there who realized the first lady was watching. On the short ride back to the White House she marveled at the slim, tall officer's rhythm and athleticism.

A wonderful professional relationship developed between Mrs. Nixon and me during my assignment to her detail that would have a positive impact on me much later in my career. In March 1971, after eighteen months assigned to her detail, I was transferred back to the president's detail. One evening shortly after going back to the shift, I was standing post inside the White House by the front door at 11 p.m. The post was only thirty feet or so away from the grand staircase. Mrs. Nixon and her close personal friend, Helene Drown, came strolling down the staircase shortly after I had taken the post. The two of them were chatting and appeared to be just enjoying each other and looking at the pictures and the decorations in the East Room and Blue Room. After fifteen minutes they headed back to the grand staircase and Mrs. Nixon noticed me standing my post. She smiled and headed in my direction with Mrs. Drown nearby. The first lady stopped about three feet away, smiled, and commented, "So, you are too good for me now that you are on the first team, huh?" With a grin and sassy twirl she turned and headed for the grand staircase. The first lady and Helene Drown were chuckling as they disappeared up the stairs.

President Nixon bought two beach houses on Biscayne Bay in 1969 next to his friend Bebe Rebozo in Key Biscayne, Florida. The houses were a ten minute-drive from downtown Miami. A fenced presidential compound was created that included a Secret Service house, a home owned by Robert H. Abplanalp, and a helipad in addition to the two Nixon houses and Rebozo's house. On presidential visits, Air Force One would land at Homestead Air Force Base, approximately thirty-five miles southwest of Key Biscayne. President and Mrs. Nixon would helicopter directly to the compound. There was no official presidential office or formal staff operations at the compound when the president and his family visited Florida. Selected staff members would stay in the nearby Key Biscayne Hotel to support the visit. Visits to Key Biscayne were usually for a couple of days of rest and relaxation.

Nixon would swim inside an area protected by a shark screen in front of his house. When he was in residence, each morning a Navy scuba diver would swim throughout the screened area to make sure it was safe for the president. Nixon enjoyed relaxing rides with friends and family on Rebozo's house boat, Coco Lobo. Even though they were closely followed by two boats with Secret Service agents and a boat with a press pool, Nixon knew this was the price of being president. The press was able to keep a distance away due to their telephoto lenses.

The lenses also gave those that wanted the opportunity to check out the beautiful women in skimpy swimwear unaware someone was spying on them.

Occasionally Nixon would helicopter from his Key Biscayne compound to Walker's Cay, a renowned bill fishing resort in the Bahamas. Walker's Cay was about 175 miles northeast of Key Biscayne located in the northern Abacos. Industrialist Robert Abplanalp had a 99-year leased for Walker's Cay and a number of other nearby islands with the Bahamian government.

On the helicopter rides over any of the islands in the area you could look down and see sharks in the water. The sharks could be seen swimming between coral and seaweed formations. Arriving at the small runway on Walker's Cay, President Nixon had the choice of either riding in the golf cart or walking to the marina. There he would chat with guests and staff before getting on board Abplanalp's yacht, the Sea Lion. The boat ride from Walker's Cay to Baby Grand, another one of Abplanalp's private islands, was about thirty minutes.

There were times President Nixon would helicopter directly to the helicopter pad at Baby Grand. The secluded island included a main house on a bluff with a small swimming pool. From the patio there was a beautiful view of the island and other tiny uninhabited cays. The original residence had been a small one-floor house without a swimming pool. After the purchase, Abplanalp renovated the house, adding the second floor and a large fenced patio with a pool. The new house had five bedrooms, a den, living room, dining room, and kitchen. A locked storage area under the house was used to store expensive wines. Also on the island were three, one- and two-bedroom cabañas, and a small shack used as a security room. The cabañas were used by the military aide, who had the "football" with the nuclear codes, someone from the staff, and the Secret Service supervisor. There was also an out-building that was used for storage and as a communications center.

Above the dock overlooking the small harbor was a caretaker's house. It was below the main house, which had a 360-degree view. The island was covered with mangrove trees and shrubs and other island growth. Along the beaches were sea oats and sea grapes. A coral/sand road leading from the main house went through the mangrove trees next to the communications/storage building, past the alternate helicopter pad and the old seaplane ramp. There was a large blood orange tree near the cleared area at the top of the seaplane ramp (this was used as the helicopter arrival/departure point).

Proceeding on, the road passed near one cabaña and over a bridge on the way to Mermaid Beach, a beautiful half-moon private beach a quarter-mile long with white sand. Mermaid Beach was Nixon's favorite place to swim. An elevated two-bedroom cabaña, where the ID agent and I stayed during the visits to Baby Grand, overlooked the beach. The road turned to the left and paralleled the beach with the view of the beach protected by the mangrove shrubs. An opening between the cabaña and the mangrove shrubs led to a path through the sea grapes and sea oats to the secluded white sands of Mermaid Beach. The crystal clear blue water lapping the shore was always inviting.

At the other end of the beach was another opening off the road through the mangrove trees and sea foliage to a large elevated cabaña with a thatched roof and a wood rail around the exterior with the sides open. Relaxing chairs and a table made the cabaña the perfect place to rest out of the hot sun and enjoy the enchanting scenery. A well-worn old barbecue near the cabaña had been used by Abplanalp for entertaining many times in the past. Abplanalp was an accomplished grill man and had a frying pan that nearly covered the top of the fifty-five gallon drum that had been converted to a barbecue. The pan had an appropriately long handle that he wielded with two hands like an experienced chef on the Food Channel.

You could see Nixon loved the solitude and privacy that his closest friends provided for him in the Bahamas, Key Largo, and Key Biscayne. They seemed to have a sixth sense about Nixon and the amount of privacy he desired. Each of them had an unobtrusive way of being available when Nixon wanted to walk, go for a swim, take a boat ride, or just talk. Nixon was not all business as portrayed by the press and as many people thought. He enjoyed his time with his two friends individually and together. He especially enjoyed the privacy he had with his family in Key Biscayne and San Clemente.

When Nixon decided to go to Mermaid Beach, he sometimes drove a golf cart. Driving the golf cart was one of those rare moments when the world's most powerful person could do one of the little things in life that gave him control. Even though Nixon could drive the golf cart the quarter mile or so to Mermaid Beach for a relaxing swim, he usually walked, accompanied by Abplanalp and Rebozo and his ever-present security detail. When he got to the beach, one agent would enter the water at either end of the area where Nixon would swim. A third agent would be selected by the supervisor to swim out thirty yards and sprinkle a black ink liquid into the water along the route where Nixon would be swimming. The agents understood the ink would create a screen so the sharks could not see the swimmers. The ink stayed suspended in the water for a while so the president could have a good swim.

On some occasions Mrs. Nixon and Mrs. Abplanalp would come to the beach after the men. The first lady would generally wade into the water but not go for a swim. She enjoyed sitting on the beach or in the cabaña taking in the scene while reading a book or magazine. When Nixon got out of the water he normally walked along the beach with

Mrs. Nixon or one of his friends. It was his time to relax, think, and be with friends.

On my first visit to Mermaid Beach, Assistant Agent-in-Charge Bill Duncan was the supervisor and P. Hamilton (Ham) Brown was the shift leader. I accompanied Mrs. Nixon when she arrived at Mermaid Beach. Duncan had just given agent Brown a small bottle of the inky solution to sprinkle into the water to keep the sharks at bay. The first lady found a place on the beach to sit on her towel, while agent Brown dove into the water. Duncan and I found a high point on the beach to watch everyone. Brown swam about twenty feet beyond Nixon and sprinkled the black solution parallel to the beach. When he was through I watched Brown tighten the bottle cap and toss the bottle further out in the clear blue water.

Joining Duncan and me on the beach Brown unfortunately mentioned to Duncan that since there was only a little bit of the solution left he threw the bottle away. Brown was frustrated to learn that the bottle was the only one we had on the trip. Duncan and I watched and chuckled as Brown swam out beyond the shark screen and retrieved the bottle.

The press, staff, day shift, WHCA, and other support people generally all stayed at the hotel on Walker's Cay. Abplanalp provided boat service to Baby Grand for those that needed it. The midnight shift stayed at the Key Biscayne Hotel in Key Biscayne. During presidential visits to the Bahamas, a Marine or Army helicopter normally transported the presidential group to either the airstrip at Walker's Cay or the helicopter pad at Baby Grand. The back-up helicopter was used to transport the working Secret Service midnight shift from Homestead AFB to the helicopter pad at Baby Grand.

❖ ❖ ❖

STORIES FROM INSIDE THE PERIMETER

The Secret Service suffered a personal tragedy during a visit by President Nixon to Key Biscayne on May 26, 1973. An Army helicopter transporting the midnight shift to Baby Grand crashed into the water just offshore from the landing site. According to agents on site, as the Army Sikorsky helicopter approached the helicopter pad over the water, the helipad was illuminated by lights from various small vehicles that were on the island along with handheld lights. Slowing as it neared the shoreline, with the landing pad fifty meters away, the pilot suddenly veered to abort the landing. He rolled the aircraft onto its side, beginning a 360-degree swing to make a second approach. In the pitch black of night, while swinging around for the new approach, the pilot unknowingly flew his aircraft into the water.

After the crash the Sikorsky sank front end down and came to rest on the sandy bottom with the rear rotor emerging from the water. Some of the agents and other support people at the pad immediately went to the dock to get boats for a rescue mission. Agents and staff at Walker's were notified of the emergency situation and appropriate notifications were made by the command post there. There was an immediate departure of several boats from Walker's Cay to assist with the tragedy.

Inside the helicopter there must have been a frantic scene with agents trying to orient themselves and get out of the downed craft. According to information from the scene at the time, the co-pilot managed to exit a side window and swim to the surface. When he surfaced fuel had already leaked from the downed aircraft, contaminating the surface water. Choking on the fumes and fouled saltwater the crew repeatedly dove down to the entrance door trying to get it open. The task was made extra difficult by the fact that the door, when in the upright position, opens with the assistance of gravity. So trying to pry open the door in an upside down position without gravity took a number of dives before the crew could wrest the door open enough to secure the release of the trapped agents. Meanwhile the agents had been huddled together breathing the air bubble that remained inside after the crash.

When the rescued group of agents finally got to the surface they gathered and realized agent Cliff Dietrich was missing. Agent Dietrich, who had been knocked out in the initial crash, did not make it. He was found sitting in his seat with his seatbelt still engaged. According to rumors it was later determined the altimeter had not been reset when the helicopter departed Homestead AFB, leading to the aborted landing and subsequent crash.

Dietrich's tragic death led to a total review of military and Secret Service procedures in the use of helicopters. New training classes for the Secret Service, military personnel, and commercial airlines cabin personnel on water crashes was initiated. His death also led to design changes in helicopters and aircraft that better directed passengers to the exits in emergencies.

❖ ❖ ❖

When I look back on my days at PPD, my memories are not only of the business at the White House, Camp David, San Clemente, and Key Biscayne. I remember some of the more personal moments when we saw Richard Nixon enjoying time alone or with others. The Secret Service's concern for his privacy allowed him on occasions to escape from the walls, fences, alarms, cameras, and support people to enjoy precious moments with his family and friends.

President Nixon enjoyed swimming as an exercise to keep in shape. When he first arrived at the White House, the president regularly used the White House pool that had been built with private money for President Roosevelt in 1933. The long pool was not as narrow as modern-day lap pools, but it was not overly wide. Several times a week before dinner President Nixon would stop by the pool on his way to the White House residence to swim laps. He would strip naked in the changing area and swim alone in the pool. One of his accompanying Secret Service agents would stand a post in the hallway leading from the dressing room to the pool. From this vantage point the agent could see the mirrored wall at the far end of the pool and monitor the president in the reflection as he swam his laps. This was the same pool President Kennedy was reported to have used when he lived in the White House. The pool was covered over in 1970 and a new White House press area was built over it.

✤ ✤ ✤

I enjoy reminiscing about visits to Camp David. There were deer roaming on the property. One deer in particular was gentle and not afraid of people. It used to come around Aspen Lodge after dark and would eat out of our hands. The Camp David visit I remember best was a midnight shift in the winter, when there was a considerable amount of snow on the ground. One of the agents made a snow bunny, over a foot tall, and set it on the railing at the rear of Aspen Lodge. Over the course of the night other agents added to the bunnies on the railing. By morning shift change over thirty sculpted snow bunnies adorned the railing. Nixon, who was an early riser, was surprised and pleased to see the array of snow bunnies on their deck. He commented to one of the agents before the morning shift change how much he and Mrs. Nixon were enjoying the bunnies.

✤ ✤ ✤

President Nixon arrived in San Francisco for a meeting and dinner on August 21, 1969 with the president of South Korea, Park

Chung Hee. As the motorcade arrived at the St. Francis Hotel, the ever-present anti-war demonstrators were alongside the hotel out of view of the president and first lady. Next to the demonstrators was an area that had been designated by the staff advance agent for a large group of pro-Nixon union members. There were lots of police in the area, including some on horseback. Someone in the group of demonstrators was holding up a big hand-painted sign that read, "Pat likes dick." The sign could be seen from the presidential suite. When Special Agent-in-Charge Taylor saw the sign from the suite, he told agent Dennis Shaw to take off his equipment, coat, and tie. Shaw was tall, big, and athletic, having played football in college. Taylor directed him to go downstairs and get rid of the sign. Shortly after going outside, Shaw joined the pro-Nixon union group and soon a fight broke out between the peaceniks and union workers. In the ensuing fracas the sign was destroyed and Shaw returned to his shift.

❖ ❖ ❖

Nixon, along with his son-in-law David Eisenhower, used to drive golf balls in front of the Key Biscayne house into the water while other family members watched. Rebozo always had a bucket or two of range balls available for the president and his guests. David Eisenhower and President Nixon wore the same size clothes. There were occasions in San Clemente, Key Biscayne, and at the White House when the president would be looking for a pair of shoes or a shirt, only to find out he was too late since it was being worn by his son-in-law.

❖ ❖ ❖

The loneliness of the presidency is something I observed on occasions in my White House assignment. Watching an animated

Nixon smile and laugh while engaged with his family and friends and then seeing him walk solo along the beach at San Clemente and at Abplanalp's beautiful Mermaid Beach sometimes presented a radical change in Nixon's mood. When Nixon was concerned or troubled about something he would become quiet and isolate himself from others for a period of time. His body language when walking was completely different. Instead of a bounce in his step with his head up and shoulders back, a reflective Nixon would have his head bowed, shoulders stooped, and his stride labored as he trudged down the beach.

❖ ❖ ❖

Whether taking Mrs. Nixon to the Ozarks to visit a furniture factory, to Elizabeth Arden on Fifth Avenue in New York City, to a campaign event, or to a school in Belgrade, Romania, I remember her as always upbeat. The first lady took an unusual amount of time to talk to teachers, staff, children, workers, volunteers, and vacationers. She projected an interest and a genuineness that left a good impression on those who met her. Her schedules were often grueling and by the end of the day she would be spent. She enjoyed a quiet evening on the road in her room. I do not recall her ever complaining about her schedule or engaging with people.

❖ ❖ ❖

President Nixon had significant impact on the Secret Service and their responsibilities. The Secret Service in 1970 under Public Law 91-217 had the name of the uniform contingent protecting the White House changed from the White House Police to the Executive Protective Service. At the same time, the responsibilities of the Secret Service were broadened to include protection of family members of the vice president and establish protection for foreign diplomatic missions in the immediate area around Washington and in other cities in the United States, territories, and possessions as prescribed by statute.

In a controversial move, the Nixon White House suggested a new formal dress uniform for the Executive Protective Service suitable for holidays, state visits, and other special and ceremonial events. A white uniform trimmed in gold with white cotton gloves included a European-style formal hat as part of the new dress uniform debuted in 1970. However, the hat was only worn for a short period of time because the hats were ridiculed by the press and others. Much of the criticism was that the new hat was too formal, too European looking, and it was soon sent to the graveyard.

In 1970 protection of foreign dignitaries visiting the United States was the responsibility of State Department Security. When French President Georges Pompidou arrived in the United States in March 1970 on a state visit he first had a state dinner at the White House and then scheduled stops in Chicago and New York City. Pompidou was viewed by some as anti-Semitic, and the Jewish communities in the cities to be visited by him geared up for his arrival. The visit in Washington went well. There was concern by some, however, about Chicago and New York.

In Chicago it was rumored that Mayor Richard Daley was less than enthusiastic about the French president's visit. Due to friction between Daley and the Nixon Administration and concern over the alleged anti-Semite bias by Pompidou, full support by the Chicago Police Department seemed to be lacking. The perceived limited police support may also have been caused by less aggressive manpower requests by the State Department security contingent. Mayor Daley greeted President and Mrs. Pompidou at the airport but had chosen not to attend a dinner at the Palmer House before Chicago's Council on Foreign Relations and Alliance Franchise.

When Pompidou arrived at his hotel, according to press reports, a large crowd had assembled outside; many were Jewish, upset with the President of France. At least one person broke through the security entourage and spat in the face of Claude Pompidou, President Pompidou's wife. He was livid and outraged and was ready to return to France. When President Nixon learned of the attack he immediately directed the Secret Service to assume control at once of the Pompidou Security Detail from the State Department.

President Nixon then called President Pompidou right away and apologized to him. The French president indicated he would cancel his trip to New York and return to France the next day. Nixon was able to get Pompidou to agree to finish his scheduled visit to New York with the Secret Service. In a surprise move, President Nixon traveled to New York City to replace Vice President Agnew and attended the dinner honoring Pompidou. Nixon wanted to personally convey his apology to President Pompidou. Neither New York Governor Nelson Rockefeller nor New York City Mayor John Lindsay attended the New York dinner honoring Pompidou. Both were reported to be looking ahead at the Jewish vote in the fall elections and alleged conflicts in their schedules prevented them from attending the dinner.

❖ ❖ ❖

In the aftermath of the Chicago incident, the State Department was relieved of the responsibility of providing protection to visiting "Heads of State and Heads of Government." By executive order, Nixon directed the Secret Service to assume those duties as well as the protection of designated American dignitaries who traveled abroad on behalf of the president. Later in 1971 the change was enacted into law by Congress.

The Nixon campaign staff had updated and rewritten the manual for presidential campaigns in 1968. Once Nixon was in the White House they did the same on how they presented the president to the public. It was their desire to portray the president in the most favorable light in every environment. Often that meant putting him in an elevated position surrounded by people below with their arms extended upwards. The advance staff was obsessed with developing the various access control zones to ensure no offensive signs were in the immediate area of the president that would be shown on the six o'clock news. It was equally important to them that no loud vocal opposition would disrupt an event. Public relations/perception seemed to be the main focus of the president's senior staff.

Speech sites were layered with children often closest to the president, and VIPs were admitted by name into a strictly controlled area directly in front of the president. Right behind this area would be an area for special guests with admission by ticket only. Finally the remainder of the viewing area would be filled with the public. When a controlled access area was not full of people, often the staff advance agent would hand out special admission tickets to the general public on the street, or else people in attendance in the general public area would be moved from a more remote area to the closer one.

On some occasions, by expanding controlled access areas to unknown persons, a problem would result. If someone the staff perceived as a problem ended up in a controlled area, the advance would claim to the police or Secret Service the person had a counterfeit ticket and ask that he or she be removed.

Staff conflicts with the Secret Service over access control, picture identification badges, location of demonstrators, and need for security posts occurred often and many times were very contentious. The staff wanted to spontaneously stop along parade and motorcade routes, while the Secret Service wanted all stops to be identified and properly secured. Agents needed to be pre-posted and a screening point leading to the "spontaneous" area needed to be identified. Even though a stop to shake hands along a motorcade route, outside a hotel or convention center, or at a sporting event seemed to be spontaneous, it was not. All stops were strictly secured and controlled by the Secret Service.

Nixon's staff was concerned about the pictures that would be taken that could end up in the papers or on the evening news. Screening out people who they deemed undesirable became an art with them. One case that ended up in the courts happened on a visit to North Carolina. The ticketed event was being held in a large athletic field house. Once entering the site people presented a ticket and were directed to one of several doors to get to their seats. The vast majority were directed to doors leading inside the arena. Visitors were profiled (long hair, anti-Nixon signs, anti-war shirts, or just generally did not seem to be a Nixon supporter) and were arbitrarily determined to be undesirable and were sent through a door taking them back outside. Without their ticket, which had been confiscated, they were unable to get back into the arena.

❊ ❊ ❊

The Secret Service continued to grow in 1971 both in responsibility and in numbers of people, when I was transferred back to the shift. I had received a good evaluation while on the first lady's detail and was on the promotion list to the GS-13 supervisory level. After seeing most of the GS-13 positions filled on the detail I asked for a transfer back to the field. Several people intervened suggesting that if I stayed I would be promoted.

I was ready to return to the field to get back to a nine to five, weekend off work environment so I could spend more time with my family. The assignment to the first lady's detail had allowed me to take the children camping, hiking, and to the beach. I had the time to coach them in basketball and softball. But with the 1972 campaign less than a year away I was hoping to get my batteries recharged before entering the next hectic phase of my career.

My request for a transfer was treated well by Protective Operations and the Office of Investigations and I received a transfer to the Seattle Field Office. My reassignment in July 1971 from the Presidential Protective Division was preceded by a house-hunting trip. Arriving at the Seattle Field Office for a courtesy call on Special Agent-in-Charge Elmer Moore, I was pleasantly surprised when he asked me if I would like to live in Tacoma and work out of my home. It was a great opportunity for me and I of course immediately agreed.

Finding a home that was large enough for Ginny, Michael, Robin, Leslie, and Jamie did not prove difficult. With the depressed housing market due to layoffs at Boeing I located a three-bedroom, two-storied home with a partially finished basement on Stadium Way in North Tacoma overlooking Commencement Bay, for $29,000. The master bedroom had a nursery as part of the suite. The house on the uphill side of the dead end street had a large backyard with a fairly steep gully that went under a railroad trestle two hundred feet below and out into the bay. I returned to Washington, D.C., anxious to get packed and head for the Northwest.

❖ ❖ ❖

Growing up in Tacoma had been a wonderful experience. By the time I was eight years old life in the Endicott family was fishing, digging razor clams at the Pacific Ocean and steamer and butter clams in Hoods Canal and Puget Sound. Trips to the sound and canal were also used for gathering oysters and Dungeness crabs. The summers were family ventures to pick raspberries, strawberries, wild blackberries, and corn. The fall found our clan searching for chanterelle mushrooms in the nearby forests and making apple cider in our backyard with our cider mill. The entire year was spent fishing either in Puget Sound for salmon and bottom fish or in the many lakes within an hour's drive of our home for trout.

Family vacations usually included other relatives and were scheduled around visits to local lakes, Puget Sound, Hood Canal, and the Pacific Ocean. We often camped in one of the numerous state parks. My father's uncle, Jerry Endicott, owned a resort at Pacific Beach, Washington, where we sometimes enjoyed camping and swimming during August. Summer days were normally in the 60s and 70s and occasionally got into the 80s, while winters were cool and wet with a snow or two, but no prolonged freezing temperatures.

My father's work projects at home and away dominated our spare time much of the year. Most of the work was done at our house, building brick walls, flower boxes, making a patio, pouring concrete walks, building a fire pit, or erecting a huge block and concrete garage. My father was a generous person, often offering our help to family and friends alike. Activities at the South End Boys Club were another priority since my mom and dad had helped establish the Parent's Club to raise money to support the club. Their group eventually raised enough money to build an indoor swimming pool.

When I was twelve years old my dad told me if I wanted to go to college I was going to have to get a scholarship. I knew he meant an athletic scholarship. With dad working in the Hod Carriers Union and being on unemployment during part of the winter I knew he would never have the opportunity to help any of his six children financially. Instead, he taught us the rewards of hard work and a moral and ethical legacy that I carried with me through life's journey.

❖ ❖ ❖

Over the years I came to understand that to be successful takes a lot of hard work and a certain fire in the belly. People often talked about luck, good or bad. I am a person who does not believe in luck. It is hard work that is the cornerstone of success. In my experiences luck is attained by using our ability to reduce the chances of failure so that when a critical choice needs to be made there is a greater chance of success. If individuals do not work hard to increase their chances of success they will fail many times. If you work hard to increase the opportunity to succeed you will still sometimes not attain your goal, but I see this as being unsuccessful, not as failing. Life has taught me that cutting corners is a sure path to failure.

❖ ❖ ❖

When I received the assignment to reside in my home town I sensed the next couple of years would be non-stressful and relaxing. Working on check forgeries and counterfeit cases with the Postal Inspection Service, Tacoma Police Department, and the Department of Special Investigation agents (DSI) at Fort Lewis and McChord Air Force Base was something I looked forward to doing. I was sure I would renew acquaintance with some of my old high school buddies. I was looking forward to the cross-country drive and moving into our new home overlooking the bay.

Ginny and I filled our small Chevrolet Vega station wagon with our four children, our cat, Charlie One Eye, Rags, our dog, our caged rabbit Thumper, and our suitcases right after the 4th of July and headed west. We received more than our fair share of stares from gas station attendants and people at rest stops and restaurants when they saw our big white rabbit in the cage, our cat, dog, and four children crowded into our car. We drove directly to Tacoma without taking any sightseeing side trips.

Soon after arriving we closed on our house and shortly thereafter our furniture arrived. We had plenty of help from family and friends with the relocation. We put Thumper's cage on a stand in the backyard near the house. We all loved the view and privacy of our new home.

❖ ❖ ❖

A week after moving into our new home I received a call early one morning before I left for work from Mrs. Lockwood who lived across the street. She told me that our son Jamie, who was not yet two years old, was outside on the hood of my car wearing just a diaper. I brought him into the house, closed the door, and locked it. Setting him down in the kitchen I watched as he returned to the front room and moved a chair so that he could unlock and open the door. I went to a hardware store and purchased a lock to install high enough so he could not undo it. The next day when I came downstairs Jamie was on the kitchen floor playing with all the pots and pans. Everything in the kitchen cabinets was on the floor. I put a lock on the outside of the nursery door, which was a few steps from my bed.

❖ ❖ ❖

A few weeks after getting settled in our new residence I received an assignment to assist the advance team for President Nixon's visit to Grand Teton National Park in Jackson Hole, Wyoming. There was an

Interior Department Lodge on a lake that was operated by the National Park Service and used by VIPs. President Nixon was going to overnight in the lodge as part of a trip emphasizing environmental issues.

The advance team and support agents stayed at the Jackson Lake Lodge owned by Laurence Rockefeller. Three days before the president arrived, the park rangers arranged for two of us to get fishing licenses. Early the next morning four of us caught enough eight-inch trout for breakfast for those in our group who wanted some. Eating fish for breakfast that was only out of the water two hours was a very satisfying culinary experience and brought back memories of growing up in Tacoma.

❖ ❖ ❖

Returning to the Northwest, I kept busy working with Postal Inspector Willie Clinton and detectives Gene Brame and Bob Hubert of the forgery squad at the Tacoma Police Department. A few days later I went out in the morning to feed Thumper and he was missing. I was upset and knew the kids would be devastated. The cage door was locked but our pet rabbit was missing. Sometime later in the fall I heard Michael and Robin talking about the men living down at the bottom of the gully behind the house. I interjected myself and questioned them about the men. They mentioned that hobos lived in the woods near the railroad tracks. There was no question for me about the fate of Thumper. I guess the bums had a good rabbit stew one evening. We did not allow the kids to play in the gully anymore.

In the fall I headed off on a dignitary protection assignment to the East Coast. It seemed that hardly six weeks would go by before it was off on another assignment out of town.

❖ ❖ ❖

On the personal side, living in Tacoma allowed me to spend time with relatives and friends and take advantage of the outdoors. My parents left in early October for Keno Bay, Mexico, for their annual six-month winter vacation. They stayed in a trailer park across the street from the Sea of Cortez and returned in late May. The trip down and back gave them an opportunity to stop and visit friends and relatives. I was playing handball several days a week with Lew Overbo, my basketball teammate at Lincoln High School. We played downtown in the old Elks Lodge building. Dick Franklin, my closest friend, who I went to school with from second grade through the first year of college, was only twenty minutes away. We spent a lot of time together.

❖ ❖ ❖

With the New Year came an assignment to Abidjan, Ivory Coast, in mid-January 1972 to support a visit by the first lady. She would be visiting multiple West African countries during the trip. Advance teams comprised of White House advance staff, Secret Service agents, WHCA personnel, and technical support agents assembled in Washington, D.C., for briefings. The teams then flew together on a USAF C-141 to Africa. Each team was dropped at the site of their visit. We were the next to the last team to be dropped off in Abidjan, Ivory Coast.

The State Department provided full support for our team through our embassy in Abidjan. The biggest problem we faced initially in the Ivory Coast was that President Houphouët-Boigny did not have anyone on his staff he felt sufficient confidence in to put together the visit of the first lady. Houphouët-Boigny was going to use an aide to his next-door neighbor, President Omar Bongo of Gabon, to lead his advance team. We needed the team in Gabon to complete the initial phase before we could begin work on the official schedule. In the meantime we took care of logistical arrangements with the embassy and the Ivorian police.

We spent one Sunday at the American Embassy cabaña on the Gulf of Guinea. We were warned ahead of time by embassy personnel that the undertow at the beautiful white sand beach was treacherous and not to go into the water. With our van loaded with food, soda, and beer we arrived at the remote beach ready for fun. As enticing as the blue water was, we decided to relax for a while before organizing a game of touch football. It was decided the teams would be the Secret Service, technical support, and WHCA versus the staff advance and embassy support. The game got more competitive as more beer was consumed. The arrival of additional embassy staff brought renewed life to the teams.

Getting ready to run out for a pass I noticed a young, unaccompanied boy about twenty yards away approaching the water. It was useless to yell due to the roar of the surf. I began running as fast as I could toward him when one of the waves knocked him over. Nearing the water I could see he was caught in the undertow and I dove into the salty water. I felt his arm brush my hand and managed to grasp his wrist. I let the undertow take me out and I worked my way to the surface as I had been advised by people at the embassy. Hugging the young boy as we came out of the water I returned him to the beach where his parents were anxiously waiting. Two minutes later the football game was once again consuming everyone's attention.

Our advance team was led by agent Jurg Mattman of our Paris Field Office, who spoke fluent French. Mattman was nicknamed Pierre by our team during the trip. He was a great asset to the team and understood the country, its people, their customs, and the limitations of the decision-making process. Mattman, who was appreciated and liked by everyone, was calm and had a low-key approach that kept everything on track.

When we encountered a problem with the government carefully controlling the number of vehicle badges allowing access to events at the palace and other government sites, Mattman said he knew how to take care of it. He plastered one-third of the windshield on the driver's side of our International van with various identification cards, baggage tags, small flags, visa documents, and other important, official-looking papers with official stamps. When the visit took place we were at the head of the motorcade and even though we did not have proper identification for access to any of the events, at each entry point, when the guards saw our windshield, they immediately snapped to attention, saluted, and granted us access. Mattman and I privately laughed about the security at the entry point.

Mrs. Nixon's trip went well as she was greeted at a small village and had a dinner at the palace. She once again showed me that she was not only a good person but a great diplomat. During the one-night visit she took time to acknowledge my presence and thanked the advance team for their support.

❖ ❖ ❖

Returning to Tacoma I knew that the 1972 presidential campaign details were beginning to be assembled and would be announced by the spring. Most agents were hoping the details would not be activated before the early summer. Work on my check forgery and counterfeit cases plodded along. Just about the time I got caught up on my work the teletype would go off and I would be on my way to another foreign dignitary detail or special assignment. So much for what I thought would be a more a restful and relaxing time in Tacoma, Washington.

When I received notice of an assignment to the presidential campaign detail providing security for Maine Senator Edmund Muskie, I was relieved to read I would be on the second rotation. I thought the sixty-day delay in reporting would give me time to get everything up to date. But the teletype went off and I was off for one more dignitary detail before the 1972 presidential campaign started for me.

When I finally joined the campaign, agent Jimmy Johnson was the detail leader and Barney Boyette was his assistant. Our protectee, Senator Muskie, had made a huge mistake early in his campaign. Before the New Hampshire primary the conservative *Manchester Union-Leader* newspaper published a letter making the claim that Muskie had made disparaging remarks about French-Canadians. Later, after the primary, the newspaper made accusations against Senator Muskie's wife, Jane, concerning her drinking and her inappropriate language. In an attempt to defend his wife, Muskie made a moving speech outside the *Manchester Union-Leader's* offices. Muskie gave the emotional speech during a snow storm and the press reported he cried. Muskie said he did not cry and what appeared to be tears were due to the snow flakes. After the incident Muskie was no longer looked upon by the press and many Democrats as a strong leader. His position in the campaign quickly eroded and it was only a matter of time before the mistake would be fatal.

❖ ❖ ❖

Shortly after I reported for assignment, Muskie officially withdrew from the campaign but was allowed to keep his detail through the Miami Democratic Convention July 10-13. Senator George McGovern was nominated to be the Democratic Party's presidential nominee and Senator Thomas Eagleton was selected to be the vice presidential nominee on the last day of the convention. Immediately after the convention I was released and returned to Tacoma.

❀ ❀ ❀

On June 17, 1972, five men were caught burglarizing the office of the Democratic National Committee in the Watergate building complex in downtown Washington, D.C. Several of the people involved with the Watergate burglary were associated with the Committee to Re-elect the President (CRP). White House press secretary Ron Ziegler shrugged everything off as a third-rate burglary.

The stay in Tacoma after the Democratic Party Convention proved to be a short one. During the vetting process, vice presidential nominee Senator Eagleton had failed to disclose that he had twice received electric shock therapy for nervous exhaustion. He began having difficulty on the campaign trail as a negative press criticized him harshly. When the information initially broke it looked as if Eagleton would survive the press questions with the support of McGovern. However, on July 31, realizing the shock therapy was dragging their ticket down, Eagleton withdrew from the ticket. When McGovern replaced Eagleton with R. Sargent Shriver I was off to Maryland. The '72 campaign, which I thought was over for me, began anew.

When I reported to the Shriver detail, agent Barney Boyette was the detail leader and agent Kevin McCarthy from the Philadelphia Field Office was his assistant. I had very much enjoyed working with Boyette on the Muskie detail and was delighted to see him again. He and I had bonded during the campaign period when he had selected me for a number of special assignments.

This was the first time I had ever been around the Kennedy family. Sargent Shriver, his wife, Eunice (Kennedy), and their children Bobby,

Maria, Timothy, Mark, and Anthony were part of the Kennedy clan. Shriver was bright and hard-working; he had been the first director of the Peace Corps under the administration of his brother-in-law, President John F. Kennedy. In 1968 he was designated U. S. Ambassador to France where he served under President Nixon until 1970. Shriver was a sociable, fun-loving, happy-go-lucky person. Eunice and Sargent Shriver were very warm, gregarious, and family-oriented. Nominee Shriver often spent time with his children playing, kidding, and cajoling them. The younger children were typical hyperactive kids. Teenagers Robert and Maria were on the campaign trail a great deal of the time getting to know many of the agents.

The campaign itself is a blur of plane rides, motorcades, speeches, and campaign stops. Most of my memories are of the children. Timmy Shriver on more than one occasion attempted to use extortion to get money from me. One time we were at a church in Baltimore, and Shriver was addressing a large group of black parishioners in the basement hall. I was standing post inside the room by the door when Timmy Shriver came into the room. He pulled me into the hallway and asked me for money for the soda machine. He told me if I did not give him change he would go inside with me and cause a scene. Looking him in the eye I said, "Go ahead." Refusing to be extorted, I turned and went back into the hall. He announced one more time inside the room for me to give him the money or he would start screaming and interrupt the proceedings. After being rejected a second time he left to look for a better score.

Probably the most unusual place that I ever had to accompany a person I was protecting was when Shriver decided to have a sauna at one of the hotels on the campaign trail in Milwaukee, Wisconsin. We had a short rest at our hotel between stops. Boyette came up to me and said Shriver was going downstairs to take a quick sauna and I should go with him. When we got into the locker room Shriver was trying to beat me into the sauna. He quickly undressed, wrapped a towel around his waist, and on the way to the sauna said to me, "Don't forget your gun, Endicott."

Entering the sauna I was without my radio but had a small hand towel wrapped around my gun. Shriver was sitting on the bench talking with the only other person in the sauna. He was being his cordial and gregarious self as he was earlier when he had challenged me to bring my gun into the sauna. Now as I sat in the sauna with my gun next to me he began to bust me about having a gun in the sauna. The other person in the sauna seemed to be enjoying the unfolding scene. Shriver, in a very playful mood, was joking, laughing, and playing to his audience. I sensed the hotel guest was amused by the banter going back and forth between the vice presidential nominee and his Secret Service agent. Shriver asked if I had ever had a gun in a sauna before and if it would rust. Once he got all the wind out of his lungs he calmed down and we found ourselves alone in the sauna. Ten minutes later we were back in the locker room showering and heading for his next campaign event.

On a brief rest stop to the Shriver compound at Kennebunkport, Maine, agent Boyette decided to take a minimum number of staff since we were only going to be there one night. He wanted to give as many agents as possible to a chance to spend a couple of days at home or get some rest in Washington. I worked out the logistical details with him so we took two reduced personnel shifts.

❖ ❖ ❖

The Shriver home looked more like a small hotel than a private residence. The beautiful New England-weathered structure was an appropriate vacation home for a member of the royal Kennedy clan.

Taking many trips to the Pacific Ocean when growing up in Washington State, I had never seen any houses even close to those in Maine. Sitting on a small rise surrounded by beach and surf, the residence was a sight many could never imagine and most would never see. The Shriver family arrived midday at their beachside residence. The weather was clear and warm with a nearly cloudless sky. Our small shift managed to get a quick bite to eat after our day shift. We got some sleep before returning that evening to work the midnight shift.

It was a very quiet, balmy, cloudless night with a slight breeze when I reported to work the midnight shift. Sitting in a folding chair on the back patio that was right next to the house offered me a commanding view of the backyard leading to the beach. There were two bedroom windows on the second floor right above me. Looking at the starry sky, I got up and slowly walked around the patio trying to find the Big Dipper. I was struggling, trying to stay awake, when I sat back down in the chair around three in the morning. There was a quiet muffled conversation above me that got my attention. Realizing the upstairs window was secretly being opened, I looked up in time to see a wastebasket coming out the window and being turned upside down. Instinctively I rolled off the chair as the water from the wastebasket hit my vacated position. Some of the water splashed on me as Maria and Timmy tried to control their laughter while they closed the window. The next evening we had a good laugh on the chartered aircraft as we flew to the next campaign stop.

The last and most vivid memory of the Shriver campaign occurred at the Shriver residence in Maryland. Unbeknownst to any of the agents, Shriver had decided to take his car for a ride after he and his daughter Maria had washed it. When Maria stepped in front of the car to try to stop him from leaving, her father continued slowly creeping forward until she lay prone on the hood. As she gripped the hood by the windshield wipers her father stepped on the gas and sped up. Shriver went through the front gate surprising everyone with Maria spread-eagled on the hood, screaming. It took several minutes to get one of our Secret Service cars out the gate to try to chase them down. However, the agents in the car were unable to locate Shriver. About ten minutes later Shriver returned to the residence with his daughter in the same position on the hood of the car as when he left and still screaming. He got out of the car laughing about the quick spin he just completed with Maria plastered to the hood of his car.

❖ ❖ ❖

The Vietnam War continued to be the major issue in the country as peace activists Sen. George McGovern and Sargent Shriver campaigned crisscrossing the country. Unlike President Nixon and Vice President Agnew, McGovern and Shriver did not have any significant anti-war demonstrations on the campaign trail. When the election was over, President Nixon won re-election in a landslide with 60.7 percent of the votes and 520 electoral votes.

I returned to Tacoma and fortunately did not have to get involved with the inauguration. Once again, however, I found myself working dignitary details. It began to dawn on me that the number and types of assignments I had been assigned to over the last year and a half had made me aware of a lot of things going on in our organization. Speaking to other agents and supervisors when on the road, I realized my databank of people, processes, and issues had greatly expanded.

Nixon and Kissinger, who had been conducting secret negotiations with the North Vietnamese, announced an end to all offensive operations. Meanwhile the daily scenes of body bags in Vietnam on the evening news were replaced by the Watergate scandal.

Nixon was sworn in for a second term on January 20, 1973. The Watergate affair had been going no place until Judge John Sirica in January 1973 meted out very harsh sentences to two of the leaders of the burglary with direct links to the CRP. One of the two, John McCord, decided to tell all in exchange for a lighter sentence. This set off a Senate investigation of the Watergate affair and vaulted *Washington Post* investigative reporter Bob Woodward to the forefront of the fiasco. His renowned "Deep Throat" informant was born out of the investigation. Over the next year and a half the investigation, hearings, and leaked information would keep the scandal on the front pages of the newspapers and as the lead story on the evening news programs.

❖ ❖ ❖

Secretary of State Henry Kissinger and Le Duc Tho of North Vietnam signed the Paris Peace Accords on January 27, 1973, and received the 1973 Nobel Peace Prize for negotiating the end to the Vietnam War. Later some would say that the holes in the agreement led to the United States barely getting the troops and embassy people out of the country. Nixon called it a "Peace with Honor." Those opposed to Nixon painted it as a loss. Either way, the troops were home and there were no more losses. There were, however, many civilian deaths as North Vietnam conquered the south.

Terrorism was regrouping and developing on the horizon. Regional terrorist groups such as the Palestinian Front for the Liberation of Palestine (PFLP), Palestinian Liberation Organization (PLO), and the Red Brigade were moving from regional terror groups to global, state-sponsored organizations. Terrorist activities were becoming transnational. I was beginning to pay attention to it. But I was in Tacoma and the terrorist threat was not something I had to worry about.

Working counterfeiting and check forgeries kept me busy, along with frequently being on the road with visiting foreign dignitaries.

A temporary assignment for the visit of South Vietnam President Nguyen Van Thieu to the United States in March 1973 brought me to Washington, D.C. There was much controversy over the secret Paris peace agreement negotiated by National Security Advisor Kissinger and North Vietnamese politburo member Le Duc Tho and the fact that President Thieu was not involved. Nixon knew he needed to cut our losses and kept Thieu totally in the dark. The state-sponsored trip to Washington was a reward for his long relationship with the United States.

President Thieu made the rounds of Washington, meeting with people at the State Department, Defense Department, and the White House. His visit was short and out of the normal spotlight.

❊ ❊ ❊

The last dignitary detail that I remember while assigned to Tacoma was with Crown Prince Hassan of Jordan. Late in his visit we were at the Newporter Inn, Newport Beach, California, and encountered an unusual set of strange events. The crown prince and the security details were staying in two full units of a four-unit, two-storied townhouse. The crown prince and his wife had the lower unit. His security detail had the upstairs in the same unit. The Secret Service had the second unit. It had been agreed with the manager at the Newporter that for security reasons the third and fourth units would remain empty. The hotel, built in 1962, was situated on twenty-six acres on a bluff overlooking the Pacific Ocean and had just over four hundred rooms.

A call from the switchboard operator to the Secret Service command post was received about 11:30 p.m. The operator reported an unauthorized phone call emanating from the unoccupied end unit in the building where the crown prince was staying. Since I was the midnight shift leader, I immediately dispatched two agents to secure the unit. One agent was directed to the rear area and the other was requested to take a post at the front door. The operator had advised that the manager would be right down with a master key. I contacted the Los Angeles Field Office intelligence agent, the Los Angeles advance agent, and the technical security agent in their rooms and asked them to report at once to the command post.

With the manager, Lonnie, several of us went to the end unit. As we opened the gate to the front area the agent on post advised that there was an obvious sign that an unauthorized entry had been made in the end unit. There was an "L" cut in the front window screen, typically used by burglars. Calling over the radio to the back post, the agent there reported the sliding glass door leading to the private patio and pool was wide open. A loud knock at the front door failed to receive a response and the manager used a pass key to let us enter. Two agents were relocated to secure the adjacent unit. A methodical search of the rooms found all of them to be empty. Turning our search to the second floor rooms was also negative.

Next, we shifted to the adjacent vacant unit. After getting no response from knocking on the front door we used the master key and entered the unit. Turning on the light we could see woman's apparel—underwear, a skirt, blouse, and shoes—scattered on the floor. Also on the floor were men's shoes and articles of clothing. Approaching the bedroom door we could hear moans of passion. Hesitating a moment I pounded twice on the door, then opened it a couple of inches and announced in a loud voice, "This is the United States Secret Service. Who is in here?"

There was a pause before a man offered his name. The manager gasped and said he would be right back. After ten minutes he returned to tell me that a prominent local businessman was in the unit. It seems he came into the lobby asking the night receptionist for a key to the room. Not wanting to tell an important customer no, she gave him a key. According to the manager, the man was with a woman who was not his wife. Apologizing to the unauthorized guest, we left the downstairs unit. A search of the upstairs unit also turned out to be negative.

Our technical security agent and another agent went through the attic that was open area, allowing movement between the four units. When it was reported the attic was clear we were satisfied that everything was safe and I accompanied the manager and our ID agent to the front desk. The telephone operator was asked to explain exactly what had happened. She said she received a call asking for an outside line. The operator said that the male caller sounded as if he had been drinking. She said she began running the plug over the board looking for the room that was making the call. Just as she identified the downstairs end unit as the location, she said the person on the other end hung up. She said she had called the manager and then notified us of the call.

The next morning after breakfast I met with the manager. He advised that the FBI had served a search warrant on the end unit at eight that morning, shortly after my shift had been relieved. The manager said the federal agents were searching for a listening device believed to be hidden in one of the rooms. It turned out this particular unit had been occasionally occupied by Martha Mitchell, wife of United States Attorney General John Mitchell, who was the head of the Committee to Re-elect the President. In fact, it was rumored she had once been forcibly removed from the room at the direction of her husband because of calls she was making to media people.

There had been rumors in the press at the time that a listening device had been placed in the room by the infamous "Plumbers" of the Watergate scandal to monitor Martha Mitchell whenever she stayed in the unit. Apparently that was how they knew about the calls she was making. It was our speculation that the mystery person who visited the room the previous night went there to surreptitiously remove the listening device. The person must have been successful, apparently, since the FBI found nothing, according to the manager.

Crown Prince Hassan returned to New York City for an overnight before returning home. He had one of his staff people stop at McDonald's ahead of time on his way to the airport and buy hamburgers for the crew and passengers of the regularly scheduled Royal Jordanian Airlines flight on which he was returning to Jordan. The hamburgers and French fries arrived for all the passengers just before takeoff.

❖ ❖ ❖

In Tacoma everything seemed to have settled down by the summer of 1973. The travel had stopped and with the weekends off our family had a lot of time together. The quiet summer gave us time to go to the ocean, camping, hiking, clam digging, and fishing. It was the most cherished time of my stay in the great Northwest.

CHAPTER TWO

TERRORISM REARS ITS HEAD
1973 - 1975

TERRORISM REARS ITS HEAD 1973-1975

Peace in the Middle East since the twelfth century has been tenuous, and very often non-existent. Prior to World War I, the Middle East was a multi-ethnic, multi-religious area controlled mainly by the Ottoman Empire (1300-1922). For hundreds of years, the borders changed with the flow of power throughout the region. After the discovery of oil in the early 1900s it became an extremely valuable commodity and lead to attempts by the British and other European countries to dominate the region.

As oil became more and more of a focus for global powers, the British and French tried to gain influence with the various countries in the region. During World War I, the French diplomat Francois Georges-Picot and Briton Mark Sykes made a proposal to their governments to create a secret pact, known as the Sykes-Picot Agreement, carving up the Middle East region between the Palestinians and the Jews. The secret agreement itself, however, broke an earlier promise of independence between the British and the Sharif of Mecca, Hussein bin Ali. The Sharif was responsible for the holy cities of Mecca and Medina and the safety of people performing the Hadj, the pilgrimage to Mecca. Other countries in the region tried to exert their influence without success; the British and French remained in control.

On November 2, 1917, British Foreign Secretary Arthur Balfour wrote a letter to Lord Rothschild about plans for a Jewish homeland in Palestine. The letter reflected the position of the British government and was referred to as the Balfour Declaration. It set forth the British position in developing a homeland for the Jews, while the rights were maintained for other people in the area. Many governments in Europe were trying to position themselves to have a say over the flow of oil from the region. In 1920, the League of Nations put Palestine under a mandate administered by the British.

In 1921, during the British mandate period, the British decided to split Palestine. The 75 percent of Palestine located east of the Jordan River was designated an autonomous political subdivision. The Emirate of Transjordan was created on that land, leaving Palestinian Arabs and Palestinian Jews to divide the other 25 percent. As a result of the creation of the Emirate of Transjordan by the British, the 1917 Balfour Declaration was never implemented. There was a tremendous amount of tension in Palestine after the creation of Transjordan. Palestinians and other Arabs in the region began attacking Jews living in Palestine. They wanted the Jews to leave and to keep the remaining land for themselves.

Many Jews, migrating from Europe, could no longer get into Palestine and found themselves stuck in refugee camps in Europe. They became extremely frustrated with the camps and the lack of movement on the earlier promises of a homeland made in the Balfour Declaration. The Jews were very organized, however, and began fighting back, hoping to carve out a section of Palestine as their homeland. They believed that in order to be successful it was necessary to rid the area of the British. So they began making attacks against both the British and Palestinian Arabs. The region continued to simmer and boil for years.

There was mistrust of the British by both the Palestinians and Jews. It seemed many members of the League of Nations resented British colonial rule after World War II. While the British global colonial empire was deteriorating, the British continued to be the dominant outside force in the Middle East. With their 75 percent share of Palestine and a new name, the Hashemite Kingdom of Jordan was now officially recognized by the countries in the League of Nations. The struggle to carve out their portions consumed the Palestinians, Jews, and other Arab nations. Neither the Palestinians nor the Jews had an army and fighting between them continued to escalate as both spawned terrorists groups in an effort to gain territorial advantage. The Jews were fighting for the creation of a homeland, while the Palestinians and their Arabs neighbors were fighting to annihilate the Jews.

❖ ❖ ❖

On November 29, 1947, the United Nations General Assembly, which had replaced the League of Nations in 1945, passed Resolution 181, partitioning Palestine into areas for the Palestinians and the Jews. The Jews were ecstatic, while all Arabs totally rejected the partitioning of Palestine. The U.N. plan gave roughly 45 percent of what remained of Palestine to the Arabs and 55 percent to the Jews. A small portion of the land around Jerusalem was allocated as an international zone. The Palestinians, who had previously lost over 75 percent of their land to Jordan, were once again seeing their homeland carved up.

By April 1948, Palestinians and Arabs began attacking the Jews as the end of the British mandate drew near. Initially the British tried to remain on the sidelines, hoping to keep their defensive positions; however, in the end it did not work. The Jews continued their attacks on the British, and the defensive tactics of the British caused them to cede land to the attacking Jewish forces.

Resolution 181, outlining the end of the British mandate, had previously set the partitioning of Palestine to be completed by August 1, 1948. The United Nations, however, voted officially to end the British mandate on May 14, 1948, when the United States, joined by a majority of the United Nations member states, officially passed U.N. Resolution 181. The next day, May 15, a Jewish state of Israel was declared and admitted to the United Nations.

Lebanon, Syria, Egypt, Yemen, Jordan, and Iraq immediately declared war on the new state of Israel. They were more determined than ever to destroy the Jews. Their armies invaded Israel from Jordan, Syria, and Egypt. There were no U.N. forces at the time to ensure implementation of Resolution 181, and all attempts by the United Nations, the British, Arabs, the United States, and others to negotiate a stop to the fighting were unsuccessful.

When the war was finally over, the new state of Israeli had expanded its territory and had more land than originally allocated by the U.N. partition plan. The area originally designated as Palestine, instead of being split between the Palestinians and Jews, ended up with a kingdom of Jordan, the state of Israel, and the Palestine area. Unlike Israel and Jordan, the Palestinians found themselves without a country, without a state.

Arab nations took in the displaced Palestinians and put them in refugee camps. Many Palestinian refugees found themselves living in unbelievably squalid conditions in crowded camps located in various Arab countries around the Mediterranean. Palestinian children grew up for decades in these camps developing an intense hatred of Jews and Israel. Meanwhile, Jews began flooding into Israel from Europe, Russia, and other areas.

With their dreams of a homeland shattered, the Palestinians regrouped to continue their violent confrontation with Israel. Even though they were given some support by their Arab neighbors, the Palestinian cause remained unresolved. The Palestinians seemed like bastard children that could find no one willing to help them with their terrible living conditions while they tried to regain their land. The Middle East continued to simmer with raids by Egyptian and Syrian forces and Palestinian terrorist gangs being conducted across Israel's borders.

The Suez Canal, which was built between 1859 and 1869 to connect the Mediterranean Sea with the Red Sea, begins at Port Said in Egypt on the Mediterranean coast and ends at Suez on the Red Sea. Initially, the canal was owned by Egypt and France, but in 1875 external debts caused Egypt to sell its shares to the British. In a move to protect their investment, British troops took control of the Suez Canal in 1882 and remained there until 1952.

Egyptian troops were one of the groups that had been conducting periodic intrusions along their border with Israel since 1948, when the state of Israel was born. In a political move to isolate Israel, the Egyptians denied them use of the Suez Canal in 1950. Raids by Egyptian Fedayeen (Muslim holy warriors) and retaliatory attacks by the Israeli Defense Forces (IDF) increased in the early 1950s. In July 1956, President Gamal Abdel Nasser nationalized the Suez Canal to gain control of the payments to help fund his project of containing the Nile River by building the Aswan Dam. Egypt agreed it would pay $81 million in installments to the shareholders of the nationalized Suez Canal Company and gained complete control of the canal.

A secret agreement between France, Britain, and Israel led to an invasion of Egypt by Israeli troops on October 29, 1956. The Suez Canal was now in control of Israel. The Soviet Union protested vigorously at the United Nations, while President Eisenhower, who had not been forewarned of the invasion, was furious over the collusion between Israel, France, and Britain. Eisenhower joined with the Soviet Union to protest the invasion and threatened to sell off the United States' reserves of British pounds unless a cease fire was declared. The threatened sale forced a cease fire and the withdrawal of Israeli troops.

By March 1957, the pressure being exerted by Eisenhower, coupled with an address at the United Nations by Canadian Minister of Foreign Affairs Lester Pearson, had a positive effect. Pearson requested the creation of a United Nations Emergency Force to replace the British troops. This led to the withdrawal of British and French forces and the first use of "peacekeeping troops" by the United Nations. Pearson received the Nobel Peace Prize for his efforts, while British Prime Minister Anthony Eden was forced to resign.

The Suez Canal incident led to the continuing deterioration of Israel's relationship with Egypt, Syria, and Jordan, and by 1967, the Syrians were lobbing shells into Israeli villages from the Golan Heights. Raids across Israel's borders from Egypt and Jordan escalated.

An incident in April 1967 caused great concern throughout the region, when Israel air forces clashed in an aerial dog fight with Syrian aircraft. Seven Soviet-provided Mig jets were downed while Israel lost only one of its jet fighters. Rhetoric calling for the annihilation of Israel escalated and blew like a hurricane throughout the Arab world.

Using routine troop movements as a cover, Israel strengthened its border positions in May 1967. In a totally unexpected move on June 5, 1967, Israel made a preemptive strike against their enemies, catching Syria, Egypt, and Jordan by surprise. The avowed enemies of Israel were caught flatfooted and, five days later, when the Six Day War was over, Israeli troops occupied the Golan Heights, Sinai Peninsula, West Bank, and Gaza Strip. Israel not only controlled much of the land designated for a Palestinian state, but also had control of additional land belonging to Egypt, Syria, and Jordan.

Repeated efforts over the next five years by the United Nations, the United States, the Soviet Union, Egyptians, Syrians, Jordanians, and Palestinians to resolve the Middle East crisis failed. All United Nations resolutions calling for the return of the land captured by Israel were either withdrawn or vetoed by the United States in the U.N. In retaliation for the failure of the United Nations to resolve the crisis by

1973, Arab states were threatening to withhold selling oil to the United States and other Western countries.

Meanwhile, attacks across the borders on Israel continued. The Soviet Union, the main weapons supplier to Egypt and Syria, had re-supplied their allies with aircraft, armored vehicles, artillery, ammunition, and other weapons. In addition, the Soviets provided the Egyptians with advanced radar systems and surface-to-air anti-aircraft missiles.

The stalemate between Israel and its Arab foes continued, as they were locked in a classic "Catch-22." The Israelis would not sign an agreement to withdraw from the seized territory until they had an agreement providing them with peace and security. The Arab states would not sign an agreement on peace and security until Israel withdrew from the occupied areas. The support of Israel by the United States put the United States firmly in the middle of the Palestinian-Israeli conflict.

❖ ❖ ❖

I was surprised when in September 1973 Barney Boyette called me about accepting a transfer to Washington, D.C., to the Protective Support Division (PSD). He was the deputy agent in charge there and told me PSD was going to expand the Kissinger detail. Boyette and I had first met in 1966 when he was a senior instructor at Secret Service Special Agent Training School in Washington, D.C. The two of us were reunited during the 1972 campaign, when he was the assistant leader of the Muskie detail and again later with vice presidential nominee Sargent Shriver. During the campaign, Boyette and I developed a friendship and mutual respect for each other. He often gave me what I saw as important special assignments conducting advance security arrangements, or working special projects. It was another one of those occasions where I wondered, "Why me?"

Boyette indicated over the phone that I would have a good chance of a supervisory promotion to GS-13 if I were willing to take a transfer to PSD. According to him, Robert Latham the agent in charge of PSD, was a hard-working taskmaster and a stickler for details. Lapham, according to Boyette, was looking for energetic young agents to help with the new and growing responsibilities of the Protective Support Division. Boyette suggested that once an agent earned his stripes with Lapham, he allowed a great deal of latitude in decision making.

My time in Tacoma had been extremely busy and challenging. There had been hardly a six-week period of time that I was not assigned to an advance detail, foreign dignitary detail, special project, or the presidential campaign. My boss in Seattle, Elmer Moore, gave me a lot of freedom, requesting I report once every two weeks to the Seattle office. I worked out of Tacoma Postal Inspector Willie Clinton's office or the check squad at the Tacoma Police Department with Bob Hubert and Gene Brame. It had been a great opportunity for me to spend time with my family and friends. Being near my mom and dad was a special treat.

I knew all good things usually ended and realized the career opportunity I was facing. Boyette, my mentor, was a good salesman and closed the deal. He told me I would be advised in October of my official reporting date.

As national security advisor, Kissinger's initial Secret Service detail began in 1971 and was small; agent Jack Ready was in charge with no more than a half-dozen agents. Agents Ned Hall and Bill Bacherman were among those helping Ready.

In an apparent move to better manage the State Department, President Nixon nominated Kissinger to replace Secretary of State

William Rogers in September 1973. Rogers had been attorney general during the Eisenhower administration and had a long history of working with Nixon. According to conversations I had years later with Nixon, Rogers was asked to retire because he was not strong enough to battle the bureaucrats at the State Department. Kissinger's appointment was approved by Congress on September 22, 1973.

After assuming his new cabinet position, Kissinger opted to retain his now-expanding Secret Service coverage. It was unprecedented for security personnel from the Treasury Department to provide protection for the secretary of another cabinet position. Protective details for cabinet secretaries were routinely assigned from security agents within their own departments. The secretary of state traditionally used State Department security agents for his protection.

By keeping his Secret Service protection, however, Kissinger would not only have the best security in the world but would have a certain independence from the State Department bureaucracy. Preserving his Secret Service detail allowed Kissinger to use his detail agents to send and receive selected messages to the White House through "back channels," thereby keeping the State Department sometimes in the dark.

The use of back channel messages by Kissinger to communicate with President Nixon facilitated the flow of information between them. It allowed the two of them to restrict information to those in the State Department who might not agree with Nixon.

I believe what I just wrote is true, so don't read this wrong, because the vast majority of communications went through normal State Department channels. But when there were very sensitive negotiating issues during shuttle diplomacy and several other projects, the use of back channels limited some in the State Department from knowing what was going on and helped cut down on leaks.

Years later, when I provided private security for former President Nixon, he said to me during several conversations concerning foreign policy, "Mike, it is the president's responsibility to formulate foreign policy, and it is the State Department's responsibility to carry it out." Nixon would continue by saying, "The Georgetown crowd at State doesn't agree. They think they set policy, not the White House." Nixon indicated this was one of the reasons he selected Kissinger to replace Rogers at the State Department. Nixon said Kissinger was better able to carry out the policies generated by the White House than Rogers was.

※ ※ ※

The 1970s were an extremely violent time not only in the United States but globally. Terrorists were hijacking aircraft, bombing buildings and cars, and kidnapping government and military leaders. Some attacks were domestic, driven by the likes of the IRA (Irish Republican Army), ETA (Basque separatists) and the Weather Underground (United States radical students). Other attacks were conducted internationally by such groups as the Popular Front for the Liberation of Palestine (PFLP, PFLP-GC), the Palestinian Liberation Organization (PLO), the Italian Red Brigade, the Japanese Red Army, the German Red Army Faction, also known as the Baader-Meinhof Gang, the Black September group, and the FLAN (Puerto Rican terrorist group). These terrorist groups were some of the major ones causing havoc all around the world.

※ ※ ※

On October 6, 1973, two week after Kissinger became secretary of state and seven years after the Six Day War, to the surprise of everyone, including the United States and Israel, Egyptian and Syrian armies attacked Israeli troop positions. The Egyptians attacked from the west, crossing the Suez Canal and overrunning Israeli positions. While Egyptians engaged the Israelis, the Syrians did the same to Israeli troops in the Golan Heights. Syria initially gained back all of the territory it had lost in 1967. In the beginning the war went badly for Israel as the Egyptian army crossed the canal heavily armed with anti-tank weapons under a Soviet-designed protective umbrella of sophisticated overlapping systems of radar, shoulder-fired anti-aircraft missiles, anti-tank missiles, and mobile anti-aircraft missiles.

The Israeli forces initially suffered heavy losses of aircraft, tanks, and other armored vehicles, which prevented them from counterattacking. The Israelis quickly drew up a plan to neutralize the Egyptian aircraft defense systems. Meanwhile, President Nixon responded to the surprise attack by immediately ordering a re-supply of ammunition, armored vehicles, and other war material for Israel. He had virtually the entire U.S. fleet of Air Force C-141 aircraft flying re-supply missions, while the Israelis were preparing their counterattack.

In the Golan Heights, the Israeli army had been caught off guard by the ferocity of the surprise attack and was forced to retreat as they suffered heavy losses. With the United States re-supply mission in full swing, the Israeli Army regrouped and counterattacked, soundly defeating the Syrian army. In fact, the Syrians, who initially recaptured the Golan Heights, were pushed out of the heights and beyond where their lines were when the war began.

General Ariel Sharon made the first move of the Sinai counterattack by crossing the canal into Egypt. Using Egyptian equipment with Israeli troops dressed in Egyptian uniforms and speaking Arabic, he and his troops penetrated Egyptian security check points using false documents printed in Arabic. The Egyptian equipment and uniforms had been captured during the 1967 Six Day War. General Sharon was able to breeze across the Suez Canal into Egypt between the Egyptian Second and Third Armies, where his unit got behind the Egyptian lines undetected. General Sharon and his Israeli Special Forces immediately began destroying both radar and defensive missile sites.

Soon Israeli reconnaissance aircraft entered Egyptian airspace and were able to direct their jet aircraft to destroy other key Egyptian defensive sites. With their position in the Golan Heights secured, together with the success of the Sharon mission west of the canal, the Israeli Air Force took total control of the skies. Israel's aircraft cut the Egyptian supply lines on the west side of the canal, while their troops on the east side of the Suez surrounded the now isolated Egyptian Third Army.

Egypt's mentor, the Soviet Union, fearing defeat of the surrounded Egyptian troops, moved the war into the political arena by publicly threatening to send in Soviet troops to help the Egyptians. Nixon, not wanting to have outside military forces become embroiled in the foray or to see the Egyptians suffer a humiliating defeat, told Soviet leader Leonid Illyich Brezhnev that Secretary of State Henry Kissinger would travel to Moscow to work on an acceptable cease-fire proposal for presentation to the United Nations.

⚜ ⚜ ⚜

About three weeks after agreeing to the reassignment to PSD, Boyette called to tell me that my transfer orders had been approved for December. He then asked if I were available to travel to Moscow on behalf of PSD to assist with advance security arrangements for a visit of Secretary of State Kissinger. I did not know at the time that the trip was for Secretary Kissinger to negotiate a cease-fire with the Soviet Union. PSD agent Matt Daley, who had several previous advance assignments in Moscow, would be the team leader, according to Boyette. I was advised it would be a good opportunity to get familiar with Moscow. Though I had made a number of trips overseas, this would be my first visit to a communist country.

With the stage set for my support of the Kissinger detail, I traveled to Washington to meet with Boyette, where I was introduced to Daley. Our pre-trip meetings at PSD included information on Moscow, the schedule, our support team, and an intelligence briefing by our Foreign Intelligence unit. Daley did a good job of briefing me on the communist environment we would be visiting. Agent Daley's normal routine for travel to Moscow was to bring chewing gum, pantyhose, and girlie magazines to give to our KGB counterparts and other support people. He also brought several bottles of whiskey to give away. Thanks to him, I developed an interest in local customs and an appreciation of developing relationships with our counterparts around the world.

Special Agent-in-Charge John Simpson of Protective Operations asked to see me before my departure. In a briefing at his office, he provided me with information to pass on to the KGB concerning a Nixon visit to Moscow in the spring of 1974.

On our arrival at the Moscow airport, we were met by a representative of the U.S. Embassy General Service section, members of the KGB Committee for State Security, airport immigration officers, and custom officers. Our passports with visas were presented, along with appropriate entry documents that we executed on the plane. Our bags, which had been searched, were brought to us and we were transported to our hotel by the KGB. Daley and I rode in a KGB Chaika sedan, which was similar to the Checker cabs being used at the time in the United States. The oversized, boxy Chaika sedan had considerable leg room in the rear compartment with drop-down seats on the back of the front seat.

Cloth curtains that covered the rear window and door windows allowed total privacy in the rear compartment.

As we moved quickly out of the airport and down the wide street heading for our hotel in the center of Moscow, we pushed the door curtains aside to see the sights. Speeding through sparse traffic, our KGB officer alerted us as we approached several huge, symbolic tank traps on the outskirts of the city. The strategic military defensive structures were made of three heavy metal I-beams welded together in the form of an X. The grossly oversized traps were on a small hill next to the main road, easily visible to the passing traffic. They marked where the Russian forces stopped the Nazi tanks advancing on Moscow during World War II.

Continuing our ride into the center of the city, we saw statues of various Russian heroes that were strategically placed in front of buildings and at intersections, especially as we entered the more populated area. An unusual tall chrome structure caught my curiosity and our KGB escort officer proudly announced that the statue was dedicated to their space program. It was of their first Soviet cosmonaut, Uri Gagarin. After that we passed a circle with a statue of Lenin, who was the first head of state of the Soviet Union. Actually his name was Vladimar Llyich Ulyanov, but he used Lenin when he was in exile and led the overthrow of the Czar Nicholas II in 1918. He continued to use it after the overthrow.

Our small motorcade soon crossed a bridge over the Moskva River, where we could see the Kremlin and the dome of St. Basil's in Red Square. We were treated to a ride past the Kremlin before arriving at the nearby Sovetskaya Hotel. It had been interesting to see the statues, buildings, and unique sights on the ride into the city. But the Kremlin, which means fortress, was the highlight of our ride. Located in the center of Moscow at the confluence of the Moskva and Neglinaya rivers, it is surrounded by a high red brick wall. Moscow and the Kremlin date back to the late eleventh century, when wood was the main construction material. In the fifteenth century, red bricks replaced the wooden churches, walls, and buildings of the Kremlin. Today, besides being the seat of their government, it continues to be an armory and repository for national treasures.

Red Square, where the annual May Day parade takes place, encompasses one side of the Kremlin. At one end of Red Square there is a wide entrance across the street from the Moskva River where the multi-colored, domed St. Basil's Cathedral is situated. At the other end of the square, facing the center of town is the State Museum of Natural History. Lenin's mausoleum is near the middle of the square close to the Kremlin wall opposite Moscow's only department store, GUM. The mausoleum is made of deep red granite blocks, doubling as the podium and grandstand for the annual May Day parade. There are other churches, museums, and historical buildings both in Red Square and inside the Kremlin walls.

When our small advance team arrived at the government-controlled Sovetskaya Hotel, we were required to immediately surrender our passports at the registration desk. In the Soviet Union the government requires all hotels to register every visiting foreign guest with the local police. We were told to return in a couple of hours to retrieve our passports. The Sovetskaya was an elegant, majestic old hotel, operated as a guest house by the Soviet government. The hotel was used only for housing local and visiting government officials, trade groups, and other dignitaries. After registering in the lobby, we each received a small slip of paper, stamped with an official seal, which contained our room number.

I stood in the middle of the lobby of this venerable old hotel for several minutes soaking up the history. The Sovetskaya was right out of the 1920s with its huge, high-ceilinged lobby, overstuffed furniture, and the imposing, wide grand staircase leading to the rooms upstairs. The Baroque pictures and graceful draperies in the lobby reinforced the imagery of a by- gone era. Two small elevators that held only three or four persons without bags were not the primary conveyance of the guests of the hotel. Unlike most hotels in the United States, in Moscow most people used the grand stairs to get to their rooms, even if it were five or six floors above the lobby.

My fascination with the hotel continued as we ascended the stairs to reach a lobby area on our floor. Here an elderly woman sat behind a large wooden counter/desk. In the Soviet Union elderly women are often called "Babushka," which translates into grandmother in Russian. Our floor director exchanged the official piece of paper for our room key, which was chained to a wooden ball, over half the size of a baseball. The babushka, who only spoke Russian, admonished us through the translator not to take our keys outside the hotel. She cautioned us that we needed to exchange the key for the official stamped paper at her desk before we left the hotel, since the paper was required in order to gain re-entry to the hotel. Lastly, the babushka told us the floor and room number of the private dining room where we would eat and the times the meals would be served. This was the normal treatment that government guests received while staying at the Sovetskaya.

Our KGB host assigned a car and driver to our advance team for our visit, thereby creating an easy way for them to keep close tabs on us much of the time. Our floor lady was designated the coordinator, ordering the car when needed and releasing it at the end of each evening. The U. S. Embassy also provided transportation, as needed, for the other members of the team, especially the Intelligence Division agent. The KGB could have provided transportation for the entire team but those that worked out of the embassy used embassy cars.

Our rooms, which were good sized, were monitored by the KGB with audio surveillance in all rooms and video in some. My bed was not quite full-size and had hemp webbing instead of box springs, a four-inch firm stuffed mattress covered with linen, and a heavy woolen blanket. The bed with its heavy wood frame was not necessarily made for comfort, though I must say I slept like a baby on the firm mattress.

The bed headboard, chairs, desk, and coffee table looked like they were from the same factory that produced the lobby furniture. There were no closets or bureaus in the room; however, there was a very large armoire. When I opened the seven-foot-high cabinet's double doors, the left side had several shelves, three or four drawers, and space at the bottom for shoes. The other side of the cabinet contained an open space for hanging clothes, with a shelf at the top. An old, late 1940s-style box television was on a small table that stood about two feet off the floor.

The desk in the room was a basic three-drawer type with a pen, pad, and telephone. On the desk was an ivory-colored phone without a dial. It was simply a drop off of the switchboard. Much of the highly polished wood floor was covered with a large red, Asian-style rug. The large bathroom had a white tile floor with white walls and ceiling. The sterile bathroom fixtures included a large bathtub with legs, a hand-held shower, a pedestal sink, and a European-style toilet. Overall the room was very comfortable and had a view of Red Square and the Kremlin, which were only a fifteen minute walk away. At night portions of the Kremlin walls and buildings were lighted, as were the red stars atop buildings.

Once we unpacked, Daley asked our floor monitor for our car to take us to the U.S. Embassy. Ten minutes later our Chaika arrived out front to pick us up. The driver gave us a big grin as he gladly accepted the gift bottle of whiskey presented by Daley. There was very little traffic in Moscow in 1973. Top government leaders were driven in black Zil limousines, other government officials, KGB staff, and important visitors were driven in the large Chaika sedans. Also traveling the streets was the Lada, a smaller, four-person sedan used mainly by mid- and upper-level government officials and the KGB agents. The Lada was available in limited quantities for purchase by citizens who could save enough money. Since Lada cars were primarily used by the police, government workers, and local officials, deliveries of new cars to Soviet citizens could often take well over five years.

The Chaika and Zil cars all had curtains in their rear compartments that were normally drawn. Some of the Lada cars also had the privacy curtains. All Soviet cars had distinctively numbered license plates that allowed traffic police, who controlled all major intersections, to immediately identify the level of the person riding in the vehicle and the area from which the car was licensed. All drivers knew the road protocol at intersections. Lada cars with KGB, ministry, other government agencies, and private license plates were driven in the normal traffic lanes. Privately owned vehicles were required to make way for all government vehicles. When one of the Zil motorcades was on the road, all intersections were controlled and all other cars were required to pull over to the curb and stop.

There were very few traffic lights in Moscow, with the entry points into the Kremlin being the exception. Uniformed traffic officers working in elevated control booths were used to expedite the traffic into the Kremlin. From their perch they could see the traffic lights, changing them with a push of a button to ensure that the flow of traffic into and out of the Kremlin was given priority. When we rode in the Chaika with or without our KGB counterparts, we received special attention by the uniformed officers and were given courtesy of the road.

❖ ❖ ❖

In 1973 the vast majority of people living in the Soviet Union did not own a car, and would never own a car or even ride in one. Muscovites commuted everywhere using their feet, buses, subways, and trains. Walking was a significant part of almost everyone's daily commute. I do not recall seeing a taxi during our 1973 visit.

Winter in Moscow usually begins in early September, when men and women start wearing boots, heavy overcoats, and head coverings. There was not much variation in the style or color of their wool coats. Most men wore a fur hat (shapka) made of muskrat, while Russians with money could be readily identified by their beautiful red fox hats. Women mostly wore a scarf on their heads, but some wore fur hats similar to the ones worn by men. The women's scarves were generally in subdued colors and the hats made of muskrat. In fact, most clothing worn by both the men and women was generally dark: black, brown, or blue. I don't remember seeing any bright colors—reds, yellows, greens, or light blues—on my first visit in 1973.

Muscovites walked the streets very purposefully with their heads down and very little eye-to-eye contact with others. Shops and stores along the streets had signs in the Cyrillic alphabet identifying what the shopper might find inside. There were no signs, posters, or pictures indicating what type of products were sold inside. In some small food shops you could see gallon jars full of canned vegetables or fruit sitting on the window sills. Some shops had small lines where people waited to buy bread. The streets, sidewalks, medians, and nearby grass areas were dirty from the unwashed sand that had been mixed with the salt to keep the roads free of snow and ice. I was told the streets remained dirty until the rains of spring washed Moscow clean.

STORIES FROM INSIDE THE PERIMETER

❖ ❖ ❖

As our car neared the U.S. Embassy, the cold war efforts of a closed society were clearly recognizable. Movable metal barricades were located along the sidewalk outside the length of the embassy preventing anyone from walking in front of the building. Numerous uniformed Soviet border guards were stationed on the street side of the barriers. People were not allowed to walk on the sidewalk in front of the embassy. The border guards carefully surveyed people in the area and stared into each passing vehicle. Vehicles entering the diplomatic compound were forced to almost stop as they ran the security gauntlet before turning into the embassy compound.

Uniformed police vigilantly scrutinized each occupant of our vehicle as our driver negotiated the last cordon of security, entered the embassy grounds under an archway, and came to a stop in the covered area. A US Marine security guard approached our vehicle asking us to show our passports before directing us to the enclosed reception area where another Marine again carefully scrutinized our passports and identification after we got out of our car.

Once cleared, we were issued temporary identification and entered the embassy, while our KGB car and driver remained outside the compound to await our return. Inside the embassy, Daley and I followed the Marine's directions, making a courtesy call on the "Deputy Chief of Mission (DCM)" and the CIA station chief. Ambassador Jacob Beam had left and a new ambassador had not been named yet. During the meeting with the DCM we were advised that Kissinger would be staying at one of the Lenin Hills guest houses and meeting at the Kremlin with various Soviet leaders about the Egyptian/Israeli war cease-fire.

The meeting with the CIA station chief was in a small, cramped office area where his staff was located on an upper floor of the embassy.

Our intelligence agent, who joined us in the embassy, had previously advised us the station chief was covert and spent most of his time in the office of his official cover role. All Secret Service agents receive top secret clearances when they enter the agency. However, when agents are assigned to a protective division, they are required to have a special CIA clearance. The clearance, issued by the CIA, allows Secret Service agents access to CIA personnel, documents, and some of their work areas. Before we had departed Washington our clearances had been forwarded to the Moscow station chief.

The covert head of the CIA worked a routine position within the embassy. Being covert meant the person holding the position was not a declared spy to the Soviet government. Normally only the ambassador and his assistant knew the dual role of a covert CIA chief.

During the meeting we provided our room numbers at the Sovetskaya and were told of the monitoring capabilities of each room. Daley and I were advised the CIA area was small and cramped and there would be times we would see and hear things about ongoing meetings and exchanges of information. We spent time with the CIA station chief going over Kissinger's schedule and the current situation on dissidents, activists, and potential troublemakers in Moscow. We were advised we were welcome to visit and work out of the CIA office anytime we wanted.

It was decided by Daley and our ID agent that, due to the cramped size of the office, they would limit access to the CIA work area to the two of them and me. We all agreed there was just no reason to expose other agents to the ongoing intelligence activities in the CIA's office. Some on the advance team were a little put off by this decision, but most understood that the restriction was not personal.

After our meetings with the DCM and the CIA we visited the office of the General Services section and the State Department

Regional Security Officer (RSO). During our meeting with the RSO, we were informed that the official exchange rate for rubles was four to one dollar. He mentioned the money handlers at the tourist shopping area on Arabat Street, referred to simply as "The Arabat," offered to exchange money on the street for twenty rubles to one dollar. The Russian ruble was not a convertible currency; however, U.S. dollars could be exchanged at the embassy for Russian rubles at the official Soviet government rate. We were cautioned that changing dollars on the street could lead to being arrested and all money confiscated. Police, we were told, would sometimes secretly observe a street money transaction and seize both currencies immediately, declaring the rubles to be counterfeit. He cautioned us to be extremely careful of exchanging money.

We purchased enough rubles at the embassy to get by for a couple of days. The RSO went over the size of his Marine detachment and outlined the support his staff would be able to provide. He said we could rely on Marine support at the very least to assist with command post duties, suite security, and baggage control. We were advised the Marines would also be used for the transportation of classified messages. The schedule as known at the time, both official and off-the-record, was reviewed and we discussed a schedule of courtesy calls on our Soviet counterparts for the next day.

A visit to the embassy cafeteria provided an opportunity to have a relaxing cup of coffee and see the extent of foods and drinks provided to employees, visitors, and guests while in the embassy. A bonus of the visit turned out to be an opportunity to purchase some beluga caviar. A Russian national working in the embassy was offering two-ounce glass containers of caviar for $10 each versus almost $50 each back home. Having never had caviar before in my life and realizing a good value when I saw it, I ordered four containers for my departure.

When we left the cafeteria, our Intelligence Division (ID) agent headed to the communication center, while Daly and I stopped by the administrative office. We were told we could use the embassy commissary if we needed snacks, alcohol, sodas, or other items. Continuing our work on the upcoming visit, Daley made appointments with various embassy personnel for the next day to discuss and schedule logistical support. We also had the opportunity to meet several Russian nationals, who would be working with us during the visit of Secretary Kissinger.

It was during this visit that agent Daley made me aware of the need to have nationals working with our team repeat instructions back to make sure they understood what they were told. Nationals, he told me, were notorious for indicating by nodding or saying yes they understood your instructions, but in reality they did not. The nationals by and large were loyal, good, and hard working. Daley purchased a case of beer at the commissary as we left to make a courtesy call at the Marine House before returning to the hotel.

❖ ❖ ❖

The Marine Security Guard (MSG) detachment, which is an integral part of all U. S. embassies, resided at a separate, secure building called the Marine House. They provided security for the embassy and the ambassador, but were also an important part of the social fabric of the embassy. The Marines played a leading role in many of the embassy parties and such annual celebrations as Easter, Fourth of July, the Marine Corps birthday, Thanksgiving, Christmas, and New Year's. They provided help and assistance to any embassy employee who needed it. The Marines usually showed a movie once a week, which embassy personnel attended. Expatriates (expats)—foreigners who work at other embassies, especially Western ones—found the Marine House a warm and friendly place to relax, enjoy a drink, and engage in friendly conversation.

Weekly cocktail mixers at the Marine House were regularly attended by both embassy personnel and expats. For Secret Service agents it was the place to get a soda, cold beer, shot of whiskey, see a movie, work out, or have a friendly conversation. Secret Service agents had an open invitation to visit any Marine House any time they wanted. Daley introduced me to the gunny (gunnery sergeant), who was NCOIC in charge of the Marine Security Guard Detachment. He advised us of the movie schedule and when the next social was scheduled. The gunny was delighted when Daley presented the Marines with the case of beer. As we departed a couple of girlie magazines were left on the bar.

❖ ❖ ❖

Back at the hotel that evening in the room assigned for our dining we had our first Russian meal in the Sovetskaya. In the room was a table that would seat at least twenty persons set for our small advance team. On the table were various size platters with sprats (sardines), smoked tongue, fresh sliced cucumbers, grated carrots in a sweet dressing, and coleslaw. Clustered on a tray in the center of the table were several half-liter bottles of beer, two liters of carbonated water, a half-liter bottle of vodka, a pitcher of juice, and glasses of various sizes.

When the server arrived he put a basket of sliced black bread on the table with butter. We were told that boiled vegetables, meat, and potatoes would be served a little later. Tea, coffee, and dessert came afterwards. The meal was filling, but the cuisine was different than what I normally ate. Having grown up on seafood, pasta, and beef with plenty of potatoes, vegetables, mushrooms, berries, and other fresh fruit, the blandness of our dinner was somewhat surprising. Returning to our rooms after dinner, we stayed in that evening, trying to rest and get adapted to the new time zone, seven hours ahead of New York.

❊ ❊ ❊

For the next two days our schedule was very busy with visits to the Kremlin, the Lenin Hills guest house, the Bolshoi Opera House, the airport arrival point, and the embassy. Daley and I had meetings with the KGB in their office at the Kremlin building, not at the Lubyanka Square headquarters building a mile away. During Soviet times the Lubyanka building was the most evil and feared building in the Soviet Union, because it housed the infamous Lubyanka Prison. It was there where dissidents over the years had been imprisoned and tortured. The number of people put to death in the prison was reported to be in the thousands. At the center of Lubyanka Square was a statue of Feliks Dzersihinsky, founder of Cheka, the original Russian Secret Police. Cheka was the forerunner to the GPU and OGPU, which eventually became the KGB.

The relationship between the Secret Service and the KGB was very interesting to me, when considering our divergent responsibilities and assignments within our individual societies. KGB agents and Secret Service agents, who both understood the great abyss that divided them in executing their mandated responsibilities, developed a normal, professional relationship. We all tried to maintain our focus, keeping a safe environment for the person we were jointly protecting. The KGB coordinated all aspects of our visit, providing manpower, motorcade security, and building access control. They allowed us to survey the sites Kissinger would visit, except, of course, the Kremlin. The Secret Service did the same for the KGB when one of their dignitaries visited the

United States. They offered to take us to the renowned Moscow Circus, the Bolshoi, or one of their museums. We were unable to accept their offer. During a break in our scheduled meetings they took us to the GUM department store, located in Red Square, a short distance from St. Basil's Cathedral with its brightly painted dome. St. Basil's, which had been commissioned by Ivan the Terrible, was built between 1555 and 1561.

Shops and stores in Moscow were small and tended to have limited but specific goods, shoes, coats, clothing, bread, meat, vegetables, and fruit. They did not have large retail stores. There was only one department store to serve all of Moscow, called GUM, which was government-owned, three stories high, and located in Red Square. It was a very large building with small shops providing various goods to the citizens of Moscow and visitors to the city. The goods were mainly manufactured in Russia with some from other Soviet countries. Upstairs on the top floor was a store selling military clothing and accessories. With the assistance of our KGB host we were allowed to purchase wide brown leather military belts with brass buckles that had a star, hammer, and sickle embossed on them. There were all types of military hats, brass, epaulet insignias, red stars, and other military memorabilia that could be purchased. The two members of our EOD team accompanied us to the store and purchased several dozen belts with buckles. They had earlier told some of us that the Soviet Army buckles cost $2.50 USD (United States dollars) at GUM and could be sold at their base in Germany for $25 each. I bought half-dozen belts with buckles and an assortment of other items for myself and as gifts.

❧ ❧ ❧

On the fourth day of our advance, and with our security plan set, we went to the airport to meet the USAF C-141 bringing the limousine, equipment, and support personnel for the visit. What a beautiful sight to see the big lumbering Lockheed Starlifter slip out of the clouds and glide down the runway to a soft landing. When President Kennedy ordered the development of the aircraft in 1961, he could not have imagined how useful and how long the Boeing C-141 would support our country's needs.

Little did I understand at the time how integral a part of my life the C-141 would become over the next six years. Our advance team, along with our KGB counterparts, embassy personnel, and customs/immigration officers, were waiting ramp-side to greet and process everyone. Once the plane parked, passports and declaration statements were collected and the rear bay opened. The communication trailer was off-loaded first, and to the amazement of our KGB friends, the White House Communication Agency advance team was speaking directly with the White House switchboard before the paperwork was processed. Our Russian friends were absolutely stunned with our technical capabilities.

Soviet customs and immigration offices reviewed the manifest and checked the passports of everyone aboard the aircraft. When everything was found in order they signaled the embassy vehicles loaded with the support agents to depart for their hotel. Next, our vehicles and the communication trailer were cleared by the KGB and driven to the U. S. embassy, where they were stored inside the compound, under observation by the Marine security detachment. I accompanied our support agents to the Rossiya Hotel, where they would be staying. With 3,600 rooms, the Rossiya was the largest hotel in the world at the time. Our arriving team was pre-registered, and I provided all passports to the front desk clerk for processing. As had been the case at the Sovetskaya, she said they would be ready in a couple of hours.

When all the Secret Service agents received their official stamped receipts, we moved to a side area for a short briefing. The support agents were provided information about Kissinger's schedule, their post assignments, reporting times, the Sovetskaya Hotel phone number, and emergency contact phone numbers, along with Daley's and my room numbers. They were also given directions to the embassy, information about the embassy cafeteria, and the dollar to ruble exchange rate. Agents were advised of the KGB technical eavesdropping capabilities in their hotel rooms. All team members were also admonished not to get involved with any women while they were in Moscow. They were cautioned that more than likely anyone they met in the hotel bar, sightseeing, shopping, or anywhere else would be a KGB operative. The agents were also told the location of the nearest dollar store (Beryoskia), where they could purchase souvenirs and Russian vodka. By the time I departed the Rossiya the agents were fully briefed and prepared for the arrival of Secretary of State Kissinger the next day.

❖ ❖ ❖

With my supply of rubles from the communication officer in hand, I headed for the Arabat with one of the Russian nationals from the embassy. This was my first visit to the Arabat and it contrasted greatly with the Moscow I had seen over the last several days. Instead of people with heads bent, walking purposefully, there were tourists, mostly from other Soviet republics or the East Bloc countries, some dressed in traditional garb, walking the streets. Many chatted as they peered into the shops appraising the glass, lacquer boxes, matrioshka dolls, hats, scarves, and other goods. Old shops, bars, small eateries, and apartments were interspersed over a three-block area. The buildings were three to five floors high. Tourists and Muscovites made this one of the busiest streets in Moscow.

Taking the three-block walk from one end to the other I encountered money changers and hawkers selling rubles and souvenirs. If a person accepted a money changer's offer he would be taken to a nearby alley to complete the transaction. The money handler tried to keep the police at bay while the deal was consummated. Russian vodka, crystal, tablecloths, matrioshka dolls, caviar, samovars, lacquer boxes, and other Soviet souvenirs could be purchased at a government-sponsored Beryoskia hard currency store on Arabat Street. There were a number of Beryoskia stores throughout Moscow where goods could be purchased with hard currency.

❖ ❖ ❖

Kissinger and his staff arrived October 22 aboard a Boeing VC-137 Stratoliner that was part of the USAF 89th Airlift Wing, which maintained the presidential fleet. As Secretary Kissinger walked down the ramp he was given the standard VIP greeting by a senior government official. People were introduced, shook hands, chatted, and slowly walked to their assigned motorcade vehicle. Departing the airport, our motorcade was surrounded with a cavalcade of police vehicles. Using red lights and sirens, the cars made a quick, uninterrupted trip directly to the Lenin Hills guest house.

The Lenin Hills compound, where Kissinger and his senior staff stayed, had a number of guest houses surrounded by an unusually high stucco wall. Several tall, massive wooden gates allowed entry to the compound at various points. The identical, two-storied guest houses, set back about forty yards from the fence, were constructed of beige and tan sandstone blocks. The wood-frame windows and tile roofs, along with the well-groomed grounds, landscaped with evergreen trees and shrubs, created a rich country feeling. A few steps up and off the circular drive, double wooden doors invited guests into the stately manor.

Inside Kissinger's large guest house were more stately wood doors, jambs, and staircases, along with furniture, rugs, drapes, and oil paintings that gave a sense of old Europe. The furniture in the sitting area was similar in style to that at the Sovetskaya.

Outside, concrete walkways and worn paths wove their way around the compound, affording Kissinger and others an opportunity to walk the grounds. There were times during the visit when Kissinger would take a walk in order to have a private conversation with executive assistant Larry Eagleburger, press secretary George Vest, or one of his other staff members. Kissinger would stroll near the guest house quietly chatting, asking questions, and discussing his meetings. He was acutely aware of the technical capabilities of his Soviet adversaries, seeming to always have his guard up.

This was my first time being around Secretary of State Henry Kissinger, and everything during the trip seemed to go smoothly. Kissinger visited top Soviet officials, including Secretary General of the Communist Party Leonid Brezhnev, Premier Alexsei Kosygin, and Foreign Minister Andrei Gromyko, at the Kremlin. We were restricted in the number of Secret Service agents allowed to accompany Secretary Kissinger inside the Kremlin office building. This was no different than restrictions on KGB agents entering the White House and other U.S. government buildings on their visits to the United States. Once Kissinger was inside the Kremlin for his meetings, the accompanying agents were taken to a side room until the secretary of state was ready to depart. The working agents were offered tea, coffee, water, cookies, and vodka while they waited.

Meetings, receptions, and social activities seemed to flow with no glitches. Kissinger was interesting, dynamic, and intriguing. There was something charming and charismatic about him, with his deep, heavily German-accented voice, projecting his public persona. The thoughtful way he addressed and spoke with people, as well as his self-assured walk, his intellect, and his smile were all disarming. Kissinger undoubtedly understood exactly who he was and what he wanted to achieve. He proceeded with a self-control that exuded his confidence. There was no hint of arrogance or self-importance when he was in the public arena.

❖ ❖ ❖

It fascinated me to see the KBG and the Secret Service work so very well together. There was an understanding that when they came to the United States, we would offer a similar support system to them. Moreover, we knew they provided access and activities we would not be able to do back home. We never discussed the differences in our cultures or political issues. However, one evening when Kissinger was at a social function at the Bolshoi, several of our security detail personnel were in a side room with our police counterparts during intermission. A KBG general, in uniform, offered me a glass of vodka (they drank on duty). Even though I was off duty I declined, but closely observed him as he drank his vodka, while asking me about my impressions of Moscow. While we spoke for several minutes, I mentioned their mass transportation system was better than ours and that there were fewer cars than I expected.

The general made the comment that there were many differences between Americans and Russians. "For example," he said, "Russians begin drinking in the morning and stop in the evening while Americans begin in the evening and quit in the morning."

We both laughed heartily. It was during this trip that I observed that Russian vodka was packaged in half-liter glass bottles with a tear-away type cap. Since it was the Russian tradition to finish a bottle once it was opened, there was no need for a reusable cap.

❊ ❊ ❊

The visit to Moscow gave me a chance to take a good look at the grand scale of travel afforded Secretary Kissinger. His limousine and follow-up cars were flown to the city visited, along with additional agents. A special communications system accompanied the cars and agents, allowing Secretary Kissinger a continuously open line directly to the White House switchboard when needed. I was surprised there was such a large cadre of press who accompanied Kissinger aboard his aircraft. As Kissinger's aircraft departed I knew I would be coming back to Moscow to head up the advance team the next time he visited Moscow. In less than one hour after Kissinger's departure, our support C-141 was loaded and cleared for takeoff.

While the advance team returned to the States, I remained in Moscow for a private meeting with a senior KGB officer to pass along the message from agent Simpson. He wanted me to give them a "heads up" on the spring visit of President Nixon. Earlier during the visit special arrangements had been made through our KGB contact for a courtesy call on a Colonel Bychkov to convey the message from Simpson. A briefing paper on Colonel Bychkov's background included information that he had been declared persona non grata by the Canadian government in 1958 for espionage and was ordered out of Canada at the time. The report included the information that he was fluent in English.

Not too long after the C-141 departed, I returned to the Sovetskya. A Chaika limo picked me up at my hotel a half hour later for the five-minute drive to the Kremlin office of Colonel Bychkov, senior officer of the KGB's Ninth Directorate responsible for dignitary protection. On arrival I was escorted to an office on the second floor, where Bychkov's assistant greeted me. After introductions, the assistant led me through a door to Bychkov's office. However, instead of finding myself in Bychkov's office, I was in a small area, two feet from another door. On the other side of the second door was Bychkov's office. The two-door private office set-up was normal in Soviet buildings. Bychkov was introduced and we shook hands as he led me across the room to a couch along the far wall. Interestingly, the entry doors remained open during our meeting, allowing the assistant to monitor our conversation and take notes from his own desk.

The high-ceilinged office featured a large, clean desk with an adjoining small table holding about twenty telephones, none of which had dials. I had also noticed the absence of dials in the hotels and various government offices we visited since I arrived in Moscow. Of the approximately twenty phones on the table one was red and the others were beige. A few feet away from the desk was a small conference table and on the other side of the table were a couch and two over-stuffed chairs positioned around a coffee table, where Bychkov had led me.

Bychkov sat in one of the chairs, motioning for me to sit on the couch. From my seat I could see the entire room. I knew from my briefing paper that Colonel Bychkov spoke English and I was pleased to see he was not going to use an interpreter. As we exchanged greetings, he directed his assistant in Russian to bring tea, water, and cookies. I was surprised, but thankful, there was no vodka. We had been chitchatting about the just completed Kissinger visit when his assistant returned with the refreshments. The colonel was pleasant, speaking very good English, and was well-versed on the visit of Secretary of State Kissinger.

We continued our conversation, sipping our tea and nibbling on sugar cookies, while the assistant retreated to his office. I had just begun explaining to Colonel Bychkov the purpose of my visit when suddenly we were interrupted by one of the telephones on the table ringing. Bychkov shouted to his assistant in Russian, obviously giving him instructions to answer the phone. The assistant rushed into the office, but cautiously approached the table with the multitude of phones. With a confused look on his face, he picked up a phone; the ringing continued. Hanging up, he quickly picked up a second phone, and a third, as his boss continued loudly trying to direct him to the instrument that was ringing. None of the assistant's actions ended the ringing, so the frustrated assistant turned toward his boss, shrugging his shoulders.

Bychkov, who had fully turned his chair to better observe his assistant, was obviously embarrassed, frustrated, and agitated by the continually ringing phone. Loudly raising his voice again with instructions, the colonel glared as his assistant lifted another receiver off another wrong phone that did not end the ringing. A totally exasperated Bychkov leaped to his feet, screaming at the failure to resolve the ringing phone problem. Quickly he moved around the conference table toward the bank of phones next to his desk. His frightened assistant immediately retreated to his office while Bychkov reached down to pick up a receiver, ending the ringing. With a hidden smile on my face I thought I had just witnessed a Laurel and Hardy, Three Stooges, or Abbott and Costello movie routine.

By the time Bychkov finished speaking on the phone and returned to our discussion, he had regained his composure. We completed our conversation concerning the spring visit of President Nixon, and my KGB driver returned me to the embassy. An embassy car took me to the airport for my return flight to the United States.

Relaxing on the flight home, I began thinking about the advance assignment in Moscow that had been extremely interesting and informative for me. I didn't realize at the time, but it was to be the first of many trips I would make behind the "Iron Curtain" over the next three years. During my stay I took the opportunity to take walks and jogs around the streets and parks of Moscow, trying to get a feel of the communist country I had grown up seeing as our feared adversary. My impression of the people of Moscow in 1974 was that they had the most basic of lifestyles. The faces, eyes, and body language of ordinary citizens projected a fear, loneliness, and hopelessness of their strictly structured lives.

City residents lived mainly in towering apartments, using their balconies as a root cellar to store vegetables and other food to survive the winter. Many residents had a parcel of land a couple of kilometers outside of the city called a dacha on which they grew vegetables and fruit, canning some of the crops for the long, cold winter. Meats were also canned by people at home for eating in the winter months. Those living on farms or in rural areas grew and stored their own winter supply of potatoes and other vegetables. There were no commercially frozen foods for sale in the Soviet Union stores and no freezers in citizen's homes. There were few restaurants in Moscow except in the hotels. There were no fast food restaurants, no pizza parlors, or delicatessens.

During my outings on the city streets I could see the lines at bread stores and the limited amount of food and other goods on many of the stores' shelves. This was something I had not expected to encounter. No matter what the people of Russia were taught or told about the citizens of the United States, nor what we were told about the citizens of the Soviet Union, there was no comparison between their lifestyles and ours. Looking back, it was during that first trip to Moscow that I realized while I was growing up in Tacoma, Washington,

I never really understood or appreciated our freedom. People raised in the United States are born with freedom. They accept it, take it for granted. After October 1973 I had a different perspective of freedom. I cherished it. My love of freedom would be reinforced many times over the next fifteen years as I visited oppressed and poverty-stricken societies around the globe.

Telephones were non-existent for the masses living in the Soviet Union during my visit. The government-operated Intourist Hotels were huge, being used mostly by vacationers from the Soviet Union and Eastern European countries. Other hotels, which were much smaller, were owned and operated by factories, and were used only by business travelers. Visiting government officials, office workers, and important business leaders were provided rooms at government-run hotels or guest houses. The Soviet electronic and telephone systems were 1940s' vintage by United States standards. Here it was 1973, and there were no telephone books, no switchboards, and virtually no private telephones. Only a few government offices had a switchboard, while most factories had individual phones without a switchboard or central information center.

I thought about the people in our country back in the 1960s and '70s that believed the Soviet Union offered an acceptable alternative lifestyle. We had no idea about the difficulty of the lives of the people living in Moscow. No telephones, no cars, no single-family homes, families living in one or two-bedroom apartments, shopping every day for food, hardly any movie theaters, few restaurants, no fast food, no pizza; not exactly what Americans were looking for in 1973. However no one ever knew since we were never told about the differences. Their lifestyle was never reported here.

❖ ❖ ❖

With the Moscow advance behind me, I took a house hunting trip to Washington, D.C., to find temporary quarters until my home in Tacoma was sold. My wife, Ginny, and I, getting ready for the transfer to Washington, were having a hectic time packing, not to mention squeezing in our Thanksgiving dinner before we departed on our cross-country drive. We sold our home, but had to make arrangements to close the deal by mail since there was not enough time to close before we left.

We loaded the car, deciding to drive the southern route across Route 66. This was attractive to us, since neither Ginny nor I wanted to drive in snow if we could avoid it. We also wanted to stop at a couple of sightseeing places for our children, Michael, Robin, Leslie, and Jamie. It was our plan to make the drive to Washington in six or seven days. Our first planned stop, the Grand Canyon, was limited due to a heavy snow storm. I stood on the rim of the canyon, looking out across the spectacular vista as large snowflakes melted on my face. The kids spent a short time looking at the falling snow before running back to the warm car.

The next planned stop was the Bristol Caverns in Tennessee. However, in between, we spent several nights at hotels with pools where the children enjoyed the water. The day before the caverns we made an unscheduled stop at an alligator farm in Arkansas. This was one of the highlights for the children, because the farm also had snakes to look at. The elderly owner's hands were both scarred from many snake bites. He impressed us all as he held a snake while speaking about his friendly snakes and alligators during the tour of his museum. He kept offering the children a chance to touch the snake he was carrying, but they excitedly declined. Our visit to the Bristol Caverns was the first time any of us had visited an underground cave. The caverns had many of the usual stalagmites and stalactites with a lighting system that presented the interior in a colorful and memorable way. Also, one of the unique features of the Bristol Caverns was a walk along an underground river that at one time had been used by the Native Americans when making attacks on settlers in the area or as an escape route from the settlers.

Overall we made good time crossing the country, with routine stops for fuel, food, bathrooms visits, and stretching our legs. Checking into a motel before dinner and departing after breakfast allowed for a relaxing pace. Ginny and I shared the driving, making sure we stopped whenever the children asked. Arriving in the Washington, D.C., area the first week of December I checked our family into temporary quarters in Arlington, Virginia. We could remain in these quarters for up to six weeks at the government's expense while we located permanent housing.

❖ ❖ ❖

In my first meeting at Protective Support Division with Lapham and Boyette, I was told I would be assigned to the Kissinger detail. Lapham indicated first that he wanted me to work around the office for a month or two. He wanted me to work with agent Ed Dansereau, who had come over to the Secret Service from the CIA after the Kennedy assassination. Dansereau was one of the most dedicated, focused, organized, and hard-working individuals I had the pleasure of working within the Secret Service. He was a taskmaster, with a disciplined approach toward his work. Dansereau was in charge of some administrative matters, drafting operational manuals, and coordinating training of agents assigned to the support division. Lapham wanted to see what I could do and wanted me to fully understand the operations of PSD.

❖ ❖ ❖

During my earlier trip to Moscow with Kissinger, he had met with Secretary General Brezhnev, Prime Minister Kosygin, and Foreign Minister Gromyko concerning the October 1973 Egypt/Israel War. Secretary Kissinger and Kosygin then drafted an outline of United Nations Security Council Resolution 383, ending the hostilities and declaring a cease-fire between Israel and Egypt. In New York the resolution was passed by the U.N. Security Council, but the cease-fire negotiated by Kosygin and Kissinger did not hold. Brezhnev, who was furious, retaliated by announcing a proposal to send Soviet and U.S. troops to the Middle East, but President Nixon refused to agree.

Feeling betrayed by the United States, Brezhnev had his ambassador to Washington, Anatoly Dobrynin, inform Nixon the Soviet Union was going to unilaterally send troops into Egypt. According to press reports at the time, Kissinger huddled at the White House with Defense Secretary James Schlesinger, CIA Director William Colby, and White House Chief of Staff Alexander Haig. It was also reported since Nixon had gone to bed that Haig decided not to waken him. A response was sent to Brezhnev refusing to join the Soviet Union and warning them not to get involved. At the same time the press widely reported to our friends and enemies around the world that the United States raised their military preparedness, known as Defense Condition (DEFCON) from 4 to DEFCON 3, the highest peacetime level.

The implication was abundantly clear to Brezhnev and the rest of the world that the United States was prepared to use nuclear weapons. Brezhnev was forced to back down and a global crisis was averted. Some historians believe Nixon created the nuclear crisis to distract attention from his problems with the brewing Watergate scandal. Brezhnev and Nixon both had interest in assuring that Egypt not be perceived as losing the war. Israel in its aggressively mounted counterattack had completely surrounded the Egyptian Third Army on the Sinai Peninsula. They were in position to annihilate the Egyptian forces when Kissinger intervened, negotiating a face-saving end of the war with Prime Minister Golda Meir, and a second cease-fire was declared. To this day the Egyptians celebrate the 1973 war as one of their biggest military victories.

It was during the 1973 war that the oil-producing Arab states finally united, refusing to sell oil to the United States or any other Western country. The birth of the oil embargo became a big bargaining chip, a new weapon that helped put a united Arab face on Middle East diplomacy.

❊ ❊ ❊

Kissinger held both the titles of secretary of state and national security advisor when I arrived at PSD in December 1973. President Nixon had authorized Secret Service protection for National Security Advisor Kissinger in 1971 due to his high profile and threat level. Kissinger was a brilliant global, geopolitical, strategic thinker, receiving the utmost respect from President Nixon.

Kissinger was not exactly an absent-minded professor, but he had a penchant for leaving his briefcase unattended in meeting rooms and bathrooms. On several occasions he completely forgot his briefcase and it was retrieved by agent Bill Duncan, a supervisor with Presidential Protective Division (PPD).

As National Security Adviser, Kissinger's initial Secret Service detail was small; agent Jack Ready was in charge with a half-dozen more agents assigned to the three shifts. One of the agents assigned was the colorful Walter Bothe from our New York Field Office. The balding, outgoing agent, who was gruff sometimes, had a huge heart and seemed to almost always have a smile on his face. Kissinger liked his rough exterior and Bothe's aggressive New York style. I believe

Bothe became Kissinger's favorite agent. Early in the assignment it was established that, besides protecting Kissinger around the world for his secret meetings, it was Ready's job to keep Kissinger's briefcase secure.

✤ ✤ ✤

Now, just so you know, Secret Service agents are trained and instructed not to carry bags, packages, luggage, umbrellas, and briefcases for the various people they protect. However, there are times that rules are made to be broken. As a supervisor I never asked another agent to carry anything for any of the persons we were protecting; however, I did expect normal courtesy when outside of the view of the general public.

Less than two weeks after I reported, Boyette advised me that Kissinger would be taking a fifteen-day, thirteen-nation trip to Europe and the Middle East. Boyette asked me if my family was settled enough for me to travel to Jerusalem. He was looking for an advance man to make security arrangements for a December 17 meeting between Kissinger and Prime Minister Meir. They were going to be discussing the new Middle East peace agreement. I agreed to head up the advance team to Jerusalem.

The 1973 war was over but the final settlement between Israel and Egypt still needed to be worked out. On his trip Kissinger would also be attending the opening session of the Middle East Peace Conference scheduled for December 22 in Geneva, Switzerland, right after his visit to Israel.

This would be my first trip to the Middle East so, before departing, I had several meetings with agents Mike Cohen and Jack Renwick of our Foreign Intelligence Branch. The two of them spent time updating me on international issues and terrorist groups. While the focus of the majority of agents in the Secret Service was domestic threats, in PSD our focus with Kissinger was international terrorism.

The time I spent in the Foreign Intelligence Branch got me up to date on all the terrorist groups that were focused on the Middle East. Lod Airport, serving Tel Aviv, was where, in 1972, three members of the Japanese Red Army massacred twenty-six passengers and injured seventy-eight others. The airport massacre was planned and supported by the general command of the Popular Front for the Liberation of Palestine. Israel suffered another terrible tragedy on September 5, 1972, when the group Black September kidnapped and massacred eleven Israeli Olympic athletes in Munich, Germany. Tension was high as I arrived at the Lod Airport with my advance team.

To prepare for the visit of Secretary Kissinger, I had meetings in Tel Aviv with embassy personnel and Shin Bet (Israeli Security Service responsible for counterintelligence and internal security). Initial meetings at the embassy were to coordinate entry of agents, technical and communication support, and to review the schedule. A courtesy meeting with the station chief of the CIA and a meeting with the legal attaché (FBI) brought me up to date on the recent terrorist threats and Shin Bet security structure.

The first get-together in Tel Aviv with Shin Bet went very well. After the meeting with Shin Bet, their liaison agent advised me that their security service had never had an opportunity to talk in depth about protection issues with a member of the Secret Service. Since we were going to be in Tel Aviv for two days before leaving for Jerusalem, I agreed to meet privately with two representatives of the Shin Bet. The meeting was a give and take session. They were interested in the type of threats we normally faced with the people we protected, what type of searches were conducted prior to their arrival, what motorcade configurations we used, and what our fire power was. We spent several hours discussing what they did versus what we did.

Surprisingly, Israeli security for Prime Minister Meir and other government officials was very low key in spite of all the terrorism, bomb attacks, and perceived threats. I was startled to learn that neither the follow- up cars used by the Israeli security details nor the vehicles used by persons being protected by Shin Bet were armored. It was also interesting that police escorts were normally not used for Shin Bet motorcades of their top government leaders, and they routinely traveled in two-car motorcades. Reading between the lines in 1973, unlike today, there seemed to be an unspoken agreement between the Israelis and Palestinians: you don't try to assassinate our leaders and we won't try to get yours.

Operationally, the Shin Bet follow-up cars had a second rearview mirror for the supervisor sitting in the right front seat. The vehicles also had hand holds bolted inside the vehicle above front and back doors assisting their agents in getting quickly in and out of the security car. Shin Bet agents carried semi-automatic handguns but there were no shoulder-fired automatic weapons visible.

Driving the road from Tel Aviv to Jerusalem we saw many rusting hulks: trucks, cars, and armored vehicles that had succumbed to the torrent of Arab gunfire during the 1948 war for independence. Our advance group arrived at the King David Hotel, which was built in 1931 of quarried pink sandstone (Jerusalem stone). In fact, zoning regulations required that all buildings in Jerusalem must be built of Jerusalem stone. The King David Hotel had a rich history, including at various times hosting three monarchs who fled their countries: King Alfonso of Spain, Emperor Haile Selassie of Ethiopia, and King George II of Greece. The British were using the King David Hotel in 1946 as their military headquarters when the south wing was blown up by the

Irgun and Stern Gangs, Israeli terrorist groups led by Manachem Begin and Yitzhak Shamir, who were both later elected prime minister.

In 1960, Paul Newman and Eva Marie Saint were in the magnificent hotel gardens during some of the filming of the movie *Exodus*. The King David Hotel is situated on the side of a hill with a stunning view of the Old City less than three hundred meters away.

There were several formal sit-down meetings in Jerusalem with Shin Bet, the Israel military, and other vested groups, to map out the Kissinger visit. The schedule and all security issues were critically reviewed with the pros and cons of Kissinger's visit carefully dissected. Everyone seemed to have the same concern about his safety: his mode of transportation. This had definitely been identified as problem number one. Everyone knew Secretary Kissinger would have the greatest exposure and vulnerability when traveling back and forth from Tel Aviv to Jerusalem.

After going over all the options, it was agreed that transporting Kissinger in a helicopter would provide the quickest mode of transportation with the least exposure to terrorist attack. We knew of the SA-7, Surface- to-Air-Missile (SAM), shoulder-fired weapons that the Soviet Union had supplied to the PLO. To thwart that threat it was agreed that two helicopters would be used when transporting Kissinger. The helicopter not carrying Secretary Kissinger would fly directly behind and below his helicopter. This neutralized the ability to hit the lead helicopter with the heat-seeking, shoulder-fired SA-7.

The remaining security issues were relatively easy to resolve. Our follow-up car would be positioned directly behind the limo and Shin Bet would have a security vehicle directly behind us. Shin Bet agreed to use marked police escort vehicles to lead the motorcade and they offered assistance by providing security personnel to be posted at each location visited by Kissinger. At government-secured sites, such as their Parliament building, the Knesset, and the prime minister's residence, we would only need a detail advance agent present ahead of time. Shin Bet advised us that they would be responsible for all security posts at those locations. They did ask for an agent to assist at the main entry check point to ensure there were no access problems for the Kissinger party. The presidential fleet aircraft transporting Kissinger would be given special security at Lod Airport. Our armored limousine and follow-up car arriving by C-141 would be secured by Secret Service agents from a twenty-member jump team, also on board the C-141. Our motorcade cars would be secured in an open, fenced area at the King David Hotel where Kissinger, staff, agents, and other support persons would be staying.

❖ ❖ ❖

On the evening before Kissinger arrived in Tel Aviv, Intelligence Division agent Mike Cohen and I took a cab to dinner at a popular restaurant on the east side of Jerusalem, outside of the Old City. The meals were served downstairs in a cave motif restaurant. Our dinner of lamb, rice, and vegetables was very good, as was the Israeli wine. Cohen and I spoke very little of the upcoming visit. Instead we enjoyed the music flowing throughout the dining room. After dinner we decided to stretch our legs and walk back to our hotel through the Old City. It was around 10 p.m. when we set out on foot. Entering the Old City through the Lion's Gate, agent Cohen and I were enthralled walking the narrow alleyways of East Jerusalem.

In the calm of the warm evening we could hear children playing as we strode down the ancient cobblestone walkway. The chatter and laughter began getting louder, and we soon encountered eight or ten young children using a collapsed soda can to play their local version of soccer.

The two of us stood watching for a few minutes when the kids motioned with their hands and feet for us to join them. We each went to a different team, and when the game started the action was quick with the kids having the advantage of playing regularly in the dimly lit, ancient street. Cohen and I enjoyed the ten-minute skirmish with them. The kids were laughing and seemed to appreciate the game, oblivious to the reality of their poverty and the tension with the Israelis. The kids probably did not fully appreciate the fun Cohen and I had during the short scrimmage.

After giving the kids high fives, we waved as we continued walking toward the hotel. It was awesome realizing we had just played soccer with an empty soft drink can on a cobblestone walkway bordered by a huge stone wall that dated back long before the birth of Christ. Proceeding around a curve in the street, less than a hundred meters ahead, we encountered a group of heavily armed Israeli soldiers on patrol. Directly behind the soldiers was an armored personnel carrier with a soldier manning a machine gun mounted on top supporting his comrades on the ground. The reality check created by the appearance of the patrol caught us by surprise. Here we were, two Americans, walking through the eastern section of Jerusalem at 11 o'clock at night without a care in the world. The stark reality of the armed soldiers jolted us awake and took some of the glow off the encounter with the kids. We double-timed it to the Jaffa gate with a much greater alertness about our surroundings. Arriving back at the King David Hotel, we relaxed in the bar with a drink before retiring for the evening. I can still hear the kids laughing, see the smiles on their faces, and remember the crumpled soft drink can.

❖ ❖ ❖

As if tensions were not high enough already, on December 17, 1973, the day Kissinger arrived from Lebanon, Palestinian terrorists used phosphorus grenades to attack and destroy Pan Am Flight 110 on the ground at Fuimico Airport just outside of Rome, killing thirty people. There was no need for us to ratchet security up another notch since we were already there.

Secretary Kissinger's in and out visit went very well with an unprecedented level of security. His only activity was a scheduled meeting with Prime Minister Meir. The meeting with the prime minister, at her office in the Knesset, is forever etched in my mind. The final settlement of the 1973 Egyptian/Israeli war was still being negotiated.

The prime minister, followed by her entourage of at least four of her top military advisors, greeted Kissinger as he exited his limousine in front of the Knesset. Walking next to Kissinger, she led this group of Israel's most powerful men into her office. It was quite a sight to see, the diminutive, homely Golda Meir, with her nicotine-stained fingers, frumpy dress, and hunched shoulders, escorting a sea of testosterone into her office. Defense Minister Moshe Dayan and the other military officers were casually dressed in brown wearing neatly pressed pants with their shirts collars open. The Israeli coterie joined by Kissinger, who was dressed in suit and tie, sat on a sofa and chairs around a coffee table arrayed with maps to be reviewed.

Shortly after the group sat down there was a photo opportunity for the traveling press. Escorted by Israeli and American Secret Service agents, the press entered the room, immediately creating organized chaos with the flashing and clicking of the still cameras and the bright lights and microphones of the camera crews. The writing press separated from the cameras and began jockeying for position trying to get the best vantage points. They were hoping during the inane chitchat between Kissinger and Meir to pick up something vital or a slip of the tongue. The camera crews and still photographers circled the group like vultures, hoping for an award-winning picture. I wondered why there needed to be so many pictures taken in such a short period of time that would be seen by so few people. When State Department press secretary George Vest signaled the photo opportunity had ended, the members of the media were escorted from the meeting room and the doors were closed.

Well over an hour later, when the doors opened, signaling the end of the meeting, it was difficult to see inside. As the entourage rose and walked toward the door, you could not see anyone's face, including that of the pint- size prime minister, through the low-hanging fog of cigarette smoke. Kissinger and Meir appeared relaxed as they approached the door and stepped out of the grey haze into the foyer. There they paused, smiled, and shook hands for the press. In my twenty-five years of traveling the globe, I have had the opportunity to see and/or meet some of the most powerful world leaders. No one, however, had the charisma of Prime Minister Golda Meir, the short, pugnacious, Russian Jew who grew up in Milwaukee, Wisconsin. She exuded a self-confidence and power not often seen in world leaders.

The motorcade left the Knesset and took the party directly to Lod Airport for the departure. As the USAF Boeing jet sped down the runway and disappeared into the night sky heading for Portugal, there was a sense of relief that our security plan with the helicopter flights, our motorcades, and meetings had gone off without a hitch.

❖ ❖ ❖

The next morning I received a call from agent Bush in the operations center in Protective Support Division requesting my presence in Switzerland to assist the Geneva advance team during the visit of Secretary Kissinger December 20-22. That afternoon I flew to Switzerland, where I checked into the Intercontinental Hotel before meeting with the lead advance agent. After the meeting I walked to the nearest department store to buy an overcoat. Since I had just arrived from Israel, with its 75 degree temperatures, I had lightweight clothes. I was not prepared for the cold winter Geneva weather.

During the visit to Geneva I would be assigned to patrol a half-mile of the motorcade route outside the main gate to the conference complex that the Swiss authorities had respectfully declined to secure. I was given an Uzi submachine gun with a sling to carry under my new wardrobe. Back at my hotel room I cut a slit in the right coat pocket and lining, enabling me to grip the automatic weapon as it hung over my shoulder through the right pocket and lining. Walking with the coat unbuttoned no one would be able to see the Uzi as I ambled up and down the motorcade route. However, with a quick forward thrust I could be ready for action in a split second.

After modifying my new coat, I received a call from agent Cohen, who was still in Israel. Cohen advised me that an important message was being sent for me through the Geneva ID agent. He requested I respond per the message. When I picked up the message it outlined a procedure for me to follow in order to meet an Israeli the next morning at a local outdoor café.

With a flower in my lapel and the *International Herald Tribune* under my arm I arrived at 8 a.m. at the outdoor café as instructed. Ordering a cup of coffee I began reading the newspaper. Soon, a man with the proper-colored flower in his lapel sat down; speaking very good English, he introduced himself. We chitchatted for a few minutes until his coffee arrived, as he told me about himself, his affiliation, and the concerns about a serious threat against Secretary Kissinger. According to my morning guest, there was ample reason to believe a vehicle would be coming into Switzerland with weapons and people who wanted to harm Kissinger. He briefly sketched out what he believed would happen. The conversation then switched to Jerusalem, New York, and Washington, D.C, as we finished our coffee and shook hands.

As he departed, the Israeli casually slipped a piece of paper into my folded newspaper. Returning to the hotel I read the note. It contained a description of a car, including the license plate number, mentioned that four people were riding in the car, and alleged weapons were in the trunk. The note was given to the ID agent, who passed it to the Swiss intelligence liaison contact.

When Secretary Kissinger arrived at the Geneva airport for his visit to the opening session of the Middle East Peace Conference, I was already on post walking my beat. Several hours later, after his visit to the conference complex, I discontinued when the secretary's motorcade passed by on its journey to his hotel. My newly acquired overcoat with special modifications was used each time the secretary visited the conference. Then it was packed to bring home. I knew it would be very useful during the upcoming winter months in Washington.

❖ ❖ ❖

Shortly after returning to our temporary residence in Virginia, we closed on the sale of our home in Tacoma by mail. Christmas was somewhat subdued due to our unsettled circumstances. However, we enjoyed the many Christmas lights around the area, especially the national Christmas tree on the ellipse, south of the White House. We purchased a home in a new home development in Lake Ridge, Virginia, about twenty-five miles south of the White House. There were several other agents with children living in the same development. My wife was a real trouper, accepting most of the unpacking chores and getting Michael and Robin in school. She never complained when I had to go out of town on an assignment. I was reunited with my good friend

Major Sims, who was assigned to the Marine Corps Base Quantico. His wife Pat ended up teaching Michael and Robin at Lowell Elementary School in Lake Ridge.

Back in PSD I was working full time with Dansereau on office projects. He was one of those individuals that stirred strong emotions. Dansereau was liked by many, but criticized by others. Under the tutoring of Dansereau my operations and logistical skills blossomed. The two of us soon became very good friends, and I realized working with Dansereau was going to have a profoundly positive impact on me and my career. Latham and Boyette monitored my progress with Dansereau as they continued to shuttle me back and forth with the Kissinger detail.

Besides being responsible for the security details assigned to Secretary of State Henry Kissinger and Secretary of Treasury William Simon, PSD also provided agents for temporary assignment to the Presidential and Vice Presidential Protective Divisions. PSD, through Dansereau, was responsible for the general training of all agents reporting to protective details in Washington, D.C.

While working in the office with Dansereau I had the opportunity to interact with agent Bill Bush, who was the logistical coordinator for the security needs for the Secretary of State and the Secretary of the Treasury details. Bush, a good old boy from the Deep South, was underestimated by many people. Lapham and Boyette would not have had him performing one of the most challenging jobs in PSD if he were not the best in operations and logistics. His Southern drawl and focused thoughtful speech patterns disarmed many who dealt with him.

In a role reversal, sometimes during lunch Bush enjoyed entertaining agents in the office by talking with some of our New York City agents using a quick, short, choppy Southern rural accent that confused almost everyone. The New Yorkers, not to be outdone, responded in rapid fire speech with a heavily laden Brooklyn accent. These mostly unintelligible exchanges would have people on the sidelines listening, smiling, and shaking their heads. Hardly anyone within earshot could understand either Bush or the New Yorkers. The exchange would always receive a hearty laugh when the performance was over.

Bush took me under his wing, teaching me the logistical ropes and briefing me on the procedures for staffing the State and Treasury details. He explained the coordinating process for acquiring agents to travel on temporary assignment with details, post assignments, and advances. Wilson Livingood, my early mentor at the White House in 1969, was now Special Agent in Charge (SAIC) working in the Office of Protective Operations. Bush coordinated all of his support requests with Protective Operations. Livingood would process the manpower requests and fill both temporary and full-time manpower needs with field agents. I spent as much time as I could with Bush trying to find out how the system worked and as much as I could about the Kissinger detail needs. Bush had been coordinating support for the Kissinger detail from its inception. He was the repository of important institutional knowledge that was so necessary for me to fully understand the issues and political process. He was the first one to alert me to the controversy between State and Treasury about Secret Service protection of Kissinger.

Over time Bush explained the tenacity of Lapham in developing proper support for Kissinger. Lapham presented a challenge when dealing with Secret Service headquarters and the White House. He doggedly perused unprecedented requests for armored vehicles and other support to precede (National Security Adviser) Kissinger on his overseas travel. Lapham was able to get his requests fulfilled most of the time. Bush, along with Doc Watson and Chuck McCreedy of the identification support section at PSD, nicknamed Lapham "Bull Dog."

McCreedy and Watson were retired military who brought wisdom and stability to a fledging identification section. They were like two peas in a pod, calm, informed, and helpful. The two of them developed a badge, pin, and credential system for identifying staff, agents, communication support, and others. This included specially designing, purchasing, and issuing pins used by all Secret Service agents. They also provided identification for support staff, law enforcement personnel, foreign dignitary details, campaign details, and other temporary details. Other federal agencies consulted with Watson and McCreedy on design and sources for their identification needs.

❧ ❧ ❧

Working most of the time with Dansereau at PSD, I would periodically receive a temporary assignment with the Kissinger detail. It seemed most of the assignments would take me to the Middle East or one of the communist countries to conduct advance security arrangements. Less often the assignment would be for a few days, to fill in for one of the shift leaders or a supervisor on the Kissinger detail. During one of my first temporary assignments to the Kissinger detail there was an interesting and amusing story making the rounds. It was a tale concerning a conversation between National Security Adviser Kissinger and agent William Bacherman that reportedly took place during the early days of his detail. The story concerned an indictment on January 12, 1971 of Roman Catholic anti-war activists Father Daniel Berrigan and Father Phillip Berrigan.

The Berrigan brothers were leaders of the Harrisburg Seven, a high profile anti-war group. In fact, alleged threats by them against

Kissinger were the reason that President Nixon directed the Secret Service to provide protection for Kissinger. When the Berrigan brothers were indicted for plotting to kidnap Kissinger and blow up tunnels under the U. S. Capitol it was reported in the media. On the morning the indictments were reported in the *Washington Post* newspaper, agent Bacherman was the working supervisor. He accompanied Kissinger, riding in the front seat of the limo, dropping him at his White House office.

Kissinger apparently read the newspaper article about the indictments while in his office. Later, when he returned to his car, Kissinger approached agent Beckerman, mentioning the article and the indictments. Then reportedly in his deepest, most heavily German-accented voice, Kissinger asked agent Bacherman, "What will you do if they try to kidnap me?"

Bacherman, according to the rumor, waited a moment, appearing to evaluate his response. Then, the story goes, he responded, "Don't worry, Dr. Kissinger. They will never take you." After a short pause he finished the sentence, "Alive." The word among the agents in PSD was that Kissinger was not sure if Bacherman was serious or not.

❖ ❖ ❖

When I reported in 1973 to PSD, Secretary Kissinger was the most heavily threatened person protected by the Secret Service. President Gadhafi of Libya had reportedly put a bounty of $250,000 on Secretary of State Kissinger's head. Threats against Kissinger during his global travel were heightened during his visits to Israel and Syria. I tried talking with Jack Renwick and Mike Cohen of Intelligence Division to keep up on terrorist threats and the terrorist movement.

I was on temporary assignment with the Kissinger detail, filling in as shift leader, when visiting President Houari Boumedienne of Algeria was scheduled to have a meeting with Secretary Kissinger at the State Department the second week of April 1974. The normal routine was for the secretary, as a courtesy and sign of respect, to greet the arriving dignitary curbside at the State Department for a photo opportunity. After the photo opportunity the secretary would then escort his guest to his office via his private elevator for discussions. President Boumedienne was on an official state visit, meaning the U.S. government was picking up his expenses as well as those of six staff members during his visit. As part of the protocol, Boumedienne was staying as a guest of the government at Blair House. As a head of state he qualified for a Secret Service detail, which was on the same radio frequency as ours.

Detail leader Jack Ready and I were on post at a desk outside of Kissinger's seventh floor office, near the private elevator. We were waiting to be notified of the departure of President Boumedienne from Blair House so Kissinger could go downstairs to greet him. Ready had previously spoken with the Blair House command post, requesting a call alerting us when Boumedienne departed for the five-minute drive to our location. When I heard the Boumedienne security detail radio transmission advising they had just left Blair House, I advised Ready, who was not wearing a radio. He walked into Kissinger's outer office and passed the information to Kissinger's secretary. Returning to the desk Ready asked, "Did the Blair House command post call?"

"No," I responded, telling Ready I heard the departure on my radio.

Ready intercepted Kissinger as he came out of the side door of his office, sending him back. He turned to me announcing, "The command post is going to call when the guest departs." Picking up the phone he started dialing.

While Ready was calling, I alerted him that I heard their follow-up car advise, "One minute."

Ignoring me, Ready asked the Blair House agent if the visiting president had left Blair House. Quickly hanging up the phone, a shaken Ready told me to get the elevator at once and hold it. He went directly into Kissinger's office through the side door as I used the key to activate the elevator. An agitated Kissinger came out of his office in a rush with Ready trailing. I was holding the elevator door open for Kissinger and Ready. To my surprise Ready stopped short, and with a Cheshire Cat grin on his face, raised his hand to his chest, waving goodbye to me as the elevator door closed. I had occasionally seen a frustrated Kissinger upset, boil over, and become vocal toward his staff, but never at the Secret Service. I knew what was coming. As the elevator started down with just the two of us, the terribly upset secretary turned, looked me in the eyes, and with a raised voice said, "How could this happen?"

Pausing, my reply was, "We f----d up."

The frankness of the answer seemed to catch Kissinger by surprise. He just hung his head and waited for the elevator to arrive in the lobby. As the door opened Kissinger could see the Algerian president with his entourage beginning to board the nearby public elevator. Quickly, Kissinger joined President Boumedienne on the larger elevator and when the door closed he apologized for not greeting the president on his arrival. Kissinger calmly told his guest the Secret Service had screwed it up. Kissinger escorted the Algerian president into his office for a private meeting and then to the dining room for a luncheon. This was the only time I saw or heard about Kissinger becoming frustrated enough by his detail to raise his voice to an agent.

❖ ❖ ❖

In late February I returned to Israel to make arrangements for a February 27-28, 1974, visit by Kissinger. It was nice to meet old friends and continue the development of our relationships. Kissinger had been to Israel several times since my December advance assignment. By the time I returned, the Shin Bet had the security routine down pat. There were the usual intelligence reports concerning the PFLP, PLO, and other groups. Concerns about terrorist attacks during the visit had not abated. Kissinger would be arriving from overnight stops in London and Damascus and would be staying overnight at the King David Hotel.

When he arrived at Lod Airport, we went by motorcade to visit a new display at the Yad Vashem Holocaust Museum and then to Jerusalem. The schedule was fairly light with meetings with government officials, including Prime Minister Meir. The day Kissinger arrived I went out for dinner after he was in the hotel for the evening. The limo, as on previous visits, was being secured by members of the jump team in a somewhat isolated area at the rear of the hotel.

Coming back from dinner I saw one of the agents on the midnight shift heading for the limo post. He was carrying a pillow and alarm clock as he headed to the car. I stopped him and asked what he was doing with the clock and pillow. He indicated the car was in a secure area and he would be resting in the limo. I was really agitated and tried to control my disappointment. I told him the hotel had been targeted on various occasions by terrorists and there was no fixed Israeli security post in the area of the car. Inasmuch as there was limited Israeli security, it was strongly suggested he return the pillow and clock to the command post. Back in the hotel I stopped by the command post and reiterated to the shift leader that the clock and pillow needed to be returned to the CP.

The next morning the Shin Bet liaison agent approached me when I came to the lobby for coffee. He mentioned that two of our agents had been out on the town with two women who worked in the hotel the previous evening. I was told the ladies were terrorists that Shin Bet routinely monitored. Since the terrorists were under observation by

Israeli security agents all the time our agents were with them they had not been in any danger, according to my Shin Bet contact. But I was advised it would be better if the agents found someone else to take them out on the town. I spoke with the two agents and passed the Shin Bet information on to them.

After briefing me about the two women terrorists I was advised that one of the off-duty American military security guards from our airplane met a young lady while out on the town the previous evening. According to Shin Bet, the Air Force guard tried to enter the secure area at Lod Airport to give his new friend a tour of the airplane at 11:30 in the evening. The guard was denied entry to the base itself by Israeli airport security. He was told only authorized people were allowed into the classified area. No fuss was made with the couple at the gate once security had concluded there was no indication the guest was a terrorist, and they were allowed to leave. Shin Bet advised that a report was written on both incidents. Both of these situations were handled privately by me with the individuals involved. These two incidents plus the walk through East Jerusalem on my previous visit gave me a new understanding of the potential threats against agents anytime we traveled, but especially visits to the Middle East.

❖ ❖ ❖

On returning to Washington, D.C., I learned of a rumor going around that there was a disagreement between Secretary of Treasury George Shultz and Secretary of State Kissinger over the use of Treasury Department Secret Service agents for the protection of the secretary of state. The issue with Treasury Secretary Shultz was not the cost of the security coverage, since Treasury was already billing State for the actual costs of the protection. Secretary Shultz and Director H. Stuart Knight of the Secret Service were concerned about the drain on their manpower and other assets needed to take care of Kissinger. Some in Treasury and in the Secret Service felt the Kissinger agents and assets could be better used supporting traditional, mandated Secret Service details and other responsibilities. Secretary Kissinger, I found out, had won the initial round in the battle, keeping his Secret Service detail. However, I knew the battle was not over by a long shot. I was sure it would go on for months.

✤ ✤ ✤

In PSD my work with Dansereau was going very well as I developed an understanding of the format for drafting operational manuals and the training process of new agents. Agent Bush seemed to always be busy arranging manpower requests to augment one of the details, making advance assignments, requesting military aircraft to transport cars, juggling cars, or making airline reservations. His operations center at PSD was always busy but also had a constant buzz with many agents dropping by to chat. I continued to find myself spending as much free time as I could with him to get the latest update on issues in headquarters and the Secretary of Treasury detail. Just sitting and listening to him on the phone helped me adapt to the mental juggling needed to run an operations center. I saw Bush upset once in a while but never saw him lose control.

Quick visits with Watson and McCreedy allowed me to refill my identification pin needs and find out the latest scuttlebutt from a different perspective. Both of them had regular meetings at headquarters and contact with staff, support, and other details. Being friendly and outgoing, they had a knack for finding out what was going on in our organization. We traded stories.

STORIES FROM INSIDE THE PERIMETER

❖ ❖ ❖

Though I did not work with his detail every day, I found Kissinger extremely interesting and intriguing. He had the public persona of a bright, strong, aggressive problem solver. On the private side he was often seen in public with attractive and many times well-known women. Though Kissinger laughed and enjoyed a good joke, with his inner staff he tended to be all business. To me he was one of those people who thrived on high pressure, operating at warp speed. People operating so far out front can sometimes get way ahead of their staff or switch gears too quickly, losing some people. Kissinger had surrounded himself with smart, global-thinking, talented people. When on rare occasions he got too far out in front of them or switched gears too quickly and they fell behind, an agitated Kissinger could become boisterous with his staff. His loud verbalizations of his frustrations were not meant to demean or embarrass anyone. His sometimes aggressive approach to problem solving was normally one-on-one or in very small groups. It was not unusual for a Secret Service agent to be within earshot. To his credit, the cadre of bright and capable staff people with Kissinger did not seem to be offended by his infrequent outbursts.

One of my memories of seeing Kissinger's frustration was in Damascus during a shuttle diplomacy trip. After negotiating with President Hafez al-Assad, Kissinger got into the limousine and told the driver, Special Officer Hank Schwobel, to take him to the guest house. The car pulled up to the guest house and staff aide L. Paul (Jerry) Bremer opened the door. Just then Kissinger, deep in thought, realized he had made a mistake and did not want to be at the guest house. Perturbed, Kissinger screamed at Bremer to close the door and "Get the f---k out of my life." Bremer quickly closed the door and the limousine departed.

I could see Bremer was embarrassed as he turned to go back into the guest house.

❖ ❖ ❖

Protection of Kissinger continued to require more and more Secret Service assets as his threat level and exposure increased. Secret Service headquarters and Secretary of Treasury Schultz were becoming highly concerned about the continuing escalation of resources required to support the secretary of state. According to sources in headquarters, new discussions with the State Department were leading to an agreement that security personnel from State would begin a joint operation with Kissinger's Secret Service detail for thirty days. At the end of that period, State Department security would once again assume full responsibility for protection of the secretary of state.

About halfway through the thirty-day joint operations period I was on temporary assignment outside the seventh-floor State Department office of Kissinger with agent Walter Bothe and a State Department security agent. Kissinger was preparing to fly to the Western White House at San Clemente for meetings with President Nixon. I was holding the private elevator door open for the secretary, agent Bothe, and the State security agent to step inside. Entering the elevator, Kissinger casually and slowly looked the three of us up and down. With a smug grin on his face Kissinger announced to agent Bothe, "Walter, when I get to San Clemente I am going to talk to President Nixon about the need for State security."

Kissinger proceeded to advise Bothe that by the time he got through meeting with President Nixon, the State Department security detail would be gone. Then he announced to no one in particular, "I have never lost a bureaucratic fight before in my life and I am not going to lose this one."

Our flight to California was routine as we arrived at El Toro Marine Corps Air Station near Irvine. A helicopter was waiting to take Kissinger on the short flight to the helicopter pad at the U. S. Coast Guard station next to the Nixon presidential compound. Getting off the chopper, the four of us took the short walk to Nixon's residence. As Kissinger left us at the gate to Casa Pacific, he commented to agent Bothe to be ready to, "Say goodbye, to them, Walter."

Later, when his meeting with Nixon was over, as Kissinger approached Bothe at the gate he had a smile and said, "Tell them bye, Walter." The next day the State Department agents returned to Washington, D.C., without their protectee. Kissinger understood that, with the White House deeply embroiled in the Watergate scandal, Nixon did not need a disgruntled secretary of state. I believe the president also understood the advantages of having the security detail outside of the State Department.

※ ※ ※

I continued working with the Kissinger detail as needed, otherwise spending most of my time at PSD working on my projects. My short assignment with Dansereau was in the fifth month. I was busy not only with new projects, but there were ongoing discussions about Kissinger's travels and threats with Boyette and new Kissinger detail leader James Cantrell. Boyette had the approval of SAIC Lapham to organize, reorganize, and change the Kissinger detail as he deemed necessary. During my periodic discussions with Boyette I could see the wheels turning and knew that changes would be coming down the road. However, I needed a better understanding of the detail before I could advance any recommendations.

Threats against Kissinger kept growing, though most were directly related to his leading role in trying to develop a Mid-East peace agreement. Unlike Kissinger's secret meetings to end the Vietnam War and his private negotiations on the opening with China, Kissinger's shuttle diplomacy strategy required high visibility. Many Arab nations and some of the Palestinians were united in their desire to destroy the Israelis, to drive them into the sea. Terrorist groups were working against any peace agreement. Some groups were domestic to the Middle East and attacked Israeli settlements, while others were transnational groups planning attacks against Kissinger and other symbols of the West. The PFLP, PLO, Fatah, Red Brigade, Red Army, and Baader-Meinhof Gang led the attacks on Western culture. Libya President Colonel Moammar Kadhafi and President Assad of Syria had changed the landscape, elevating terrorism in the early 1970s, when they began sponsoring international terrorism.

Traveling overseas with Kissinger was a tremendous challenge for both the agents on the Kissinger detail and the Secret Service Foreign Intelligence Branch. Venturing into the Middle East with the secretary of state was always very stressful. I often thought of the Kissinger Secret Service detail being like the lion tamer entering a cage filled with growling lions, in a circus tent packed full of screaming people where most of them were rooting for the lions. Protection of the secretary of state was difficult enough on its own, but with the addition of the terrorist dimension his protection was constant on-the-job training. The Secret Service did not have training manuals on terrorism and there was no specific, headquarters-directed anti-terrorism plan. Everything was in the hands of Lapham, Boyette, Cantrell, and the agents on the detail. The Secret Service Intelligence Branch headed up by Mike Mastrovito was extremely capable and helpful in assessing and coordinating the flow of appropriate information to the Kissinger detail. Jack Renwik and Mike Cohen worked closely on a regular basis with the Support Division, especially the Kissinger detail agents. They seemed to be on all the high-threat trips.

Of all the countries visited by the secretary of state, Syria was the most dangerous. Many terrorist organizations had a close relationship with the Syrian government, so it was inevitable that those in the government, who did not want a peace agreement, would try to prevail. Often we had specific, detailed threat information on visits to Syria, requiring the advance team to prepare for a worst case scenario on all visits into the Middle East. Some detail agents, in a direct conflict with Secret Service policy, began routinely carrying a personal handgun as a back-up weapon on visits to the Middle East. I became worried during one trip when a member of the Syrian security detail offered an agent $1,000 for his back-up weapon. When the agent seemed to be considering the offer I took him aside. It was mentioned to him privately that the weapon could be found later at the site of a terrorist attack. That ended any conversation about selling guns.

✤ ✤ ✤

A last-minute assignment found me traveling to Damascus, Syria, to assist the advance team preparing for a Kissinger visit scheduled for March 1, 1974. A specific threat against Kissinger had been passed to our Foreign Intelligence Branch through the intelligence community. A credible source had alleged there would be an attempt on Secretary Kissinger during the visit to Damascus. The understaffed advance team headed up by Jimmy L.C. Miller of our Los Angeles office was already in place when I arrived in Damascus to assist. Meetings with President Hafez al-Assad to discuss an Israeli disengagement proposal and a tour of Umayyad Mosque were the only things on Kissinger's schedule.

The renowned Umayya Mosque, which was built between 709 and 715 A.D., served as the most important central gathering place for Muslims outside of Mecca. My assignment while in Damascus was to coordinate the security at the guest house, where Kissinger slept and his staff was headquartered during this visit.

Damascus was a closed city with a very heavy security presence. The movements of Secret Service and support personnel both on duty and off duty were strictly controlled and monitored. Identities of our Syrian liaison support coordinators were unknown to the advance team. The Syrian, who maintained contact with the team and coordinated at the highest governmental level, had simply been introduced as "His Excellency Number One." The United States did not have an embassy in Syria. Instead we had a U.S. Interests Section that had been established on February 8, 1974, in the Italian embassy. Thomas J. Scotes was the principal officer. On June 16, 1974, Scotes was designated the chargé d' affaires. Our Interests Section, which had a small staff, coordinated our activities through administrative officer Gary Lee. Five years later, on November 4, 1979, Lee, while assigned to our embassy in Iran, became one of the 52 American Embassy employees held hostage in Teheran for 444 days.

During our stay in Damascus, the advance team was without the usual Intelligence Division advance agent on site. The Syrian government, several years earlier, had hung a person they claimed to be a CIA spy in the square in front of the main market. The body allegedly hung there for several days and as a result of the hanging no U.S. intelligence agents traveled inside Syria. Our ID agent did not accompany the advance team to Syria, but remained in the area, where contact was maintained through phone calls and the secure message center at the Interests Section.

STORIES FROM INSIDE THE PERIMETER

Secretary Kissinger arrived in Damascus March 1, 1974, for an overnight visit to continue his meetings with President Hafez al-Assad as part of the shuttle diplomacy. He landed amid very tight security, departing in a motorcade composed of over twenty motorcycles, our follow-up car, and two pickup trucks with armed troops positioned outside and behind our security car. Behind the pickups were several large troop trucks full of soldiers. In addition, there were several other security cars plus a dozen staff cars.

Before the departure, the traveling agents were advised by advance agent Jimmy L.C. Miller that there would be regular and irregular Syrian troops armed with shoulder weapons positioned along the entire motorcade route. We knew it would be confusing and stressful seeing men not in uniform along the route carrying automatic shoulder weapons. Everyone also understood that all intersections would be controlled by the military. As our motorcade sped out of the airport, the follow-up agents could be seen openly carrying Uzi machine guns in the station wagon with the windows down. The agents on heightened alert had turned in their seats and were pointing their weapons out the windows.

As the motorcade sped down the main road outside the airport, a motorcycle went down, throwing a leather-clad officer and his bike sliding into the path of the oncoming array of security vehicles. Sparks were flying as the officer used all his skills to keep out of the path of the swerving cars, station wagons, and trucks. Fortunately all vehicles managed to keep from hitting either the sliding motorcycle or the officer. His leather boots, pants, jacket, helmet, and lots of luck allowed him to walk away from the near- tragic accident. When we arrived at the main circle on the road to Damascus the road narrowed and the motorcade slowed down. There were uniformed security personnel at every intersection and along the way as we maneuvered our motorcade down the streets to the government-provided guest house.

Kissinger and his staff worked out of a Syrian guest house, which had offices, a meeting room, dining area, and several bedrooms. The first day there were meetings with President Assad and a dinner. Most everyone, including Kissinger, was awakened early the next day as the Syrians were called to prayer from a minaret less than a block away. As the second day wore on Kissinger began to fall behind schedule and by the final meeting with Assad he seemed really tired. Instead of visiting the mosque after the final Assad meeting as scheduled, Kissinger told Cantrell he wanted to return to the guest house to rest. Upon arrival he announced his decision to cancel the visit to the Umayya Mosque to his Syrian hosts.

At the guest house there was a plethora of security people. In addition to the normal Syrian guest house security detail, there were motorcade security officers, drivers, motorcycle cops, close support agents, and other Syrian agents. Most had been standing by to accompany the motorcade to the mosque when the visit was cancelled. There must have been over fifty Syrian security personnel and agents loitering in and around the guest house grounds. Shortly after Kissinger cancelled his visit to the mosque a buzz began making the rounds of the Syrian security detail. The advance team had picked up information the Syrians were talking about a recovered bomb targeting Kissinger that had been located hidden at the Umayya Mosque. Agent Miller immediately moved the motorcade cars around to the secluded walled area at the rear of the guest house, where it would be out of sight of curious onlookers.

Miller and the rest of the advance team had a meeting with detail leader Cantrell to review the latest intelligence and assess our options. One of the latest pieces of intelligence received from our ID support agent alleged an attempt would be made on Kissinger when his motorcade returned to the airport. An in-depth discussion led to a decision by Cantrell and Miller to make special arrangements with "His Excellency Number One" during Kissinger's motorcade to the airport. Our Syrian host was requested to provide a second "dummy" motorcade complete with a full-size limo, follow-up cars, police vehicles, and staff cars. The number of Syrian security people in the rear area was reduced.

Meanwhile, an older American sedan and station wagon were provided by Administrative Officer Lee from the U.S. Interests Section assets. The two cars were inserted near the end of the primary motorcade parked at the rear of the guest house. Agent Grady Askew of our Atlanta Field Office volunteered to ride in the limo in place of Secretary Kissinger. When Kissinger quietly exited the rear of the guest house, he was ushered into the embassy sedan at the back of the motorcade. The normal follow-up crew joined Kissinger in the old station wagon behind his sedan. A second follow-up crew escorted agent Askew to the limousine and took their places in the normal follow-up. Askew, with a nervous grin on his face, settled into the rear seat of the limo and waved to the security detail. The only people outside of our agents that saw what we did with the motorcade and Kissinger were a small cadre of Syrian security personnel.

With red lights flashing and sirens screaming, our motorcade raced for the airport, while the smaller "dummy motorcade" was about a mile ahead of our caravan with lights blinking and sirens wailing. As the two motorcades barreled toward the airport, our advance team anxiously awaited Kissinger's arrival. When the motorcade carrying Kissinger arrived at the airport he was whisked aboard the aircraft along with his Syrian escort for a final handshake in the safety of the plane. When the aircraft lifted off, our concerns about the hidden Umayya

Mosque bomb and the alleged attempt to attack the motorcade were replaced with relief that Kissinger had departed safely, bringing a quiet and subdued mood to our group.

We headed back to the hotel to wrap up everything. There was no celebrating the departure of the secretary. Everyone on the advance team, including our support agents, were asking, "Did we dodge a bullet?"

The next day, as we were getting ready to depart for the United States, agent Miller received a report from our ID agent advising that the informant on the original threat to the motorcade had been re-interviewed. According to the report, the informant advised that the attempt along the motorcade route as the limo headed for the airport did not materialize because the assassins did not know for sure in which car Kissinger was riding. We knew then and there that the only people who saw Kissinger get into the station wagon were agents and a few Syrian security people in the privacy afforded at the rear of the guest house. There had to be a leak in the Syrian security detail.

※ ※ ※

Returning to PSD, I found I had less time to spend with Dansereau on our regular projects; instead I was in meetings with Boyette, Cantrell, and our Foreign Intelligence Branch. Boyette had decided to do a complete review of our security plans and intelligence assessments. The most troubling issue we were beginning to address was, "Do we have the same threats and/or threat level in the United States as we have overseas?" If we do, then what new procedures do we institute?

We were acutely aware that changes in security procedures were usually driven by the Presidential Protective Division and there was not a real terrorist threat against Nixon. We realized that the public here at home was not ready to see agents carrying shoulder weapons openly. What was needed more by the Kissinger detail—extra people, additional weapons, up-dated procedures, or something else?

About this same time, Special Officer William (Shelly) Shellhammer, one of the Kissinger detail drivers, approached me about some ideas he had about carrying our shotguns and automatic weapons. He drove both limos and follow-up cars for our detail in Washington, D.C., and on the road. Shelly was a "gun nut" and "gadget man." He had many good ideas, not only on carrying our shoulder weapons, but how to maximize access to them both inside our follow-up car and when carried in public. His insight on increasing our fire power was reflected in several designs he developed in prototype cases for carrying our shoulder weapons.

Shelly had two "soft packs" made to hold our Uzi machine guns. The bags were made of black imitation leather, designed to allow the agent carrying the bag quick access. Agents toting the soft shoulder bag would put the sling over their shoulders. The agent could unzip the back of the bag and grip the weapon inside out of sight of the public while in close proximity to Kissinger. The bags used strategically placed strips of Velcro, allowing the agent to push the weapon down and forward out of the bag for immediate use. The soft packs augmented the hard, more cumbersome Secret Service-issue metal briefcases currently being used throughout the Secret Service to transport the Uzi.

Shelly also developed special soft material ammunition units that strapped to the back of the front seats in the follow-up vehicle that held additional Uzi clips and shotgun shells. His new carrying cases solved the problem of quicker access to our machine guns. Shelly continued to refine his work over the next year and provided a number of useful accessories to assist the working agents.

Boyette and Cantrell were evaluating proposals for additional manpower, weapons, and procedural changes. I spoke with them several times while I was home.

❖ ❖ ❖

March 16, 1974, found me heading for Moscow to take care of advance arrangements for Kissinger's March 24-28 visit. Kissinger was scheduled to meet with Soviet leaders in preparation for President Nixon's Moscow summit meeting in June. My trip with Daley five months earlier had prepared me for this assignment, and I was looking forward to the challenge of dealing on my own directly with the KGB. When we arrived on Saturday afternoon the embassy was closed but the usual staff support from the embassy greeted us along with the KGB representatives. We were quietly and efficiently escorted through the immigration and customs control stations and transported to the Rossiya Hotel.

Once we were processed in the lobby, we received our room keys from the babushka on our floor. There was a short team meeting to brief the newcomers in our team on the do's and don'ts of Moscow. It was agreed we were on our own for dinner in the Rossiya, which had a regular lobby with some shops, bars, and restaurants. One of our team members mentioned there was a hockey game Sunday night and wanted to know if I could get tickets. Our KGB contact was waiting in the lobby and seemed anxious to help us and said he would check on the tickets and let me know the next morning.

Sunday was spent sightseeing and walking around Red Square. In the evening the KGB escorted us to the hockey game between the Wings of the Soviet and Red Army Team Number One. Upon arrival we waited in the lobby area while one of the KGB agents and someone from the office went into the arena. A few minutes later they returned escorting a group of somewhat disgruntled fans. We were then led to our seats in the front row right behind the glass on the blue line. It didn't take a genius to figure out the people who we saw leaving had been ordered to give up their seats so we could watch the game. It made me uncomfortable to realize what I had just witnessed. I made a mental note to never again ask for tickets at the last minute.

I must say at the time I was not a big hockey fan, though I had been to a couple of games and had seen several on television. But this game was totally unexpected; it was like none I had ever seen. There was a flow and a motion in the game like a ballet; no high sticking, no slashing, no bullying, or roughing the opponent. Each team raced up and down the ice at breakneck speed, around the rink in full control, all the time respectful of their opponents. It was Swan Lake on ice. The fans cheered and clapped as if this were a championship game. Our group enjoyed the action and cheered at every good play.

The next morning, when we made a courtesy call on Ambassador Walter Stossel, Jr., he asked how our Sunday was. I told him about the hockey game. He was surprised by our attendance at the game. Ambassador Stoessel told us it was their championship game, comparable to our Stanley Cup back in the United States. Stoessel said the teams were the top two in the Soviet Union and people waited all year for tickets to the game. He told me he understood there were no tickets available and asked how we got the tickets. He smiled and nodded his head when I mentioned the KGB.

The Secret Service had some electronically made tapes that could be played during private meetings and conversations that would not allow the KGB to filter out the external noise and understand what we were saying. These tapes were available for Kissinger and his staff and would be set up by one of the technical people when needed. I mentioned to our team members that there would be a meeting in my room each day at 4 p.m. Privately, it was suggested to each person that he bring a book, magazine, or paperwork, since I was going to play a tape.

Kissinger was scheduled to meet with the Soviet leadership to work on issues to be addressed at the June/July summit meeting between Nixon and Brezhnev. In the first meeting I had with the KGB a proposal was made by the KGB to schedule a helicopter to take Kissinger to a government dacha compound on the outskirts of Moscow. We were advised that the compound was similar to Camp David. Kissinger would be there for two nights for substantive meetings with government leaders. When it was determined rooms were not available for our shift agents, a car or helicopter was requested to make our shift changes. There was a short discussion between our KGB counterparts about the transporting request, and they decided the dacha proposal would be scrubbed. Later, I found out that their helicopters did not have night flying capabilities and therefore could not accommodate shift change flights for our 4 p.m.-12 a.m. and 12 a.m.-8 a.m. shifts.

Once everyone arrived at our afternoon meetings I announced the agenda and turned on the tape machine to drown our voices. For the next hour we read, did paperwork, looked at magazines, or napped. At the end of the meeting, once the tape was turned off, I thanked everyone and outlined our evening activities. In between our daily activities we worked on our manpower needs, technical support, and other issues in small groups away from the prying eyes and ears of the KGB. Also, at each meeting with the KGB and others I would conspicuously position my briefcase on the floor near me so that everyone was readily aware of it. I kept the case with me at all times, during meetings, at meals, while sightseeing and shopping, and I never opened it in the presence of

Russians. Between playing the tape and the placement of my briefcase I was sure the KGB's interest would be piqued.

Overall the advance period went very well. After completing our work there was plenty of time to sightsee, shop for souvenirs, make visits to the Marine House, and go to the Beryoskia for vodka to take home. The C-141 with the limousine, a twenty-man jump team of agents, and communication support arrived without incident and were soon in place. Everyone was quickly cleared and ensconced in the Rossiaya Hotel. A hand-out that outlined the schedule, assignments, and other pertinent information was provided at a short meeting off to one side of the lobby.

Kissinger arrived at Vnukovo Airport on the VIP arrival side and was met by a government greeting party. He was transported to the Lenin Hills guest house. On the first day of the visit, when Kissinger returned to the Lenin Hills guest house after a morning meeting at the Kremlin, he walked into the office room, where the staff was typing reports, briefing papers, and other documents. Kissinger smiled and said hello to the joint State Department and embassy staff working in the room. Everyone seemed to be surprised, but especially pleased that the secretary of state had taken the time to stop in the staff office and say hello. Turning to leave, Kissinger asked his top assistant, Lawrence Eagleburger, to accompany him for a walk. I lagged behind them.

Once outside, away from the monitored rooms, Kissinger asked his assistant if the typewriters being used were the ones from Washington or the embassy. When Eagleburger said he thought they were from the embassy, a slightly agitated Kissinger directed that the special typewriters from Washington be used. He said he was worried about the Soviets using special techniques that enabled them to monitor the documents when typewriters were used that were not encrypted.

Walking to the command post I was thinking, "Alright, alright, so Kissinger is concerned and smart about security." I was impressed. During the visit Kissinger met with Brezhnev, Kosygin and Gromyko preparing for the upcoming summit.

The visit was short and went well. When Kissinger left I had a feeling I would not be returning for the summit meeting. President Nixon would be here and I think Boyette and Cantrell felt I could be used more effectively at another location.

❖ ❖ ❖

On March 30, 1974, Secretary of State Kissinger married Nancy Maginnes, who worked as a foreign policy aide to former Governor of New York Nelson Rockefeller. Kissinger and Maginnes met when they worked together on a Rockefeller foreign policy foundation. With his marriage Kissinger moved from his Waterside Drive townhouse to a townhouse on P Street in the Georgetown section of Washington. They honeymooned in Acapulco, Mexico April 1-April 9.

Kissinger spent May 1974 traveling between Israel and Syria conducting the most challenging legs of his shuttle diplomacy. In thirty-four days he traveled over 24,000 air miles. Our Damascus advance team was headed by Special Agent-in-Charge Don Edwards of the Secret Service Uniform Division and was supported by a twenty-person jump team, armored limousine, an explosive ordinance team from the Army, and an ID agent in Israel. The jump team would provide car security, assume fixed security posts, and be used to assist with other security needs. Edwards had been personally selected by SAIC Cantrell to coordinate the advance. Edwards told me he would focus on handling the negotiations/liaison with the Syrians while I would coordinate much of the day-to-day activities.

I was looking forward to returning to Damascus, which is the oldest continually lived-in city in the world. On my last visit there I did not have a chance to do any sightseeing. As we got off the plane at the Damascus airport we knew that various Arab countries, Palestinians groups, and a number of international terrorist organizations were working hard to derail any peace settlement. The extremely violent government-sponsored terrorists would do anything they could to disrupt the negotiations. A pre-departure intelligence briefing identified not only threats against Kissinger, but also against staff and agents in Damascus, who were specifically being targeted by some of the terrorists. Edwards had been fully briefed on the threats during Kissinger's last visit to Damascus and told about our suspicion that someone in Syrian security was leaking information on Kissinger's movements to outsiders. According to the briefing, staff and agents were being targeted for kidnapping as a way to disrupt the peace talks.

As was customary for them, the Syrians did not identify the senior people working with our advance team. When Edwards and I went to the first meeting we were introduced to "His Excellency Number One," who I had previously met, and "His Excellency Number Two." Adnan (no last name), our escort, who we later learned was a captain in the Syrian Air Force, was also present. Adnan was responsible for coordinating our schedule and took routine care of all our needs. Our ID agent in Israel identified His Excellencies One and Two as high-level Syrian security services operatives. In an attempt to lower our vulnerability, Edwards executed a plan to shift responsibility for threats to our Syrian counterparts.

First, Edwards passed on our suspicions of a leak in the Syrian security detail and the threats against our agents and the accompanying staff. He then told our two hosts it was in the interest of President Assad that the Kissinger visits proceed without any outside disruptions.

Edwards cautioned that from time to time he would provide information in writing identifying what we thought were specific and serious terrorist threats. He also told our hosts that the information on the threats would be provided in writing to His Excellency Number One, who would be required to sign a receipt acknowledging he received the information. Continuing, Edwards advised His Excellency Number One that either he or his assistant would be required to ride in a car directly ahead of Kissinger during all motorcades. It was emphasized to Adnan, who was translating, that the motorcade would not move unless one or the other was present. Finally, Edwards presented our host with a paper that outlined a specific threat and had him sign a copy.

As far as the motorcade and routes were concerned, at Edward's request the Syrians agreed to provide several secured motorcade routes between the airport access route and the downtown guest house to be used by our motorcades. In addition, Edwards said that he, not the Syrians, would determine which of the routes would be used. His Excellency Number One readily agreed. It was also agreed that a "dummy motorcade" would either lead or trail our motorcade as requested by Edwards. Finally, our armored limousine needed a secure area where our agents would provide protection when it was not in use. According to intelligence estimates, security of the motorcade routes required 10,000 regular and irregular Syrian soldiers.

The advance team was housed at the Umayya Hotel. We fondly referred to it as the O MY GOD hotel. The old hotel had a small elevator, a grand staircase, and a lobby that was fairly good sized. At one end of the lobby were a bar, small tables, chairs, and a couple of couches, while at the opposite end was a small café. It was quicker and easier to use the grand staircase to get to our rooms on the fifth floor than wait for the elevator.

❖ ❖ ❖

A USAF support C-141 arrived with the armored limousine and a twenty-man jump team two days before Kissinger's first scheduled visit. Our vehicles were secured around the clock at a hangar at the Damascus airport by two members of the jump team. Meals were brought from the hotel to the airport by Syrian security officers for the agents. Between the advance team, the jump team, and our EOD support we had over twenty-five people staying in the Umayya Hotel. During our visit to Damascus everyone would be under house arrest. Adnan advised us that no one in our party was supposed to leave the hotel without him being notified. He told us if anyone left the hotel without telling him, strategically placed security agents in and around the hotel would follow them. Adnan, who was outgoing and gregarious, wanted to be friends. He worked hard, going out of his way to please everyone. We knew this had to be an important assignment for him.

It was our understanding that all the costs for our stay in Syria were being paid by the Syrian government. Before paying the bills the government forwarded them to Administrative Officer Gary Lee at the Interest Section for approval. At the Umayya Hotel a running tab would be kept at meal times in the café and a running tab would be kept at the bar during the afternoon and evening. After each meal was over, one of the advance team members would sign for everyone and make sure the agents that were securing the cars at the hangar were fed. The bar tab would be signed once or twice a day. Dinner sometimes would be served at a huge table in a private room big enough to accommodate the entire team. Most times, however, we ate in small groups in the café.

One evening early in the advance, several of us sat in my room and kidded and joked about Adnan for over an hour. The next morning when Adnan showed up, he took me outside and nervously admonished me, "Michael, you need to be more careful what you say in your room." He then added, "Also, be careful talking in the cars."

�֍ �֍ ✖

During his first two visits to Damascus, Kissinger stayed overnight at a Syrian government guest house. There was a minaret a block from the guest house where the muezzin called the people to prayer early each morning. The call to prayer woke Kissinger earlier than he wanted, so after the second visit he decided to spend his nights in Israel. Not wanting to offend his Syrian hosts, he did not mention the early morning call to prayer as his reason for not spending the nights in their guest house. Secretary Kissinger would normally arrive in Damascus in the morning. He would sometimes stop at the guest house before his first negotiation session with President Assad at his palace office. In between the morning meeting and an afternoon meeting Kissinger would go to the guest house for talks with his staff and have lunch. Depending on how much energy he needed, he sometimes took a short rest before going to the palace. At the end of the day Kissinger would board his aircraft and return to Israel. After two nights in Israel he would repeat the cycle returning to Damascus.

Soviet Foreign Minister Andre Gromyko would routinely come to Damascus after Kissinger had made two or three visits to consult with President Assad. The meetings between Gromyko and Assad in Damascus would take place while Kissinger was in Israel. I received advance warning of the impending visit when Adnan would ask me to move to another room so that the head of security for Gromyko could stay in my room. After changing my room three times I asked Adnan if I could have our technical person "bug" another room for them so I would not have to change rooms so often. Adnan smiled but declined our offer.

A week or so after the shuttle trips began we received information from our ID agent in Israel that a PLO-supported terrorist group, the Democratic Front for the Liberation of Palestine, had infiltrated the Israeli border town of Maálot. Hoping among other things to disrupt the Kissinger peace negotiations, the DFLP took a group of about one hundred teenagers hostage in a Maálot school. After ten days of negotiations between the terrorists and the Israelis failed to resolve the hostage situation, Israeli Special Forces counterattacked. During the counterattack the terrorists machine gunned the children being held in a dormitory; over twenty of the children were killed and seventy injured.

❖ ❖ ❖

With the intricate security plan set and Kissinger visiting every third day there was a considerable amount of down time. Adnan was gregarious and enjoyed talking and being with the agents. He loved to take us for rides into the countryside, including the valley leading to Lebanon and one of the passes leading into Damascus. Several times these rides ended up at a quaint restaurant for lunch. It was essential for Adnan's ego that we know how important he was. He expressed a great deal of knowledge of Damascus and the surrounding area. However, on one ride into the countryside, we rounded a turn on a narrow road in the hills and found ourselves confronting an anti-aircraft battery of surface-to-air missiles.

On another occasion, we drove to the hills overlooking the Lebanon border, and Adnan suggested we get out and enjoy the beautiful vista. From our vantage point we could see the rolling hills and farm houses across the valley in Lebanon. However, below us in the wooded area we could see men, tanks, and other military equipment on maneuvers. When he realized that there was a military training exercise in progress, Adnan quickly ordered us back into the cars and drove from the area.

Adnan especially enjoyed taking groups of agents to lunch or dinner. The meals were in a local restaurant serving very good Mid-Eastern fare, where Adnan always proudly picked up the tab. When Kissinger was not in town, many of the men would get up late, have something to eat, and pretty much lounge around the hotel. We drank the hotel out of beer on several occasions. This happened not because of the volume we were drinking but was due to the limited amounts the hotel ordered. When the beer ran out we would give Adnan a difficult time about proper stocking of the bar. We asked him if we should have some brought over on the next plane from Israel. The real problem with the lack of beer was the Syrians and other Middle-Eastern countries were Muslim and most people did not drink alcohol. If you put a team of twenty-five young men in a small hotel in a Muslim country, you will have a beer supply problem.

Lee, the administrative officer, would come by periodically to check with me, asking if we needed anything. He was super-efficient, cordial, and enjoyable to be around; occasionally he would stay for lunch. One day about two weeks into the visit Lee came by the hotel and advised me our bar bill for the first two weeks was almost $10,000. I told him, "No way."

Lee said it didn't really matter since, "The Syrian government is paying the bills."

I was really agitated, not wanting to believe we actually drank that much alcohol. The next afternoon, with Kissinger still in Israel, Adnan came over and joined some of us for lunch. Throughout the early afternoon twenty men ate, with many having a beer or two with their lunch. Around three in the afternoon I asked for the bill, which was in Arabic. Before signing the tab I asked Adnan to translate it for me. Looking it over, he said we had 20 lunches and 115 beers. I told him I had been keeping track and we only had 36 beers. Adnan glared at me, then, getting a very serious tone in his voice, he abruptly said, "Michael, sign the bill. You are not paying for anything."

The light went on. I now understood why our bar bill was so high and why we went out to eat so much. Obviously, there was a kick-back system that took care of our hosts on everything we ate and drank.

❖ ❖ ❖

In Damascus it was difficult for us to tell how the talks were going. There was no western television to watch and no *Herald Tribune* or other English papers for us to read. Kissinger would arrive, visit with President Assad, rest at the guest house, have more meetings, and return to Israel. Since we had no idea how long we would be in Damascus, as the days piled up it was a challenge to keep the agents focused. About three weeks or so into our assignment, an attractive Mid-Eastern woman of about forty came into the hotel café in the late afternoon. She was accompanied by a couple of younger, attractive women. They had a snack and juice. She started coming in most afternoons during the week. The woman was generally accompanied by one or two young ladies. She and her friends were outgoing, talking with everyone in the café. Of course, it was mostly Secret Service agents enjoying a beer before dinner in the café. Some of the men enjoyed talking with her and her friends, since they all spoke English.

After a few days I introduced myself, discovering that the older woman worked at the Iranian Embassy a few blocks down the street from our hotel. According to her, the other ladies all worked for her. I sent a message to our ID agent with her name and all the other information I had gathered. The next day I found out she worked at the Iranian Embassy as a receptionist. According to the report, part of her job was providing support and young women to Arab businessmen and diplomats who came to the Iranian Embassy in Damascus. Also, the intelligence report indicated she had provided compromising pictures of some men with her girls to various Arabic newspapers in the region. Speaking to our agents in small groups, I briefed them on the situation. They were cautioned not to get involved outside the café with the women.

✣ ✣ ✣

Car security and the visits of Kissinger were going well, with any early wrinkles ironing themselves out. During one of the secretary's earlier visits, we were at the guest house, where Kissinger was resting while waiting for the afternoon meeting with President Assad. We were totally caught off guard when a message was received that President Assad was ready to see Secretary Kissinger. Everyone scrambled to get the motorcade assembled, the security people ready, the staff in their cars, and Kissinger in the limo. As we started to leave, Edwards realized that neither His Excellency Number One nor His Excellency Number Two were in the lead car. He immediately stopped the limo and quickly escorted Kissinger back into the guest house to wait for one of our hosts to arrive. Kissinger did so without as much as a question. As you can imagine, Adnan and the other staff people were going crazy. They wanted the motorcade to leave at once, after all, "The President called," Adnan admonished me. He was visibly upset as he continued trying to convince us of the need not to keep the president waiting. Edwards told him that there was an agreement that the motorcade did not move unless one of our hosts was present.

As he continued pleading with us, Adnan's face paled and you could see pure fear in his eyes, but Edwards held firm. By the time His Excellency Number One arrived we were over fifteen minutes late in departing. After that our Syrian counterparts made sure one or the other was always with us at the guest house.

❖ ❖ ❖

Adnan took several of us out to dinner one evening to a very good restaurant near our hotel that had a belly dancer. The Syrians were not big drinkers, but that particular evening there were several bottles of scotch, vodka, and wine on the table in addition to beer. After we had dinner and a few drinks, the belly dancer came out and performed. She was very attractive and dressed in their typical costume including a silk cloth covering the lower portion of her face. Adnan alerted me as she neared the end of her final dances that the belly dancer would motion for me to come on stage. He cautioned it would be an insult if I did not join her on stage. Adnan said the dancer had been told I was a very important American, so it was an honor for her to have me join her in the final dance.

When the belly dancer motioned to me, I joined her on stage. As I nervously stood next to her, she rotated her hips and belly, demonstrating the motion and rhythm of the dance to me. The musicians began playing the accompanying music. At first the beat was slow, giving me a chance to adjust to the rhythm. Soon the music was fast and furious as the patrons clapped and yelled encouragingly. After several tiring minutes I was allowed to step down and returned to my table. Adnan and the rest of our party had a good laugh, shaking my hand and congratulating me.

Leaving the restaurant our entire group was all smiles. Adnan and our two security officers were feeling no pain as we walked the half-mile down the side streets back to our hotel. Arm in arm like a chorus line we were meandering down the narrow cobblestone street chattering and joking when, without warning, Adnan and the Syrian security officers took out their Russian-made 9 mm PM Markarov semi-automatic handguns. Laughing, yelling, and screaming, all together the three of them raised their weapons over their heads. They repeatedly discharged them into the night air until the clips were emptied. Adnan indicated it was a common practice to fire your weapon after an enjoyable evening. I began to understand the shots we could hear most evenings.

※ ※ ※

During the first two weeks in Damascus I would go up to the roof of the hotel almost every morning to jog at 6 a.m. After my forty-five-minute workout I would return to my room, shower, and go downstairs to have breakfast. One morning I was about halfway through my jog when an Israeli Air Force F-4 Phantom jet came screaming right over the hotel. The jet seemed to be no more than three or four hundred feet off the deck. The sound was deafening and I could feel the roof vibrate. I guessed that the Israelis wanted to remind the Syrians they were still around. This experience would be repeated again before I changed the location of my morning run.

On some mornings, after the run and before leaving for my room, I would linger on the roof. Looking out over the city to the southwest I could see Mt. Hermon. Israeli troops had occupied the southern and western slopes of Mt. Hermon since the 1967 war. Midway between our downtown hotel and Mt. Hermon was a Syrian Air Force base. A "war of attrition" was being conducted by the Syria Air Force, who made daily bombing runs on Israeli military positions on the mountain. Standing on the hotel roof I could glimpse two

Soviet-made Mig-21 jet aircraft shortly after they took off. Heading away from Mt. Hermon, they circled back toward the mountain and dropped bombs on Israeli positions. I could not see them drop the bombs nor see the bombs explode, but I could see most of the flight pattern. After completing two runs, the jets would return to the airbase. As soon as they landed, another pair of the Soviet jets would begin the next attack.

Once while walking through downtown Damascus with my silent security shadows I came upon a small Syrian shop. It was the closest food shop to a New York City deli as I had ever seen in the Arab Middle East. Stacked on tables outside the shop were desserts well-known in the Middle East. Donuts, *haghajha, baklawa*, and *kaik* were a few I recognized. Inside, the small shop was crammed with various canned, dried, and fresh goods, as well as a glass-enclosed case with cheeses, sausages, salami, and other prepared dishes. In large baskets on the floor were pita breads, rolls, and loaves of bread. From the wonderful aroma I was sure the breads and pastries were freshly baked. I was especially surprised to see the boiled hams in the glass enclosure. On top of the counter I spied a commercial meat slicing machine. Taking my time I selected some salami, ham, cheese, rolls, and mustard to take back to our hotel. Leaving the shop there was a new urgency in my steps during the jaunt back to the hotel with the bags of goodies for lunch to share with the team. I could not keep the smile off my face as I entered the hotel.

The luncheon surprise was well received by my colleagues and was repeated several more times before we left. The food at the hotel, though neither gourmet nor Western, was okay. Breakfast was the standard fare of sweet rolls, toast, eggs, and breakfast meats served with coffee or tea. Lunch tended to be hamburgers and fries. The evening meals often were lamb and/or seafood, starch, and a vegetable, often eggplant.

One memorable evening we all arrived in the bar, had a drink, and walked as a group into our special private dining area. We were startled by the table's contents. The gray mass sitting on each plate was easily identifiable as we neared the table; awaiting each of us was a plate with a Syrian delicacy, sheep brain. Looking around, everyone seemed to be waiting for someone else to sit down. Finally a comment of, "Let's go to the café," was made. I am sure our Syrian hosts were disappointed that we walked away from their special meal. So, once in a while having ham and cheese sandwiches was a nice break for the team members.

One morning the technical support team asked me if I were the one running on the roof every day. When I nodded and told them yes, they asked if I knew that everyone in the hotel could hear me. It never dawned on me that the running vibrated throughout the hotel, waking people up. After speaking with Adnan, he arranged for a Syrian car to pick me up early the next morning, so my runs could continue on a secluded ramp on the military side of the Damascus airport. I was near the hangar where the Kissinger limousine was secured. Nobody on the team said anything, but I am sure some enjoyed me using a new site for my running.

❖ ❖ ❖

A couple of weeks into the shuttle diplomacy, while Kissinger was in Israel, Adnan came to my room in the early afternoon. He was nervous and animated, telling me one of our agents was missing. Adnan said the agent had left the hotel earlier in the day, going to the church across the street. According to him, the agent met a young lady there and the two of them left the church together after the service. He excitedly continued reporting that they walked to the center of town where the security tail lost them. Adnan said that the girl was sixteen and had two brothers who were members of the Fatah section of the PLO, who were fighting on Mt. Hermon. He said he was concerned the agent might have been kidnapped. Our host said the security forces would continue to conduct sweeps in the area where the agent was last seen. Since there was nothing I could do, I left a note on the agent's room door to come and see me when he returned.

About an hour later there was a knock at my door. Our wayward agent had returned. Although I admonished him about leaving the hotel, he seemed oblivious to the seriousness of what had happened. He could not understand my concern. The agent told me he had met a girl at the church across the street a week earlier. They had spoken for a short while and he agreed to meet her today. He said after church they walked downtown, window shopped, and then went into a theatre to see a movie. The agent, who was not assigned to PSD, said he did not understand the big deal. I explained that the girl's brothers were members of Fatah, an armed faction of the PLO fighting on Mt. Hermon. When he was questioned if he remembered my earlier briefing about the intelligence concerning terrorists wanting to kidnap an agent or staff, he reluctantly shrugged his shoulders in acknowledgement. He still did not equate personal danger to his behavior with the young woman.

I tried to keep my composure as I strongly expressed to him that his behavior was not acceptable. He was advised that it was one thing if he got himself kidnapped or killed because of his stupidity but it was a problem if United States foreign policy was interrupted because of his carelessness. The agent was cautioned to follow the rules or he would be sent back to the States.

About two weeks later a very agitated Adnan came to my room and said that the same agent was gone again. He said that this time he thought the agent was with the lady from the Iranian Embassy. Adnan asked me if I knew where she lived because he believed the agent was at her apartment. I gave him the address which had previously been provided to me in the report from our ID agent. When the Syrians brought him to my room later, I relieved the agent of his weapon and instructed him to return to his field office. It was suggested he contact Gary Lee at the Interests Section to make arrangements for a return ticket to the United States. The agent was told to explain to his boss why he was sent home early and where his gun was. I did not tell him I was not writing a formal report. I was worried about the impact on his career of a formal report.

※ ※ ※

Several times during the month-long shuttle diplomacy, intelligence information that was very specific was provided to His Excellency Number One. Each time it was provided he signed our copy of the report. On one particular occasion the information dealt with the location of some weapons and people. Another time the information passed concerned an attack on the motorcade along the route. In each instance, after the Syrians had time to check out the information, His Excellency made a point of thanking Edwards for the information. He opted not to go into detail of their investigation, but he seemed happy with the information supplied.

※ ※ ※

Everyone was excited after the twelfth visit by Kissinger, when we received a call from the detail in Israel advising a disengagement agreement had been reached. All of us were elated to hear we could go home. The first thing I did was to call Bush at the Protective Support Division and request a C-141 to pick up our team the next afternoon. We knew the cargo plane would be coming out of Incirlik Air Force Base in Turkey. Knowing this would be our last night, we had a special celebration at the hotel. The next morning we were in the middle of the lobby accumulating our luggage and equipment, waiting for a Syrian military truck to arrive to pick up our gear. You can imagine our surprise when we got a message from the advance team in Israel that Kissinger would be making one last courtesy visit to Damascus to thank Assad.

Even though we were advised the traveling group would be much smaller than on the previous visits, it was going to be a race for us to get everything together. We had less than an hour and a half to notify the Syrians and Lee, assemble cars, agents, and escort vehicles. We knew everyone would have to jump through hoops to put the security plan in play. Fortunately the limo and follow-up were already at the airport. Our jump team agents were advised that our dress codes had been relaxed and to get to their assigned posts as quickly as possible. We managed to have a quick meeting with the general in charge of the troops securing the motorcade route, and our Syrian counterparts were asked to get the escort vehicles to the airport at once.

To compound everything else, the general in charge of route security was advised directly that we had disturbing intelligence of a specific nature; an attack on the motorcade would come from the non-uniformed paramilitary forces helping with route security. Because of the short notice of the intelligence on the visit, a very unusual request was made by Edwards. He requested the general to have all route security personnel place their shoulder weapons at their feet and face away from the motorcade. It was emphasized that none of his people along the route should have a weapon in their hands. Forcefully, the general was advised that anyone with a gun in his hand facing the motorcade would be shot.

The general, who had less than forty-five minutes to brief his people and get them posted, said he would try to get the dummy motorcade out to the airport. We managed to get a message to Chargé d'Affaires Scotes through Lee of the new visit. Lee performed magic, managing to get us a couple of vehicles and drivers to take us to the airport ramp and be used in the motorcade. Riding to the airport, we could see trucks dropping off security personnel along the motorcade route. Arriving on the ramp, we quickly put a small motorcade together with our limo, follow-up car, and the staff vehicles provided by Lee. We had a couple of police vehicles but not our normal contingent of motorcycles and troop trucks. Our motorcade was ready ten minutes before Kissinger touched down. Neither of our counterparts had arrived as Kissinger and a small cadre of staff exited the aircraft.

We had enough agents at the airport, but some were not our regular motorcade crew. We delayed the motorcade departure for a few minutes to see if more of our official motorcade would arrive. However, since the visit was unscheduled, we decided to depart before our full Syrian detail and motorcade arrived. Heading down the highway into town I saw an absolutely incredible sight. Syrian military personnel, uniformed and non- uniformed, were facing away from the motorcade with their weapons at their feet; amazing, absolutely amazing. The dummy motorcade with our Syrian counterparts and security vehicles for our motorcade passed us on the other side of the center divider en route to the airport about halfway down the airport access road.

We continued into the city and went directly to the palace where Kissinger had a short meeting with President Assad. While the two leaders were meeting, we had a chance to assemble our normal motorcade. After the meeting we immediately returned to the airport and Kissinger departed for Israel.

As soon as Kissinger left, we anxiously returned to the hotel and got back to loading the truck for our departure. We managed to get all our equipment, bags, and people to the airport ramp shortly before our C-141 was scheduled to arrive. When I first saw the big cargo plane swoop down out of the sky I got a lump in my throat. I was thinking "God Bless America" to myself and was thankful about the freedom we took for granted back home. As the USAF cargo aircraft coasted down the runway and we could see the American flag painted on the tail, everyone broke out cheering. Old Glory never looked so good to me. Our jump team and the EOD support team had been on the ground over thirty-three days, while our advance team had been on the ground almost forty days. When we had left the United States none of us realized we would be gone so long.

The double doors at the rear of the plane were quickly opened and the ramps put into place so the limo could be driven aboard. Our equipment, baggage, and souvenirs quickly followed. Some agents boarded through the rear and some through the door near the front of the plane. However, before we had time to close the back of the plane, the pilot explained to us that he had a problem with one of the engines. Some of us exited the plane to the ramp where we waited anxiously watching the Air Force mechanic bring out a step ladder and open the cowling to check out the engine. We had been told the pilot was talking directly with Incirlik, troubleshooting the problem with the air base in Turkey, while the mechanic was trying to find the problem.

Standing near the plane watching the Air Force mechanic, I spoke with Special Officer Bill Scholl, our limo mechanic on the trip. Scholl, who had retired after over twenty years as a mechanic with the Air Force, worked for a while with Boeing in Seattle, Washington. Scholl mentioned to me that he was aware of the problem being experienced and advised that he thought he knew how to fix it. But, he told me, he was sure the Air Force guys would not listen to him. After a half hour and no success in fixing the problem, the pilot decided to request a back-up aircraft, while his mechanic continued to try to fix the problem. Incirlik advised that a replacement aircraft would arrive in a little over two hours with another mechanic. We tried to relax while nervously waiting for the replacement aircraft. We were hopeful the new mechanic could fix the problem so we could leave at once, otherwise everything would have to be offloaded and then reloaded on the new aircraft.

When the second aircraft finally arrived, the new mechanic was given a chance to fix the problem before we moved everything to the second C-141. Scholl and I were standing not far from the problem engine as the new mechanic walked toward us. Motioning toward the problem engine, Scholl described to me how the mechanic would fix the problem. As he had predicted, it took the mechanic no more than three minutes to do exactly what Scholl described to fix the engine. We were a little more subdued as the aircraft finally rumbled down the runway for takeoff. Looking down at Damascus, I knew I would be back when President Nixon visited Syria on his Mid-East victory tour sometime in June or July.

❈ ❈ ❈

Back in the States I knew it would not be long before I would be permanently assigned to the Kissinger detail. By the end of June I was advised to wrap up my projects with Dansereau, since the Kissinger detail was going to be my new home. By the time I was finally assigned full-time to the Kissinger detail, my focus had changed. I found myself thinking once again about the difference between the security strategies used overseas to combat potential terrorist attacks against Kissinger versus those used in Washington, D.C.

On June 10, 1974, before I could really start a project, Kissinger accompanied President Nixon on a ten-day tour of Europe and the Middle East, going to Egypt, Saudi Arabia, Syria, and Israel. I headed for Damascus ahead of Air Force One to conduct the security advance for Kissinger. Working with the president's detail was a snap. Most of the time when Kissinger accompanied the president, we were along for the ride. Standing on the ramp waiting for Air Force One to arrive I was speaking with the Air Force advance person. It was mentioned that Air Force One would be accompanied by several Soviet Mig jets. The advance agent told me he had spoken with the Syrians and requested no escort. I advised him that every time Kissinger arrived he was escorted by the Mig jets once the plane entered Syrian air space, though sometimes the Soviet-provided jets were not in close proximity.

The military advance person quickly got on his radio and spoke to Air Force One advising them of the possibility of the Mig escort. Shortly after he spoke with the president's plane it entered Syrian air space with the Mig jets nearby. As they advanced toward the airport the Migs positioned themselves closer to the wing tip. When Colonel Ralph Albertazzi, the presidential pilot of Air Force One, made a dip with a slight roll left and right to discourage them, the Mig pilots backed off.

❈ ❈ ❈

Kissinger was attending a luncheon at the restaurant where Adnan used to take us on occasions during the long shuttle negotiations. First Lady Pat Nixon was going to attend the same luncheon. Her advance agent arrived about a half hour before the luncheon. I briefed him on the site and told him where the women's room was located. Shortly before she arrived, her agent told me Mrs. Nixon had a touch of "Montezuma's revenge" and would go directly to the restroom. He jumped at a chance to make five dollars when I bet him she would not use the restroom.

The advance agent had not gone into the room to check it out and therefore did not know it did not have a regular toilet bowl. The restrooms were old European style with a porcelain hole instead of the toilet bowls we had in America. Having used the men's room and knowing Mrs. Nixon, I was sure she would not use it. Mrs. Nixon arrived and was led directly to the restroom, but came out in ten seconds and went to her seat. President and Mrs. Nixon stayed overnight in Damascus and departed the next day for Israel. I returned to the United States.

❧ ❧ ❧

Kissinger cut short his participation in the Nixon victory tour to attend a NATO ministerial meeting in Ottawa June 17-19. Secret Service had the same weapons problems with the Royal Canadian Mounted Police (RCMP) as with Scotland Yard. No shoulder weapons and no handguns were allowed in Canada. I did not make the trip to Canada. I was in the office after returning from Syria before Kissinger went to Canada. Boyette told me he had spoken with headquarters and the RCMP was not allowing us to bring any guns into Canada.

The Ottawa visit went well, but back in the United States some time after Kissinger's visit there was a picture of King Hussein of Jordan during his visit to Canada in one of the U.S. papers. The picture clearly showed the king with his coat open with his arms raised while waving to a crowd. Stuffed in his waist band behind his belt a handgun was clearly visible. I had heard from the Israelis that they took no guns into Canada but got guns to carry once inside Canada. I guess King Hussein did the same.

Kissinger kept busy traveling after Canada, going to Belgium with President Nixon for a NATO heads of government meeting June 25-26 and then on to Moscow, Simferopol, and Minsk June 27 to July 3. Kissinger returned to Washington from Spain on July 9 and I was officially switched to the Kissinger detail.

❖ ❖ ❖

Kissinger and his wife, Nancy, were invited to stay at the District of Columbia residence of one of his friends, who was the CEO of a major U. S. chemical company. The brown brick, Tudor-style house was located on eleven acres in northwest Washington. Agents Don Stebbins and John O'Toole were working the midnight shift with me. Our command post was located in a sunken big game room off the foyer. The trophies of successful hunts, including animal heads, pelts, stuffed birds, and small game were on the walls, tables, and floor of the room. The property was divided by a fence with the driveway and house on one side and a big field with the swimming pool on the other.

We held two security posts on the midnight shift; post one was at the front door of the house, while post two was in a small grassy area at the rear of the house between Kissinger's bedroom and a six-foot-high brick wall. With only three agents working, the agent in the command post relieved post one, who took up post two. The agent at the rear post then proceeded to the command post. Around 2:30 a.m. agent O'Toole was manning the front post and Stebbins came into the command post from post two to speak with me. He told me of a prank he wanted to play on O'Toole and removed a very large moose head with antlers from the command post wall. Stebbins put the moose head out of sight behind the brick wall near the bedroom and then returned to his post. At three a.m. I went out to relieve O'Toole at the front of the house, while Stebbins waited patiently in the back for O'Toole to relieve him. When O'Toole arrived, instead of going to the command post, Stebbins quietly snuck around the brick fence and picked up the moose head.

It was a cloudy, dark night with no moon and the cloud cover hiding the stars. I quietly positioned myself around the side of the house where I could observe the front area while at the same time see the brick wall and O'Toole. Stebbins carefully lifted the moose head above the fence, resting the lower jaw on the top brick less than ten feet from where O'Toole was standing in the dark. All at once Stebbins began pawing the ground with his feet and loudly snorting. O'Toole at first seemed confused by the noise, but he quickly recovered, chambering a round as he raised the weapon to his shoulder. At three o'clock in the morning the sound of a round being chambered in a shotgun sounds like a jet airplane taking off. With O'Toole aiming toward the noise emanating at the fence and slowly moving in that direction, I was concerned he would fire a round. Realizing that a practical joke had gone awry, I immediately shouted, "Don't shoot! Don't shoot!"

My career was flashing before me. I could see O'Toole firing a shotgun blast at the moose head, blowing it apart, and both Stebbins and I being transferred to New York City. O'Toole responded to the sound of my voice and lowered the shotgun. He removed the round from the chamber and reloaded it into the shotgun. Stebbins, muffling a laugh, headed to the command post with the moose head. All three of us were trying to contain our chuckling as the moose head was returned to its rightful place on the command post wall. I don't know if Kissinger or his wife heard us or not and we never asked. Eventually word got around the detail about the moose head prank. It had to have come from O'Toole because Stebbins and I told no one.

❖ ❖ ❖

The Watergate scandal had been taking a toll on Nixon since the June 17, 1972, burglary of the Democratic National Committee office in the Watergate building complex. There was the Senate Committee investigation headed by Sen. Sam Ervin (D-NC) that found out about the White House tapes, among other things. One of the tapes was found to have an eighteen-minute gap. Nixon's secretary, Rosemary Woods, said she had inadvertently erased some of the tape while transcribing it. Between the disclosures of the White House taping system and the eighteen-minute gap, Nixon was doomed.

Many politicians, the press, and prominent private sector leaders were calling for Nixon to resign. It was generally acknowledged that Nixon did not have the votes to survive impeachment by the House of Representatives. However, in the Senate it was believed there were not enough votes to impeach him. Impeachment by both houses of Congress was required to drive a sitting president from office. Things got worse for Nixon as the summer wore on in our nation's capital.

❖ ❖ ❖

It was a typical hot, humid summer evening on August 8, 1974, as Kissinger's limousine approached the northwest gate entrance to the White House on Pennsylvania Avenue at 7 p.m. One of the Uniform Division officers on the sidewalk approached our limousine and notified the security post to open the gate. As the working supervisor, I was in the right front seat of the limousine. I was aware this was going to be a historical evening and was pleased to be part of it.

As we slowly entered the grounds we could see a large crowd of people gathered on the Pennsylvania Avenue sidewalk outside the White House fence holding a candlelight vigil. Most of the people appeared to be young. The somber, calm atmosphere on the sidewalk was striking. There were no signs, no yelling, and no jostling; just a crowd waiting for probably the most historic event of their lifetime. Kissinger and his wife were going to watch the resignation speech live in the East Room of the White House along with other members of Nixon's staff. But first, Kissinger would visit privately with Nixon in the family quarters.

After watching the address, Kissinger and his wife left to go to the trendy Georgetown restaurant Rive Gauche for dinner. Exiting the White House grounds, we had a last look at the candlelight crowd that had grown substantially since our arrival. It seemed strange to see a large group of people in front of the White House so calm and quiet. The drive to the restaurant took less than ten minutes.

With the limousine and follow-up car on the street alongside the restaurant the word quickly spread throughout the neighboring establishments that a special guest was dining at the Rive Gauche. Groups of people began gathering on three of the corners waiting for the secretary to emerge to his waiting motorcade. The scene outside the Rive Gauche was very similar to that at the White House, as people gathered in an eerie calmness. The mood was very somber with no one conversing in normal tones. Why everyone spoke in hushed voices was something I did not understand at the time and still don't. I went in and out of the restaurant several times trying to keep track of the expanding crowd. Several hundred people were waiting when I interrupted Kissinger as he finished his dessert. I quietly mentioned to him that two to three hundred people were on the corners outside waiting for him to appear.

Exiting the restaurant with his wife on his arm, Kissinger paused outside the doorway and surveyed the large gathering of people. Walking to the corner by the rear of the limousine Kissinger calmly raised his arm and waved politely, acknowledging the waiting throng. The scene was surreal. The men and women on the corners began a spontaneous rhythmic clapping. Just as was the case at the White House, there was no cheering, no yelling; in fact, the cadence of the clapping itself was slow and somewhat muted. Turning to get into the car, Kissinger again acknowledged the somber clapping crowd with a brief nod of his head and a slight wave of his hand. As the car left the curb for the short drive home, Nancy asked her husband, "What was that all about?" Kissinger told her that he believed the people saw him as something good in the administration and were sadden by what the nation was going through with the Nixon resignation.

The next day at noon Gerald Ford was sworn in as the thirty-eighth president of the United States. Ford, a senator from Michigan, had replaced Spiro Agnew as vice president on December 6, 1973. He was the first person appointed vice president under the terms of Article II, section 1 of the Twenty-fifth Amendment. He became the thirty-eighth president of the United States under the same amendment. On August 9, 1974, Ford became the first person to be sworn in as a U.S. president who had not been elected. Since Kissinger remained secretary of state and continued as the point man for President Ford in foreign policy, there would be no change in my assignment.

❈ ❈ ❈

There was no overseas travel the rest of August and all of September. However, Kissinger spent twenty-six days on the road between October 9 and November 9. I traveled with Kissinger on his airplane for a week to Egypt, Syria, Jordan, Israel, Saudi Arabia, Algeria, and Morocco. By the time we got to Algeria the aircraft was overloaded. Every nook and cranny was full. The crew unloaded over two dozen cases of wine and other bulky non-essential packages and left them on the ramp in Algiers. Before we departed, all of us riding in the plane were told we could bring with us only items that would fit in the overhead compartment or under the seat in front of us.

❖ ❖ ❖

The Kissinger detail was the Rodney Dangerfield of the Secret Service. They just didn't get any respect. The Presidential and Vice Presidential Protective Divisions got first selection on all new agents. They had a high level of outside support and top-of-the-line equipment available to them. The type and level of threats they received were completely different from those Kissinger received. The danger to them was mainly from the whacko, mentally ill, radical fringe groups and people who thought they had been wronged by either the president or vice president. Meanwhile the secretary of state traveled extensively overseas and his daily schedule exposed him constantly to those groups who would harm him and those who wanted to thwart American's foreign policy. Kissinger had serious international terrorist threats in addition to the normal domestic threats. SAIC Lapham, the bulldog, was tenacious in his approach to dealing with headquarters in trying to get things done. He truly led the charge, using Boyette to handle the day-to-day operations. The two of them seemed to have a very close professional relationship. Secret Service headquarters, on the other hand, was more than happy to have the detail go their own way without bothering them with a lot of supervision. It was a case of out of sight out of mind or don't call me I'll call you.

Robert Lapham, Barney Boyette, Jack Ready, Jim Cantrell, and Ed Dansereau molded a group of outcast young agents together to assume an historical assignment to protect one of the most threatened secretaries of state in our history. These vagabonds developed and implemented new procedures providing security to the first person protected by the Secret Service to experience such extensive, ongoing global terrorist threats. These renegade agents, traveling around the world, accepting assignments and projects, facing threats against themselves while developing the first operational procedures to fight terrorism, never thought of themselves as trailblazers.

Kissinger, as national security adviser, was well aware of the threats against him and the other top leadership of our country. On occasion when agents walked with Secretary of State Kissinger, he would bring up the level of his security. This happened once when I was with him. He asked about his level of security versus the president, the vice president, and the secretary of the Treasury. His questions were, "How many agents does the president have?" followed by, "And the vice president?" The follow-up question was "What about Treasury?" The investigation did not conclude with "How many do I have?" The conversation that followed seemed to almost become an interrogation by Kissinger, who clearly knew his threat level. I sensed he saw the number of agents assigned as an indication of the pecking order.

Some agents, I had heard, would gratuitously talk with the secretary about the unusually high threat level attributed to him. In retrospect I think Kissinger checked periodically to see if the number of agents on his detail had been increased. When he asked, "How many agents do I have?" was he checking on our response to increased levels of terrorist threats against him? It would not surprise me. He certainly knew his threat level as well as we did. Initially, I had thought Kissinger's interest in manpower levels was an ego thing. Maybe, I thought, he equated importance with numbers of agents. Today my sense is that his interest in numbers assigned for him dealt with his perception of the Secret Service commitment to keep him alive.

The responsibility to protect Secretary Kissinger was a very unique one for the Secret Service. In the Middle East, agents got up in the morning not knowing if this would be the day. We wondered if a bomb would go off, if we would we be attacked, or if someone would try to penetrate the inner circle. Agents did not linger on the threats; they knew the threats were there, knew they existed. But they never talked about their exposure. They just kept doing their job.

Kissinger, understanding the threat against him, must have believed it was imperative he have the protection afforded by the Secret Service to enable him to perform his mission as secretary of state. He knew the Secret Service was the world's most elite group of security professionals. The organization from top to bottom was committed to keeping the people they protected alive. The ongoing conflict between Secret Service headquarters and the secretary of the Treasury with the State Department was strictly political and not budget or security related.

Agents, though usually visible with Kissinger, faded into the background at the appropriate moments. Whether Kissinger was in Damascus, Cairo, Jerusalem, Moscow, Belgrade, Paris, Munich, or London, the agents were as visible as needed to get the job done, including times when machine guns were openly carried. Yet Kissinger could go to a private dinner with a friend, acquaintance, or business professional without an agent intruding or changing the intimate atmosphere.

The Middle East had the most potential for disaster for Kissinger and us. It was where our Uzi machine guns often were routinely carried openly. In many of the European countries, shoulder weapons were kept out of public view in carry cases or slung, out of sight, over a shoulder, under a top coat. London, however, presented an unusual and special challenge. British laws did not allow any handguns or shoulder weapons to be brought into the country by foreign security services. Through negotiation by headquarters, a very limited number of handguns were allowed to accompany the agents into England in the early 1970s. No shoulder weapons were allowed in England during Kissinger's visits, but there was an exception for visits of the president and vice president. Attempts to get authorization for the entry of shoulder weapons (shotguns and Uzi machine guns) during a visit by Kissinger were continually denied. We were allowed to bring four handguns into England and nothing else.

Our British Scotland Yard counterparts knew very well the high threat level directed against Kissinger. As the Boeing 707 carrying Kissinger landed at Heathrow an armored vehicle accompanied it from the runway to the ramp debarking area. Uniformed British military personnel carrying automatic weapons were posted in the area near the plane. When Kissinger and his party got off the plane, detail leader Cantrell had selected the four agents to carry the weapons. Our agents were met by two Scotland Yard detectives providing security. The detectives might or might not have handguns, but they never had shoulder weapons. One of the detectives sat in the front seat of the limousine and the other in the back seat of the follow-up car. Agents getting off the plane carried two aluminum briefcases that contained our automatic shoulder weapons with spare clips.

Before the motorcade left the ramp, one Uzi in a case would be placed unlocked on the floor in the front compartment of the limousine for the supervisor. The other case would be on the back seat of the follow-up car, between our agent and the Scotland Yard detective. The case was unlocked and sometimes opened, making the weapon visible to the detective. The agents were very careful to make sure only the

Scotland Yard detective assigned to our detail knew we had the shoulder weapon. The Scotland Yard representatives, who knew Kissinger's threat level, must have been appreciative of the additional fire power. They never even acknowledged the presence of the automatic weapons to our agents. It was one of those situations where no one said anything. It always amazed me that Kissinger was provided an armored vehicle and automatic weapons support at the airport when entering the country but such a low level of security while in the country.

❖ ❖ ❖

In October, when I received an assignment to go to Moscow to advance Kissinger's October 23-27, 1974 visit, I was told by Dansereau and Boyette that Secretary of Treasury Simon was currently in Moscow. Dansereau suggested I check with the Simon detail before I left for my advance, since he heard they were experiencing problems with the KGB. In debriefing the Simon advance agent before I departed, I found out that there had been a reported shake-up in the KGB. Yuri Andropov, who was the director of the KGB, had recently assumed responsibility of the Ninth Directorate. They provided security for government leaders and visiting dignitaries. According to the Simon detail agent, the KGB was being uncharacteristically difficult in dealing with the Secret Service by inserting a Foreign Ministry officer between their office and our advance agent.

Upon our arrival at the Moscow Airport, instead of being met by the KGB, we were greeted by a young, inexperienced service representative from the Foreign Ministry. Processing through immigration and customs at the airport was unusually slow and stressful. The Foreign Ministry simply did not carry the weight that the KGB did. When we were finally processed, we were transported to the Sovetskaya Hotel.

Even though our check-in at the hotel went off without a hitch, I was becoming concerned that the Foreign Ministry representative had been inserted between the KGB and us to act as a buffer to slow everything down. It was clear to me they could not provide any real help. If my instincts were right, this would make it very difficult to efficiently accomplish our mission. After getting unpacked I met my nervous Foreign Service contact in the lobby for a chat to deal directly about the whereabouts of our KGB counterparts. The answers turned out to come from an isolated, uninformed young bureaucrat programmed to be void of information. I requested a meeting as soon as possible with my KGB representative. He told me he would get back to me. In the meantime, several of us on the advance team headed out to do some shopping and sightseeing.

The next day, when I had my meeting with the KGB, it turned out to be a very structured and not necessarily informative get-together. The camaraderie and professional respect I had seen in my last two trips had been replaced with a formality that could only be meant to isolate us. The agents were aloof and formal as my request for cars, site visits, and other support received the new KGB response, "We'll get back to you." In fact, they indicated the information would be provided to us through our Foreign Ministry contact. Each day of the advance our schedule was to hurry up and wait. In addition, one of my advance agents, Jim Andersen, told me he was repeatedly getting incoming phone calls from a male who was telling him, "I like young men." The man would also request Anderson to come to a specific room.

I approached our Foreign Ministry representative and told him the calls needed to stop immediately. He was reminded that all calls into the hotel had to go through the switchboard and were monitored. If the calls did not stop immediately I advised him that I would make an official complaint through the U.S. Embassy. There were no more phone calls harassing any of our agents after that.

Two nights before the arrival of Kissinger, my explosive ordinance team from Germany arrived a day early. As soon as I was notified of the change I spoke to the manager of the Sovetskaya through the switchboard operator, who spoke English. I was told there were no empty rooms, so the men could not stay there. He said only the KGB could authorize people to stay in the hotel. Knowing it would be impossible to get approval for rooms on a Sunday evening through our ministry contact, I ignored what he said and departed for the airport.

One of the administrative employees from the embassy accompanied me to meet the two EOD members. On the car ride back to the hotel I told the explosive experts of the room situation at the hotel, asking them to bear with me and follow my directions back at the hotel. Entering the hotel with their bags in hand we stopped in the center of the lobby. One EOD member was directed to an overstuffed couch on one side of the lobby and the other to a similar couch on the other side of the lobby. Each was told to open his suitcase on the floor and lie down on the couch. As I strolled to the front desk to see the switchboard operator, both the EOD men were lying on their respective couches. The operator was staring at the two men on the couches when I announced to her not to bother the manager since my men would sleep on the couches. Abruptly I turned and headed for the grand staircase to walk the four floors to my room. At the third floor landing I was met by the hotel manager, who took me back to the front desk to speak through the operator.

He once again told me he could not put my men in a room. I quickly responded, "Don't worry, I understand. The men will sleep in the lobby tonight and we can get things straightened out tomorrow."

The manager appeared confused and baffled about what to do when he finally said, "I have one room that the two of them can stay in tonight."

I thanked him, and the men were put in a room on the fifth floor. After they were settled we accompanied the manager to his room. Once inside his room the language barrier did not matter. I opened my briefcase and took out several skin magazines. Opening them to the centerfold, I got him to understand he could take one. After giving him a couple of packages of gum and a pair of pantyhose I thanked him and went to my room. He was smiling from ear to ear when I departed.

My frustration level was very high two days later when I arrived at the Vnukova VIP area to await the arrival of Kissinger. I had no luck trying to find someone who could authorize me to put two-way radios into some of the motorcade vehicles. There were just too many unanswered questions and I was trying to control myself. Standing in the large waiting room I saw Colonel Bychkov enter the room. We made eye contact as I headed in his direction. When we shook hands he asked, "How is everything going?"

That was the wrong question to ask and I unloaded on him, complaining about everything from the insertion of an inexperienced Foreign Ministry officer between the Secret Service and the KGB, to a lack of professionalism, harassing phone calls, no rooms for EOD, to now not being able to put the radios in the proper cars. I forcefully objected about the lack of professional support and being treated like an outcast. Our voices were not elevated but anyone who saw us knew it was not a pleasant conversation.

Suddenly Bychkov stopped speaking and motioned me to meet someone. Pausing, he extended his hand and greeted a person wearing a heavy overcoat and a Russian fur hat, calling him General Andropov. As Andropov and I shook hands Bychkov introduced me to the general and then, in a voice dripping with sarcasm, he proceeded to belittle me, telling Andropov, "Mr. Endicott is not happy. He is upset that the KGB is not being nice to him."

General Andropov, who I realized was the director of the KGB and a member of the Politburo, turned to face me and asked, "Is that so?"

Another big mistake was made by the KGB and I drove a truck through the opening. Methodically I began to outline my stay in Moscow. First I told him that the professional courtesy and relationship between our services seemed to have been abandoned. Then, slowly, one by one, I listed my dissatisfactions with the treatment our team had been receiving. We began to draw a crowd as I punctuated my points by moving closer and with my right index finger began to gently but repeatedly touch his chest. As I had anticipated, Andropov was uncomfortable with the exchange.

Andropov had not come to the airport to speak with an irate Secret Service agent. He was there as the government representative to greet Kissinger. But here he was entangled in a messy conversation with a lower level operational Secret Service agent. Through my earpiece I could hear Kissinger's aircraft notify me the secretary was ten minutes out. After a couple more comments I could see how nervous Andropov had become. I quickly backed off when I was sure General Andropov had just enough time to get to the ramp area before Kissinger would deplane. (Little did I or anyone else suspect that eight years later, Andropov, would be named to replace Brezhnev, upon his death November 10, 1982, as the new Soviet Union General Secretary.)

The motorcade was on the ramp when I got to the arrival point and I put my radios in the limousine and our follow-up car. This was an evening arrival and Kissinger was taken directly to the Lenin Hills guest house. The next morning our KGB detail had several extra agents and seemed friendlier than before. The ice may still have been on the grass but there was no question in my mind it was beginning to thaw. On the third day of Kissinger's visit I was truly surprised when two members of the KGB, not on the detail assigned to Kissinger, showed up at the guest house asking for me. They wished me a happy birthday and gave me a box with three bottles of Moskva vodka and a large can of Beluga caviar from Colonel Bychkov. It was not hard to understand how they knew it was my birthday, but I was intrigued that after the confrontation with Bychkov and Andropov at the airport they had decided to make a special event out of it. The remaining two days of the trip went very well as the KGB reverted to their friendlier, easygoing ways. Professional courtesy returned to our relationship.

The trials and tribulations created by the KGB were passed on earlier, before Kissinger arrived, to the CIA chief of station. During the meeting with him I was briefed on Andropov's background and the struggle with the Secret Service being created apparently by him. According to the CIA, Andropov had personally taken the top position in the Ninth Directorate and was reverting to hardcore cold war tactics. The CIA was interested in the internal shake-up that seemed to be taking place. After the airport confrontation with Andropov I thought the KGB was upset with me and said so to the station chief. There was no opportunity for me to talk to him again during the secretary's visit.

After Kissinger departed I met with my KGB liaison, thanking him for their support. I also asked if it were possible to have a tour of the old monastery area in the basement beneath the Kremlin, where the monks used to sleep. The State Department Regional Security Officer and his wife and another embassy employee were allowed to accompany me on the tour.

When we were escorted to the lower level, we entered a narrow arched passageway made of stone. The hallway was about seven feet high and maybe six feet wide. It was dank and dimly lit, with lighting being provided by bare light bulbs hanging from extension cords strung down the center of the hallway. On either side of the passage were small cells where the monks used to live when the Kremlin was an active monastery. The doors to some of the rooms were ajar and we could vaguely see icons hanging on the walls of most of them. We entered several of the rooms to get a closer view, but with no lights in the small cells it was still difficult to really see the details of these very old religious paintings.

Our friendly guide provided no information on the cells, monastery, or the icons. Afterwards we were taken to the state dining room where very large, beautiful paintings hung on many of the walls and gold leaf adorned the scrolled trim throughout the room. Some of the paintings were portrayals of religious scenes dating to the time of Jesus Christ, while others were of battle scenes. I asked our guide about the significance of the paintings and was told the scenes depicted early life. From the state dining room we visited several small receiving rooms. Each had a beautiful fireplace as the central attraction. One fireplace was made of jade, another was adorned with amber, and others with special stones.

Before returning to the States I took time to make one last call on the CIA. When I mentioned the special tour I had been given I was advised that the underground tour was rarely given to Westerners. The chief of station indicated he was sure I had gained the respect of the KGB after my exchange with Andropov.

❖ ❖ ❖

I got back in PSD for two days before heading for Bucharest, Romania, where the secretary of state was going to meet with President Ceausescu and Foreign Minister Mancovescu. Our advance team was staying at a hotel downtown. I found out from our sources in the embassy that my room had both audio and video coverage by Romanian security. We only had three days to set up the security for the visit, which was plenty of time, except the head of Romanian security did not respond to the embassy's request for a meeting with me.

After not hearing from Romanian security for two days I spoke with the CIA office and got the name of the general in charge and had an embassy car take me to his house. When the general personally responded to my knocking on the front door I told him who I was and that we needed to have a meeting or their president and foreign minister would not be meeting with the secretary of state. I suggested if he had any questions about me to send a message or call his KGB friends. We met the next morning and worked out all the issues for the visit. That afternoon the car plane arrived with the limo and agents to stand post. One of the agents on the C-141 was my old friend John Novak. We had not seen each other for quite some time.

This was the first time for both of us to travel to an East Block country and we thought we could just go down the street and find a restaurant to get caught up on old times. Well, we walked for quite a while when we saw what appeared to be an eatery in an old house. It was dark out and none of the signs were in English. As we headed up the walkway approaching the house we could see a half-dozen or so tables covered with white tablecloths. Novak and I entered, sat down, and were greeted by an elderly woman, who put a menu on our table. Novak opened the menu and started to smile and laugh. He told me we were in trouble because he had never seen the language in the menu. Novak said there was not even a hint as to what was on the menu. We tried to see if we could establish a line of communication by saying fish, steaks, salad, vegetables, and other food groups.

We were making no headway, so we took out a piece of paper and drew a picture of a fish, chicken, pig, and cow as the owner looked over my shoulder. Using hand gestures and circling the pictures we believed we had placed an order but we were not sure what they would be cooking. The meal of salad, chicken, vegetables, and potatoes washed down by two beers was delicious. It was followed by some cake and coffee. The price of the meal was less than three dollars each. As spoiled Americans we left a hefty tip.

The next day Kissinger's airplane arrived right on time. He was greeted by government officials and embassy diplomats. Detail leader Cantrell trailed the secretary down the stairs and immediately motioned to me that he wanted to speak with me. Taking a few steps to the side, Cantrell said for me to wait here because Kissinger wanted to speak with me when he was through with the receiving line. Wondering what he could possibly want I waited until he walked over to me. The secretary said to me, "Mike, I am making a quick, short-notice trip to Damascus and need you to get there right away to set everything up." He told me that reservations had been made for me on an Aeroflot flight that was leaving in a little over half an hour. He said I would have less than twenty-four hours to get everything ready. Kissinger finished up by saying that the agents would check me out of the hotel here and bring my clothes to Damascus. Cantrell, who was standing next to the secretary as he briefed me, gave me a piece of paper with the flight information on it. As the two of them walked to the motorcade I stood in place thinking, "Did what just happened really happen?"

One of the people from the General Service Office at the embassy walked up and said he would get me on my flight, but we needed to hurry. The first thing I noticed when boarding the Aeroflot flight was how much higher the belly of the plane was off the ground compared to our Western planes. I was directed to my seat in the last row of the six seats in the first class section. The door was open to the coach section and I could see it was more than half full. A goat and several chickens were in the aisle toward the rear of the plane. When the flight attendant closed the door I realized it was oval, like on a submarine. Passengers needed to step up over the door frame when getting in and out of the rear compartment.

There were only three of us in the front section; I hesitate to call it first class. The meal served on the flight could be best described as intriguing. Once when the door to the rear cabin was opened I could smell food being cooked in the back compartment. We had two plane changes and I managed to get a couple of hours of sleep.

Arriving in Damascus the next morning I expected to be met by my Syrian friend Adnan. Instead a representative from our Interests Section and a colleague of Adnan's assisted me through immigration and customs. I told them I was disappointed when Adnan was not there but learned he was escorting a visiting group of women from Canada so he was not available. I was told it was a very busy time in Damascus and the Umayyad Hotel was full as were all the hotels normally used by Westerners. I learned from my Syrian counterpart that hotel rooms were going to be difficult to find. He asked how many people were going to need rooms. The representative from the embassy gave me a folder with messages and returned to his office.

Sitting down with my contact I reviewed the messages. The C-141 transporting the limo and a jump team would arrive with the limousine and twenty passengers at 2 p.m. I also found out that the Kissinger visit would be short and not complicated. Since the jump team was going to arrive in the early afternoon, rooms for them were going to be the highest priority and the biggest problem. I was afraid the Syrians were going to have to take drastic measures to secure all our room needs. I knew I would have a revolt if I put the agents and mechanic on the C-141 in non-Western rooms.

My Syrian contact and I went over the room requirements, Kissinger's schedule, and motorcade security. He made several calls trying to get the room issue resolved with no luck. Motorcade cars, security, and schedule issues were resolved within the first hour. At 11 a.m., with the room issue still not resolved, my contact decided to go to an early lunch. I suggested we could continue working on how he was going to solve the room problem. He took me to the restaurant where Adnan and I had often gone for lunch.

Sitting at one of the tables brought back memories of my thirty-nine days in Damascus. Before our order came there was a commotion at the restaurant entrance. Ten or more well-dressed, attractive women were entering followed by Adnan. When he saw me he stopped, threw his arms up in the air, and shouted across the room to me, "Mike, I am Adnan, the meanest mother f----r alive." He then rushed to my table and gave me a big hug. After he got his party seated he came back to our table and asked how everything was going and if there was anything he could do. I told him about the room problem, asking if there were a suitable solution. I mentioned there would be twenty-one of us, and if he could get us four or five rooms we would be happy. Adnan thought for a couple of moments then told his colleague the name of a hotel for us to use. He said the hotel was full but that people there should move to another hotel that he identified. Adnan indicated some people were out for the day so someone from the hotel would have to pack their bags and move them. He told me we might have to have people sleep on the couch, in chairs, and doubled up in the beds, but they would get as many rooms as possible. Finally he said it was going to take a while to move everyone and change the linens. He said he thought the rooms could be available by four or five.

When I left to meet the C-141, my Syrian contact departed to begin acquiring enough rooms for our group. At the airport I made arrangements for sandwiches, two cases of beer, one case of water, and one of soda for the people arriving on the support aircraft. When the plane arrived, I assembled everyone on the ramp and collected their passports and had them fill out an immigration arrival document. A representative of immigration took the documents to be processed. The limousine was off-loaded and parked ramp side next to the terminal.

The agents were brought to tables where the food and drinks were located. I told them about the sandwiches and drinks, and I explained that we did not have any rooms right now but should get some in a couple of hours. It was mentioned that we might end up with four or five in a room because all the hotels were full. It was obvious that two members of the team were disgruntled and I could see them complaining to Hank Schwobel and Glen Bosman, our driver and mechanic. I heard Schwobel tell them, "Hey, you've got sandwiches and beer and when he fixes the room problems you will have a place to sleep. But you do what you have to do." He advised them if it were him he would leave it alone.

Two young agents that I had never seen before approached me about ten minutes later concerning the rooms. They were very upset with the situation and said so to me. They complained about the long hours and poor conditions. I took several minutes to explain, among other things, that I didn't even have a change of clothes and had tried to sleep during three plane changes. I knew they had been on the road for a week and were tired and frustrated. When I told them that sometimes we have to suck it up, they became even more upset. They became verbally abusive and out of line. I mentioned I had things to do and needed to leave. They again complained about me and the lack of support. "Well, if you don't like it here then you can go back to the States, because I don't have time to deal with whiners," I told them.

Asking for their guns I gave them the phone number to the Interests Section and told them to call and make arrangements to fly back home. They were advised their weapons could be retrieved in headquarters. After directing them to a phone in the terminal I went over to the other agents. Some were smiling when Schwobel walked over and said he told them they didn't know how good things were and if Mike says there are no rooms there are no rooms.

In the early evening Kissinger arrived for a meeting with President Assad concerning the Middle East peace process. After the meeting he departed, returning to his previous European schedule. That night I was in a room with six other agents. I slept on the floor and for the first time in three days I had a shower and a change of clothes.

❖ ❖ ❖

Besides the advance assignments to arrange security for the secretary of state, I also traveled with Secretary Kissinger on a couple of trips to Europe and the Mediterranean region. In PDS, Boyette was transferred to the vice president's detail in December 1974 and was replaced by Jim Legette. It was going to take some time for him to get up to date on the Kissinger detail. I had been reviewing for several months the level of security Kissinger had when in Washington versus overseas, such as Europe and the Middle East.

In Europe, with the exception of England, the Soviet Union, and other communist countries, automatic shoulder weapons were carried openly at the airport and in some government buildings. The shoulder weapons were also present but not carried openly by our government-provided security outside the airports during visits of Secretary of State Kissinger. Our foreign hosts, again with the exception of England, usually provided a marked police lead car and another vehicle full of plainclothes officers augmenting our agents.

In the Middle East, at the airports and during the visit, shoulder weapons were carried openly by both the host country's security and the Kissinger detail. In Washington, D.C., normal security for Kissinger included only Secret Service agents in the traditional two-car motorcade: an armored limousine and an unarmored follow-up car

Secret Service Intelligence Division constantly monitored domestic and global threats of both individuals and groups against Kissinger. Early in 1974, Colonel Moammar Kadhafi, President of Libya, was reported to have put out a $250,000 bounty on the assassination of Kissinger. The Kadhafi bounty, coupled with threats by various other Palestinian and Mid-East terrorist groups, made Kissinger the most threatened person the Secret Service was protecting. In fact, we believed him to be the number one target of terrorists and those governments sponsoring terrorism.

Before developing new procedures, it was going to be necessary to conduct an assessment of intelligence information to better understand the serious nature of the terrorist threats against Kissinger. Working with Intelligence Division I was able to do a comprehensive review of major terrorist attacks beginning with the February 1970 attack by the Popular Democratic Front for the Liberation of Palestine and the Organization for the Liberation of Palestine in Munich against an El Al bus transporting passengers. Three terrorists attacked the bus using grenades and guns, killing one and injuring eleven passengers. The terrorists were captured by the airport police. This appeared to be one of the earliest attacks that was state sponsored. It was followed closely by the Japanese Red Army hijacking of a domestic flight in Japan, March

31, 1970. The Red Army hijackers ended up going to North Korea, where they vanished.

The prime minister of Jordan, Wasfi Al-Tal, was assassinated November 28, 1971 in the lobby of the Sheraton Hotel in Cairo, Egypt, when his government-provided security detail failed to show up. Though no one took responsibility, it was believed by many that it appeared to have been the work of the Black September group.

There were over a half-dozen attacks in 1972 and 1973, which were tied to various groups including: Black September (Munich 9/5/72), Japanese Red Army (Lod Airport 5/30/72), and an attack and hijacking by Palestinian terrorists on a Pan Am aircraft at Rome's Fiumicino Airport on December 17, 1973, for which no one claimed responsibility. Admiral Luis Carrero Blanco, Prime Minister of Spain, on December 20, 1973, was assassinated when a car bomb exploded, hurtling his car over the roof of the church he had just attended. On August 19, 1974, Rodger P. Davies, United States Ambassador to Cyprus, and his secretary were assassinated by snipers at the U.S. Embassy in Nicosia.

Syria, Libya, North Korea, Iraq, and Egypt were some of the states which were actively involved in providing money, training, and other support to global terrorist operations. Syria openly allowed training bases and camps to be set up in Lebanon's Baka Valley for a number of terrorist organizations, while other Mediterranean countries were reported to be providing covert terrorist training camps.

It became abundantly clear that the increases in terrorist attacks were by state-sponsored groups who were opposed to Israel and against the United States' participation in the Middle East peace process. Secretary of State Kissinger, as the symbol of our involvement in the process, needed to be neutralized by the terrorists. To remove him would be a huge setback in the search for a Palestinian and Israeli peace accord. The Secret Service was going to be required to accept the fact that the terrorist threats against Kissinger were not limited to when he traveled into the Middle East region. In conversations with the leadership at PSD, it was decided to contact our Washington Field Office and begin to ratchet up Kissinger's security not only in Washington, but also when he traveled domestically.

By January 1975 a plan was beginning to develop and agent Ralph Basham, who was assigned to the Washington Field Office, was the contact for implementing this project. Basham was a very bright, results-oriented agent. He had developed a great deal of protective experience while working with many protective details out of the Washington Field Office.

To get the elevated security started, the Kissinger detail began using a "route car" to precede Kissinger's morning motorcades to the State Department. Two agents departed in a car ahead of the limousine looking for suspicious vehicles and people along the motorcade route. Additionally, an ID agent from the Washington Field Office was assigned to participate in Kissinger's daily schedule by supporting activities outside the State Department building in Foggy Bottom. Again this gave us another pair of eyes in the outer security ring to help find a problem before it got to the agents accompanying Secretary Kissinger.

To assist the detail, Basham coordinated new procedures with the Washington Metropolitan Police Department. He arranged for the placement of a police bomb car along the motorcade route between Kissinger's P Street townhouse in the Georgetown section of the city and the vehicle entrance to the Rock Creek Parkway. Much of the area was crammed with cars, parked bumper to bumper, on both sides of the street throughout the neighborhood.

To assist the detail, Basham coordinated new procedures in meetings with the Metropolitan Police Department. He arranged for marked police vehicles to check vehicles parked between Kissinger's

Georgetown residence and the Rock Creek Parkway each morning before the secretary departed for the State Department. As was the case with our Secret Service route car, the police were looking for people and/or vehicles that seemed to not fit into the neighborhood. To add more depth to the heightened security, the police also began license plate checks on cars parked along the route checking for stolen cars. The final layer of security was a bomb sniffing dog that was routinely employed by the police to check cars along the Georgetown route.

Basham was transferred to the Kissinger detail and was assigned to my shift. I gave him a crash course on shift leader responsibilities and had him take over day-to-day operation of our shift. Having worked so many different details at the field office, agent Basham was full of fresh new ideas. Initially with Basham on board I kept busy doing advances, special projects, or filling in as supervisor. With the end of the high-profile shuttle diplomacy, the Kissinger detail had settled into a routine by the first of the New Year. The end of the 1973 Mid-East war and the success of the shuttle diplomacy seemed to give everyone a little break. Terrorist acts continued, but they did not seem to threaten the process as much. Secretary Kissinger's threat level remained high, but his exposure had been somewhat reduced due to increased security procedures and his successful shuttle diplomacy.

❖ ❖ ❖

Kissinger was busy with travel to the Middle East during February 1975, visiting Israel, Egypt, Syria, and Saudi Arabia to work out the second Egyptian-Israeli disengagement agreement. Then there were trips overseas to give updates to Germany, the Soviets, the United Kingdom, and Iran. I traveled on the secretary's plane during the February trips. March was more of the same type of travel for Kissinger, but I was busy working projects to continue upgrading security to counter the terrorist threat.

With the infusion of good young talented agents like Ralph Basham and William Montgomery from the Washington Field Office, the Kissinger detail moved in a new direction. By the spring I was now spending more time working with the shift and riding in the car with Kissinger and was less involved with working on advances and projects. The change of pace gave me the opportunity to evaluate where I was in my career and see what other opportunities might be available.

My many days of traveling overseas with Kissinger during the shuttle diplomacy, coupled with conversations to which I was privy due to the proximity to people and events, gave me an interesting insight into national and world events. What the Kissinger era brought to the Secret Service few outside of the Protective Support Division really understood. There was an extraordinary amount of political jockeying that led to the Secret Service protecting Secretary of State Kissinger. Yes, the detail was a drain on manpower. Sure, there was an unusual amount of travel. Without question, many of the agents were free spirits or outcasts who would never have been on the draft list of the presidential and vice presidential details. The strength of the detail was the leadership. This included Robert Lapham, Barney Boyette, Ed Dansereau, Jim Cantrell, and Bill Bush, who were a dedicated group of risk takers.

It was their collective leadership, filling key positions in PSD with bright, talented agents, and then standing behind all of the agents assigned to PSD, that kept Kissinger alive. They selected agents to fill leadership roles on the shifts, take care of advance security arrangements, and work on special projects. Colorful agents like Walter Bothe and Bill Pots, and visionaries like Ralph Basham, Chuck Owens, and Don Stebbins worked together, developing procedures and strategies to counter terrorism. Drivers and mechanics such as Hank Schwobel,

Glenn Bosman, Bill Scholl, Bennie Hurst, and Bill Shellhammer were loyal and dedicated to the organization and to their assignments. They contributed greatly in the Secret Service's march against terrorism.

❖ ❖ ❖

Internal discussions by agents on the detail about using semi-automatic handguns had gone on for a number of months. It bubbled to the surface as I was preparing to transfer to Vice President Rockefeller's detail. Even if it weren't feasible to arm all Kissinger agents with semi-automatic weapons, there was sentiment from the agents on the detail for arming at least one agent accompanying the secretary on all of his movements.

In 1974 the Secret Service was exclusively using revolvers. Often during evening activities in Washington, D.C., Kissinger would be accompanied by only two or three agents plus the limo and follow-up drivers. Even with our Uzi soft pack it was not always possible to have the machine gun readily available. Those working in close proximity with Kissinger understood the need to have more firepower. Our six-shot, two and a half inch .357 magnum handguns were okay for protection before terrorism began to surface as a serious threat to the people we protected, but by 1974, they would be almost useless in a terrorist attack.

The consensus of the Secret Service agents with Kissinger was that the terrorist threats required the use of weapons with more firepower. One agent with a semi-automatic handgun just might be able to lay down enough firepower for another to evacuate Kissinger. These concerns were raised within the leadership at PSD. Lapham, Jim Legette, and Cantrell began mulling over the request for handguns with more firepower.

The Kissinger detail was the Secret Service's laboratory, the dedicated front line in the fight against terrorism. As I mentioned earlier, there were no procedures or policies in place on how to deal with terrorism when the Secret Service accepted the responsibility of protecting the secretary of state. As a lesser, but politically sensitive, detail: there was little leadership from the headquarters level when it came to terrorism. On the intelligence side the Secret Service developed an excellent research program, identifying terrorists, organizations, and groups. The Foreign Intelligence Branch provided a broad range of information under the leadership of their Special Agent-in-Charge Mike Mastravito with the leadership of agents Jack Renwick and Mike Cohen.

The Secret Service Foreign Intelligence Branch broadened and strengthened their relationships with some of the foremost anti-terrorist intelligence organizations around the world. The Israelis were especially helpful on both the intelligence and operational side. My assignment to the Kissinger detail gave me opportunities in the Middle East, the Soviet Union, England, and Central Europe to live history and exert a leadership role in the Secret Service's fight against terrorism. My relationships with Jack Renwick and Mike Cohen of our Foreign Intelligence Branch helped me develop an understanding of the terrorist threat that the Secret Service faced with the secretary of state that few had. I knew that one day the procedures and practices developed during the Kissinger era would be helpful to both the Presidential and Vice Presidential Protective Divisions. It would only be a matter of time before terrorism would hang over the heads of all the people the Secret Service protected.

When I reflect back at the historical significance of the Kissinger detail it is abundantly clear the shift to neutralize terrorist threats was initiated without the normal leadership role of the Presidential Protective

Division or oversight by headquarters. Wilson Livingood was the guardian angel of PSD. He watched over the Kissinger operations and provided the backing, trying to make sure Lapham and Boyette got what they needed. To everyone else it seemed, "Out of sight out of mind." If PSD had failed in the protection of Kissinger I believe the negative implications for the Secret Service would have been much greater than November 22, 1963, in Dallas, Texas.

President Nixon talking with Umpires and children after softball game.

Nixon talking with wives at a picnic.

President Nixon at Picnic talking with author, Mike Endicott.

President Nixon signing wine bottle used to toast
last night with Secret Service.

President Nixon with the agents he hosted at his house on his last night with Secret Service.

President Nixon with members of the City of New York Emerald Society
Police Pipe Band.

President Nixon with the detail softball team.

President Nixon with the agent's wives at a softball game.

Governor Reagan autographed picture, 1968.

Governor Agnew during 1968 Presidential campaign.

President and Mrs. Eisenhower 1968.

To Mike Endicott
With appreciation + best wishes

7-31-85

Richard Nixon

Presidents Reagan, Carter, Ford and Nixon, 1981.

Vice President Mondale with my wife Ginny and myself, 1978.

Vice President Rockefeller with my wife Ginny and myself, 1976.

President Thieu of Vietnam at Andrews Air Force Base, 1973.

President Nixon with marines Kelly Noordamn (left)
and Michael Endicott, Jr. (right).

President Nixon with children at a picnic.

Secretary of State Kissinger briefing the press on an airplane.

President Nixon holding Daved Endicott, with Michael Endicott and
daughters Leslie (left) and Robin (right).

President Nixon on Halloween with trick-or-treaters Carol Rossazza
and sons Keith and Mark, as well as Daved and Ryan Endicott.

President Nixon with Mike Endicott and Gary Ross after
final toast in Nixon's home.

President Nixon with children at a softball game.

CHAPTER THREE

INSIDE THE SECRET SERVICE
1975 - 1980

INSIDE THE SECRET SERVICE 1975 – 1980

My promotion to the operations supervisor position with the vice president's detail in April 1985 united me with Boyette. Jimmy Taylor was the agent in charge, Boyett was his deputy, while Dave Grant was assistant agent in charge. Taylor I knew by reputation. He had interrupted the assassination attempt by Arthur Bremer on Governor George Wallace during the 1972 political campaign. Grant was a shift leader when I was assigned to the White House from 1969 to 1971.

The new team of President Ford and Vice President Rockefeller was in place when I reported to the detail. For the first time in the history of our country, we had a president and vice president who were both appointed. Ford initially replaced a disgraced Spiro Agnew as vice president, and then became president when Richard Nixon resigned in shame due to the Watergate affair. Rockefeller was appointed to succeed Ford as vice president.

The Vice Presidential Protective Division had an operations position with a well-known reputation as a highly stressful assignment. Of the two previous holders of the position, one retired with a high blood pressure problem, while the other retired with a heart problem. They both were approved for disability retirements due to work-related illnesses. I never once thought about the stress. The operations office consisted of one full-time agent, one agent rotating from the shift for a six-week assignment, and the operations supervisor. I did away with the full-time agent shortly after reporting.

In addition to coordinating the day-to-day schedules of the agents with the vice president, the operations supervisor coordinated the activities of the vice president and his family with his staff.

The coordination included the travels of Mrs. Rockefeller and their two sons, Nelson Jr. (14) and Mark (11), who resided either at Kykuit, on the Rockefeller family estate, at Pocantico Hills in Westchester County, N.Y., or their Fifth Avenue apartment in New York City. Kykuit is Dutch meaning "lookout." It was the location of the Rockefeller summer house built in the early 1900s by John D. Rockefeller, father of Vice President Rockefeller. Kykuit had a commanding view of the Hudson Valley and Hudson River. Nelson Jr. and Mark both attended the Buckley School at 113 East Seventy-third on the Upper East Side of Manhattan.

The operations supervisor monitored various special projects assigned to agents and worked with the three shift leaders in designating agents to conduct advance security arrangements for the vice president and his family. This position worked closely with agent Dennis Dwyer, who was in charge of the family detail in New York. On the vice president's detail the operations supervisor contacted the Office of Protective Operations on all manpower and other support requests. When I reported to the operations position, Wilson Livingood of Protective Operations was still coordinating manpower and special requests with all the protective details.

In 1974, Congress designated the Chief of Naval Operations residence at One Naval Observatory in northwest Washington, D.C., as the official residence of the vice president. When I reported, renovations at the Naval Observatory were still underway and I became involved in assisting agent Ben Locket with some aspects of his special project coordinating the opening of the residence.

Vice President Rockefeller lived at his private residence, at 2500 Foxall Road N.W., Washington, D.C., during the week, and traveled to New York for the weekends. His wife, Happy Rockefeller, and their two boys resided at their apartment in New York City during the week.

The Rockefeller family normally spent the weekends at their estate in Pocantico Hills.

When the work at the official residence was finally completed in late 1974, Vice President Rockefeller held a Christmas reception for his staff, agents, press, and friends to show off the renovated house. He and his wife only spent one night at the official residence during his vice presidency. He instead preferred to continue living at his Foxall Road residence

Interestingly, Vice President Rockefeller's staff referred to him as "Governor." It seems they saw his position of vice president as a step down from governor of New York. Rockefeller's schedule took him from Washington, D.C., to New York almost every weekend. He would depart on Friday afternoons, flying out of Andrews AFB into Westchester County Airport aboard the USAF McDonald Douglas DC 9 assigned to him. From there he would travel via his private helicopter to the Rockefeller family estate in Pocantico Hills. On some occasions he would fly the DC 9 into LaGuardia Airport and travel by car to his New York City apartment on Park Avenue. Rarely was the full weekend spent in New York City.

An agent from the shift would routinely be assigned to travel to New York the day before the scheduled arrival of the vice president to coordinate security issues with the New York Field Office and room assignments with the Tarrytown Hilton. Due to the long hours and boring routine of the New York visits, agents on the detail did not see the New York advance as the most desired assignment. In fact, many of the detail agents were not enamored with the routine of the weekly visits to New York by the vice president. Being isolated in the small bedroom communities in Westchester County required agents to drive into New York City to get away from the microscope of local scrutiny. During the summer the Rockefeller family would spend some time at their beach house in Bar Harbor, Maine.

❖ ❖ ❖

President Ford took a lot of heat from the press and Nixon haters when, on September 8, 1974, he gave Nixon a full pardon for any crimes he may have committed while in office. Ford indicated it was time to get Watergate behind us and move forward.

In September 1975, President Ford survived two assassination attempts. The first attempt was on September 5, when Lynette "Squeaky" Fromme, a member of the Charles Manson cult, tried to shoot Ford as he walked through Capitol Park in downtown Sacramento, California. Dressed in a red robe with a large hood Fromme loitered with other people along the route Ford was walking. When he stopped to shake hands, she surprised everyone when she pointed a gun at him. Agent Larry Buendorf grabbed the gun before she could squeeze the trigger and threw her to the ground. It was later determined that there wasn't a round in the chamber of the gun.

A little over two weeks later, on September 22, Sara Jane Moore fired a handgun in the direction of President Ford as he exited San Francisco's St. Francis Hotel. A bystander, seeing her raise the gun to fire at President Ford, grabbed her arm, causing the bullet to miss. In fact, it ricocheted off a wall and wounded a cab driver. Oliver Sipple, the bystander, is now in the history book for saving the life of President Ford. Fromme is serving time in the Federal Medical Facility, Carswell, Texas. Moore is currently serving a life sentence in a federal women's correctional facility in Dublin, California.

❖ ❖ ❖

My Rockefeller detail assignment gave me an insight into the support system the Secret Service and military provided to ensure the efficient movements of the vice president and his family domestically and overseas. The weekend travel of the vice president to New York offered an opportunity for me to develop effective manpower usage models to reduce the number of agents going to New York and provided a cost savings to our detail. In addition, it gave me an opportunity to begin to understand the unique, cyclical manpower requirements of the Secret Service in relationship to presidential elections, off-year elections, and domestic and foreign travel.

In deciding to streamline my office, the full-time assistant position was discontinued, but I kept the temporary position active by continuing to rotate someone from the shift every six weeks. The shift leaders made the selection as to who came to my office for the rotating assignment. In addition to giving me a chance to evaluate the logistical skill of agents, this assignment could be used by the administrative office when evaluating agents for promotion. It also became a valuable source of information flow between our office and the shift agents.

In the evenings some shift leaders would send one of their agents to the Executive Office Building to routinely drop off paperwork and/or pick up office supplies after our office was closed. There were occasions when I could tell someone had gone through my unlocked desk. So I would periodically make notes on a make-believe trip overseas and insert a few dates and names. I would hide the note on top of my desk under the pad or in a drawer and then wait to see how long it took before shift agents started to ask about any upcoming foreign travel.

Special Agent-in-Charge Taylor, Boyett, and I developed a great professional relationship. Taylor was laid-back and tended to be very quiet. He was one of the most professional people I had ever met. His language and demeanor were exemplary. As Taylor became comfortable with my operations and logistical skills he, like Boyett and Lapham, gave me a lot of latitude in developing procedures that benefited our detail. Agent Livingood, our contact at Protective Operations, was a very dedicated, bright, hard-working individual. I believe he understood protective responsibilities as well as anyone in the Secret Service. Working closely with Livingood allowed me to develop a greater understanding of the system and gave me a chance to develop new cost-effective procedures. Livingood gave me a tremendous amount of latitude, encouraging me to develop new procedures and tactics. There was a mutual respect and openness between us that was beneficial to our protective responsibilities and the organization. He approved our cost-effective approach to operations inasmuch as it did not detract from the overall security mission.

In our office I would brief Taylor almost daily and Boyett frequently so that neither would be surprised by what we were doing. After several months of regular briefings Taylor said that it wasn't necessary that I brief him quite so often. I expressed to him my desire to continue regular briefings so that he was able to answer any question that might arise about our operation procedures. Taylor was giving me a tremendous amount of freedom in developing new procedures and the overall decision-making process. I wanted to make sure he knew everything we were doing and not be caught off guard by anyone in headquarters. The briefings continued but on a less frequent schedule.

Joseph Canzeri was in charge of Vice President Rockefeller's advance office. He had been with Rockefeller since 1962 and was recognized within the political community as an outstanding political strategist and advance man. Canzeri, a can-do person, personally handled advance arrangements for all big events. He selected political operatives from a long list he kept in his desk to lead and assist on routine vice presidential events. Canzeri took care of many personal chores for Vice

President Rockefeller. We developed an unusual respect for each other and an enduring personal relationship. He loved to tell stories about his travels and projects with Rockefeller. Canzeri once confided in me that he made arrangements for secret meetings between Rockefeller and his wife to be Margaretta Fitler Murphy, better known to the public as "Happy" Rockefeller.

Early in 1976, Rockefeller announced his decision not to be President Ford's running mate during the 1976 campaign. In the spring of 1976, Canzeri headed a four-man team to pre-advance an around-the-world trip for Vice President Rockefeller and his wife. Ron Thompson, assigned to the White House Communications Agency, Chuck Maguire of the State Department, and I joined Canzeri on the team. The trip was going to be twelve days around the world. When we left for our first stop, we all knew the trip was going to be a lot of work with little rest. Many of our flights would be overnight. Canzeri and Maguire worked out the logistics so almost all of our flights were on Boeing 747 aircraft. McGuire made arrangements for us to be seated at the table in the upstairs lounge area so we could work during the flights. In addition, we had seats where we could sleep if and when the opportunity presented itself.

❈ ❈ ❈

Canzeri scheduled us to start with three relaxing days and nights in Paris to coordinate the French part of the trip. We were able to take care of the Paris visit through several meetings at the U. S. Embassy. We had an opportunity to eat at several upscale restaurants before departing on a late afternoon flight to Teheran, Iran. During the flight we wrote the situation report for France and prepared ourselves for the next nine days of serious travel.

When we arrived at the Teheran Airport late that evening, we were met ramp-side by our Iranian hosts. Exiting the commercial aircraft I immediately saw three armored cars with machine gun-toting guards who were waiting for us. The need for us to have armored cars and security details brought home the problems that Shah Mohammed Reza Pahlavi was experiencing at the time. Religious turmoil in Iran was beginning to be a serious problem for the shah. He was using his intelligence service, SAVAK, to try to neutralize his religious opposition. In less than three years the shah would flee into exile, ending up in Egypt. After a meeting with our hosts, we were whisked to our hotel for a short rest. We got about four hours sleep.

In the morning our diligent security detail transported us in the heavily guarded motorcade to the American Embassy, where Maguire filed the Paris situation report. After coffee and rolls, our day began with a strategy meeting at the embassy.

My second meeting, with SAVAK, the Iranian secret police, at the Marble Palace, required me to leave the embassy meeting early. An embassy car drove me the short distance to the palace, where I was joined by George Cave, the CIA contact from the U. S. Embassy. With SAVAK able to exert tight control the security plan went together quickly. Cave and the SAVAK representative were able to give an overview of the problems being faced by the shah with the religious leaders. After the relaxing meeting, Cave asked if I would like a ride back to the embassy or did I want him to call for an embassy car. Watching him put on his overcoat as he spoke, I realized it had Kevlar body armor inserts. Without commenting about his armored coat I told him, "I'll go with you."

Outside we approached his nondescript, older Plymouth sedan. As I buckled my seatbelt I watched the CIA agent take a .45 caliber handgun out of his waist holster and place the weapon next to him on the driver's seat. While reaching under the front seat and removing a second gun, he told me there was another gun in the glove box if I wanted one. After putting the second gun on the seat, Cave turned to me and said, "I have had three attempts on my life in the last thirty days. Are you sure you want to ride with me?" Removing the .38 revolver from the compartment, I held it securely in my hand and replied without any trepidation, "Let's go."

It was about a one-mile drive to the embassy. Cave sped down the road with his eyes constantly surveying vehicles and people along the way. We arrived at the embassy in record time and I returned the revolver to its place in the glove compartment.

The remainder of our stay was busy but uneventful. We were cloistered inside the U. S. Embassy compound until our evening departure. The ride from the Marble Palace to the embassy was the highlight of the visit to Iran, but a close second was my first taste of high-quality Iranian caviar at a reception at the embassy.

❖ ❖ ❖

During the all-night flight to Kuala Lumpur, Malaysia, our team worked on the situation report for Iran. Thinking about the friendly relationship between the United States and Iran and our reliance on their oil, I was worried about the radical religious fundamentalists who were fomenting unrest against the shah. There was no question Iran was going to present a big challenge for our country on the international scene, and the visit itself would test the Secret Service going into a troubled country.

The cabin staff on our flight was very helpful providing meals, snacks, drinks, and other support when requested. We had a short stopover in New Delhi, India, before arriving at our destination of Kuala

Lumpur, Malaysia. The visit to Kuala Lumpur and then to Singapore were long on work and short on rest. We had hotel rooms at each of the Asian stops but had little time for sleep between meetings, visiting sites, and eating. We were hitting our stride with McGuire and Canzeri chairing the meetings, setting up site visits and meetings with appropriate representatives of the government and security.

While in Singapore I commented to one of the locals on how clean the streets were kept. He mentioned to me that each neighborhood was required to keep their streets and sidewalks clean. The entire neighborhood would be fined if they did not do a good job. Also in Singapore I was told it was against the law to spit in the streets or on the sidewalks. Individuals were fined for violations. I wondered what would happen in the United States if we required our communities to be responsible for keeping the streets and sidewalks clean.

The overnight flight from Singapore to New Zealand was interrupted by a two-hour stopover at 3 a.m. at the Sydney, Australia, airport. We were met at the airport inside the international arrival area by an American Embassy team assigned to the Sydney/Canberra visit. McGuire and Canzeri had seized the opportunity to meet our counterparts and organize an agenda and meetings for our return in less than two days. We did manage to get our trip reports for the last two stops drafted before we arrived in Wellington and drove to the American Embassy.

After meetings at the embassy and with the locals, we took a drive through the countryside to Christchurch, where the Rockefellers would be staying. To our surprise, at the end of the busy day when we arrived at our hotel in the evening the streets were empty and all the bars and restaurants had closed. We did manage to get something to eat and drink at our hotel before a short night in bed. We completed our work the next day and took a flight to Sydney. We were all beginning to feel the effects of the long hours, missed meals, overnight flights, and the lack of any sort of daily routine.

The flight to Australia allowed us to complete most of the New Zealand report. Thanks to the previous meeting in Australia, we were able to go directly to our hotel on arrival. I managed get the most sleep since we left Paris that night in Sydney. However, when I got up for breakfast, both Canzeri and I were somewhat disoriented. I was having trouble with my balance. Walking down the hallway to the elevator I noticed that if I put a hand against the wall I wasn't dizzy, but as soon as I released the wall I had trouble walking. Anytime I stood I was dizzy but it would abate if I held an arm, the wall, or a piece of furniture. During my first meeting of the day with the police I mentioned my dizziness problem. After the meeting the police made arrangements for me to visit a local doctor.

The doctor told me that my circadian rhythm was out of kilter. He said due to the irregular eating and sleeping schedule of the past eight days my body cycle was confused. The doctor said that I was experiencing what is commonly referred to as "combat fatigue." He gave me some medication that he thought would help. By the time I caught up with the rest of our team shortly after noon the medication was beginning to work.

Canzeri, however, was now in much worse shape than I was when I woke up. He was not able to stand on his feet for any extended period of time. He stayed in his room during the morning meetings. In the afternoon the Australian military flew us to Canberra aboard a C-130 to pre-advance the Australian War Memorial Museum that would be part of Vice President Rockefeller's schedule. Canzeri stayed on board the aircraft while Thompson, Maguire, and I visited the museum.

Canberra had the most impressive war memorial I had ever seen. The scenes depicting fighting in the jungles of Vietnam were fascinating. I was speechless looking at the devastation and the anguish of the wounded. I began thinking of the many friends I had that served there. I also thought of the tens of thousands that gave their lives for our country. I was sure that many in the United States probably were not aware of the support we received from Australia in the Southeast Asian theatre.

We all breathed a collective sigh of relief on our return military flight. We were taken directly to the Sydney airport, where we boarded our commercial flight for our last stop, Tahiti.

One thing about traveling with Canzeri, he knew how to relax and enjoy life after the mission was over. With the stop in Australia over, the working portion of our trip was behind us. We flew to Papeete, Tahiti, to spend two nights relaxing and recharging our batteries before our flights to Los Angeles and Washington, D.C. We agreed on arrival to forget the Australian trip report until the flight to Los Angeles.

The new hotel where we stayed near the beach at Papeete was unique. In addition to rooms on the beach, some of the rooms were in clusters of four or six units on stilts a hundred yards offshore. A small boat was used to transport guests to their rooms. It was the most relaxing time I had ever had. With no schedule, no report writing, and nothing to do, we rested, slept, had a drink or two, and ate without leaving our rooms the first twenty-four hours. With our batteries recharged, on the second day we ventured out for some souvenir shopping and a meal in a wonderful restaurant. However, we still spent most of the time in our rooms. We finished our last trip report before we changed planes in Los Angeles. When we got back to Washington, we were all ready for the routine grind the next day at our respective offices.

Overall the trip went well. It was a great opportunity for the agents in our detail to become exposed to foreign travel. We had two C-141 USAF planes, each with an armored car and a jump team of agents assigned to assist at stops as needed.

Since Rockefeller had announced he was not running for re-election, his schedule was pretty light when he returned to Washington. He did some fundraisers for the Republican National Committee and also attended the Republican Nominating Convention at Kemper Arena in Kansas City, Missouri, August 16-19, 1976. He did a number of campaign stops between the convention and Election Day.

❖ ❖ ❖

President Ford received the presidential nomination after defeating a strong challenge from former Governor of California Ronald Reagan. Agents I knew on the Reagan detail said that Reagan had a meeting with President Ford after he was nominated and was expecting to be asked by Ford to be on the ticket. According to agents on the Ford detail, the president was expecting Reagan to tell him he would like to be on the ticket. The meeting allegedly was held with both of them waiting for the other to bridge the gap. When Reagan was not lured onto the ticket and did not ask to be on the ticket, Senator Robert Dole (R-KN) was nominated at the convention.

Sometime after the convention, Canzeri shared with me a story about a young lady who had an appointment to interview Rockefeller. According to Canzeri, the interviewer gave him a gift box of Oreo cookies, each one individually wrapped in foil. He said that Oreos were Governor Rockefeller's favorite cookie. Canzeri said that the woman, Megan Marshak, caught Rockefeller's fancy and, after the interview, ended up being hired as a press consultant. When Marshak was still around after several weeks, Susan Herder, Rockefeller's staff chief, in a cost savings move, hired Marshak at a lower salary to work permanently in the press office, according to Canzeri.

During the fall, Rockefeller maintained his normal routine, leaving for New York on Friday afternoons. On one particular Friday afternoon in the late fall, I received a phone call from the advance agent at Andrews Air Force Base, who advised that the senior staff and agents were aboard Air Force II waiting for the vice president. The advance agent asked for information on the current status of the departure of Rockefeller from his office. After checking, I called the advance agent, telling him Vice President Rockefeller was in his private office with Marshak. This was not the first time or the last that the departure of Air Force II was delayed on a Friday due to Rockefeller and Marshak "meeting" in his private office.

The 1976 campaign turned out to be a breeze for our detail. Vice President Rockefeller campaigned for the Ford/Dole ticket, but with a fairly relaxed schedule. With limited travel, little overtime was worked by the shift agents.

❖ ❖ ❖

For me, as a member of the Secret Service, one of the key moments of Rockefeller's participation in the 1976 campaign was a political rally at the Broome County Airport in Binghamton, N.Y. Among the crowd was a small group of young people heckling Rockefeller. They got under his skin. With Republican vice presidential nominee Dole standing nearby, a frustrated and upset Rockefeller responded to the disruptive demonstrators with an obscene gesture using his middle finger. The traveling photographers were delighted to be able to capture the vulgar finger gesture.

Several days after his return, the vice president's press office gave me several copies of the photograph. The photo not only showed Rockefeller giving the finger to the unruly demonstrators, but off center in the picture were fans of Rockefeller carrying a sign that read "Endicott Loves Rocky." The supporters of former Governor Rockefeller had traveled from the nearby city of Endicott, New York, to attend the rally.

❖ ❖ ❖

The 1976 election was won by the Democratic Party team of Jimmy Carter and Walter Mondale. During the campaign, the nominees were provided Secret Service details composed mainly of agents assigned to field offices. The normal routine for the Secret Service after the election when there was going to be a change of administrations was that the Presidential Protective Division would take the security and logistical leadership positions with the president-elect. Protection of the vice president-elect would continue to be coordinated by the nominee operation center with the Vice Presidential Protective Division providing key leadership support on the detail right away.

Taylor and Boyett attended a meeting at Protective Operations concerning the Mondale transition detail. When the two of them returned to our office, Taylor told me he proposed and headquarters agreed the Vice Presidential Protective Division would coordinate the operations and logistics of both Vice President Rockefeller's and Vice President-Elect Mondale's details. Poking fun at me, Taylor said, "I am sure you approve of my decision, don't you?" He laughed and indicated that it would be a great opportunity for us to meet and work closely with the Mondale staff. Taylor indicated it would be our chance to expose the Mondale staff to the level and type of support available to a vice president. He knew I would like the idea of having the Rockefeller and Mondale agents as a pool to use as needed.

Taylor said that protection for the Mondale children, Ted, William, and Eleanor, had been declined by the vice president-elect. He also said the Mondale staff had passed on to Protective Operations that they would like two of the supervisors from the nominee detail to be transferred permanently to our division if it could be worked out. With the assistance of the additional agents assigned to our office, the coordination of both the daily and travel schedules of Rockefeller and Mondale went smoothly. The larger pool of agents made it easier to find people for special assignments and advances. This unique situation gave us an opportunity from the very beginning to familiarize the Mondale staff with the normal routines of our permanent Secret Service detail. Also, for us, we were able to see firsthand the ins and outs of the staff process and who the players were. It was an invaluable experience.

Senior Staff Assistant Michael Berman was designated the contact point for Mondale's schedule. During the initial days of the transition, the staff was involved mainly with transition meetings. Vice President-Elect Mondale and his family went on vacation to the Caribbean. Once senior staff positions were filled and working staff were identified and brought onboard, my office worked directly with Mondale's scheduling staff.

By the first week of January things were beginning to settle down and take shape. Berman advised that Mondale was going to take a one-stop trip overseas shortly after the inauguration. I went through the usual procedures for overseas travel with Berman, requesting State Department support, military aircraft support, White House communications support, and advance teams. When mentioning that we normally transported an armored car, follow-up car, and support agents on a C-141 prior to the arrival of the vice president, Berman said he did not think the White House would authorize the use of a military aircraft. He said we should be prepared for the request to be denied and added that it would probably be suggested we use the local U. S. ambassador's armored limousine.

Berman then asked that the request for military support be put in writing. I spoke with Taylor about my conversation with Berman. A justification request for a C-141 was prepared, signed by Taylor, and forwarded to the White House military office. As Berman had predicted, our request was denied by the Carter White House. The request was denied on the grounds it was not cost-effective to fly the armored limousine overseas. We were advised to use the ambassador's armored vehicle instead.

In a later meeting Berman mentioned to me that we should not fly cars and agents domestically on C-141 aircraft either. He said this issue was being driven by the White House and was a cost-effective issue. Berman knew a lot of details, including the hourly cost of using a C-141. I mentioned to him that the C-141 aircraft that supported the Secret Service were U. S. Air Force Reserve assets and the pilots and crews routinely flew training missions each month to keep up their skills. The costs of these flights were already in the Air Force budget and did not add costs to our budget.

Ignoring what I had just said, Berman continued by telling me the Secret Service should use local assets when available or else drive an armored vehicle in support of domestic travel of Vice President Mondale. It was clear the White House was going to make big changes in military aircraft support of the vice president's detail. I was more than a little concerned because, by law, the United States military was required to support the Secret Service in performance of their duties at no cost, per the 1976 Presidential Assistance Protective Act.

The Carter White House either did not accept our position that the aircraft and crews were flying anyway and there was really no additional cost to the government or they had simply decided to ignore it. It was made clear by the White House to the Secret Service at the highest levels that our vehicles should be driven or trucked to support the vice president. We were also told to use State Department vehicle assets on overseas travel. My explanation to Berman that the level of protection of cars assigned by the State Department to our ambassadors was lower than Secret Service vehicles was ignored. The cost savings aspects were not open to discussion. It was very clear from my conversation with Berman that the decision on armored cars had been made at the highest level in the government, President Carter.

I had no idea if Secret Service headquarters played the Presidential Assistance Protective Act card. My sense is if they did, the White House simply decided to ignore it. As the operational supervisor responsible for putting forward and coordinating the security plan for the vice president, I was extremely frustrated with the White House and disappointed with my own headquarters.

In an effort to put the imprint of the "People's President" on his administration, President Carter set precedent by being the first president to walk the inaugural parade route from the Capitol to the White House with his family. Carter also requested the traditional inaugural luncheon not be scheduled. He was focused on removing the images of what I believe he saw as the Imperial Nixon White House.

In a split with past tradition, President Carter gave Mondale an office in the West Wing of the White House for his day-to-day activities. Meanwhile, Mondale retained the traditional office of the vice president in the Executive Office Building. Two days after taking office, Vice

President Mondale visited the Executive Office Building to see his office. Taylor asked me to come to the office to meet the vice president. He said he wanted me to explain the various assets and procedures that were used in support of the vice president and his family.

As I entered the office, a tanned Mondale appeared relaxed sitting in a comfortable overstuffed chair. With an unlit Churchill Cuban cigar in his hand he waved in my direction, asking me to sit down. Noticing I had eyed the cigar, the vice president said he liked Cuban cigars and had a friend who got them for him. Taylor introduced me to the vice president, asking that I explain the support available to him and his wife through our operations office. I explained to Mondale that our office coordinated the use of armored cars (limo/sedan), a vehicle for Mrs. Mondale, and U. S. Air Force assets at Andrews Air Force Base. The communication support provided by the White House communications was outlined as was the C-141 cargo aircraft used to fly support personnel. Vice President Mondale was also alerted to the capabilities of our Technical Support Division to maintain a secure, bug-free environment at his residence, office, and at places where he stayed or meeting sites outside of his office and residence. Vice President Mondale was also advised of the specific support he would receive on travel overseas.

After the briefing I answered several questions from Mondale and then decided to use the meeting to lobby for support aircraft. I mentioned to Mondale the benefit of using the C-141 for his car and agents. The vice president made me immediately aware that he knew of our request and that it had already been declined. In the discussion that followed, Mondale lit his cigar and mentioned that he did not have a problem with the trappings of government. However, he advised that President Carter did. Mondale said that he and Carter wanted to do away with the "Imperial White House" created by Nixon. He offered his unsolicited opinion, "Nixon is evil, evil." Mondale added that things were going to change.

❖ ❖ ❖

At that time, in 1977, I was neither a Nixon fan nor a detractor. However, I was taken aback by Mondale's comment about Nixon. He was the first political person I had been around who expressed such distain for another politician in my presence.

Vice President Mondale indicated he would be using his "off the record" car, not the limousine. He said he would not fly the vice presidential flag or seals. He said he had declined Secret Service protection for his children, Teddy, Eleanor, and Billy. It was pretty clear that image, as defined by the White House, was going to affect some of our logistics. I was pretty sure at the time that cost was really the reason for some of the cutbacks.

When I got back to my office, I began thinking about the cars and planes. Before the Carter presidency, the issue of transportation of armored vehicles had been left up to the Secret Service and the military. Transporting vehicles went back at least as far as President Kennedy's administration and probably Eisenhower's. According to the Presidential Protection Assistance Act of 1976, the United States military, as specified in the legislation, was directed to honor all requests for security assistance for the president and others the Secret Service protected. The legislation identified the military support to include weapons, equipment, and personnel and specified that the support be provided at no cost to the Secret Service.

In the past when the vice president traveled, one of his armored cars and often a follow-up car were flown to the location to be visited. If a Secret Service limousine were pre-positioned, as was the case in

New York City or Los Angeles, it might be used by the vice president depending on other requirements. The Secret Service expected the president's limousine and the follow-up to always be transported to sites he visited. The Secret Service made their request directly to the military through the White House Military Aide's office or the Vice President's Military Aide's office. At the direction of the White House, everything changed with President Carter. All aircraft support requests were required to go through the White House.

❧ ❧ ❧

A few months later, Mondale was once again scheduled to travel overseas. A written request to fly vehicles on a C-141 was sent to the White House Military Aide's office. This time, to make it "cost-effective," a justification was written showing twenty agents would also travel on the C-141. Transporting the agents on the military aircraft would save the Secret Service the cost of commercial airline seats and an extra night at a hotel for the traveling agents. It would also reduce the number of agents needed to support the visit by 25 percent to 50 percent. Taylor signed the C-141 memo, but once again our support request was denied by the White House Military Office based on not being cost-effective. When I was advised of the denial I began thinking about the next request and how I could get a support aircraft approved.

Our division was required by the White House to drive armored cars in support of the vice president's domestic travel or use pre-positioned cars. Due to the wear and tear on the cars, the Secret Service began to ship the armored limousines by truck, because driving them was beating up the fleet. Since it was more cost-effective to ship them than fly them, the White House would not approve Air Force support.

However, shipping a car for a single stop would take it out of use for four or five days and sometimes longer.

The assistant director of Protective Operations had a study conducted to see what increase in assets would be needed to meet the need to truck our limousines. We knew an increase in the fleet would mean more pre-positioned cars and more armored cars for shipping. It was the assistant director's position that we needed enough armored car so that there would always be some that could go out and not have to wait for ones in the field to be returned.

A memo was sent to the undersecretary for law enforcement at the Treasury Department, who was responsible for the Secret Service. The memo requested an increase in the armored car fleet to meet our ongoing needs because of the extended time shipping took them out of service. According to insiders at Secret Service headquarters, the memo eventually made its way to the desk of President Carter. His initials and a brief remark in the margin showed his micro-management.

Not all of the armored cars requested by the Secret Service were approved and the policy on transportation of armored cars was modified. The Secret Service was given authorization to request aircraft support through the White House Military Office, which was managed by President Carter's cousin, Hugh Carter. The Vice Presidential Detail was given permission to fly the armored cars on USAF C-130 propeller planes in support of the vice president. The C-130 planes were also authorized to shuttle agents for security post assignments at sites ahead of the vice president.

The support C-130s were Air Force assets assigned to National Guard units and coordinated out of Arkansas. They were "cost-effective" in the picture being viewed by Hugh Carter. In retrospect, it was Hugh Carter, who was in charge of the White House Military Aide's office, carrying out the president's policy of denying the C-141 requests.

❖ ❖ ❖

The Carter administration had decided to use zero-based budgeting for determining costs with all government agencies. Livingood called from Protective Operations and mentioned zero-based budgeting. I prepared a document for him listing all costs. Those costs that were required for the successful completion of our mission were listed first. Other costs were listed below the required ones. Later in the year Livingood told me he needed information on manpower, equipment, overtime, and travel for a budget projection. I was very busy and did not have time to get heavily involved with the report he was writing, so I simply forwarded the information he requested.

However, the next year my operations desk was fairly quiet and when Livingood called I suggested that if he sent the report to me I would compile the information needed and write the report for him. Basically what was being requested was a financial report on projected expenditures. I believe they wanted the report to cover five years; two six-month projections, a one-year projection, and a three-year projection.

Thinking about my last four years in the Secret Service, I let my mind absorb random parts of the puzzle for the better part of a day. Then I began breaking down our budget factors, identifying the impact of the presidential election, off-year elections, and overseas and domestic travel based on how long the administration had been in office. As I researched, I began to understand political and international issues that affected a first-term administration versus a second-term one, things like off-year Congressional elections and developing foreign policy in a first term versus extending it in a second. Next I reviewed the type of travel a vice president did, such as in and out, airport stops, major speeches, multiple stops, and overnights. In each case I was able to project average manpower usage and overtime needs. The exercise was especially good for me since by the time I was through I realized I knew more about what affected our protective detail costs than anyone in the Secret Service.

What I did not realize initially was that I had discovered the major components of the cyclical costs affecting the entire Secret Service budget. I had the key to budget projections and their impact not only on Protective Operations but also on agents assigned to the Office of Investigations. I knew Livingood was very busy and when I was through my report was forwarded to him. Neither of us took time to discuss the report with each other.

Nine months later I got a call directly from the head of our Financial Management Division who wanted to know how come my projected costs were so close to actual costs. I gave him an abbreviated version of the presidential cycle, the types of travel, manpower support, and an overtime cost analysis over the phone. There was a few seconds of silence and then I was surprised when I was asked if I could give a briefing to a selected group of the financial staff.

The next week I made a formal presentation to supervisors in the Secret Service Financial Division. In between I had briefed Livingood on my projections. During the meeting I was able to break down our costs based on cycles of the first-term and/or second-term presidency. I was also able to tell them how I projected costs based on travel days and types of travel. After answering all their questions, I retreated to my office. It felt good to have provided the information that would not only allow a much more accurate projection of our protective costs but of the whole Secret Service. I knew how my projections affected field costs and was confident after the briefing that the financial side would see it also.

Back in the office I began thinking about the Secret Service becoming computerized. (I knew there was a project to install computers starting with headquarters.) In a follow-up to the budget projections, my internal computer began heading in a new direction when the staff office gave me a copy of an update of the projected travel. As part of my budget review I had developed a formula identifying four categories of presidential travel and the manpower needed to support each. A category A visit was an airport rally and normally required five to ten support agents. A category B visit was an in-and-out visit for a breakfast or lunch. A category C visit was an in-and-out for a major fundraising luncheon or dinner and required fifteen to twenty support agents. A category D visit was an overnight with a dinner and/or other function and would need twenty to thirty agents.

Explaining everything to Livingood, I requested a meeting with someone from our expanding computer program group. Sitting down, I outlined for them my ability to know as much as six weeks ahead of time the vice president's schedule. It was mentioned that the travel schedule could be classified by the activity and designated as an A, B, C, or D visit. Each letter would identify roughly the number of post agents needed and the number of hotel rooms that would be required. This, I suggested, should allow for more efficient manpower coordination by Protective Operations and the Office of Protection. Agents could be put on standby three or four weeks ahead of time, and airline flights and room reservations could be projected. I believed this would be a big morale booster for agents. Many became anxious on Friday afternoons at 3 p.m. waiting for the teletype to go off announcing protective manpower needs that required travel over the weekend.

The meeting took two hours and lots of notes were taken as I walked through the entire planning schedule and the cost savings effect. But it was not going to happen. Unfortunately for me, the computerization of the Secret Service was in the infancy stage and the money and support was not there to move into the areas I envisioned.

❖ ❖ ❖

Supervisor David Grant retired without a lot of notice and we were one supervisor short until he could be replaced. Taylor asked me if I would ride with Vice President Mondale a couple of mornings a week to his office and also rotate as standby supervisor every third weekend until Grant was replaced. This would allow him and Boyette to work their normal schedules until a replacement for Grant was named.

For me, this simply meant coming in a little earlier than normal during the week and riding with the vice president to his office. Either Taylor or Boyette would take him home at the end of the day. Working every third weekend was not a big inconvenience for me either. In fact, it led to a very interesting and amusing Saturday with Vice President Mondale. Sitting in the security room one Saturday morning I was summoned by the agent on post at the front door of the VP residence at the request of Mondale.

Vice President Mondale was waiting for me when I arrived. He told me that he needed to take his son William to the dentist for a scheduled appointment. He apologized for not notifying us earlier and said we would leave as soon as the men and cars were ready. Then he dropped the "bomb." "Mike, I would like to visit that place where you are supposed to take me to relocate if something happens. We are going to do a surprise inspection. Don't tell them we are coming." Pivoting around, he went back inside the residence to get his son.

I immediately radioed the shift leader Jerry Terry to bring up the cars; we were going to the dentist. When Terry arrived, I advised him of the location of the dentist and the surprise inspection. I asked him to give the site a heads-up call through the radio room. We made a quick stop to drop off William. Vice President Mondale accompanied William into the office and said "Hello" to everyone there. I spoke with Terry and he advised me that we did not have the phone number for the site we were going to visit and he was having a problem getting the White House communication center to understand who he wanted them to call. I had been monitoring his contact with the White House communication center on my radio and thought agent Terry may have been too cryptic with them. I was worried about arriving at our next location without giving them advance notice. I advised Terry to break Secret Service rules and use the name of our arrival point when we departed the dentist's office. It didn't work. The communication center still did not realize where we were going.

Upon arriving at the classified site, Vice President Mondale and I got out of the car and approached the pedestrian gate. I pressed the "squawk box" talk button and announced it was the vice president of the United States here for a visit. I also announced my name and that I was with the Secret Service. After several announcements and requests for response over about a five-minute period of time, Vice President Mondale, in a rather serious tone, said, "Mike, I am going back to the car. Get me in there." Walking away, he said, "I am not leaving until I get in there." I began to realize that this site probably got a lot of people pushing the talk button and advising that it was someone important.

After another frustrating four or five minutes, an individual came out of the facility, dragging a black trash bag and heading for the dumpster. The individual ignored my attempts to speak to him and acted like I did not exist. When he put the bag in the dumpster and headed back to the entry point, I announced in a somewhat loud voice, "I am Michael Endicott with the United States Secret Service. Look over my shoulder and you will see a limousine. Inside that limousine is the vice president of the United States. If you want to keep getting a paycheck and working for the military, I would suggest you come over here and look at my credentials."

There was a short a pause and then two rather slow steps before he turned and walked over to the gate, looking first at the limo and then at me and my Secret Service credentials. It only took ten seconds and much of the color was gone from his face. He now realized that the vice president of the United States was in fact paying a surprise visit to his workplace.

The next insurmountable hurdle was when I asked that the vehicular gate be opened so we could secure the two cars. The person I was talking with did not have the combination to the vehicular gate. He did mention that he was able to open the pedestrian gate, adding that everyone working this day was TDY (temporary duty).

I went to the car and VP Mondale accompanied me through the gate to the entrance of this "relocation" site. Inside he met the senior person on duty and Mondale explained that he would like a tour of the facility. He indicated that he wanted to meet all the people working this shift.

The tour took about fifteen to twenty minutes. At the end of the tour the vice president explained the issues he had and the questions he would like answered. The senior person acknowledged he would do as the vice president requested. Then Mondale turned to me and said, "Mike, make sure this gets taken care of."

Returning to the cars, we departed for the dentist's office and picked up his son. When I dropped the two of them off at the residence, Mondale had a smile on his face and said to me, "I bet that will shake some people up."

As luck would have it, on Monday morning I was assigned to take Mondale to his office. We arrived at the courtyard at the Executive

Office Building. Mondale normally walked to his office in the White House from there. Captain Matheny, one of the military aides to the vice president, was waiting. As the vice president exited his car he said, "Matheny, what do you want so early?" He replied, "I am here to see Endicott, sir."

I had a smile on my face. Once the vice president was out of earshot, Matheny said, "What the hell went on Saturday?" He told me that there had been a special meeting of the Joint Chiefs of Staff on Sunday evening about what happened on Saturday. I suggested we go somewhere and talk.

Matheny led me to his office, and I told him what had taken place. He advised that there were a lot of questions and that I needed to go to a meeting at the Pentagon concerning Saturday's surprise visit.

After several meetings over the next couple of days, I called our Liaison Division and asked if the Secret Service agent assigned to the military could accompany me to the next meeting and take over for me. Agent Ned Hall, who I knew from my days at PSD, was the liaison representative to the military. He met me and we rode together to the meeting at the Pentagon. The meeting at the Pentagon went fairly well and I thought most of the Secret Service issues had been resolved. I took Hall aside after the meeting and mentioned that since he was now participating I could stop coming to the meetings and return full time to the vice president.

Hall laughed and said I should continue to attend the meetings for a while longer. He seemed genuinely amused by the whole situation. After attending more meetings than I thought I needed to, I wanted to get back to my regular job. A couple of mornings later, while riding with Vice President Mondale from his residence to the office, I asked for his help. I told him that after all the meetings I had attended if the "military could not fix the problems without me then our country is in trouble."

I advised the vice president that I needed to get back to my operations job full time to better serve him and his staff. I requested that he get me out of the meetings. He told me, "Okay." Later Matheny told me I no longer needed to attend the meetings. That afternoon when I rode back to his residence with Mondale, I thanked him for getting me released. Mondale, with a Cheshire cat grin on his face, said, "Next time we will visit that place up in Pennsylvania." Looking him in the eye I replied, "Not on my watch you won't."

Grant was finally replaced by Richard Lefler, who had been head of the Secretary of the Treasury Detail. Lefler was a contemporary of mine out of the Los Angeles Field Office. He was closely associated with the Special Agent in Charge of Los Angeles, Robert Powis. There were recent rumors Powis was going to be reassigned to headquarters. When Lefler arrived I was delighted to go back to my operations job full time.

❖ ❖ ❖

As I mentioned earlier, Vice President and Mrs. Mondale declined protection for their children, Teddy, Eleanor, and Billy. I truly believe that they both felt that they wanted their children to have as normal lives as they could. I do not think their decision was either an image or cost issue.

Teddy Mondale at age twenty was your normal, motorcycle-riding, high-testosterone teenager. He seemed to have few restrictions placed on him, coming and going at all hours. Stories about some of his adventures and escapades abounded within the detail. I only heard a couple of them. Teddy Mondale had a motorcycle that he liked to ride. One night when his mother and father were out of town for the weekend he came in late. He drove his motorcycle on the grass around the observatory, digging ruts in the beautifully manicured grounds. Berman and I talked about Teddy and the motorcycle escapade on Monday morning after I had received a call from the command post at the vice president's residence. Berman said he had made arrangements to have the damage repaired.

On another occasion when his parents were out of town, Teddy returned after an evening out with a girlfriend in tow. About three a.m. the security room got a call from Teddy advising that his friend was stuck between floors in the dumbwaiter. Members of our uniform division responded and were able to get her released. The unanswered question that everyone asked was, "Did she have her clothes on?"

It still remains unanswered.

Eleanor Mondale, who was six teen when her father was elected, was a well-endowed young woman. She often dressed provocatively in cut-off shorts and tight tee shirts when walking around the grounds. The last year or so of her father's term she developed the habit of climbing out of her third-story bedroom window and down the fire escape to go out at night. She would run across the observatory grounds, climb the fence, and get into a waiting van. It would drive off for a Georgetown bar. Unbeknownst to Eleanor and her friends, one of our Secret Service agents would follow them in a car. When they left the Georgetown bar the agent would shadow the vehicle back to the Naval Observatory. Eleanor would reverse her route in returning to her bedroom.

I understood that Taylor, our detail leader, struggled with his obligation to tell the vice president about her antics. Though he never spoke to me about his dilemma, I believe he spoke to the vice president.

❖ ❖ ❖

Mondale, like many Minnesotans, enjoyed fishing. He and his longtime Minnesota friend, Fran Beffera, would make an annual trip into Canada to fish. They flew on a twin-engine Grumman seaplane referred to as a "goose" out of International Falls, Minnesota, to Lake Manitou in Manitoba, Canada. Beffera had a rustic cabin on a small island in Lake Manitou. The two of them were able to fully enjoy the remoteness and the dependency on each other. They did their own cooking, washing, and cleaning as any other campers would do. They caught, cleaned, and cooked their fish and other food.

Other times they stayed at a friend's cabin or home on other lakes. Most of the agents who went on the fishing trips were volunteers. These were the men who really enjoyed fishing and the wilderness. This was an opportunity for them to relax and fish. They caught walleye, northern pike, and huge lake trout (up to twenty-five lbs.).

One of the problems our detail faced going to Canada was the issue of handguns. Carrying guns when traveling to Canada (like Britain) was a problem for the Secret Service. Each visit required negotiations with the Royal Canadian Mounted Police (RCMP) as to the number of guns, if any, that could be brought into the country. A meeting by headquarters with the RCMP representative in Washington determined that no weapons could be brought into Canada during Mondale's vacation trips. Taylor sent Boyett and me to meet with RCMP representative Howard Comba in Regina, Manitoba.

Comba was responsible for the area of Saskatchewan where Mondale would be fishing. We were met at the airport by our jovial RCMP host. Boyett, with his Southern friendliness and gregarious personality, hit it off right away with Comba. As an active law enforcement officer, he seemed more attuned to our weapon problem than his Washington colleagues. During the meeting Boyett explained our concerns about traveling without weapons into a remote region of

Canada. Comba smiled and nodded his head while saying that American hunters were allowed to bring shoulder weapons into his country every day. He said that there would be bears and other wild animals in the woods where we were going, adding that there would be no problems if we brought two shotguns for protection. He said he would take care of the paperwork if we provided him with the information on the weapons. It was agreed that this would be taken care of at the local level and there would be no need to bring the shoulder weapon issue to anyone outside our immediate group. With smiles all around and a new friend living in Regina, Canada, Boyette and I returned to our office. Taylor was appreciative of the solution to the ongoing weapons problem.

On some fishing trips Mondale made there were logistical issues that presented unique challenges. A remote lake where Mondale stayed in a friend's cabin had no place for the agents. Taylor asked me to travel to the area and make arrangements for the detail to stay at a lodge on a nearby lake and resolve boat, food, and other issues. I was able to fly in, make all the arrangements, and return to International Fall in the early evening.

The shift change was going to take over one hour, since the shift would have to take a boat across the lake and then walk about half a mile to the nearby lake where Mondale was staying. They then boarded a boat there and proceeded to Mondale's cabin. Due to the length of time it took to make the shift change, the agents decided they preferred twelve-hour shifts instead of the traditional eight-hour shifts.

The biggest challenge logistically for a fishing trip was when Mondale went to a much more remote lake almost up by the Arctic Circle, where he stayed in a friend's vacation home. As usual, he and Beffera flew in by seaplane. The area was really remote with no support facilities at all. To accomplish our protective mission, it was necessary to devise a plan using a CH-46 military helicopter to fly in boats, motors, a full tent camp (tents, cots, sleeping bags, cooking facility), and other equipment. The nice thing about working with our military on the tent camp was that this was their area of expertise. They put the plan together in no time, getting the necessary clearances from the Canadians. The CH-46 helicopter was used to take everything needed plus the advance team and the working shifts two days early in one lift. It gave them a chance to get everything set up before Mondale arrived. When everyone returned, they brought back fresh walleye and trout fillets that were shared with others.

Agent Harry Ludwig, who was an outdoorsman, enjoyed advancing the fishing trip. He was adaptable, dependable, and very resourceful. When he returned to Washington, he described the winds and weather factors that almost led him to have to abort their departure. Agent Ludwig said that if it had not been for the incredible skills of the helicopter pilot the lift could have been delayed for several days.

Mondale and Beffera had a tradition of going ice fishing in the Duluth area during the winter. Arrangements were made for snowmobiles, clothing, and other winter needs with the Arctic Cat Company to have the agents properly equipped and clothed for the severe weather extremes. The agents accompanying the vice president told me that some of the lakes used for ice fishing had a number of shacks that were used by the ice fishermen. A kerosene heater could be put into the fishing structure to keep the occupants warm. According to reports, a chainsaw would be used to cut a hole in the ice and special metal holders with red flags would be placed next to the hole. The fisherman's line held down the red flag. When a fish took the bait the spring-loaded flag would snap up and set the hook in the fish. The fisherman would then either reel the line in or pull it in by hand.

❖ ❖ ❖

My relationship with the scheduling office was challenging as we tried to understand and adjust to each other's needs. Making adjustments to accommodate a new system that required us to use more personnel due to an aversion to using military support was very frustrating. Consequently there were adjustments required by our office and the vice president's advance office. Staff assistant Becky McGowan, who was new to their office, was great on the political side but inexperienced in the complex operations and logistic details. I was trying to adjust to a changing policy on the use of available military support by the White House. Between trying to developing new logistical plans and bumping heads with McGowan initially, Berman would be asked to intervene. Over time things smoothed out with McGowan even though we did not always agree.

A trip for the vice president to visit Arizona, Colorado, Oregon, and Idaho had been considered for November 1977. For a reason unknown to me, after initial planning everything was cancelled. The trip was put back on the schedule for the second week of January 1978. In a mid-December staff meeting I suggested to Berman he was crazy for making a trip up the Rocky Mountains in January. When I mentioned that the weather would be a major problem, it did not faze either Berman or McGowan. In fact, Berman sarcastically asked, "So, what are you, a weatherman now?"

I simply pointed out that the potential for delays due to weather could very well require last-minute cancellations and changes to the itinerary. I knew this would be the most logistically challenging trip I had been asked to put together since Mondale became vice president. For two days my views on the weather were made known to anyone who would listen and some that did not want to hear about it. Berman had the final say and I had not garnered his support. After quietly listening one last time to my concerns about the weather, airplane, and helicopter issues, he made the decision the trip was a go as scheduled.

In reviewing the schedules, there were two major concerns about the weather: 1. The helicopter would be unable to fly from Grand Junction, Colorado, over the mountains to Steamboat Springs if the weather turned bad; 2. I knew I could get a twenty-man jump team of agents into Steamboat Springs, but possibly would not be able to leapfrog them out of there for their next assignment. These concerns were passed on to the staff and my superiors. McGowan was not concerned and did not suggest any back-up plan. Taylor, who had full confidence in my logistical team, felt any problem that came up would be handled by us.

Tackling my manpower problem with headquarters ended up being a somewhat frustrating exercise in and of itself. The initial request to Livingood of Protective Operations for an extra twenty agents on standby in case the agents in Steamboat Springs got stuck was denied. Livingood, like Berman, questioned whether I was now a weatherman. However, I knew with Livingood I just needed to put a logical plan together and he would approve it.

On a subsequent call to Livingood it was suggested that he provide me the names of twenty agents from one of our larger offices, such as Los Angeles or Chicago. This would make it easy for everyone, I told him. With the names I would make all the arrangements for transportation and rooms and would only activate them if I needed them. Livingood was a little skeptical but finally agreed when I assured him no money would be spent unless the team got stranded in Steamboat Springs. It was made clear that no money would be wasted.

When it came to the Grand Junction/Steamboat Springs problem with the helicopter, I spoke to agent Charlie English before he headed to Colorado to conduct the advance in Grand Junction. I asked English to make arrangements for twenty-seven rooms on a standby basis in case we needed to overnight in Grand Junction. It was explained to him that if the weather did not co-operate the helicopter would not be able to make the high altitude evening lift from Grand Junction into Steamboat Springs. It was agreed that the information about the rooms would be provided ahead of time only to his advance team, the chief of police, and SAIC Taylor.

When Air Force II lifted off, Taylor had been fully briefed not only on the Grand Junction and Steamboat Springs situations, but a couple of other potentially small problems that were covered with backup plans. The trip progressed as I had thought. As predicted, the weather became an issue in Steamboat Springs and the twenty standby agents were activated and sent to Portland, Oregon, to cover for the jump team stranded in Steamboat Springs.

When Mondale returned to Washington, Taylor told me that Air Force II was lowering the landing gear preparing to land at Grand Junction, Colorado, when Jim Johnson, chief of staff to Mondale, told him that Vice President Mondale would need to go to a holding room; because of bad weather the helicopter could not get into Steamboat Springs that evening. He told Taylor arrangements would have to be made for rooms for an overnight. Taylor simply said, "OK."

As Vice President Mondale and the other passengers deplaned, agent Charlie English stood on the ramp handing out keys and room assignment lists for the local hotel he had selected. Taylor said that Mondale's schedule was adjusted and he flew by helicopter to Steamboat Springs the next morning. My jump team was unable to get to Portland, Oregon, but the standby agents made it. Mondale completed all his scheduled activities through the rest of the week with a few adjustments we anticipated also due to the weather.

The final stop for the vice president before heading to Andrews Air Force Base was a press event in Colorado at the Denver Airport.

Shortly after the departure from Denver, staff chief Johnson asked SAIC Taylor for my home phone number. Jim Johnson said VP Mondale wanted to thank me for my work on the trip. I received a telephone call at my residence in Lake Ridge, Virginia, about 7 p.m. from the White House switchboard operator announcing that Vice President Mondale wanted to speak with me.

When Mondale came on the line it was apparent he had been made aware of my crucial assistance in the success of his trip. He mentioned several things in addition to Grand Junction that he knew I had arranged that made a difference between success and failure on the trip. After he thanked me for my hard work he said he had an assignment for me. He then advised me that former vice president and fellow Minnesotan Hubert Humphrey was dying. He said that if Humphrey died before Air Force II crossed the Mississippi he would go to Minneapolis and bring Humphrey's body to Washington for the funeral. If Humphrey died after the Mississippi crossing a military jet would be sent to bring his body back the next morning.

Mondale then asked me to take care of notifications and get everything ready for the funeral. After Mondale hung up, I sat down and thought "Why me?" as I called Livingood at home. I knew what he would be thinking when I reached him at his residence about 8 p.m. Friday night. After I told him about the call from Vice President Mondale, Livingood suggested to me that I should coordinate the arrangements for the funeral as the representative of Protective Operations. He said that since it was Friday night it would be difficult to put a team together out of the Washington Field Office.

Livingood said, "Mike, you know everyone who will be involved and are the best person to put it all together." He ended the conversation by asking me to keep him advised as things progressed.

I worked over the next couple of hours out of my house contacting the duty officers for the Secret Service Washington Field Office, Secret Service Liaison Division, Capitol Police, Washington Metropolitan Police, and Andrews Air Force Security Police advising them of the situation with Humphrey. Liaison Division was requested to provide a copy of the government plan of the funerals for former vice presidents. A general meeting was scheduled for 2 a.m. with all the police agencies and representatives of the Capitol, where Humphrey's body would lie in state, to go over the plan.

Before heading into Washington, I dressed in warm clothing, put on a heavy military jacket, and grabbed a good pair of gloves. It was very cold out with snow on the ground. I didn't expect to return home until sometime on Sunday.

The initial meeting went well and I laid out a schedule for meetings over the next twenty-four hours at each site. As advance agents were scheduled and contacted me, I set up site meetings with them for later in the day. Going to each site overnight I developed preliminary estimates of manpower needs and the number of site advance agents needed.

Humphrey died Friday evening, January 13, 1978. Early Saturday morning a USAF special mission aircraft transported his body to Andrews Air Force Base. Agents from the Vice Presidential Detail, the Washington Field Office, and Liaison Division were assigned to Andrews Air Force Base, Capitol Hill, motorcades, and other appropriate sites Saturday morning. Midday the special military flight arrived with Humphrey's coffin. Meetings were conducted all day Saturday and into the evening at each site. I provided Livingood a general number of agents needed for post standing. Lists of names were made available identifying post agents to assist at each site. Late Saturday night all plans were reviewed during a general meeting at the Capitol.

Overnight Saturday, I was able to go over everything and put together the final schedule and manpower need for each site involved. I finally went to my office in the Executive Office Building around 4 a.m. and got a couple of hours of rest before reporting to Capitol Hill to observe the arrival of the hearse carrying the body of Vice President Hubert H. Humphrey. When the casket was carried into the rotunda at the Capitol, I got in my car and went home. Other than the short rest at my office I had not slept in forty-eight hours.

❊ ❊ ❊

On Monday morning I arrived early at the office. My boss, Jimmy Taylor, who had come in earlier with the vice president, heard me come into my office. Calling me into his office, Taylor told me that before I said anything about the call from the vice president for me to sit down so he could tell me what happened in Colorado on Friday. He said when Johnson told him about the vice president wanting to call and thank "Mike" for all his hard work, Taylor said he told Johnson, "You don't know Mike Endicott, do you?" He said Johnson said, "What do you mean?"

"Mike doesn't care about the vice president calling him; he wishes you guys would have listened so he would not have had to spend so much time working on the trip," Taylor said he told Johnson.

I smiled at Taylor and thanked him for his support. We spoke about the trip and some of the other backup plans that bailed out other parts of the trip. I asked about Humphrey and the funeral. He said everything went well at the Capitol and President Carter was going to the funeral, not Mondale. Walking away I thought to myself that Taylor really did know me. I must admit that after the Rocky Mountain trip McGowan and I worked much better together.

❧ ❧ ❧

In the spring, Robert Powis was promoted and transferred from the Los Angeles Field Office to assistant director, Protective Operations. The promotion placed one of the top field office administrators in charge of all protection. Powis was especially respected for his strategy and management of criminal investigations. Our paths had crossed over the years but I had never worked for him.

I knew a number of people who worked for him and most had nothing but high regard for him. I knew others that were outside of Los Angeles that did not like his aggressive New York style. Frank Wood, Special Agent-in-Charge of the Portland Field Office in Oregon, had once shared with me that he did not care for the fact that Powis had sent Los Angeles agents into his Portland district. The agents made a counterfeit buy without consulting him first. Wood said agents from Los Angeles also dismantled the counterfeit printing operation and took it back to Los Angeles without telling him. I sensed that Powis' and my strong personalities would clash one day.

The next time Mondale was scheduled to go overseas it was an extensive trip with many stops. I decided to take a different approach in my aircraft support request. Speaking with Taylor and Boyett, I repeated my view that the White House was never going to approve a support aircraft. However, my sense was to make a request that would positively show that the use of a support aircraft had nothing to do with cost effectiveness, but with image. I was sure it was the fact that the Carter White House perceived the use of C-141s as part of the Imperial Nixon White House that prevented them from using those cargo aircraft.

I knew they would not approve anything I submitted, but I wanted to show them the fallacy of their cost-effective position.

For the extensive overseas trip Mondale was making I made a request for a KC-135. The KC-135 is a Boeing 707 with only a couple of small windows. It is less costly to fly than the C-141 and is often used for Congressional delegations and official White House group travel. Within the military the aircraft is used for transportation of personnel and with a bladder inserted is used for refueling aircraft. A KC-135 was stationed at Andrews AFB as part of their fleet.

With the approval of Taylor, a request for the KC-135 was submitted to Protective Operations. I believed I had painted the White House in the cost-effective corner. The potential problem I saw was Powis, our new assistant director of Protective Operations. With his strong, dynamic leadership Powis was known for his aggressive approach to problem solving. I was worried he would believe he could solve the unsolvable problem and not request the KC-135.

The memo requesting support was sent. It outlined that the KC-135 would be used to transport forty-nine agents in support of the vice president. The cost savings over the use of commercial aircraft was projected at $250,000. The request was made about ten days before the vice president's trip but one week before the support aircraft needed to depart.

In an unusual move, Taylor asked me to accompany him to his meeting with Assistant Director Powis and his deputy, John Simpson, concerning the support aircraft request. During the meeting, Taylor carefully went over the justification memo I prepared on using the KC-135. Assistant Director Powis expressed, strongly, his desire that we have two C-141 planes with cars and agents on board to support the mission. He believed that Secret Service armored vehicles were superior to State Department assets and should be used. He also said that it was more cost-effective than the KC-135. Taylor indicated that he did not believe that one C-141 aircraft, let alone two, would be approved. He explained to Powis and Simpson in detail our previous attempts and failures to get C-141 support. He pointed out that we had already identified the superior quality of Secret Service armored cars and the effectiveness of using C-141s for transportation of cars and jump teams jointly and each request had been denied.

The White House knew very well our position on Air Force Reserve officers flying our missions to keep up their monthly flying hours and there was no cost impact on the Secret Service. Taylor renewed his request for the passenger aircraft to Powis. I was somewhat surprised, not when he denied the request, but when Powis directed me to cancel my commercial reservations. In denying the request, Powis said not to worry as he would get us an aircraft. I was getting ready to say something when Simpson intervened after he saw the surprised look on my face, and said, "Mike, give Powis a chance. I think he can do this." To his credit, Taylor continued the in-depth discussion trying to get Powis to change his mind.

At the end of the discussions Taylor turned to me saying, "Speak up now, Mike, or don't say anything when we get back to the office."

In the discussion that followed I shared with Powis and Simpson the comments Vice President Mondale made about the Imperial White House and Nixon. Explaining my experiences with the Carter and Mondale staffs regarding trucking cars, the use of off-the-record cars, the ban on using official seals and flags, coupled with President Carter carrying his suit bag without any clothes in it all led me to believe this administration was obsessed with image. Carter was hung up on his "People's President" image, I offered to Powis and Simpson. If I were correct, I explained to Powis, the cost-effective requirements by the White House were a charade and when we met them they would still not agree to let us use C-141s. If the issue were truly image then there was only one way to unmask the charade: we had to actually put a cost-effective request on the table other than the C-141. I felt strongly that the KC-135 request would never be accepted by the White House on its own and as a fall-back position it would be dead before it arrived.

I had the feeling Powis did not necessarily disagree with my assessment. With his direct, aggressive management style, however, I was sure he still believed he could prevail with logic. Simpson suggested to Taylor and me that if Powis did not get the C-141s he would request the KC-135. As the meeting ended I expressed my opinion that if we did not go forward with the KC-135 request first, we would lose everything, and encouraged Powis one last time to paint the White House into a corner. The justification memo I added would expose the aircraft support issue not as being about cost-effectiveness but one of image. Powis thought for a moment then repeated to me, "Cancel the tickets."

Simpson, trying to broker the situation, once again asked that we give Powis a chance to resolve the problem. As Powis left the meeting I advised Simpson privately, "If you go forward with the request to the White House Military Office, you will be asked to submit a written justification." Having already prepared a C-141 request, I told Simpson to call me and I would get it to him. Taylor and I talked on the short walk back to our offices. Neither of us was elated at the idea of not pursuing the request for the KC-135 first. We were satisfied, however, with the opportunity we had to make our case. We both agreed Powis would not prevail.

It took about ten minutes for Taylor and me to leisurely walk from headquarters to our EOB office. A few minutes after arriving Simpson called. I returned to headquarters with the justification memo and Simpson assured me not to worry. He said Powis had a meeting scheduled at the White House the next morning (Friday). "Powis will get the planes," Simpson volunteered.

The next afternoon I ran into Simpson at headquarters. He told me the C-141 request had been declined, but the KC-135 request would be submitted on Monday for its Wednesday departure.

On Tuesday morning Simpson called and asked, "Did you cancel the reservations?"

"Do you think I am crazy?" I responded.

Simpson told me I was going to need them. The KC-135 request had been turned down also.

The overseas trip for Mondale went well without military aircraft support. The trip did require me to almost double the number of agents supporting the vice president. Taylor and Boyett knew how frustrated I was with both the White House and our own organization. I think they were worried I would provoke an incident that would not benefit anyone. Before I had fully settled down I found myself on the way to Italy.

❖ ❖ ❖

President Carter had sent his wife, Rosalynn Carter, to Rome for the installation of Pope John Paul I on August 26, 1978. Thirty-four days later, to the shock of the world, Pope John Paul I died. Vice President Mondale was selected to attend the funeral of John Paul I as the representative of President Carter. SAIC Taylor asked me to lead a team of agents to coordinate the vice president's attendance at the funeral. It was quite unusual that a supervisor like me would be selected for this assignment. I had mixed feelings about traveling but realized I could not turn my boss down.

Call it a reward or recognition by Taylor that I needed to get out of the office for a breather, either way I packed up for a ten-day trip to Rome and the Vatican. Using the debriefing forms in the Support Division and talking with our Foreign Intelligence Branch, I had a pretty good picture of the security issues when I arrived in Rome. A meeting at the U. S. Embassy gave me further insight into several issues that had developed during the earlier visit of the first lady. Two issues were raised by the embassy. One was the demand that the Secret Service follow-up car be positioned directly behind the first lady's limousine and the second was the fact that the Secret Service blocked the exit of vehicles from the small parking lot next to St. Peter's Basilica, used by VIPs. At the end of the meeting I was told privately by a representative of our State Department that the Carabinieri would defer to the Secret Service in placement of the security vehicles, so it was important to leave that decision to them. The Carabinieri were both the Italian federal police and the Italian military.

During a private meeting with the chief of station of the CIA I was advised the Carabinieri was struggling with a confidence crisis after former Prime Minister Aldo Moro was kidnapped by the Red Brigade on March 16, 1978 and executed on May 9, 1978. Five Carabinieri guards in a security car accompanying him were killed during the kidnapping. It was a huge embarrassment for the Italian police since the press reported that Aldo Moros' security detail trailing in the follow-up car had left their machine guns locked in the trunk of their car. Without their automatic weapons the Carabinieri were no match for the terrorists.

After twelve years of overseas travel I knew the sensitivity of the motorcade alignment. The meeting with the Carabinieri went well and when we got to the issue of motorcade security, I asked for their suggestion on placement of our follow-up car. Without hesitation they said our Secret Service follow-up would be directly behind the limousine.

The rest of the meeting was routine. The overall security plans, motorcade routes, intersection control, security vehicles, and police support at the various stops were agreed upon with only minor changes. We then spent several days surveying the sites, conducting route surveys, making lists of people authorized to enter the security zones, and developing post assignments for our security jump team. Hospital routes to be used in an emergency were agreed upon as were counter-terrorist teams and other special needs.

The next big challenge was going to be the security detail at the Vatican for the funeral. During our initial meeting at the embassy it was pointed out to me that the Vatican was upset over the Secret Service delaying the departure of cars in the small private parking next to St. Peter's Basilica. At Vatican events such as the death of a pope, the pecking order for special guests began with heads of state followed by heads of government with the lesser guests last in line. Protocol required that royalty have unfettered access to the tiny parking lot. Ceremonies at the Vatican were steeped in history with the protocol for events developed hundreds of years ago. Royalty existed long before there were presidents and prime ministers.

Earlier the embassy staff indicated the small parking lot could barely handle thirty cars, and the Secret Service parked Mrs. Carter's twelve-car motorcade in the lot. If that were not bad enough, the embassy representative said a number of the royalty had to wait until the American motorcade departed before they could leave. I advised the people at our meeting that this would not be a problem and the Mondale motorcade would not create any problems. My mind had been working overtime to find the solution to the problem.

Our entourage of embassy staff, Secret Service, Swiss Guards, and the monsignor in charge of Vatican security walked around the basilica to review the funeral plans. We were being fully briefed on the ceremony: where everyone was seated, security posts, and the protocol of the ceremony. After we resolved the issues concerning the ceremony, we walked to the side of the basilica where the parking lot was situated. There was some tension in the air and I sensed everyone thought this was going to be a contentious issue.

When the monsignor turned to address me our entire group was staring. He paused and asked, "What do you need in the parking lot?"

Without any delay I responded, "Can I park a car, here, near the steps leading up to the basilica, at three in the afternoon on the day of the funeral?"

The monsignor replied, "Yes."

To everyone's surprise I said "Thank you," and walked away. I could sense the lack of understanding by our survey group as we walked back to the Vatican. I knew no one had any idea what was going to happen.

I was waiting for the inevitable question, "What are you going to do?" Our entourage walked in silence. After several minutes the monsignor walked up to me and asked the question. Smiling, I advised him that at three o'clock I would park a vehicle in the approved spot and when Vice President Mondale's motorcade arrived the limousine would replace the pre-positioned car. The rest of the motorcade would drop their passengers near the stairs and then line up outside the parking lot along the road for the departure. Since it would be a short walk there should be no problem keeping our motorcade together.

The monsignor had a big grin on face. Nodding his head he chuckled and asked me to go with him. We separated from the rest of the group and went into the Vatican. The monsignor proceeded to give me a private tour of the Sistine Chapel and the Paolina Chapel, built in 1540 at the direction of Pope Paul III. The monsignor told me it was the pope's private chapel. I had been in the Sistine Chapel before but visiting the pope's private chapel was an unexpected treat. It was located in a long, narrow room near the Sistine Chapel. It was a very manly room with its dark wood pews and trim. On the left side wall was a fresco of St. Peter crucified upside down. The wall on the right had a fresco of St. Paul. Standing in the private chapel saying a prayer, I was in awe of the history of the room and the few people that ever had a chance to see the chapel as I did, let alone have time to say a prayer in it.

I thought we were through when we came out of the chapel. To my surprise the monsignor walked me up one floor and took me into some of the receiving rooms. I was stunned by the beauty. The huge tapestries trimmed with gold leaf, the paintings, frescoes, and artifacts were not just beautiful, they were breathtaking. I would wager that not many people except royalty, distinguished government leaders, esteemed religious leaders, and illustrious guests ever got to see these rooms. I found myself thinking, "If the walls could talk." These rooms had been used for hundreds of years and the stories affecting world history and church history must be riveting. I found out later the four reception rooms were the Raphael Rooms that were decorated by a young artist from Urbino named Raphael.

I took our advance team to tables on the Via Veneto for a relaxing evening. We were enjoying our evening of dining and watching the people walking by the tables. Agent Roy Wilson was enjoying entertaining us with a magic trick he had mastered. He had a false thumb that allowed him to make coins and other appropriately sized things disappear. As the evening wore on, Wilson was entertaining more and more people. At one point he was standing up and, in addition to the people seated, another thirty or forty had gathered to watch the entertainment. When he finished his routine everyone gave him a round of applause. As the other customers began leaving I called over the waiter to pay the bill.

Agent Wilson picked up the ten or so small cash register receipts placed in the middle of the table by our waiter. When the waiter arrived at the table Wilson took all the receipts, rolled them up into a ball, and with the waiter watching made them disappear. The waiter had a look of disbelief on his face as we told him the receipts were gone. He brought the manager over trying to explain to him what happened to the bills. We all had a good laugh as Wilson made them reappear.

The night before Mondale arrived we went to a small Italian restaurant recommended by the embassy for an early relaxing evening. Waiting to order I was thinking about the tour of the Vatican. It had been a highly emotional "Why me" time for a Catholic from Visitation Parish in South Tacoma. This was the highlight of my time in Rome. My thoughts were interrupted when a tanker truck parking in front of the eatery caught my attention. It looked like a heating oil delivery truck to me. I watched as the driver unrolled the hose and put it through an open window into the restaurant. He came inside and pumped the house red wine into a large wooden barrel in a small alcove. When we ordered our meal the waiter drew two carafes of the house wine from the same barrel. We enjoyed the meal, especially the wine.

The visit itself was routine and went very well. There were no security problems, political issues, or other hitches during the visit. The vice president's arrival and departure motorcades at the basilica caused no problems and the monsignor thanked me after our motorcade departed the small lot. After the ceremony, I had a chance to go to dinner with the vice president's private secretary, Penny Miller, and several of the Congressmen who were part of the official delegation. The food and drink was delicious and the meal lasted several hours. I don't know which Congressman bought the meal, but they were on a different per diem than the Secret Service. The next day the vice president and his party returned to Washington, D.C.

I returned to my operations desk in the Old Executive Office Building with a renewed energy. Taylor and Boyette were right about me needing a chance to get away from the pressures of the operations job.

❋ ❋ ❋

During 1978 the use of the C-130s had becoming a problem due to breakdowns, most of them minor. There were three basic issues with the support aircraft that were beginning to gnaw at me. The first issue was their reliability. There were a number of cases where the support aircraft had mechanical problems and needed to be repaired or replaced before our mission could be completed. The second problem was the fact that the C-130 aircraft did not have a VIP insert with kitchen and restrooms, as the C-141s did. This was not an issue of food as much as one of privacy and hygiene inasmuch as we flew men and women together on many flights. A bucket sitting under a wood frame with a toilet seat and lid attached referred to as a "honey bucket" had to be used as the restroom. A privacy screen separated the restroom from the passengers. Lastly, the prop aircraft did not have commercial airline type seats. Agents were seated along the sides of the aircraft in webbed seating.

During the summer and early fall of 1978 there had been several times when support aircraft had mechanical problems during a mission and were required to be replaced in order to complete our mission. While flying in the webbed seating on the sides of the aircraft might prepare the military for parachuting out of the aircraft or rapid deployment of men and equipment for combat, for people dressed in suits and ties the cramped conditions were not optimal for performance of their mission, especially since, on occasion, agents would have to report for post assignments within a very short time of the C-130 landing.

My frustrations with using the C-130 came to a head during the second half of 1978. First of all, breakdowns were becoming all too frequent. Second, Vice President Mondale had a heavy travel schedule in late October in support of Democratic incumbents and other candidates during the 1978 off-year elections. I approached my new boss, Jerry Parr, who had replaced Jimmy Taylor, to express my frustrations with the support aircraft. It was my sense that Protective Operations was not willing to argue with the White House over using the C-130s and I told him so.

I had prepared a final draft of a very strongly worded memo to AD Powis about the situation with the C-130s. Knowing that the Office of Protective Operations would not be happy to see the memo, I advised Parr I wanted to forward the memo to headquarters soon. I wanted to do it before I chickened out. I was careful to tell Parr it was not my desire to bring him into this conflict and he did not need to approve or sign the memo. I indicated I knew it would not be received well but that I was willing to send it with just my signature. Parr had previously seen several drafts of the memorandum and said he would look at the final draft of the memo before making a decision. The bottom line of the memo clearly outlined that I felt we were going to find ourselves in one of two very uncomfortable situations. If the mechanical problems continued, we could be required to make a choice of either canceling a visit by the vice president or allowing him to visit a site not properly secured. The other possibility, equally as serious or maybe more so, was that a mechanical problem could cause a plane to go down with some agents on board being hurt or worse. After reading the memo Parr said it could be sent out over my own signature.

I was a little surprised when, before I had a chance to send the memo, I was asked by agent Lefler, who had replaced Livingood in Protective Operations, to coordinate two weeks of campaigning by

Mondale and President Carter. Due to the tension between Protective Operations and me I knew my relationship with their office was not the greatest. They knew firsthand the frustrations I had over aircraft support. I knew, however, that the type of coordination that was needed to make the two weeks successful for the White House would be difficult for Protective Operations to accomplish on their own. It wasn't necessarily that Gus Holmes, their logistics person, was not up to the task. They knew if they gave the task to me they would not have to get involved at all and the plan would be cost-effective.

Vice President Mondale was going to be traveling for the last two weeks of the campaign in support of off-year election candidates and incumbents. The vice president would do joint appearances with President Carter on the two weekends before the elections. In an effort to be efficient and effective, I agreed to coordinate all the logistics as long as my office would be able to coordinate the movement of C-130 aircraft for agents and cars. This type of duel use of agents was right up my alley.

Lefler knew I would be able to bring all assets together to maximize our resources and minimize the number of agents needed. Under my plan, pre-posted agents supporting the vice president would perform double duty supporting President Carter also. This would lessen the need for a larger number of extra agents, and at the same time provide adequate support for the president and vice president.

My plan, in addition to saving money, would also save wear and tear on our agents. The travel of our two top leaders would require support by probably three, twenty-person security jump teams that would leapfrog using C-130 aircraft. Also, we would use several C-130s to transport our armored cars. Due to the smaller cargo area of the C-130 there was not enough room for a car and agents to ride together. I thought of how much more efficient and cost-effective we would be if we used C-141s that could transport both the cars and the agents together. It was agreed with Lefler that PPD would take care of the transportation of President Carter's cars and I would move the vice president's cars around the country and coordinate the transfer of all of the agents for Carter and Mondale.

The success of my cost-cutting planning was to neutralizing any negative impact on the president, vice president, or our agents while making sure we had reliable transportation to leapfrog the jump teams and armored vehicles. If a C-130 were taken out of service I knew I would need an alternative means of transporting the cars and/or our agents to make sure no campaign stop would be cancelled.

Anticipating breakdowns of some C-130s, I asked five of the vice president's advance agents if they could get standby private aircraft from charter companies at the local airports. It was necessary that a charter company would accept a "Government Transportation Request" (GTR) for an aircraft large enough to transport twenty agents if needed. The five advance agents all confirmed they had aircraft that could be used. They reported that they could get the Secret Service billed for the actual cost of any aircraft that was pressed into service. If a C-130 that was flying a car needed to be replaced I knew we could find one with the military.

I spoke with agent Lefler and explained the potential problem and asked for authorization to charter five aircraft on a standby basis in the event of a problem with one or more of the C-130s. I made sure he understood that no money would be spent unless we activated the aircraft. We had a spirited discussion about the use of the C-130s and the recurring breakdowns, but I got nowhere with him.

I knew mentioning that we should be asking for C-141s would exacerbate the situation, but there was no question in my mind that using them would resolve all our problems. Finally, in frustration, I brought up the C-141 issue with Lefler. That pretty much ended the conversation. The bottom line was Lefler would not approve the use of the standby charters or request C-141 support. Before our conversation ended I reminded Lefler it was the military's responsibility to support the Secret Service per the Presidential Protection Assistance Act. I told him I did not believe the C-130s met our responsibility to the president and vice president. Lefler continued to deny the standby request.

By the time our conversation was over I was really worked up. Since no money needed to be committed ahead of time I was sure that Livingood would have approved the standby request. I was more frustrated than I had ever been since joining the Secret Service. It was Friday afternoon and the first C-130 with a jump team on board was scheduled to leave Andrews AFB for South Dakota within the hour. I had no one to talk with inasmuch as my bosses, Jerry Parr and Barney Boyette, were on the road with the vice president. In total frustration I picked up the phone and requested that the White House switchboard connect me with Hugh Carter in the White House Military Office.

When Carter answered the phone, I introduced myself and told him I was responsible for the travel of Vice President Mondale. Then I asked him if he had ever heard of the Presidential Protection Assistance Act. There was silence on the phone. I explained to Carter that the Presidential Protection Assistance Act directed the military to support the Secret Service in the performance of their duties at no cost.

Then I fibbed and told him I had just re-read the act and that nowhere in the act was his name listed. I challenged him, asking by what authority he was denying the use of military assets to the Secret Service. He remained silent, letting me talk. I expressed my serious concerns about the reliability of the C-130 and the dilemma I was facing coordinating the travel of agents and transportation of cars to support visits of President Carter and Vice President Mondale. I requested that

Carter approve support by the more reliable C-141s instead of the C-130s. He immediately denied the request.

I was well aware that he was responsible for our use of the C-130 military aircraft. He was the person who denied our requests to use C-141s. Before hanging up I told him that when the planes started breaking down he would have to correct the problem or President Carter and Vice President Mondale would have to cancel some of their stops.

I was on an emotional roller coaster but amazingly calm inside. The last year of frustration was being vented and it was clear to me what I needed to do. I did not want to cause injury or the death of the president, vice president, or an agent on my watch. I did not want the president or vice president to have to cancel any of their stops. I asked Carter once again to replace the propeller-driven C-130s with the C-141 jets. Without hesitation he denied my request.

Calling Lefler, I told him about my conversation with Hugh Carter and my admonition about fixing the problem I was predicting. I mentioned to Lefler that the first support aircraft with a jump team on board was leaving Andrews Air Force Base soon and I would be leaving for home shortly after it departed. Before hanging up the phone I again asked for approval of standby charters. When he denied my request I admonished Lefler, "Don't call me when the first plane breaks down. It is going to be your problem."

About an hour later, before I left the office, I received a call from the Andrews operations desk reporting the C-130 heading for South Dakota with twenty agents on board had a problem. According to the call it was a mechanical problem on board. Agents had to use oxygen masks until they descended below 10,000 feet. It was my understanding the aircraft would have no problem completing the flight to South Dakota but needed to fly at the lower level. I was advised the aircraft, however, would have to be taken out of service and a replacement would need to be found.

Immediately Lefler was advised by phone of the problem and that I was leaving for the weekend. On Monday when I arrived at the office I found out that all the C-130s had been cancelled and C-141s had taken over the missions. Lefler never talked to me about the problems over the weekend or afterwards.

During the following week Lefler advised Parr in a phone conversation that Assistant Director Powis and he had a meeting with Hugh Carter to discuss the C-130 issue. Parr told me he was advised that Carter had told Powis and Lefler the vice president's detail was using C-130s due to the lateness of their aircraft support requests. Parr said, according to Lefler, Carter said I was not giving them enough time to secure C-141 support.

With my frustration level elevating I responded to Parr that this was pure unadulterated "bull shit" and I was not going to accept that answer. I mentioned to Parr that I knew about the luncheon meeting between Hugh Carter, Powis, and Lefler from my sources. I heard that the C-141 issue was a side issued dealt with after the luncheon meeting was over. With Parr standing at my desk I called Lefler and told him that Hugh Carter was not correct. All my requests were made in adequate time to schedule C-141 aircraft.

Lefler got upset with me when I suggested that he had not properly supported our detail and did not care about the safety of our agents. A heated exchange followed with the call ending abruptly when I hung up. Parr was still standing just a few feet away, listening to the conversation. I stood up, trying to get my thoughts together. Looking at Parr, I said, "I am going home and I don't know when I will be back." Parr had a surprised look on his face but did not say anything. Without saying another word I left everything on top of my desk and drove home.

Four days later, when I felt I had made my point, I returned to work. Parr was supportive and told me he had removed the final draft of the C-130 memo from my file and sent it to headquarters. The tense situation I had with Protective Operations moved up a notch when they received the memo. I heard from several sources that Lefler and Powis did not appreciate the memo I wrote. It reinforced their opinion that I was not part of their team. There was backroom talk that I needed to leave my protective assignment.

When we had a mechanical problem with another C-130 less than two weeks later, I wrote a draft memo that made the last one look nice. I told Parr I did not want him to sign it. In fact, I did not even show the memo to him. While sitting at my desk trying to work up the nerve to hand carry it to headquarters, Boyett walked into the office. This was his first day back from his Arkansas vacation. He stopped by my desk and put a large manila envelope on my desk. As he walked away Boyett said, "I think you will find these articles interesting."

Taking the articles out of the envelope I noticed two of them were from a local Arkansas newspaper. I read both articles with interest since they were about Arkansas National Guard C-130 aircraft that were having mechanical problems. The articles identified the number of breakdowns, crashes, and deaths that had occurred since the breakdowns started. The reports indicated all C-130 aircraft were being grounded until the problem was fixed.

Putting the only copy I had of my memo and two of the newspaper articles in the manila envelope, I walked over to Lefler's office. Entering his office I could feel the tension as I put the envelope on his desk. I avoided eye contact as I turned to leave. Not wanting him to speak I said, "If I were half the asshole you think I am, I would have given this to you officially."

With that I was out the door. When I got back to my office, I told Parr and Boyett what I had done. Both were smiling and chuckling as they told me they had already received a call from Lefler announcing the immediate suspension of the use of C-130s. Lefler indicated to Parr that a memo would follow.

In late November 1978 I found myself in the battle of my life trying to save my career. Protective Operations had not been prepared to confront the White House and were displeased with my approach to problem solving even though I had repeatedly assisted them with difficult logistical issues. Lefler approached me in December, advising that I had been assigned to Protective Operations for over five years and it was time for me to return to the field for supervisory experience before I could be promoted to the next level. In other words, you have pissed us off enough and are not a team player, so goodbye.

Even though I was near the top of the promotion list to the GS-15 level, I was being told I needed to get some field administrative experience in an office first. For me this was the kiss of death. Unsuccessful intervention on my behalf by several supporters failed to change anything. Powis' assistant SAIC Lefler made it abundantly clear that, good, bad, or ugly, I was not going to be promoted while assigned to Protection Operations. I was sure the message was coming from the assistant director. Lefler and I did not always see eye to eye and had our share of disagreements, but he was usually straightforward.

I felt I was getting paranoid and asked myself, "Am I caught in a power play with the front office of Protective Operations? Does Powis really want field-trained people on the protective details with field supervisory experience? Is my aggressive and sometimes abrasive style causing the problem? Am I being black-balled?" These were the thoughts rumbling through my head.

Paranoia runs rampant sometimes when you have dedicated so much time and effort to a cause and are unceremoniously shoved out the door. I knew, however, that if I ever wanted another promotion I would have to take an assignment in the field. The challenge for me was to make sure I did not get buried in one of the large field offices on the way out the door.

Lefler arranged a meeting with the Office of Investigation for a discussion about openings at the GS-14 level. Before the meeting I received a call from a supporter telling me there was an opening for an assistant at the GS-14 level in Kansas City. When I got to the Office of Investigation for my meeting I was offered a position in the third tier of supervisor responsibility in either New York City or Chicago. We spoke for a few minutes about the offer when I asked about the opening in Kansas City, where my old Kissinger boss, Jim Cantrell, was the Special Agent-in-Charge. I could tell they were surprised with the question about Kansas City. I sensed they wanted to say no but did not have a good reason. After several minutes they said they would speak with Cantrell first and let me know. The next day the deteriorating situation with Powis and Lefler in Protective Operations was over when I was told I would be going to Kansas City, Missouri.

✤ ✤ ✤

Meanwhile I had suffered a personal failure, when earlier in 1978 my wife Ginny left me and our four children for another man. Several weeks after she left I was surprised to come home and find the house empty and Michael, Robin, Leslie, and James gone. In fact, everything had been moved out of the house while I was at work, except my clothes, a bed, and some things in the kitchen. I went to court immediately. The judge who held the hearing issued a directive that required the children and all the household goods be returned to me at once.

Three months later Ginny and I reconciled and she returned to the house, but I realized too late she just wanted a divorce with the children. She had me arrested for abuse, but later we went to court to have the charges dropped. However, the judge would not dismiss the charges without an investigation by family services. Once their report exonerated me of being abusive the charges were dropped. The situation at home continued to deteriorate as my wife constantly pressed for a divorce so she could start fresh in a new life with her friend. We executed a separation agreement and property settlement papers just before I left on my reassignment to Kansas City.

The Shah of Iran was overthrown by the Iranian Revolution on January 16, 1979 and fled to Egypt. On February 1, the Shiite cleric Ayatollah Khomeini returned to Iran after fourteen years of exile in France. Less than month later I would be driving west to report to my new assignment, Kansas City, Missouri.

❖ ❖ ❖

In late February 1979 I packed my clothes, took a small television set, and said good-bye to Michael, Robin, Leslie, and Jamie. My wife and I had signed a child support and a property settlement agreement. Everything I owned, including the car and house, was given to my ex-wife. The drive through the mountains of West Virginia was a challenge. It was snowing heavily and the roadway was covered with compact snow and ice. At one point I lost control of the car and the left front tire hit the curb or a pothole really hard. The front end began to vibrate a little. Anxious to get to my new assignment, I continued driving even though the looseness in the steering mechanism was more than I liked.

About a hundred miles outside of Kansas City the vibration began to worry me and I stopped to have a mechanic look at the problem. He recommended that I not continue and said a part needed to be ordered to fix the problem. He said it would take two to three weeks to get the part.

I called my friend, agent Mike Cohen, who had been transferred from Protective Intelligence Division to St. Louis, Missouri, and told him of my predicament. Cohen said he was coming to the gas station to pick me up and drive me to Kansas City. When I arrived in Kansas City Cantrell assigned me an office car and I took up temporary residence at the house in Independence being rented by the Truman Protective Division. The house was used as a command post for former First Lady Bess Truman, who lived across the street. It was fully furnished and had a bedroom upstairs that offered privacy. I wanted to get a feel for Kansas City before deciding in which area of the city to look for an apartment. While I commuted the eight miles from my temporary residence Cantrell kept me busy learning the ins and outs of administering a field operation. The relaxed, slower pace of the field work helped me through the difficult changes in my personal life. I missed the children and talked to them regularly.

On one afternoon a tornado alert warning went off at work and everyone in our office was told to leave and return to their residences. Exiting the Federal Building to my car I became concerned when I saw the dark grey clouds in the direction I would be traveling. Driving toward Independence I watched as the clouds ahead went from grey to black. Looking in the rearview mirror I could still see some sunshine and clear blue sky, but it had diminished greatly. Extremely anxious and concerned about driving into a tornado I pulled over to the side of road to get my thoughts together and figure out what to do. My total experience with tornadoes had been occasionally seeing them on the evening news (we didn't have the Weather Channel back then).

Continuing to stare at the two-lane road I noticed that the cars in the left lane driving into downtown had their windshield wipers operating and were wet, making me even more nervous. Not knowing if I should continue driving to the command post or go to the airport and return to Washington, I sat nervously on the roadside for several minutes more. Finally, realizing I was the only one stopped, I edged back into the traffic flow with the ominous black clouds directly overhead.

In a few minutes the sun was gone and I was driving using my headlights in total darkness. With the windshield wipers having a difficult time removing the torrential rain, I slowed to below twenty miles per hour. Five minutes later, at three in the afternoon, in total darkness, I parked at the curb of the Truman detail house and rushed up the sidewalk. As I entered the house one of the detail agents urgently yelled to me to go to the basement immediately. When I got downstairs I was told the news was reporting a tornado in our area. A few minutes later, when the all clear signaled was given, I went outside. It was astounding; even though it was still quite dark outside, I could see the street and yards. It looked like a bomb had hit outside with several trees down and large tree branches strewn across the lawns and street.

When I came back inside the residence one of the agents mentioned a tornado had set down about six blocks away, picking up a school bus and tossing it nearly a hundred yards. He said fortunately no one was hurt since the driver had followed routine procedures and exited all the children and was lying in a nearby ditch with them. It took me a good week to realize I had to be able to cope with the tornado alerts and warnings or leave Kansas City.

Immersing myself in work, I took my time looking for a furnished apartment and enjoyed getting to know Kansas City.

Running became a passion as I burned up excessive energy every day after work. With the opening day of the baseball season my love of baseball brought me to Royal Stadium several times. In late April I committed to an apartment in North Kansas City that would be available June 1.

I was surprised in May when I received a call from the Vice Presidential Detail advising that Vice President Mondale would be visiting Kansas City and he had asked to say hello to me at the airport on his arrival. Most of my time in the office was being taken up on administrative matters and I was not scheduled to be involved in the nuts and bolts of the vice president's visit. However after the call, I volunteered to go to the airport early to meet the support agents, who would be arriving two hours prior to Mondale.

When the agents arrived on the USAF C-130, I recognized agent Chuck Zaboril as he exited the aircraft. He had been one of the shift leaders on the Presidential Protective Division when I reported there in 1969. Sensing he was upset I approached him and shook hands. Zaboril, who was the team leader, said he wanted to talk to me about the support aircraft after things settled down. The jump team and Zaboril gathered with the advance agent and everyone received their assignments. After the briefing, Zaboril and I had a chance to get caught up on old times and our current assignments.

Once relaxed, Zaboril began to describe and complain about the conditions on the C-130 support aircraft. He specifically mentioned the use of webbed seating and the "honey bucket" with a privacy screen. I was surprised to see the C-130 being used again to transport agents. I updated him on my experiences with the White House and Protective Operations concerning the Secret Service use of the C-130. He told me he had flown on many C-141s with their VIP package but had never flown on a C-130.

During our conversation, Zaboril expressed that he was disappointed, no, offended, by the two-and-a-half hour flight using web seating and the "honey bucket." We both agreed it was not the way to deliver agents for assignments, especially agents going directly on to security posts. Zaboril indicated that there was nothing he could do since this was obviously a decision made at the highest levels of Protective Operations. At the end of our conversation I mentioned I would make a call to Washington the next day to see if I could find out anything.

When Air Force Two arrived, Vice President Mondale was greeted by the normal group of state and local dignitaries. I was standing off to one side. After the handshakes and some small talk, Mondale walked over to me with his hand extended, asking how my transfer to Kansas City was going. We chatted for a few minutes and laughed while recounting the weekend inspection trip to the relocation site in Washington, D.C. I was surprised, pleased, and honored that the vice president took the time during a busy schedule to chat and say, "Thank you for your support." It is one thing to say I knew the vice president when I was on his detail and yet another to have him actually take time out of his busy schedule to say hello to me.

The next day, back in the office, I made a call to the operations desk in Protective Operations advising that the agents supporting Vice President Mondale's visit to Kansas City arrived aboard a C-130. I mentioned I had a 1978 copy of the memo from AD Powis suspending the use of these aircraft, and requested a copy of the memo rescinding the moratorium on use of the C-130. The person on the other end of the phone said he would check into it. No memo was forthcoming, but later I heard the use of C-130s had once again been discontinued.

The first of June I moved into my new furnished apartment in North Kansas City. It only took a couple of days to buy everything

I needed to make the apartment cozy. Michael, Robin, Leslie, and Jamie would be coming for a two-week visit and I wanted them to feel comfortable. Three weeks after moving into the apartment I received a call from Protective Operations. They wanted to know if I was available to travel as a supervisor to the Dominican Republic for six weeks with William Mondale, the youngest son of Vice President Mondale. He had accepted a summer job in Santo Domingo and would be staying at the home of former Dominican President Joaquin Balaguer. The vice president wanted his son to have Secret Service protection during the six weeks south of the border.

Before the trip with the young Mondale my children visited for two weeks and we had a great time. We went to a couple of Kansas City Royals baseball games. We did sightseeing in the area when I was off. They spent much of the day while I was at work with friends at the apartment complex in the swimming pool. One day while I was at work we had a tornado warning. The kids turned on the television and watched the weather report to see where the warnings were. They told me when I got home that they were a little worried about a tornado but were relieved when the television reports showed the tornadoes were a safe distance from the apartment. I shared the story of my first tornado experience with them and they had a good laugh about me pulling the car off the road.

Robin surprised me one day when I arrived home; she had done the laundry and ironed some shirts. She was only thirteen years old and a little embarrassed as she turned over one of the shirts she had ironed. It had the imprint of the iron on the back. I told her I could wear it but just could not take my coat off. We all had a good laugh, but it was really nice that she initiated the help. I was able to take several days of leave so we could spend more time together. The swimming pool was their favorite activity and when I was home I joined them. When I took them to the airport at the end of their visit I was not sure when I would be seeing them again. I hoped it would not be too long.

I arrived in Washington two days before my scheduled departure with William Mondale for briefings on the trip at the vice presidential detail. As I have written earlier, the Mondale children were authorized by law to have security provided by the Secret Service, but their parents declined the coverage on a routine basis. At the request of the vice president, agents from the vice president's detail and some from field offices were providing the support for the trip to the island of Hispaniola shared by Haiti and the Dominican Republic.

I was somewhat surprised after the meeting when I was asked to "go by" Protective Operations to see my old mentor SAIC Simpson. After saying our hellos, Simpson told me there was an opening for a new Special Agent-in-Charge of the Nixon Protective Division in San Clemente, California. He indicated the current detail leader, Pontius, had applied for a disability retirement and was on leave at home. There was urgency since Jack Ready, the assistant on the Nixon detail, had been transferred earlier in the year without a replacement and Nixon was preparing to go on a trip to China in October. Simpson said Protective Operations wanted to fill Pontius' position by the end of August.

The question Simpson asked of me was simple, "Are you interested in the assignment?" There was, however, one caveat. Since I was no longer high enough on the promotion list I would have to wait for the next round of evaluations. Simpson said it would be a temporary assignment for about three to four months until I was reevaluated and the new list could take effect. Biting my tongue about my removal from the promotion list by Lefler and Powis, I told Simpson I would be happy to go. He suggested I travel with William Mondale to the Dominican Republic and get the operation up and going there and in three weeks he said he would send a replacement to relieve me.

I told him that was going to be more than enough time for me to return to Kansas City and begin preparing for my new assignment. As I walked to my hotel after the meeting there was a smile on my face. Amazing, I thought, simply amazing; after less than four months of field work I was now qualified to head up a former president's detail. Later, as I relaxed back at the hotel, I thought that probably the last person in the Secret Service that AD Powis and his assistant Lefler wanted to offer a promotion to go to San Clemente was Michael Endicott. Don't get me wrong. I never believed either disliked me. Powis was a dynamic administrator and leader; however, I marched to my own drum beat, saw a different picture, and raised too many difficult questions. Later I heard that the Nixon job had been offered to several others, including some of the Powis "in crowd" but no takers could be found.

I was sure in my mind that John Simpson played a role in my good fortune. After working for him during the 1968 campaign our paths had crossed quite often. I believe he respected my work ethic and knowledge of operations and logistics. My broad exposure and assignments over the last fourteen years had given me a databank of excellent agents. I was looking forward to managing my own detail and developing some of the younger agents. I knew I would need some help.

❖ ❖ ❖

Luck has been a part in my life. Often when evaluating an agent, I would ask, "Are you a lucky person?" The question would be immediately followed with, "Explain your luck to me."

I believe strongly in luck. I have often been referred to as a lucky person. Whether it was school, sports, or my occupation, I approached life with my understanding of "luck." To me, luck was the ability to reduce the chances of failure so that when a decision needed to be made the odds of success were more favorable for me. It was important to me to surround myself with lucky people. In basketball one of the most basic plays is called a pick and roll. The success of the play depends on making the defensive players believe you are going to keep the ball, so when you pass the ball your teammate is open and makes a basket.

In the Secret Service it was always important for me to know where the potential failure points were. With proper vision and planning, the chances of failure could be greatly reduced. With the gift of seeing the big picture and surrounding myself with excellent support people who had a similar vision, I believed that I would not fail.

Could it be my good luck was beginning to head in a positive direction? Having been given the Nixon assignment I knew my future was in my hands.

During the commercial flight to Santo Domingo with William Mondale I began organizing my transfer to California in my head. But first I wanted to spend three weeks relaxing in Santo Domingo. This was one of those assignments you dream about: beautiful weather, a nice hotel, big swimming pool, excellent food, casinos and night clubs if you wanted something to do in the evenings. The irony of my upcoming change of duty stations and the need for me to get back on the promotion list brought a chuckle. Boy, Protective Operations must have really given me a poor performance rating. I was not thinking "Why me?" this time. I knew I had earned this promotion and would succeed.

Our detail stayed at one of the big international chain hotels in downtown Santo Domingo, while William Mondale stayed at the Balaguer residence a short distance away. Monday through Friday Mondale worked half days in an office in downtown Santo Domingo.

During the week the afternoons offered him a chance to either rest or have some type of recreational activity swimming, tennis, or the beach. Mondale met a number of young adults his age and was introduced to the Santiago night scene by them. At seventeen it had to be a great time for him, since he had so much freedom. Some evenings they went out to local clubs, while other times they gathered at one of the friends' homes for music and whatever young adults did in Santiago. I must say he seemed to be making good choices by coming home at decent hours and keeping himself surrounded with other good friends. I never saw him inebriated or observed any outrageous behavior on his part.

On two of the weekends we drove Mondale to Casa De Campo in La Romana, where he stayed at a second home of President Balaguer. Casa de Campo had a small runway for private airplanes and a very nice eighteen hole golf course. We stayed nearby at a new hotel. It was very relaxing inasmuch as William Mondale was at the Balaguer home most of the time. The drive back and forth was interesting as our two car caravan negotiated the narrow two-lane highway, dodging the land crabs crossing the road at dusk.

My three weeks by and large were quiet, routine, and enjoyable with one exception. During the midnight shift one night I was awakened by a call advising that one of the agents had accidentally discharged his firearm while on post at the Balaguer residence. Even though no one was hurt, I responded right away. Secret Service regulations required headquarters be notified at once and a report be written any time a firearm was discharged, accidentally or not. Since it was out of normal office hours, a routine call was made to Washington, D.C., advising the Intelligence Division duty agent of the incident. The culpable agent was interviewed by the shift leader and I listened and then provided a written statement.

The agent whose weapon had discharged steadfastly maintained that he had taken his issue weapon out of his holster to check something. He reported that while re-holstering his gun he inadvertently dropped it, causing it to discharge. Anyone with the basic understanding of firearms knows a revolver does not discharge when dropped. But that was his statement, so a full report was forwarded to Protective Operations. I did not hear any more about the incident.

❖ ❖ ❖

The challenges of the upcoming Nixon assignment were churning in the back of my mind. For an agent to have his own office or detail was one of the most sought-after rewards an agent aspired to attain. This was going to be a great opportunity for me in beautiful, sunny, warm San Clemente. Back in Kansas City it was going to take a Herculean effort to get everything in order quickly but I knew with Cantrell's help it could be done. Getting my personal effects ready, limited as they were, was not the major issue. I wanted to leave with all the projects I was working on in order. Cantrell was extremely competent and one of the world's nicest bosses. He had been very helpful and supportive during my short stay in Kansas City.

Midway through Mondale's six-week visit to the Dominican Republic, I was relieved of my assignment with William Mondale on schedule and traveled back to Kansas City. I had spoken to Cantrell by phone earlier and told him of the opportunity for promotion with the Nixon detail and thanked him for his support. He indicated he was delighted with the opportunity and the challenge facing me. Things moved rapidly as I either closed out or transferred the projects assigned to me. I packed up some of my possessions and decided to return after a couple of months in San Clemente to close out my apartment and sell my car.

Boarding the commercial flight for Los Angeles I had checked two bags with clothes and a few personal possessions and carried a shoulder bag with my official equipment onto the flight. Simpson had agreed that after the China trip I would return to Kansas City and close out my apartment before returning to San Clemente. On the flight I could see the voyage on which I was embarking. This was going to be the most interesting assignment of my Secret Service career. Heading on a trip down life's road with one of the most unique presidents in our history excited me. How could it be anything but exciting? I was being given an opportunity to see what made this extraordinary person tick. On that August afternoon when I checked into the San Clemente Inn, little did I realize the odyssey I would be taking with former President Richard Nixon.

❖ ❖ ❖

It was a far different Michael Endicott who arrived in San Clemente on that August day in 1979 than the young agent who had been selected to be on the White House detail ten years earlier. My experiences working the 1968 and 1972 campaigns, many foreign dignitary details, and other special assignments had allowed me a unique look at the inner workings of the Secret Service. My travels with Kissinger exposed me to terrorism and the requirement for detail planning that few agents in 1975 understood. Being responsible for the operations of the Vice Presidential Protective Division for Rockefeller and Mondale had helped me hone my logistical skills. Confrontations with the White House and my own headquarters helped me understand the political process much better than most agents at my level. I had developed a confidence in the decision-making process that left me very comfortable.

Agent Larry McCann, acting supervisor of the Nixon detail, met me on my arrival at the San Clemente Inn. He gave me a key to a furnished two-bedroom condo on top of a cliff overlooking the Pacific Ocean. McCann was the senior agent in charge of the detail pending my arrival. The son of a retired agent, McCann called Philadelphia his home. I had never met McCann and knew very little about him. After we took my bags to my condo, we headed for the command post.

On the short ride there McCann explained there was a cadre of agents and special officers under his command providing the security at the Nixon residence and the office complex. I knew agents provided inner perimeter and close proximity security. All the uniformed officers were retired senior master sergeants from the United States Marines, with one exception. The special officers provided administrative support, worked perimeter security, and drove the limousine and follow-up cars, according to McCann. He was very upbeat and positive about the group of agents and special officers working at the compound. After a quick tour of the Coast Guard complex and introductions to the men on duty we headed back to the San Clemente Inn. In a more relaxed environment in my room we continued our conversation about the detail.

Initially McCann had been all business as he briefed me on the personnel and the operations of the detail. Back in my condo, however, he relaxed as he spoke about Nixon and his upcoming trip to China. McCann was well-organized and I could tell he was appreciated and liked by the Nixon Secret Service detail. He was especially proud of Officers Jack Pettit and Robert "Doc" Walgren, who worked in the office. McCann confidently said the office would make arrangements for me to get my China visa through the Nixon staff and update my shots at Camp Pendleton. He said that a meeting had been scheduled for me with President Nixon later in the week.

I spoke with McCann about my previous relationships with Mrs. Nixon and Julie during my earlier assignment at the White House and mentioned they could be an asset for me. The rumors I had read about Nixon drinking to excess and about him being a broken man were just that, rumors, McCann told me. Finishing for the day, McCann said he would pick me up in the morning and would get a car to me the next day.

McCann picked me up early, so the first order of the day was getting a cup of coffee before some chitchat with agents on the midnight shift at the compound. A short visit with the day shift and then the office staff finished the social contacts for the morning. The first official business was a staff meeting attended by agent McCann and special officers Pettit and Walgren. They explained the administrative process and the routine reports they prepared.

Bursting with pride, Pettit told me about how unique the group of special officers assigned to Nixon was. He indicated all fifteen were retired military. There were fourteen Marine master sergeants and one U.S. Navy chief petty officer. Pettit (USMC) and Walgren (USN) were part of the large group of former military men assembled to assist with protecting former President Nixon.

I remembered my trips to San Clemente when Nixon was president and the special officer group was larger because the staff and support group for a sitting president required a much larger security detachment. Agent McCann and special officer Pettit had been busy overseeing the day-to-day operations of the Nixon detail since SAIC Pontius had left. McCann gave me a much more detailed tour of the compound buildings, posts, and the grounds of Casa Pacifica, the Nixon residence. It did not seem to have changed that much since my last visit there with Secretary of State Kissinger in 1974, except, of course, there were far fewer people around today.

McCann continued the briefing in his office with Pettit on the upcoming trip to China, advising that he was taking care of all the logistics for the trip and agent Jimmy Miller from the Los Angeles Field Office was doing the advance. Pettit told me it would take several trips to Camp Pendleton to get my vaccinations updated, unless I wanted to do them all at once. He requested my passport and advised that the visa for the trip to China would take three days. I told Pettit I would do the shots in one day. I knew it would take several days to get over aches and pains, but I preferred that to going back and forth to Camp Pendleton.

The rest of the first day was spent with officers Pettit and Walgren taking care of documents that needed to be processed concerning my change of station. Walgren was one of those rare individuals who was jovial most of the time and seemed to enjoying his job and life in general. He was proud of his navy background and was sometimes prone to salty language, but not in an offensive way. In addressing me he often began a sentence speaking out of the side of his mouth saying, "Jesus Christ, Endicott..."

Pettite, like Walgren, was proud of his military background. He ended his career in the Marine Corps as a loyal, dedicated office administrator who paid close attention to detail. Pettite and Walgren worked closely together and enjoyed kidding McCann and me. They were able to keep the atmosphere in the office upbeat and pleasant.

McCann was somewhat preoccupied with other activities in the morning and I wasn't sure if it was my new assignment, the China visit, or something else. We chatted for a little while at the end of the first day and he said for me to see Walgren about getting a car assigned. When Walgren gave me the keys to a car he invited me to join him and Pettit at Landal's Restaurant the next morning for their ritual breakfast of SOS. Many eateries on the West Coast, especially near military bases, had on their menu biscuits and sausage gravy, enjoyed by many in the military. Growing up with a World War II father I knew the Navy and Marines called the dish SOS – Shit on a Shingle. My father served in the Merchant Marines and often served SOS on Sunday mornings. Dad did not use the more traditional sausage in the gravy; instead, chipped beef was his choice.

After breakfast we drove to the compound and got the office up and running. McCann told me he needed to speak with me. I could tell by his demeanor something was bothering him. Sitting in his office, McCann told me that one of the special officers had a drinking problem. He struggled to tell me the officer had been caught a couple of months earlier drinking on duty and it was handled internally by Pontius. McCann explained to me that he and Pettite had followed one of the officers on the day shift out to his post the previous morning. He said they observed him remove a bottle of liquor that had been hidden on the property near his post assignment.

McCann said since I was so busy with first day meetings and reviews that he decided to wait one day before talking with me. He said he confiscated the bottle of liquor and sent the officer home. He said he hoped I was not upset over the delay in reporting the incident. McCann explained that his first concern was for the officer. I could tell he was worried about the officer and did not want to have to fire him. McCann said he wanted to help him recover and told me about the other incident that had never been reported.

I told McCann I needed to notify Protective Operations in order to get help for the officer. I told him not to worry about me or headquarters dismissing the officer. I let him know I was familiar with the Secret Service Family Assistance Program and would make sure he got into a recovery program. McCann was asked to have the officer report to me the first thing the next morning. In the meantime I called Secret Service headquarters and spoke first with Protective Operations and then with the head of the Family Assistance Program. I wanted to make sure the next morning I fully understood and could explain the options available to the special officer.

Back in my room that night with the sliding door open, I could hear the roar of the surf. Watching the sky turn yellow, orange, and red as the sun set I sipped on a scotch and thought about Mondale's comment about Nixon being evil. As a conservative and a registered independent I believed I had an open mind about politicians and government officials. Like the vast majority of Americans, I was very upset at Nixon during the Watergate affair. I believed Nixon did the right thing by resigning. It showed me he cared about the country. I was looking forward to where this assignment would take me, not back at where President Nixon had been.

Thinking about the meeting I would soon have with Nixon, I played it and replayed it in my head. Since arriving in San Clemente I knew the meeting with the former president would set the tone for our relationship. It was important for me to explain to Nixon that this assignment was a promotion for me. It was necessary for him to know that I wanted this new challenge. For me it was compelling that he understood that Michael Endicott was going to work with him to do the things that he wanted to do.

Reviewing my second day on the job as the sun disappeared below the horizon, I realized I had a loyal and dedicated cadre of very efficient people around me. I knew how important it was that I help our officer with the drinking problem; everyone was watching me. I was happy for my involvement in policy and programs back on the VP detail. Working with Taylor and Boyette had made me well aware how important it was to deal with problems quickly and according to the rules. I knew that since the first incident was swept under the rug they were worried the officer would be fired. McCann, Pettite, and Walgren were all watching.

First thing the next morning I spoke with the officer, getting him to acknowledge his drinking problem. He was then instructed that he had to get into an assistance program. The program could be one of his choosing or could be coordinated through the Family Assistance Program, I advised him. I gave him the phone number of the Family Assistance Program. The officer was advised his recovery would be closely monitored officially by headquarters, not by me. He was instructed to stay home and enroll in a program either through the Family Assistance Program office or on his own. I made sure he understood that the terms of continued employment required him to be in a program by the time I returned from China. He was advised that if he chose an outside program to tell McCann and it would be reported to Family Assistance, which would monitor his progress. I asked if there were anything McCann or I could do to help him personally. He seemed very satisfied with our conversation and indicated the he wanted help in his recovery from his drinking problem. Later, when we returned from China, it was confirmed he had opted to get into a program monitored by our Family Assistance Office.

❖ ❖ ❖

The day after dealing with the personnel problem I had a private meeting with President Nixon. When we sat down in his office together, Nixon immediately put me at ease. He spoke for a few minutes about the California Angels and the American League pennant race. He told me what a great person owner Gene Autry was. He told me about his annual pool party for the Angels' players, coaches, and their families. He said they served Mexican food. As we both relaxed, Nixon confided in me he was going to move to New York City. This really caught me by surprise. There were rumors he might move sometime, but this was the first confirmation of his plan to move to New York.

With excitement in his voice and a sparkle in his eyes, Nixon said he would be seeing his old friends Bebe Rebozo and Bob Abplanalp on a more regular basis. This meant that we would reopen the travel routes to Key Biscayne, Florida, and Walker's Cay, Bahamas. The former president said, "It is time for me to get back to the East Coast where the action is." He mentioned that by living in New York City people would not have to drive an hour and a half to visit. Nixon was really fired up about the move.

When it was my turn to speak I proceeded to fill Nixon in on my desire to be the head of his security. After mentioning my background in operations and logistics, I told him I was being promoted to fill Pontius' position. I made sure he understood I wanted him to do the things he wanted to do. I expressed how much I enjoyed being on Mrs. Nixon's detail back in 1969-1970. I shared details of my trip to Japan with David and Julie Eisenhower to visit the World's Fair in Osaka in 1971.

Concerning his safety, I told Nixon that there were no threats against him and that absent a specific and reliable threat he could go anywhere he wanted to go and do anything he pleased. As to his health, I offered that it was our responsibility when he traveled to know where the closest doctor and hospital were located. He must understand, however, that it was his decision to isolate himself where it could take several hours or more to receive emergency medical treatment. We both knew I was referring to Abplanalp's islands in the Bahamas.

The latter part of our chat presented me with a chance to explain my love of sports. When I mentioned I played varsity basketball and baseball at St. Martin's College in Lacey, Washington, it piqued Nixon's interest. Though he did not play in any of his college football games it was well known he enjoyed the camaraderie of being on the team and practicing with them. I knew Nixon had developed into a relatively good golfer by the time he became president. I saw firsthand that Nixon, a recreational swimmer, liked the salt water and was not intimidated by the ocean surf. During his political years, the media had reported on the many college and professional athletic events Nixon had attended. It fact, it had been widely reported in the media that, as president, Nixon had phoned Coach George Allen of the Washington Redskins giving him a play for Super Bowl VII.

Nixon told me how, as president, he had relished the honor of throwing out the ceremonial first ball on the opening day of baseball season. Living in San Clemente he told me he routinely went to the California Angels' baseball games. When he attended the games, Nixon said he would sit with Autry in the owner's box.

As I walked back to the command post I was thinking of how comfortable and at ease both of us were during the conversation. I had expected the meeting to be formal and it was not. Also, I thought to myself, so Richard Nixon is going to once again attempt to resurrect his political career. No question in my mind the odds were against him. However, the deck was not stacked. When Nixon teed up the ball, he was going to be responsible to keep it out of the roughs, out of the traps. I was interested in being on the course.

As a politician Nixon had not always succeeded. But his one real failure, albeit a big one, Watergate, cost him the presidency. I have always seen a clear distinction between failure and not succeeding. In an assignment or project, if you take all appropriate steps to succeed and do not succeed, to me you did not fail. However, if you do not take all the available steps to succeed and then do not, you have failed.

It was interesting to me that Nixon obviously thought he could overcome Watergate and his San Clemente exile. He talked only in positive terms and projected confidence that he would succeed. I wanted to be part of his resurrection and I was really looking forward to the move to New York after having met with the "man."

Returning to the command post I encountered Mrs. Nixon, who was walking from the residence to the staff building. She stopped and greeted me warmly and congratulated me on my new assignment. Mrs. Nixon excitedly told me about their move to the East Coast, mentioning she would drop her Secret Service coverage soon since it would not be needed in New York. Without reacting to her comment about the move and her detail, I asked about the Eisenhower and Cox families. We spoke for several more minutes. She smiled as she spoke about her grandchildren, Christopher Cox and Jenny and Alex Eisenhower. When we parted it was reassuring that she remembered me.

When I got back to my office I spoke with McCann about my meeting with the president. I told him of the pending move to New York City and my conversation with Mrs. Nixon. McCann said there had been rumors recently about a possible move to New York, but he was taken aback by the fact that the move would come so soon. He also said he was surprised by the decision of Mrs. Nixon to give up protection. It was decided it was important for me to talk with Simpson in Protective Operations about the move and Mrs. Nixon's decision to drop her detail. McCann said he would set up a staff meeting the next day to frame our approach to the New York City move. The remainder of the day was spent briefing Simpson, reviewing the upcoming trip to China, and trying to prepare an agenda for the next day.

The visit to China was over a week away, a move to New York City was in the future, and I needed to return to Kansas City to close out my apartment. This certainly was not what I had anticipated my first week to be like when I arrived in San Clemente.

The next day McCann, Pettite, Walgren, and I had a staff meeting to discuss the move to New York City. McCann and Pettit agreed to contact Secret Service headquarters and work while we were in China to review the options for disbanding the detail. We all knew it was imperative we take care of the special officers. It was also decided to survey the agents assigned to the detail and see how many, if any, wanted to go to New York City.

I was beginning to see Nixon's trip to China this fall as the opening volley in his well-orchestrated reentry into the "Arena." Accompanied by his son-in-law Edward Cox and Chief of Staff Col. Jack Brennan, Nixon boarded our commercial flight to China in September 1979. This would be my first trip to China and I was excited about it. Having already traveled to over ninety countries around the world I looked forward to the opportunity to add China to my list.

Agent Jimmy L.C. Miller, our advance agent from the Los Angeles Field Office, met us on the ground in Beijing when we arrived. I had previously met Miller when he had been the advance agent for Kissinger on my first trip to Damascus back in 1974. The China visit went like clockwork. Nixon stayed at the Diaoyutai State Guesthouse in Beijing. He met with Chinese officials and attended the theatre, where United States Ambassador George Bush was also in attendance. Nixon was hosted at several dinners and held his own dinner for his hosts.

In the mornings agent Miller and I would take a three-mile run before breakfast. Miller, like me, was a good athlete and in good shape. Jogging through the grounds of the Diaoyutai compound, we passed other guest houses, government leaders' houses, and support facilities. One morning after our run Miller and I were walking to cool down. We neared a school where a group of teenagers, both boys and girls, were playing half court basketball in an exercise yard a quarter mile from our guest house. Pausing, we watched for a few minutes. One of the groups motioned to us. Though not a lot was said it was clear they were inviting us to join their teams in a game. Miller and I selected two of the girls and squared off against five of the boys. The boys were laughing and kidding each other. We sensed they thought they were going to clean our clocks. In a gesture meant to give them overconfidence we gave them the ball first. Our zone defense kept them from scoring the first basket. Ignoring the girls when we got the ball, Miller and I screened for each other and drove to the basket. As the defense collapsed on us an outlet pass to one of the girls led to a score. Miller and I controlled the backboard and made sure all our points were scored by our two teammates. The boys became frustrated and before they could adjust to our style the bell rang, signaling to come into the building. We all shook hands, bowed, and thanked each other. The girls were especially happy to have beaten, no, trounced, the boys.

Being a food aficionado I enjoyed eating the various regional foods that were served at the different dinners. Definitely the meals were not the same as the Chinese food served in the United States. It was also interesting to learn the Chinese dos and don'ts of their drinking etiquette. A small stemmed glass at each table setting was filled with Mao Tai, a favorite Chinese fermented spirit. The clear liquid itself tasted like a cross between JP-4 jet fuel and kerosene.

At the big dinners the host stands and offers the first toast. Throughout the evening the host can offer two more toasts to the assembled guests. At each table Chinese participants and guests can offer toasts to each other. The person giving the toast stands, offering the toast, and raises his or her glass. With the salutation, "Goombay," everyone empties their glass. With the salutation, "Sway Bien" everyone takes a sip of the drink. All glasses are filled after each toast.

After several drinks the Chinese limit their participation in drinking the toast to the person making the toast. Sometimes the etiquette of the evening becomes a game. Chinese participants often target one of their American guests for special attention. American guests, being

Americans, meanwhile, drink to every toast. Sometimes by the end of the dinner the targeted Americans need assistance to their cars.

In the four dinners we attended there was much Mao Tai consumed. I don't remember anyone from the Nixon party leaving any of the dinners inebriated.

On our return to the United States our flight cleared customs in Anchorage, Alaska. It was disappointing for me to see a former president denied courtesy of the port by the United States Customs Service. Normally former presidents and other high-ranking United States officials, such as Cabinet secretaries, members of Congress, and state officials, are allowed re-entry into the United States after presenting an executed declaration form. However, Brennan advised me that he and Nixon were routinely denied courtesy of the port.

I watched in amazement as their customs declaration forms were carefully scrutinized. Then their briefcases and bags were searched before their entry was approved. Nixon didn't say anything at the time but told me afterwards that he thought that the denial of courtesy of the port and the custom check was at the request of the Carter White House. Vice President Mondale's words about Nixon being "evil" were echoing in my ears. I never shared Mondale's comments with Nixon and never would, but I was disturbed by the action of the Anchorage custom agents.

I thought about when I coordinated Secret Service operations for Vice Presidents Rockefeller and Mondale. Courtesy of the port was a routine request that was received for agents returning to the United States via military and private aircraft that had supported the vice president. I also requested and received the same courtesy for Vice President Mondale when he returned to International Falls, Minnesota, on a private aircraft from his fishing trips to Canada. The request for courtesy of the port was directed to the customs officer at the port of entry. Nixon never said anything about the baggage and briefcase searches. But Brennan was rightly upset. He told me he was offended at the lack of respect afforded former President Nixon. I made a note to make sure in the future that former President Nixon was given the courtesies appropriate for his position and service to the country if at all possible.

❊ ❊ ❊

The Angels were closing in on the American League West Division championship when we arrived back in San Clemente. This was a title they had never won before and Nixon wanted to be at Anaheim Stadium for the clinching victory. The Angels were one win away from the championship. The Texas Rangers were in town for a three-game series September 21-23. I told McCann to take President Nixon to the game Friday night since he had been going recently. The Angels lost the game 3-1. McCann said he could not go with Nixon on Saturday night so I decided to go with him. It would be my first time to see the Angels play.

Upon arriving at the Anaheim Stadium, Nixon and I were escorted to the owner's box by our advance agent and stadium security. Owner Gene Autry and his wife Jackie were already seated, waiting for the first pitch. Although there was a cordial round of helloes, the tension in the air could be felt by everyone. In the owner's box it was apparent everyone wanted Autry to win the championship, but no one wanted to say something that would jinx the game. Nixon pored over the lineups as the full house got ready for the first batter. Nixon cheered for all the players by name and stood with an arm in the air when the Angels scored. When the final out was made in the top of the ninth the Angels won 3-1.

The whole stadium went wild. There was chaos on the field and in the stands. Everyone in the owner's box was congratulating Autry. Nixon shook his hand, patted him on the back, and returned to his chair. After the players began leaving the field Autry and his wife came over to Nixon and invited him to join them in the clubhouse. I learned a lot about Nixon when he gracefully declined saying, "This is your night; I'll catch up with you downstairs later."

After everyone departed, Nixon and I were alone in the box. We could hear the fans yelling and screaming as they left the stadium. Nixon stood enjoying the celebration as he told me about his respect for Autry. He said he was delighted that after all of the years of commitment to the team, fans, and the community, Autry's Angels were Division champions.

A very relaxed Nixon began reminiscing about the old days before Major League baseball came to the West Coast. He told me of his support and love of the old Triple A, Pacific Coast League (PCL). He recalled the days of the Los Angeles Angels and the Hollywood Stars, teams that played in the 1940s and '50s. He said that three of the great players who graduated from the PCL were Joe DiMaggio, Ted Williams, and Tony Lazzeri. Having grown up watching the Seattle Rainiers and the Tacoma Giants I recalled Juan Marichal, Jose Pagan, Jimmy Ray Hart, Willie McCovey, and Tom Haller, who went on to play for the San Francisco Giants. After twenty minutes of reminiscing, a nostalgic Nixon excitedly said, "Okay, Mike, let's go."

We exited the box and our waiting advance agent, along with the stadium security team, escorted us to the lower level. Nearing the clubhouse we could hear the noise coming from inside. Approaching the entry Nixon lingered to survey the scene, which could only be described as complete chaos. Inside, Autry and his wife, the players, coaches, and front office people were all celebrating at the other end of the room. Champagne was being sprayed everywhere. Sportscasters, writers, and television crews seemed to be enjoying the excitement as they went about their business. It looked as if everyone in the clubhouse were drenched in champagne.

Nixon had a smile on his face as he cautiously stepped through the doorway. He was immediately approached by one of the radio sportscasters, who asked for an interview. Nixon agreed to do the live broadcast. Standing a few feet away, I relaxed and took in the victory party. This was a celebration I had watched many times before on television, only this time I was part of it. Looking around I realized Nixon and I were the only ones that still had coats and ties on in the entire room. As I continued surveying the bedlam in the clubhouse I also realized that we were the only two people there that were not yet wet.

Nixon was a few minutes into the interview when Angels' second baseman Bobby Grich, beer in hand, walked over to Nixon. They shook hands; Nixon congratulated Grich, who joined the live radio broadcast. After joining Nixon in answering a couple of questions Grich excused himself to get another beer. When Grich returned, he walked over to me, held up his new beer, pointed to Nixon and asked, "Is it okay if I pour this beer over his head?"

With a grin from ear to ear my response was, "Go ahead."

I knew that any avid sports fan would love to be part of a clubhouse celebration. I felt Nixon would not object to joining the party. In fact, after being with him less than a month I was sure he would truly enjoy being part of it. Holding the can of beer by his side in his right hand, Grich returned to the interview with Nixon on his right side. With his right hand resting on Nixon's left shoulder, Grich raised the can of beer until it was about six inches above Nixon's head. Nixon was so engrossed in the interview that he had no idea what was going to happen. Slowly and deliberately the Angels' second baseman lifted the can and, without drawing attention, cautiously tipped the beer until it began to seep out. Nixon was totally taken by surprise. Laughing, Grich quickly turned the can upside down. As the beer cascaded out of the can over Nixon's head Grich roared, the announcer gasped, and Nixon began shaking his head to clear his eyes. Observing it all I had a Cheshire cat grin on my face.

Nixon shrugged his shoulders as the cold beer ran down his back and dripped off his chin. His tan suede sport coat, tie, and shirt were soaked. Nixon shook his head to clear some of the beer out of his hair and face. As he wiped his face with his handkerchief, he looked at Grich. Nixon was laughing with a big smile on his face. What an amazing sight, the thirty-seventh president, who had experienced so many historic events, had just been properly initiated and was now officially part of the Angels' championship celebration.

Nixon shook hands with Grich and waved to others as he departed the clubhouse for the wet motorcade ride back to San Clemente. Thank you, Bobby Grich. You may not know how much Nixon truly enjoyed being made part of the celebration, but with your can of beer you made the number one fan of Autry and the Angels a wet, happy man.

With the American League Western Division Championship settled I arrived at the office Monday morning to begin addressing the serious issues concerning the move to New York City. McCann briefed me on our options and the opportunities available to all personnel. The decommissioning of the Nixon Protective Division would be handled as a "Reduction in Force" (RIF). McCann reported there were specific rules regarding a RIF that needed to be followed. He said agents assigned to the detail would be provided a list of three offices for reassignment. They should list their preferences and we would try to get them their number one choice. The special officers would be advised of openings in the Secret Service for their positions and hopefully we could get them their first or second choice. McCann and Pettit were drawing up lists to present to the staff for their review. A schedule was being developed to interview all employees to find a new location for each of them.

McCann advised me that our special officer with the drinking problem had enrolled in a program through our Family Assistance Office. We didn't like it, but we both knew the program was designed to remove us from the flow of information. I was disappointed we were not involved. It would have been nice if we could have called ahead to his new assignment and given them a heads-up.

A few days after returning to San Clemente, while I was walking to the command post, President Nixon and Brennan came walking by. Nixon stopped and spoke with me about his move to New York City. In addition to needing office space and a new residence, Nixon told me he was searching for a new chief of staff and asked if I were interested. Nixon advised me that his chief of staff, Col. Jack Brennan, (ret.), would not be accompanying him on the move to New York City. Brennan, the Marine Corp Military Aide in the Nixon White House, had accompanied President Nixon to San Clemente after his resignation, where he was appointed chief of staff. I was walking Nixon back to his office when Nixon asked me to become his senior staff person replacing Brennan in New York City. I was flabbergasted and speechless at the offer to become Nixon's chief of staff. The question caught me totally off guard. It was flattering and I was honored by the confidence being expressed by Nixon. But I had not thought about leaving the Secret Service. I was not sure I was ready. I needed to think about it and told Nixon I would get back to him. I was very happy with my position in the Secret Service and was looking forward to reaching retirement in a little over five years.

I tried to weigh all the pluses and minuses that evening as I relaxed and listened to the surf pounding on the sandy beach below. At the time I knew I had been able to meet every challenge presented to me during my tenure in the Secret Service. The difficulty I was going through in my personal life was on my mind. I thought the challenges of running the Nixon detail were not anywhere near as demanding as running a new staff for a former president in New York City. I was not politically orientated and had never thought of that as a career direction. Taking a sip of my club soda I enjoyed the tingle in my mouth and thought, "Why me?" Why, after a month of interaction with a former president, would he ask me to take such an important staff position?

The next day I thanked Nixon for the confidence he expressed in offering me such an important position. I respectfully declined the opportunity to take the staff position and indicated I would work with whomever he found to make sure the move and stay in New York would go well. I have never looked back and second-guessed that decision.

❖ ❖ ❖

McCann and I were busy decommissioning the detail. The RIF was being implemented. McCann was coordinating everything and trying to find new assignments for our agents and special officers. Our special officers were given an option to receive transfers to existing operations at other former president details or they could bid on openings in Washington, D. C., or in field offices. Pettit and McCann told me they believed most of the officers would choose to discontinue working. For the agents leaving San Clemente, most would return to the field. McCann spoke with the Office of Investigations trying to develop several options for each agent. Overall most of the agents seemed to be happy with their new assignments. I could see many of the special officers who enjoyed the camaraderie between the officers and agents at San Clemente were not prepared to disrupt their lives and transfer to a new location. They lived a comfortable life in San Clemente on their military retirement and could easily find some other job if money were an issue. I knew McCann and Pettite were right in their assessment.

Meanwhile I was working with headquarters, setting up a Nixon Protective Division in New York City. The New York Field Office would provide temporary personnel until newly assigned agents could relocate to the area. Agents transferred from the New York Field Office and the Newark Field Office would report immediately since they would not need to relocate. Protective operations had given me a suggested size for the detail and lists of names. I had developed my own staffing level based on a formulation Boyette had taught me. Take the number of shifts per day times seven, times the number of agents per shift, divided by five. To that add the supervisors, drivers, and administrative staff. Boyette had used the formula during the campaigns, at PSD, and on the vice presidential detail. It was my desire to keep the level as small as possible and Protective Operations agreed with my smaller number. Headquarters was giving me an opportunity to develop my own level of security. I settled on a twenty-person detail based on Mrs. Nixon discontinuing protection. It turned out that she and President Nixon agreed to have a special officer driver and one agent accompany her when she left the residence.

Returning to Kansas City, I closed out my apartment before the Angels lost in the first round of the playoffs. I managed to sell my car and close out the apartment in less than a week. I thanked Cantrell for his support and returned to San Clemente.

McCann and I had settled into a routine and everything seemed to be moving forward nicely in San Clemente. I was really pleased with McCann's handling of the RIF. Under his control it was flowing smoothly and all personnel were happy with their reassignments. I could not have been more delighted when McCann told me he would accept the position as my assistant in New York City. I knew that sometimes I had difficulties dealing with people, while McCann, on the other hand, had a way with the troops and no question he would be a tremendous asset to the detail and me personally.

In one of our conversations before I left for Kansas City, President Nixon had talked about swimming in the Pacific Ocean and his love of the salt water. He said that he often swam into the month of October long after most people ceased swimming in the Pacific. I mentioned growing up swimming in Puget Sound and the Pacific off the Washington coast. Like him, I had often swum in Puget Sound and the Pacific into October, especially during the warm Indian summers of the Northwest.

Shortly after returning from Kansas City, President Nixon suggested to me late one afternoon that we go swimming at Camp Pendleton. He said he liked the privacy of Red Beach, which was just a short ride away. McCann told me that Red Beach was the main beach used for amphibious landing training for the Marine Corps. He said he would contact Camp Pendleton and see if the beach were available for a swim. It was a clear, warm October afternoon when the military police vehicle met us at the San Onofre gate off of Interstate 5 just south of San Clemente and led us over the dirt road to the well-known Red Beach.

Nixon, dressed in his swimming suit, a shirt, black walking shoes, and socks got out of the car with his towel in his hand and walked the short distance to the beach. Nixon told me the water should be in the high 60s. He said that our bodies would adjust quickly to the chilly water. Knowing the water temperature would be challenging to most people, I had already suggested to the other agents if they were more comfortable they could stand at the water line, prepared to go in if Nixon needed any assistance.

Meanwhile Nixon and I slowly walked out into the ocean letting our bodies adjust to the cool water. When we were in up to our waists he said, "Let's go," and we both dove into the water at the same time. It took a minute or two for my body to adjust to the cool temperature of the water. Using breast strokes, we swam out ten yards and treaded water for a few seconds.

Nixon began his normal routine at the beach, swimming laps for exercise. I swam out ten feet beyond him and paralleled him while he swam back and forth. I could see two agents positioned on the beach. After about fifteen minutes of exercising he did a few back strokes and then rested, floating on his back. When he rolled over and began treading water I was nearby. He talked about the stimulating plunge into the water and how much he enjoyed Red Beach. Nixon mentioned he was going to miss Red Beach when he moved to New York. He said the Atlantic was much colder off New York and New Jersey than the Pacific off of California and warmer water off of Florida. After several minutes talking about swimming in the sixty-plus degree water and how most Californians would not go into the Pacific without a wetsuit after the first of September, Nixon said, "Mike, let's get out."

Drying off with his towel Nixon put on his shirt, socks, and shoes and folded the towel to sit on during the return ride to his residence. On the short ride back to the compound he again mentioned to me an upcoming trip to New York City. He also told me that his friend Robert Abplanalp was trying to buy the New York Mets. Nixon said that he would be going to Yankee and Mets games next year. Arriving back at Casa Pacifica, Nixon once again told me how happy he was that Autry had won the Division championship. He laughed when I mentioned Bobby Grich.

STORIES FROM INSIDE THE PERIMETER

❖ ❖ ❖

On the international scene things in Iran had deteriorated dramatically since my spring of 1976 trip in support of Vice President Rockefeller. On November 4, 1979, the American Embassy in Teheran, Iran, was surrounded by a large group of Iranian students, several hundred of whom called themselves the Imam's Disciples. These radical Iranian students were at the embassy every day. They were part of a continuous, twenty-four-hour anti-American protest on the embassy grounds.

The Imam's Disciples protesters surprised the embassy by charging the embassy grounds in an attempt to take it over. Since the White House and State Department were not expecting a takeover, there were a limited number of Marine security guards assigned to the embassy. By the time key people realized the demonstrators were actually trying to take control of the embassy it was too late to stop them. There were simply not enough Marines available for the defense of the embassy when many of the Marines were reassigned from defensive positions to help others in the embassy with the destruction of classified documents and equipment. Attempts to thwart the seizure of the embassy with the limited number of Marines were unsuccessful.

Initially in excess of sixty hostages were taken and several days later, when the names of the hostages were printed in the paper, I discovered Gary Lee, former general administrative officer at the Interests Section in Syria, was one of the hostages. After a week or so several of the hostages had escaped and the hostage number was reduced to fifty-two, but still included Lee.

President Carter tried financial pressure and diplomatic initiatives but was unable to get the Iranians to negotiate with him. After the hostages were taken, the three networks led off their prime time evening news broadcasts identifying the number of days of the hostage crisis. Ted Koppel of ABC News started a new program called *America Held Hostage* that reported each night Monday through Friday the status of the hostages and background information. After the release of the hostages, Koppel's program changed its title to *Nightline*. The press and much of the country were obsessed with getting the hostages released. President Carter became extremely frustrated when all attempts to open negotiations on the release of the hostages with Iran failed.

❊ ❊ ❊

Brennan was working with us on the logistics for a trip by President and Mrs. Nixon to New York in early December. The former president was going to look at office space and visit a townhouse in Manhattan they were interested in purchasing. McCann passed on the information to agent Joe Gallo of the New York Field Office. Gallo was assigned as our man in New York to coordinate all visits and was responsible for the Nixon move to New York City. He was going to be one of the shift leaders once the Nixons permanently relocated. In the meantime he was responsible for all our logistics for the trips to New York and was responsible for setting up the permanent detail. I knew of Gallo but had never met him. He had worked a lot with Vice President Rockefeller's detail on visits to New York. The feedback from many agents I knew was highly favorable on Gallo.

President and Mrs. Nixon, accompanied by Brennan, made a short trip to New York City to look at office space and potential living quarters. Several private office buildings in mid-town Manhattan, including the Chrysler Building, were visited. Space in the Chrysler Building was especially attractive to Nixon. But it seemed to me that he was feeling pressure from his detractors in Congress and in the media to move into less expensive government space.

After Nixon's resignation from the presidency, there were some Congressional people, press, and others who wanted to see Nixon lose his government pension, his government-paid staff, and his Secret Service protection. Even though it was not a majority of people who wanted to see this happen, the ones that did were very vocal. This may have been the reason Nixon settled on the less expensive office space at the Jacob K. Javits Federal Building at 26 Federal Plaza located at the lower end of Manhattan. For us his choice meant we had secured underground parking, good employee and public access control with an x-ray machine available, and other law enforcement personnel nearby.

President and Mrs. Nixon selected a three-story townhouse at 142 East Sixty-fifth Street as their new home. The residence was located in the trendy Upper East Side of Manhattan on Sixty-fifth Street between Third and Second Avenues. It was less than three blocks from Central Park. The new residence would be about half a mile from their daughter Tricia. Nixon offered a small room off the entry area for our command post.

During the December visit we were driving from the townhouse to the Cox residence on East Seventieth off of Central Park. It was the middle of the day and the traffic was very heavy. I was considering the option of using our red light and possibly a siren to help us get through traffic. Before I could make the decision, Nixon said, "Mike, don't worry about traffic. I am going to live here and we have to get used to sitting in traffic and going slowly." I thought he had just read my mind. I was beginning to see a different Richard Nixon than the one portrayed in the media. The question in my mind was, was he reacting to his detractors or was he really concerned about disrupting traffic? I was beginning to see a very interesting and intriguing man. Richard Nixon was a very complex person to me and I knew only time would tell me who he really was.

With issues of office space and residence resolved, President and Mrs. Nixon returned to San Clemente. The Christmas holidays were spent in San Clemente with a couple of visits to the Eisenhower residence at Capistrano Beach, ten minutes north of San Clemente. David and Julie Eisenhower had one child at the time, Jennie, who was not yet a year old. On one afternoon visit everyone went to the El Adobe Mexican Restaurant on Camino Capistrano for lunch and on another one Julie hosted her mother and father at their beach house for dinner.

During the dinner visit to the Eisenhower residence I had a pleasant surprise. Lew Overbo, a boyhood friend and the other starting guard on our Lincoln High School basketball team in 1960 my junior year, was visiting a few houses away on Capistrano Beach. I was able to visit with him. Overbo was and continues today to be one of the most competitive athletes I have ever known. He challenged me to a foot race on the beach that evening, not knowing I was in exceptional shape. I routinely ran three miles in a little under eighteen minutes at least five times a week. Of course, I didn't let Overbo know this. When the race was over, for the first time in my life, I defeated him in a competitive endeavor. Overbo whined, moaned, and cried and to this day has trouble admitting in front of other friends the results of our race.

❖ ❖ ❖

The visit to Capistrano Beach and the time I spent with Overbo were a welcome break from office routine. McCann and I both knew that Gallo was doing an excellent job of getting everything set up before Nixon's scheduled arrival in New York City on January 20, 1980. Once the move was over and everything settled down, Gallo would assume his position as shift leader on our detail. Gallo turned out to be just like

McCann, with a good grasp of operations and logistics and, in addition, he knew New York like the back of his hand. Agent Gallo was excited about his role with the Nixon detail and was going to continue to be a big asset to us. He was sure we could operate with smaller numbers than those initially suggested by headquarters. Between McCann and Gallo, any reservations I was feeling about getting the detail set up quickly vanished.

On more than one occasion President Nixon told me he was anxious to get to New York City. He said he wanted to be closer to the "action." He sometimes lamented that the hour-and-a-half drive from San Diego or Los Angeles airports were a drawback in seeing people in San Clemente.

❖ ❖ ❖

One afternoon I was told by Pettit that Nixon wanted to talk with me. It surprised me a little. When I went into his office he told me he wanted Rebozo to come out from Florida and take a trip in a Winnebago with him to the Grand Canyon. Nixon mentioned the trip would take place in early January and would be a nostalgic trip retracing one he took while in college. He told me that while at Whittier College, he and a couple of his buddies made the same trip during spring break. I am sure he did not think about the changes that had take place in the intervening forty-five years. I knew at the time I would be on the East Coast preparing the New York detail and relocating in the New York area.

McCann and Pettit had pretty well resolved all the issues on the RIF and disposal of our equipment when I left to go back to Washington, D.C., for meetings at Secret Service headquarters. So I asked McCann to coordinate with Nixon and put together the Winnebago trip. McCann was advised Nixon planned on using a Winnebago owned by his friend Gavin Herbert. McCann knew Herbert, who was chairman and chief executive officer of Allergan, Inc., and a close personal friend of Nixon.

In fact, Herbert bought Nixon's residence, Casa Pacifica, when the president moved to the East Coast.

McCann arranged for Herbert's Winnebago to be brought to Casa Pacifica for Nixon to familiarize himself with before I left for the East Coast. After looking at the Winnebago, Nixon told McCann they were going to use it, but he was going to ride "shotgun," not McCann. When Nixon was through discussing the departure date and route with McCann he went to his office and called Rebozo, inviting him to join him on the trip. McCann continued working with Nixon on the itinerary and the cities for the overnights.

By the time I left for Washington, the final details of the adventure to the Grand Canyon had been completed by McCann and Pettite. I wished McCann good luck and told him I would meet him in New York later.

My meetings at headquarters went well. I had a chance to go over the list of agents who were being reassigned to the Nixon detail. Some of the agents I knew or had heard of during the Rockefeller detail visits to New York City. We agreed on using agents from the New York Field Office to fill in until agents from outside the New York and New Jersey area had a chance to relocate into the area. It was agreed that a two-man intelligence team from New York would be assigned to Nixon for the first thirty days. I was pleased to be working with some of the people who had been responsible for my transfer to Kansas City. They were anxious to get Nixon settled in New York and there didn't seem to be any hard feelings.

I had been going through a divorce since leaving Washington, and it was finalized in early December 1979. After my meetings at headquarters were through, I married Stacy Parrot, who was working on the staff of Vice President Mondale. We went on a honeymoon to Williamsburg, Virginia, and then we went to northern New Jersey to find a place to live. We settled on a three-bedroom house in Ridgewood. After we got settled, Stacy returned to northern Virginia to be with her mother, who had been diagnosed with breast cancer.

When I next spoke with McCann in New York I asked how the trip went. He mentioned that at one point before they left on the trip he told Nixon a storm would be hitting one of the areas they were going to visit. Nixon's response to McCann was, "Well, just drive around it." McCann laughed as he said he advised Nixon that if they were flying they could go around it but there was no avoiding the storm in a motor home.

He said that when Nixon and Rebozo got into the Winnebago, Nixon had several bottles of very good wine that he put in one of the cupboards. Nixon then moved into the right front seat and said to McCann, "Okay, let's go." He said that Nixon relished riding "shotgun." Agent McCann said he started out driving the vehicle and the first stop turned out to be unscheduled at a K-Mart just outside of Indio, California. It seems Nixon asked Rebozo to select and open a bottle of wine, so they could have a glass. The problem began, McCann said, when Rebozo tried to use plastic glasses for the wine. Nixon apparently told Rebozo there was no way he would drink wine as good as the bottles he had brought on board from a plastic cup. According to McCann, Nixon directed him to find a place where they could buy real glasses for the wine.

McCann said they pulled into the parking lot of a K-Mart just down the highway near Indio. After they parked, Nixon asked Rebozo to go into the store while he walked around the lot. Nixon had spied a small trailer for a local radio station broadcasting from the parking lot. With McCann in tow, he walked to the trailer and spoke to the broadcaster, who announced to his listeners that Richard Nixon was in the parking lot. McCann said by the time Rebozo got back with the glasses a traffic jam was created as the lot filled up with people looking for the president. Nixon gave a lot of autographs before he continued on to the Grand Canyon.

Special officer Dick Maughn was on the trip to assist with the driving. Early in the trip McCann needed information about the route. He told me he turned toward the back of the Winnebego to address Maughn. McCann said he yelled, "Hey, Dick, what route do we take next?" According to McCann, Nixon responded immediately, "What did you say?" McCann said he was more careful when addressing Maughn after that. The trip went well but was shortened due to bad weather.

McCann said when Nixon got back to Casa Pacifica almost all of their household and office files had been packed by his staff. He told me Carl Howell, who worked for the Nixon office, would be traveling to New York City ahead of the moving vans to assist with the unpacking of both the office and household furniture. McCann said he thought Nixon and Rebozo had a really good time.

President and Mrs. Nixon traveled to New York City via commercial aircraft. When he landed at JFK Airport, a large contingent of press was on-hand. In addition to the regular news media a relatively new, all news cable network, CNN, assigned a cameraman with a sound man to cover the arrival. The CNN crew followed the motorcade and parked outside of Nixon's new residence. They managed to get several interviews over the first few days.

Gallo had two New York intelligence agents at the command post on the ground floor of Nixon's residence. They were both somewhat inexperienced but we knew that would not be a problem. We had plenty of experienced agents on the detail that could assist with intelligence issues.

❖ ❖ ❖

People would come by the house hoping to see the former president. When the limousine was out front curious onlookers stood around waiting to see if Nixon would come out of the house. There was one individual in particular that kept hanging around across the street who exhibited abnormal behavior. His behavior led me to tell the ID to find out who he was and get rid of him while the president and Mrs. Nixon were having lunch at their daughter's.

When I arrived back with President and Mrs. Nixon from their lunch with their daughter I noticed the person was still standing across the street. Inside the command post I pointed to the camera aimed at the street outside and asked the ID team how come the loiterer was still there. The agents told me they interviewed him and ran a name check. I was advised the person had a CO-2 file. People who come to the attention of the Secret Service due to letters they have written, visits to locations where one of the people the Secret Service protects is visiting or living, or anyone who makes threats against any of the people the Secret Service protects are given a file number. The files begin with the prefix CO-2 and people who have that file are commonly referred to in the Secret Service as a CO-2. Our agents mentioned the person across the street was not dangerous. They told me they had asked him to leave but he refused. When they asked me, "What can we do?" I got up, left the command post, and walked across the street, aware that the ID agents in the command post were watching. Approaching the person, I leaned forward and sternly whispered so he was the only one who could hear me, "Get the fuck out of here."

Startled, he jumped back and said, "I don't have to leave and you can't make me."

Responding immediately in the hushed tone, I offered, "Either you get the f--k out of here or I will have you committed to Bellevue Hospital."

Arrogantly he said, "You can't commit me. I will be released right away."

Purposely stepping closer to intimidate him by violating his space, I moved my face several inches from his. I wanted to be in his face, I wanted him to feel the pressure as I quietly but forcefully said, "I can have you committed for either a week or a thirty-day observation and you know it. Now get out of here and don't come back."

Quickly turning to leave he said over his shoulder, "Yes sir, Captain."

Returning to the command post I sat down without saying a word. For several minutes it was quiet, and then one of the ID agents asked me what I had said. I explained that I was sure the CO-2 understood I had the authority to commit him, and once I made the threat to do so, it convinced him to leave. An interesting side note is he never came back.

❖ ❖ ❖

With the help of the New York Field Office, the Nixon detail was able to secure office space in the World Trade Center complex. We were given space in the Customs House, the same location as the field office but one floor above them on the eighth floor. Initially we set up our administrative operations in the Westbury Hotel on Sixty-ninth Street, between Fifth and Sixth Avenues, while the space at the Customs House was made ready for us. When we moved into the World Trade Center complex my corner office gave me a spectacular view of the Statue of Liberty and Ellis Island. Sitting at my desk and looking out the window at the Statue of Liberty was a special treat. At the time the lots across the street between the World Trade Center and the Hudson River were vacant. I could see Ellis Island and New Jersey. If I stood right at the window I could see the twin towers of the World Trade Center.

It took several months for the new detail to get all permanent agents on board and get settled into a routine. I was lucky when it was decided to have a special officer assigned to drive Mrs. Nixon. We got John Kierans, who knew New York City like the back of his hand. President Nixon was getting used to his new staff, but Brennan was still trying to recruit a new chief of staff. During the initial months Nixon was putting the finishing touches on his newest book, *The Real War*.

❖ ❖ ❖

Richard Nixon was not a mechanically inclined person. Once during the unpacking process he told me how talented Carl Howell was. He said Howell assembled furniture and installed the electrical equipment. Nixon told me, "He can even put in the new light bulbs." Howell was one of those nice guys who seemed to be a "Jack of all trades." Nixon was lucky to have him. But Howell decided to return to California once the unpacking was completed and things settled down.

I was surprised one Monday morning a few weeks after Howell left when McCann briefed me on an alarm problem over the weekend. He said that the alarm from the door of the elevator mechanical room on the roof had sounded in the command post. McCann said he and agent Frank Murphy immediately responded. When they got to the roof they were amazed to see Nixon with a pair of pliers in one hand and a screwdriver in the other trying to get into the elevator mechanical room. McCann, with a chuckle in his voice, said, "Mike, how can someone who is amazed that Carl Howell could screw in light bulbs fix a problem with the elevator motor?"

McCann chuckled as he said he told the former president to stay away from the cover over the elevator motor. He said once he and agent

Murphy escorted Nixon to his den he told him he would call the elevator repair people to fix the problem.

※ ※ ※

Nixon seemed energized by the move to New York City. He did not avoid people or the press. New Yorkers and others would regularly stop Nixon on the street, in the elevator, in a restaurant, or store to shake hands, say hello, or ask for an autograph. Nixon would rise early and go out for a walk before departing at 6 a.m. for his 26 Federal Plaza office. New York City was referred to as the "The city that never sleeps" in the opening dialogue of the old television series, "Naked City." New York was coming alive at 5 a.m. as Nixon strolled down Lexington Avenue, Sixty-fifth Street, and other avenues and streets in the area around his residence. Sanitation workers were beginning their morning rounds and some would yell and wave at him. Emergency vehicles would speed by, sometimes with red lights flashing and sirens wailing. People passing him that were headed for the subway and bus stops often took time to say hello. Some police vehicles would go speeding down the street and others would slowly cruise by. Uniformed cops would pay respect by acknowledging the former president. I got a sense that many New Yorkers were pleased to have a former president living there.

There were two men, father and son, who showed up early quite often the first month to catch Nixon before he departed for his office. They had Nixon memorabilia they would ask him to sign for them. The men were interviewed by the midnight shift and determined not to be a threat. However, the shift supervisor had found out they were from Monroe, New York, thirty minutes away and had a souvenir shop. After numerous requests did not convince them to stop coming, I spoke with

Nixon before he exited the house. After telling him about the two I asked that he avoid them and go directly to the limousine. He said okay and stepped out the door. Seeing the two standing with pictures in their hands, Nixon walked directly over to the two and asked, "Can I sign those for you?"

I smiled and shook my head as I put the former president in the back of the limousine. Quietly I radioed the agent at the front post and asked him to pass on to the two individuals that this would be their last day of autographs at the house. They were told in the future to send or bring things to be autographed to Nixon's office at 26 Federal Plaza in lower Manhattan.

❖ ❖ ❖

Laurence Rockefeller, brother of former Governor Nelson Rockefeller, lived in the townhouse next door to Nixon. Shortly after Nixon moved into his new residence an elderly lady began to hang out in front of the Rockefeller house. We had our New York Field Office intelligence agent interview her and conduct a name check. The name check was negative and the interview revealed the woman indicated she was homeless and thought she was married to Rockefeller. She was nice enough and friendly to anyone who would talk to her. Some of the agents began greeting her as Mrs. Rockefeller. One day she told one of the agents she was going to have a moving truck bring her goods to the townhouse. Of course, no one believed her, especially since we thought she was homeless. A moving truck arrived the next day with her household goods. The New York Police Department was notified by our ID agent and the woman was committed to Bellevue that day for observation. She never returned.

❖ ❖ ❖

President and Mrs. Nixon would frequently take the short drive to East Seventieth Street to visit with daughter Tricia Cox and her family. On occasions their daughter would walk to their Sixty-fifth Street townhouse pushing her son Christopher in the stroller for lunch or just to visit with her parents. President and Mrs. Nixon seemed pleased to be close to their family.

❊ ❊ ❊

Nixon mentioned to me before he left San Clemente that he was going to re-open the travel routes to Key Biscayne, Florida, and Walker's Cay, Bahamas. He made a trip to Key Biscayne for a long weekend visit to Rebozo during the first month in New York City. Nixon flew to Miami on an Eastern Airlines flight one Friday around two in the afternoon. Our Miami Field Office took care of the advance security arrangements and met us ramp-side with a motorcade. Nixon and Rebozo were driven to Cye's Rivergate Restaurant in downtown Miami for dinner. It was one of the top restaurants in Miami. The owner, Cye Mandel, a good friend of Rebozo and Nixon, was originally from New York and had grown up in his parents' restaurant business in the New York Catskills. Mandel had been a longtime friend with the flamboyant and controversial Jimmy the Greek, who at the time was a sports color commentator on the CBS program *The NFL Today*. The Greek and other sports announcers often came into Cye's when they were in town covering a Miami Dolphins football game.

When Mandel seated Nixon and Rebozo in the restaurant he had a table set aside nearby for four of the accompanying Secret Service agents. A special treat that most of the agents enjoyed at Cye's Rivergate were the extra-large stone crab claws. I spoke with Mandel about our bill when the waiter did not present one. He refused to charge our agents for their meals. I urged the agents to leave a large gratuity.

Nixon stayed with Rebozo at his Key Biscayne residence. Our detail stayed at the nearby Key Biscayne Hotel just like the old days. The two of them went for a ride on Rebozo's boat and anchored in Biscayne Bay. The old Key Biscayne presidential compound where Rebozo lived had changed dramatically. The barriers controlling the traffic by the houses were no longer there. The wrought iron fence that stretched from Rebozo's residence past the two Nixon houses and the Secret Service house to the helicopter pad was gone. The Secret Service house and the two Nixon homes had been torn down, replaced by a very large and elegant two-story home. Rebozo told me the new house was owned by a Columbian and was used periodically for party scenes in the television series *Miami Vice.*

Between driving around the area and staying at the Key Biscayne Hotel I relived many wonderful memories. I was aware Rebozo was buying a new residence at a private community, Ocean Reef, an hour away near Key Largo in the Florida Keys. He told me he was looking forward to moving to the new location. Rebozo said he was going to sell his Key Biscayne property once he moved and build a new home on the other side of the helicopter pad.

Rebozo and Nixon ate in at Rebozo's house the second night and Rebozo cooked. He made his famous Cuban black beans and rice and served it with fresh fish and a salad. Nixon was delighted since he had not eaten Rebozo's cooking for quite some time.

The visit was very relaxing and Nixon got a good feel for the new Key Biscayne. It had been interesting dealing with Nixon and Rebozo during the visit. Often each wanted to defer to the other on the daily schedule. Both wanted to do what the other wanted. Nixon would tell me to check with Rebozo on the schedule and when I did, Rebozo would first tell me if there were any previous commitments. He would then ask, "Well, what does the president want to do?" In the end I would listen to both of them and then put their schedule together. They were both easy to please.

❖ ❖ ❖

Back in New York things were beginning to settle down. About a week after our return, agent Marty Venker mentioned one Monday morning that he had received a phone call from the White House switchboard on Sunday. He said the switchboard wanted to get President Nixon's private home phone number. He told me he was told by the operator that President Carter wanted to talk with President Nixon. Venker said he told the operator he would check with Nixon and get back to them. According to Venker, when he told Nixon about the call and the request for his phone numbers, Nixon calmly advised him to have the White House switchboard call his office the next day for his home phone numbers. Could it be the shabby treatment Nixon had been receiving going through immigration and customs was coming home to roost?

❖ ❖ ❖

It took Abplanalp a little time to get his schedule worked out so he could host his two friends at his renowned bill-fishing Island, Walker's Cay, located in the Abaco chain of islands in Northern Bahamas. Walker's Cay, with a small two-story hotel, several cabañas, a conference center, a full-service eighty-boat marina, a store with an apartment above it, and a restaurant in the marina along with a dive operation, was the jewel of the islands that Abplanalp had secured in a ninety-nine-year lease from the Bahamian government in 1966. Walker's, with a small landing strip, could easily accommodate propeller-driven planes and some small jets. A ten-minute walk from the hotel was a beautiful white sand beach for swimming or visitors could swim in one of the two pools near the check-in building with a restaurant, bar, and souvenir shop.

On our first trip to Walker's Cay I flew out of the Walker's Cay Airlines terminal at the Fort Lauderdale Airport with Nixon, Abpalnap, and Rebozo. We were on Abplanalp's private Grumman Mallard seaplane. It landed in the water off Walker's Cay and used the seaplane ramp to taxi to the small Bahamian customs building at the top of the ramp. The white plane with the red and blue trim was immediately greeted by the Bahamian customs agent and Abplanalp's daughter Maria, who was the manager of the facility. After clearing customs, Nixon decided not to get into the golf cart and instead walked the short distance to the marina. The former president was greeted by a large group of guests from the hotel at the marina before our party boarded Abplanalp's private yacht, the Sea Lion. The short boat ride to his secluded, private island, Baby Grand, took less than thirty minutes.

Miami ID agent John Golden and I stayed with Nixon on Baby Grand in a small two-bedroom cabaña near Mermaid Beach. The rest of the agents stayed at the hotel on Walker's. Two shift agents were present on the island with Nixon around the clock, making the relief by boat from Walker's Cay. One detail agent and the Miami advance agent maintained the command post at the Walker's Cay Hotel.

The first morning after breakfast I accompanied Nixon, Abplanalp, and Rebozo on a walk to Mermaid Beach. One of the two shift agents walked with us. Nixon engaged me in some general conversation, telling me about the coral island and the white sand beaches. He mentioned the upcoming bridge we would cross over on our way to the beautiful Mermaid Beach. After passing the helicopter landing area, Nixon said that Abplanalp had rebuilt the bridge since the White House days.

Nixon chuckled as he said Abplanalp had named it "Chappaquiddick Bridge." I knew the history about Chappaquiddick Island, where late on the night of July 19, 1969, Senator Ted Kennedy (D-Mass) was accompanied by Mary Jo Kopechne, and drove off the Dirk Road Bridge into the water. The car overturned and sank to the bottom of Poucha Pond. Kennedy got out of the car and saved himself but his passenger, Mary Jo Kopechne, was unable to get out and died in the car at the bottom of the pond.

Crossing the bridge, we continued on the sandy/coral road and strolled past the cabaña where Golden and I were staying as the road turned to the left. Nixon led us straight ahead on the path through the sea grapes and sea oats to the white sands and blue water of Mermaid Beach. Everyone walked along the water to the far end of the beach, where an elevated cabaña with open sides was located. Just as he had done at Red Beach, Nixon took off his shoes, socks, and shirt, placing them neatly on the sand near the stairs of the cabaña along with his towel.

Heading toward the beach Nixon yelled back to Abplanalp and Rebozo, telling them they should go into the water. Without delay Nixon walked into the warm water, dove in, and swam out to where it was over his head. Stopping, he began to tread water, looking back to see where his friends were. Nixon then swam parallel to the beach for ten to fifteen minutes. In a ritual I would get used to over the next ten years; he rolled onto his back and rested for a few minutes. He then did the elementary back stroke for fifty yards, completing his exercise. Nixon then spent another ten minutes in the water floating, treading water, and commenting to me about the weather, the swim, and the beauty of

Mermaid beach. Nixon told me he believed this was the most beautiful beach he had ever seen.

Rebozo and Abplanalp had walked a short distance when Rebozo dove into the water. Abplanalp watched Nixon and Rebozo for a minute or two and walked to the cabaña. Rebozo swam for a couple of minutes, then got out of the water and joined Abplanalp.

After his swim, Nixon walked to the cabaña and picked up his towel. Putting it over his shoulders he headed off, strolling toward the far end of the half-moon beach. This was his private time. He had not asked anyone to join him. When he got back he put on his shoes and shirt before joining Abplanalp and Rebozo in one of the chairs on the cabaña. The three of them chatted for a while before walking back to the house.

One of the boating excursions took us a mile or so offshore in the Sea Lion, where we anchored close to an artificial reef. The anchor was lowered and a chum bag with a frozen chunk of ground seafood scraps was put in the water to attract fish. Nixon, Abplanalp, agent Golden, and I all put a line in the water. Sitting in a chair Nixon caught a strawberry snapper. After the fish was in the boat he announced he was going inside the air-conditioned cabin. Nixon seemed out of place when he was sitting in the chair, methodically reeling in his fish. He didn't seem to relax and enjoy fishing. Abplanalp, Golden, and I caught five or six yellowtail snapper each. A couple of mutton snapper and a grouper were also reeled in and put in the cooler. The fish were filleted by the crew on the ride back to Baby Grand.

Abplanalp had his chef, Bruno Brandenberger, brought over from the hotel to cook dinner. Chef Bruno was from Switzerland, as was Abplanalp's father. Chef Bruno had worked at the Cairo Hilton in Egypt before coming to the United States to work for Abplanalp. I met the chef when he came into the kitchen. I wanted to watch him prepare the dinner. I had grown up on Washington State fish and shellfish. I was anxious to learn new things about food preparation. Chef Bruno prepped his vegetables and salad and readied seasoned flour and a mixture of two-thirds grey mustard and one-third Worcestershire sauce for the fish. He made a vinaigrette dressing of red wine and tossed the salad. While the salad was being served he began preparing the shredded carrots, green beans in a butter and lemon sauce, and boiled new potatoes. Lightly dredging the yellowtail fillets in the seasoned flour, the chef smeared both sides of the fillets with the mustard mixture. His timing was impeccable as he plated the vegetables as the empty salad plates were returned to the kitchen. Chef Bruno placed a piece of yellowtail on each plate like Picasso finishing a painting.

I had been fascinated watching the chef glide his 375-plus pound body around the kitchen. When the meal was served he had seen my interest in cooking and asked me if I would like to assist him by doing some prep work the next evening. For me it was the first of many times in the kitchen with Chef Bruno.

The weather at Walker's Cay was usually very warm in the season and in the summer months it could be uncomfortably hot. I was aware Walker's Cay had been hit on more than one occasion by a hurricane. Nixon spent most of his time in the air-conditioned house visiting with his friends or reading and writing. He would come out onto the patio with the small pool and enjoy the view from their perch on top of the hill.

Agent Golden and I stayed in the small two-bedroom cabaña near Mermaid Beach. There was no television or radio in the cabaña. Sitting on the deck as the sun slowly sank into the blue water we could hear the lapping of the waves as they rolled onto the beach. I was amazed by the sounds that could be heard on the isolated island. Insects clicked, hummed, and buzzed; the sea oats and sea grape several yards away rubbed against each other as the light breeze blew on shore. The sky was clear and Golden and I could see a sky full of bright shining stars in the darkness

Our agents on Walker's Cay staying in the hotel had two pools, one saltwater and one freshwater. The food at the restaurant was excellent and the bar friendly. The agents had brought Marie Abplanalp a gift case of Michelob beer, which was not available on the island. She treated them very well in return. It was a very relaxing time for the agents. By the time we departed everyone seemed to have their batteries recharged and had either a tan or sunburn. The Miami Field Office made arrangements with the Miami Airport Police and Eastern Airlines for us to drive ramp-side to catch our commercial flight.

❖ ❖ ❖

In New York Nixon kept busy with his writings and making a few public appearances. He made a short trip to Abidjan, Ivory Coast, to visit with his old friend President Houphouët-Boigny. Nixon had developed a relationship with the Ivory Coast president during his travels as Eisenhower's vice president in the mid-1950s and continued seeing him over the years. In fact, he invited the Ivory Coast president to the White House when he was president. Chief of Staff Brennan accompanied Nixon on the trip.

After our arrival at the Abidjan Airport, Nixon was driven to the presidential compound. As our motorcade crossed a small bridge over the moat surrounding the presidential residence, I could see crocodiles sunning themselves in the water and along the banks. I am not sure exactly what I thought I would see going through the gate, but it was not the elegance of the huge two-story residence.

We unpacked and got settled in our rooms when Nixon was invited to take a tour of the grounds by President Boigny. The trees, flowers, shrubs, and other landscaping along with the groomed lawn were impressive. When the walk ended Nixon asked President Boigny where our agents were staying. The president said they were well taken care of and pointed out the comfortable-looking building where they were being housed.

The compound looked as if it were only a couple of years old. Besides the beautiful landscape the residence was filled with antiques and art work. In my room on the second floor I noticed a pair of small gold elephant statues being used as bookends on top of a bookcase. When I went to pick up one of the elephants I had to use both hands. That was when I realized they were solid gold. It looked as if a considerable amount of money had been spent on the lavish compound.

The three-day visit to Abidjan was short but included a ride through the downtown area and the neighborhoods near the presidential residence. Two dinners and a meeting with President Boigny completed the schedule.

The first afternoon several people came to the center of the bridge over the moat with two chickens. They were accompanied by a group of locals. We had been alerted by the security force that this was a daily ritual. The two chickens were going to be thrown into the moat and people would be betting on how long they would survive. None of us participated in the betting but we observed the process from our end of the bridge.

It was interesting for me to learn some of the history of the Ivory Coast, which became a French protectorate in the 1840s. It gained its independence in 1960 after over one hundred years of French influence. The Ivory Coast developed a sound governmental infrastructure along with good schools, paved roads, and a stable political situation, thanks to the French. They also adopted French as their official language.

On the return to JFK Airport, Brennan told me he was worried about getting a gift through customs that had been given to Nixon by President Boigny. After the disgraceful custom fiasco I had witnessed in Anchorage I told Brennan to give the gift to me and I would put it in my carry-on bag. I was sure my bag would not be checked since we had courtesy of the port. When we got back to Nixon's townhouse I gave the package to Brennan. He opened a beautiful teak box that had a piece of an ivory tusk in it. The tusk had a face carved into it and was covered with gold leaf.

❖ ❖ ❖

Back in New York City Nixon got right back into his routine. His book was done and the 1980 presidential campaign was capturing his interest. We had been back for a couple of weeks when McCann said agent Venker had a woman pounding on the front door over the weekend. He told McCann she was yelling and screaming about the Vietnam War. Venker said when he carefully opened the front door she tried to push her way into the residence. McCann told me Venker said she continued to rant and rave incoherently about the war. Venker did manage to get her to leave. Later, according to Venker, Nixon asked him about the commotion at the front door. Venker told him a woman was beating on the door shouting about the Vietnam War. According to McCann, Nixon asked Venker, "Was she for it or against it?"

CHAPTER FOUR

RICHARD NIXON
1980 - 1986

RICHARD NIXON 1980 - 1986

Nixon had a book tour scheduled in April 1980 to Germany and England ahead of the May release of his new book, *The Real War*. Col. Jack Brennan, who was still trying to find a new chief of staff, was scheduled to accompany Nixon on the trip. He told me he had a meeting with Nixon at the residence prior to going to JFK Airport for the departure. When I told him I would be going out to the airport separately from Nixon, Brennan suggested we meet at Nixon's and go to JFK together. Since it was a warm April day and the command post was fairly small I waited for him outside on the sidewalk.

When Brennan came out of the house after the meeting, he was animated and mentioned he needed to make a quick telephone call. We walked together to the phone booth at the corner of East Sixty-fifth Street and Third Avenue. While we walked, Brennan told me he had spoken by phone to Dan Rather of CBS in Nixon's den about an exclusive interview with President Nixon. He said Nixon wanted the interview to be live or taped to time so that the taping could not be edited ahead of the CBS broadcast. Brennan said Rather responded that he could not make the decision alone and needed to "kick it upstairs." According to Brennan, Rather said he would get back to him the next day. He said Nixon told him if Rather could not make the decision he should call Barbara Walters at ABC and offer her the interview with the same caveats.

Brennan dialed Walter's number at the pay phone and got her on the line. I could hear him advising her of the opportunity for the exclusive interview. He mentioned the restrictions to her without telling her about his previous conversation with Rather. Brennan suggested to

Walters the interview could be a "special or on a show like *20/20*." He advised her he was leaving on a trip overseas with Nixon and needed an answer in the next two hours before Nixon departed on his European book tour. Brennan said he would call her again after he got to JFK Airport before he boarded the plane.

We hailed a taxi and went to the airline VIP room to await Nixon's arrival. After settling down and getting some coffee, Brennan went to call Walters and confirm the interview as it had been outlined to her earlier. When Brennan returned he had a smile on his face and said to me he thought the interview would be live on ABC's program *20/20*. Nixon seemed pleased when his chief of staff briefed him on the interview on his arrival at the airport.

When our commercial flight landed in Germany at the Frankfurt Airport, it received a routine escort by an armored vehicle from the runway to the gate. Getting off the plane I could see machine gun-toting uniformed militia around the exterior of the aircraft. Inside the airport terminal there were similarly heavily armed militia patrolling and on fixed posts. Prior to our departure we were advised we could bring our handguns and machine guns with us. The German police provided a marked lead car and a security vehicle to escort our cars. The promotional visit to Germany went well as Nixon publicized his new book and met with various German leaders. He seemed to bask in a public that recognized him and anxiously sought his autograph, picture, and a handshake.

The visit to London began on April 24. England had security at the airport similar to that in Germany. An armored vehicle met our commercial aircraft shortly after it landed and escorted it to the gate. Two heavily armed militias were posted on either side of our flight at the gate. Inside the arrival area and throughout the terminal we saw armed militia carrying machine guns patrolling. Unlike Germany, however, Scotland Yard would not allow us to bring any weapons into their country. They did provide two detectives to accompany Nixon. One detective rode in the follow-up car and the other I asked to ride in the front seat of the limousine, while I rode in the jump seat in the rear. The situation with Scotland Yard was strained but not with the detectives as they were just following orders. I did not give my weapon to Scotland Yard when I surrendered the other agents' guns. I knew Nixon and I would not have to go through the magnetometers. I was aware that if I got caught with my weapon in London it would create an international incident. I was very much aware headquarters disagreed with the ban on bringing guns into England. It had been indicated to me that I should carry my gun.

Nixon was staying at the Hyde Park Hotel on Knightsbridge, across the street from Hyde Park. He was scheduled to give a speech, meet government officials, and have promotional meetings about his book. He was also going to meet his friend, Parliament member Jonathan Aitken.

During the afternoon of April 25, I received a call from the Secret Service Intelligence Division duty desk agent. I was requested to pass on to President Nixon information about a failed rescue mission in Iran that had occurred earlier that morning. The information included the following: The helicopters en route to a gathering site for the rescue mission at the U. S. Embassy were caught in a sandstorm but made it to the secret airstrip in the Iranian desert. One helicopter could not continue the mission because of mechanical problems due to the storm. The rescue mission had to be aborted due to the loss of the one helicopter. At the secret airstrip were several C-130 aircraft with Special Forces and equipment to support the rescue mission. A disaster ensued after the mission was aborted, when one of the departing helicopters clipped the tail of one of the C-130 aircraft, causing the chopper to crash. All eight servicemen aboard the helicopter were killed and the C-130 was destroyed.

As I briefed President Nixon in his suite it was obvious to me he was becoming upset. Grimacing and slowly moving his head back and forth, he listened intently as I relayed the information on the failed mission and the death of eight of our troops. When I was finished his head was bowed and he thanked me for the briefing. Turning, he walked away shaking his head. I could hear him say to no one in particular, "Why didn't Carter listen to them?"

When the press reports came out later about the mission it was reported that President Carter had personally been involved in the planning of the rescue mission. It was alleged in the media that Carter had cut back by one the number of helicopters to be used in the mission. As a result of that cutback, some in the media suggested when one of the helicopters could not continue the rescue mission due to the sandstorm there was no back-up helicopter and the mission needed to be aborted.

"Why didn't Carter listen to the military?" echoed in my head as I read articles and watched news report about the failed mission. I wondered how Nixon knew President Carter had cut back one of the helicopters. Did he have an advance briefing on the mission from the White House? Or did he know from one of his sources in the military or CIA? Or was it an instinctive guess?

The visit to England was going smoothly in spite of everyone's frustrations due to the failed hostage rescue mission. Walking across the street and jogging through Hyde Park was a treat for me. I had a routine of trying to jog in every city where we spent a night.

Nixon took daily walks, mostly on the paths in and around Hyde Park. On April 30 Nixon set out on his normal morning walk accompanied on foot by two midnight shift agents. Since they planned to only walk in the park they did not take a car with them. On this day, once outside, Nixon decided to walk across the park, suggesting to the agents they look at the neighborhood on the other side of the park. When I reported to the security room at 7:30 a.m. the day shift was relieving the midnight shift. It seemed a problem had developed during the walk. Once they got into the residential area on the other side of the park, the streets did not have a north/south and east/west grid. Nixon had been on his walk for over an hour and a half and one of the agents was talking with the command post agent. The agent was having a difficult time explaining exactly where they were. Using the map in the command post the day shift was trying to plot a route to pick them up.

The day shift agreed to bring the limousine and follow-up car to pick up Nixon and the agents. The problem was the day shift was still trying to identify exactly where the walking party was. After consulting a map the shift leader decided to take two cars to pick up everyone.

I decided to let the working shifts work out the problem and left the command post. I was going to chat with the bobby in the hallway outside the suite. We had been talking for several minutes when all of a sudden his radio, which periodically cracked with static, came alive. One of his colleagues began broadcasting to Scotland Yard that masked terrorists were taking over the Iranian Embassy. The uniformed officer turned up his radio as he told me the embassy building was very near, down the road from us. As we both listened, information continued to be provided on the situation at the nearby Iranian Embassy. The reports over the radio gave no mention of the exact number of terrorists; however, it was reported the terrorists had taken a gun and radio from the bobby on the security post at the embassy. It became clear from the broadcasts that Scotland Yard was in the process of sending in reinforcements to try to contain the incident. Our bobby advised me that Nixon should not come back to the hotel until the situation at the embassy was stabilized.

Immediately, I radioed the follow-up car to determine the location of Nixon and the cars. The shift leader reported they would meet Nixon shortly. He was instructed to take Nixon for a ride once they hooked up with him. It was mentioned there were problems in the area of our hotel and to stay on the other side of Hyde Park until further notice. Once the message was passed on, I called our Intelligence Division, Foreign Intelligence Branch. Speaking with agent Jack Renwick, I advised him of the developing situation at the Iranian Embassy, including the information on the gun and radio. He was advised of the status of Nixon and the decision to delay his return to the hotel. It was agreed that the information should be passed on to Director Knight and all assistant directors. I called the office of assistant director, Protective Operations, in Washington and notified Special Agent-in-Charge John Simpson of my conversation with Renwick.

Within thirty minutes of the seizure of the embassy the perimeter of the embassy was secured by Scotland Yard. It turned out there were six terrorists and twenty-six hostages. Once the perimeter was secured and additional police were sent to our hotel, the day shift was directed to return Nixon to the hotel. The next day, as scheduled, we returned to New York. On the flight home I read an article in the newspaper concerning the developments in Iran and London. I thought to myself that I was living history.

❖ ❖ ❖

Upon our return to the United States, I spoke to Renwick, who advised me of his conversation with his CIA contact soon after we spoke. He told his contact all the information concerning the hostage situation at the Iranian Embassy in downtown London. Renwick said his contact initially thought he was kidding because the CIA had no information on the situation in London. When the contact understood it was real time information he wanted Renwick to tell him the source. The CIA contact found it incredible that Renwick would have real time information on this type of incident. Agent Renwick laughed, relishing the idea of scooping his contact on such an important international incident.

Over the first few days five hostages were released. On May 5 the Iranian terrorists killed the embassy press attaché, Abbas Lavasani, and threw his body outside. With the death of the attaché a special unit of the British SAS executed a rescue mission. Five of the six terrorists were killed during the assault and the terrorists killed another hostage. However, the remaining nineteen hostages were rescued.

❖ ❖ ❖

Meanwhile in New York, Brennan was working to finalize the *20/20* interview with Barbara Walters. The president's staff was also scheduling other appearances and interviews to promote Nixon's new book. I was becoming more comfortable as our detail personnel situation had stabilized and the routine morning walks and motorcades to the office were proceeding without any problems.

Agent Gallo, working on office space and other logistical issues, did a great job of arranging overnight secured parking for the limousine in a nearby garage managed by another federal agency. The follow-up car was kept on the street in front of Nixon's house overnight in the event of an emergency. Gallo had obtained space for our new administrative office in the Customs House located inside the World Trade Center complex. He was able to use his contacts with the New York Field Office, which was in the same building, to help secure our lease.

Gallo was being kept on the administrative staff until all the detail agents were on board and the administrative office at the World

Trade Center was opened for business. In April, not too long before he was scheduled to take over supervision of one of the shifts, he had an accident on the way home. He was traveling to his Westchester County residence in a government car that was hit by a sack of sand or small stones after he went under an overpass. The sack was being used at a construction site on the overpass. Fortunately, he was not hurt, only shook up. After two to three weeks Gallo, however, was experiencing pain in his lower neck. An examination by his doctor determined he had some damage to his spine from the accident and it was causing the problem. Gallo told me his doctor wanted to try and solve the problem without surgery. After five days in the hospital he was given a massive dose of cortisone and the next day told me he began feeling better. He took six weeks off to fully recover before returning to work. Since the only big project on the immediate schedule was the Barbara Walters' interview, McCann and I worked with the other shift leaders to pick up the slack for Gallo while he recuperated.

Brennan had been keeping us up on Nixon's schedule and the date when he was going to do the ABC interview. We sent an advance agent to the studio several days early to coordinate our security. Knowing how important the interview was, I wanted to limit the number of agents inside the studio during the live broadcast.

When President Nixon reported to the ABC studio on May 8, 1980 for his exclusive live interview with Barbara Walters, I waited in the studio while he went to the make-up room accompanied by the shift leader. This was going to be Nixon's first interview with one of the American networks since his resignation in 1974.

In the studio one of the cameramen told me privately that there was concern in the front office at ABC that the interview would not go well. He said *20/20* was going to do the live interview in fifteen-minute segments. It was shared with me that Hugh Downs, the regular host of

20/20, was present in another studio prepared to take over the broadcast in the event the Nixon interviewed flopped. He said there were three different fifteen-minute segments "in the can" that could replace the Nixon broadcast any time once a decision was made. The cameraman confided that Downs was not happy at all that Walters, who had never appeared on *20/20,* was doing the interview. He said the tension in ABC was significant surrounding the Nixon interview.

I could see that there appeared to be an unusual stiffness or anxiety on the set. There was not the usual chitchat between the various people present. Even whispered conversations were few and far between. Some of it could have been fallout from having the disgraced former president on the set. No one seemed to know how to deal with the archenemy of the press. Or it could have been tension from Walter's taking over the *20/20* program for one night. More than likely it was a combination of the two.

The importance of the interview was reflected in the fact that ABC Chairman Roone Arledge was present. Arledge, who had taken over the news division at ABC in June 1978 after successfully elevating their sports programming department, was the creator of the highly successful *20/20* program. I could sense the continuing nervousness before Nixon came onto the set. As he approached the studio, hushed-toned comments were now making the rounds on the set.

Walters, who had arrived earlier, was sitting on the set with a stack of what appeared to be 5 x 7 cards in her lap. Each card had a single question on it that she was going to pose to the former president. Walters, who had been reading and rereading the cards, arranged them in the sequence she would present them to Nixon. Next to her was the empty chair where Nixon would be seated. Watching Walters review the cards reminded me of the first time I saw her during the

1968 Republican Convention in Miami, Florida. Walters had come to the Deauville Hotel suite of Governor and Mrs. Reagan to interview California First Lady Nancy Reagan. On her arrival I met Walters at the door and accompanied her and her crew into the suite. After rearranging much of the furniture in the sitting room of the suite to get the proper setting for the interview, she sat down, took out her cards, and reviewed them as she waited for Mrs. Reagan.

As the time for the interview approached, Arledge, who had been nervously pacing and quietly talking to a few selected staff members, stopped to focus on Nixon as he entered the studio. He studied the former president, keeping his eyes on him, as Nixon sat down and a microphone was clipped to him. There were the usual greetings that protocol required between Nixon and Walters but no light conversation. Everyone on the set seemed more than a little tense. Arledge took a position standing next to the cameraman directly in front of Nixon and Walters, where he could make eye contact with Walters. I was behind another camera to the right of Arledge.

The director called for silence in the studio where you could already hear a pin drop. When the camera went on and Walters introduced Nixon to her audience before beginning her questions, the tension seemed to dissipate on the set. Quietly shifting her note cards as she proceeded, Walters and Nixon seemed to hit a rhythm. Arledge would nod his head, seeming to approve the questions and pleased with the way things were going. The first segment ended and no one interrupted either Nixon or Walters. Walters and Nixon each retreated into their own space to get ready for the next round. The cameraman looked at me, winked, and said, "One down."

In the second segment Walters continued using each card to delve into the mind of Richard Nixon. She moved effortlessly from foreign policy to personal questions about Mrs. Nixon and the family.

Arledge, a genius in the realm of television interviewing, realized the historic event taking place. He reacted immediately to the change of content. He must have been thinking the evening was not about the Nixons' personal lives. He quickly grabbed a big cue card and wrote on it, "Get back to Foreign Policy." As Nixon answered the latest question about Mrs. Nixon, Walters very adeptly and quickly rearranged her cards out of the view of her audience. She made the transition back to foreign policy, Watergate, and the presidential campaign smoothly, without missing a beat.

All four segments of the *20/20* program were of the Walters' interview of Nixon. Hugh Downs would not be called in from the bench. The evening turned out to be a win for Arledge, Walters, and Nixon. Like it or not, Downs, the longtime solo *20/20* anchor, would soon have a co-anchor, Barbara Walters.

Nixon's televised live interview in New York City with Barbara Walters on *20/20* was his official "coming out." Though she didn't know it, the *20/20* interview coup for Walters personally was due to the inability of Dan Rather to be able to quickly agree to the terms presented by Brennan.

❖ ❖ ❖

Nixon's self-imposed exile was now officially over. Since he had reopened the travel routes to Key Biscayne and Walker's Cay, he was spending more time with his two best friends and confidants, Bebe Rebozo and Robert Abplanalp. More important for him was that he could now continue down the road to resurrection. The coming out of Richard Milhous Nixon was not over; it had just begun.

With his ability to compartmentalize his personal nightmare, Nixon seemed to be at ease with himself. I made a point of traveling with him out of town much of the time the first year he lived in New York City. I wanted to try to understand who this complex man was. McCann, my assistant, would accompany me on some of the out of town trips and took Nixon alone on others.

McCann lived in Denville, New Jersey, and had a much easier drive into New York City if he came in early to take Nixon to his office. He was scheduled to work twice as many days riding with Nixon in New York as I was, so he could avoid the rush hour traffic. I lived considerably closer in Ridgewood, New Jersey, and had a much easier commute. It gave me less time with the agents but more to work on logistical issues and with headquarters.

Between the morning rides and the trips overseas, Nixon and I were developing a close personal relationship. It was not unusual when we rode from his Upper East Side residence to his 26 Federal Plaza office for Nixon to point out something about the national or international scene he was reading in the newspaper. On occasion he would mention that a policeman or fireman had been killed in the line of duty. Nixon would ask that I give his secretary, Kathy O'Connor, the name of the fund where he could make a donation. A call to the New York Field Office always led to the name of the fund. The field office was very supportive and helpful.

It was in the spring of 1980 when Nixon casually mentioned during a ride from his office to his townhouse that he was offering advice to some of his fellow Republicans. For the remained of the 1980 presidential campaign he spoke regularly about Ronald Reagan and the campaign. He told me about his strategy and what Reagan needed to do to win. He was excited that a conservative Republican had a chance to win. Nixon mentioned several times, "Conservatives would rather be right than president." He was excited and energized as he spoke about Reagan uniting the conservative base. Nixon knew key voting districts in various parts of the United States and how polls of those areas showed him Reagan winning. He specifically mentioned areas in the Midwest and Cook County, Illinois.

During one of the later briefings Nixon said that he had read press reports that Reagan was not going to visit or spend money on the 1980 campaign in New York because it was a lost cause. He told me he had sent Reagan's campaign a memo telling them that it was important to visit and spend money in New York State. He believed that a large portion of the news in Connecticut and New Jersey emanated from New York. Voters in the tri-state area were influenced by New York news, he mentioned.

It had become abundantly clear to me that Nixon wanted to be a player in the Republican Party campaign and seemed to think his counsel should be private. Nixon often spoke about talking with Republican members of Congress and political consultants. He specifically spoke of conversations with Lee Atwater, Roger Stone, and Ed Rollins and an up-and-coming young politician from Mississippi, Senator Trent Lott. Nixon seemed especially excited about Lott and his future in the Republican Party.

❖ ❖ ❖

Besides politics, and the domestic and international scene, Nixon loved to talk about the Yankees, Mets, Giants, and Jets. He didn't talk a lot about professional basketball but he was a real fan of college basketball. He loved his alma mater, Duke, their basketball team, and Coach K (Mike Krzyzewski). Initially I was surprised with his in-depth knowledge of sports in general. The longer I was around him, however, I could see he was able to hold his own with most people on more than just his favorite teams.

Abplanalp, a big Mets fan, had tried to purchase the New York Mets' Major League baseball team in January 1980 but was outbid by Doubleday Publishing. Nixon's friend had a six-seat box on the press level, which he had for years, and had recently bought a thirty-seat sky box at Shea Stadium in Flushing to watch the Mets' baseball games. When Nixon arrived in New York, Abplanalp gave him a standing invitation to join him watching Mets' games from the sky box.

Nixon was one of the most avid sport fans I had ever been around. He was admittedly an American League and California Angels' fan, but he loved the game of baseball and attended a couple of the Mets' games. One time a reporter asked him about going to the Mets, Yankees, and Giants games. The reporter said he thought Nixon was a fan of the Angels and other California teams. Nixon, forever the politician, said, "I am a fan of the Angels but have rooted for the home teams wherever I have lived."

The entire staff and security team at Shea Stadium were friendly and helpful on visits to the box. Arthur Richman, who worked in the Mets' front office, was our contact person and always took good care of Nixon and our agents. Richman had been around baseball for years and was referred to throughout the league as an ambassador for the game. Later Richman moved to the New York Yankees, where he continued to assist us.

Nixon went to his first New York Mets game since returning to the East Coast in early summer of 1980. He joined Abplanalp in his sky box at Shea. When Nixon entered the box he spent some of the time before the game meeting guests and talking baseball. There were drinks, hot food, and snacks available. About the time the game was ready to start, Nixon moved to the front row of the box to watch the game. There was no protective glass in the box. I sat next to him so I heard an excited Nixon say, "I hope I get a foul ball." Abplanalp was in and out of his seat on the other side of Nixon during the game as he greeted other special guests. President Nixon seemed to enjoy the game even though he signed baseballs, programs, and everything else put in front of him.

At the beginning of the sixth inning, Abplanalp suggested to Nixon that he should just relax, enjoy the game, and not worry about signing things. He indicated to Nixon he had signed enough already. Nixon said, "No, no, Bob, it is not a bother." I began giving Nixon things to sign only between innings after that.

Nixon and I chatted as two sports fans during the game, commenting on a play, a pitch, or an umpire's call. I knew he was enjoying the game but I could see a yearning in his eyes to be seated down below in the regular seats. I knew there would be more visits to Shea Stadium and also some to Yankee Stadium. I wondered how long it would be before Nixon would ask to sit down below.

The Mets had a hard-throwing, right-handed relief pitcher named Doug Sisk, who was one of the best relievers in the National League. He was from Tacoma, Washington, and I was hoping for an opportunity to meet him.

❧ ❧ ❧

The early summer in New York was warm and the morning walks around the neighborhood were comfortable. Nixon was going into the office every day and was working on a new book. It was getting a little too warm to go to Key Biscayne or the Bahamas to vacation so President Nixon relaxed in their air-conditioned home. Everything pointed to this being a hot, quiet summer. Gallo was with his shift and everyone had settled into the routine of our New York schedule.

❧ ❧ ❧

STORIES FROM INSIDE THE PERIMETER

On Saturday, July 27, 1980, former Shah of Iran Mohammad Reza Pahlavi died in exile in Cairo, Egypt. I was called at home on Sunday before noon by agent McCann who said he had just spoken with Nixon. The former president told him that he had spoken on the phone with Egyptian President Sadat about the shah's death. According to him, Nixon had asked Sadat for an invitation to the funeral in Cairo, Egypt. Nixon told McCann he was waiting for official confirmation and then wanted to take the 8 p.m. overnight flight tonight to Paris, change planes, and go directly to Cairo. McCann advised me he would take care of the arrangements for the trip, calling agents, making the flight arrangements, and notifying our office in Paris.

Later McCann called and said things were falling into place and he had spoken to Hal Thomas, our agent in Paris. He told me Thomas would meet our flight in Paris and travel with us to Egypt. Thomas had told him that was the earliest flight he could catch to go to Cairo. McCann said that Thomas would get a hold of the State Department Regional Security Officer (RSO) in Cairo and ask him to coordinate security arrangements and take care of our motorcade needs. Since the trip was going to be short, we agreed we would take a minimum number of agents. McCann began calling agents and when he got enough who could leave with only eight hours notice he called the U. S. Embassy in Cairo and gave them the names of everyone accompanying Nixon. They were advised we were traveling without visas or passports.

McCann amazed me. I didn't expect him to take on the challenge of planning the entire trip. I knew he was a good supervisor, but I had not realized he was such a great logistical person. He gave the agents traveling the choice of going directly to JFK Airport or joining the motorcade at Nixon's residence. Tickets and seating was all set when we got to the airport.

Boarding our plane at JFK Airport with Nixon I knew he considered the shah a good friend. When we were seated he reminded me that he visited him in Mexico during the summer of 1979. Nixon continued to reminisce about the shah's move to Egypt and his treatment for cancer in New York in the fall of 1979. Nixon said his friend, the shah, wanted to stay in the United States, but President Carter ruled against allowing him to remain here. Nixon's argument was that the shah had been a good friend for many years and should have been allowed to stay here. After the short conversation, we both told the cabin staff we would sleep through dinner and have breakfast before the arrival in Paris. About thirty minutes after takeoff we turned out the lights and put our seats back. The coffee, juice, and roll hit the spot in the morning.

Agent Thomas met us in the international transient lounge at Orly Airport as we waited to board the Cairo flight. He briefed us on his conversations with the RSO in Cairo. Thomas was confident everything would be taken care of for our stay in Egypt. President Nixon seemed pleased to see agent Thomas. He commented that he had not seen him since the White House days when he was in charge of the detail for Julie and David. I realized I had not seen Thomas since our 1971 trip to the World's Fair in Osaka, Japan.

Thanks to McCann, Thomas, the RSO, and the U. S. Embassy in Cairo, everything was set when we arrived. Our motorcade was waiting and took us to a hotel to rest before the funeral.

The weather was scorching as Nixon and the other special guests lined up behind the horse-drawn caisson carrying the shah's body. Nixon was at the head of the group of dignitaries. The formal procession through the streets of Cairo was a sight I had never witnessed before and would have been unable to imagine.

The scene was a security nightmare. As I stood with Nixon waiting for the procession to start I was thinking, "How are they going to keep everything together and moving?" I wondered if we would be overwhelmed by the hundreds of thousands of mourners along the route. Fortunately for us, just before we were scheduled to depart for the long walk our ID agent notified me that a platoon of Egyptian Special Forces under the supervision of the CIA was en route to assist President Nixon during the procession. Five minutes later the platoon, wearing black berets and carrying automatic weapons, arrived. The platoon was split, with half providing crowd control on our left flank and the other half on our right flank. I was told the troops would march on our flanks the entire route of the procession.

The chaos that engulfed the parade over the next hour required the Egyptian troops to be very physical at times in order to keep the wailing throng from blocking the route and overwhelming the procession. To the credit of the military and the Egyptian government, everyone did a great job in keeping the procession moving without allowing an extremely difficult situation to get totally out of hand.

People at least five deep were crowded on both sides of the street along the entire route as the funeral procession wound its way through the streets of Cairo. Some of the narrow roadways were cobblestone and most of the buildings were multiple-floored adobe-type structures on both sides of the street. Everywhere people were screaming, howling, crying, and waving at the passing caisson. Some were standing on the sidewalks and in the streets, others waved out the windows, while the roofs were crowded with people distraught with the death of the shah and saying their goodbyes. Not only were most people wailing and crying, but many were showering the funeral procession with flowers as it slowly passed on its way to the burial. The procession took over an hour, moving forward at a slow, somber pace. Nixon seemed moved by the outpouring of people along the way. There was no smiling, no waving as Nixon moved forward stoically, with his back erect, arms at his sides, and eyes straight ahead.

Since we left New York in such a hurry I had not properly taken into account the hot weather in Cairo. Due to Nixon's daily walks I knew he was in excellent physical condition, but as we walked in the blistering sun I began to realize dehydration could be an issue. There was no water available in the procession or along the way. I made a mental note to make sure to get him some water when we got to the burial site.

The procession ended at the Al Rifa'I Mosque, where the shah's body would be interred. At the mosque he would be united with Egyptian King Farouk, his one-time brother-in-law. The dignitaries were ushered into a large tent to rest while waiting as the caisson was moved into the mosque. Like many of the people dressed in suits, Nixon had perspired right through his suit from the penetrating heat. The local dignitaries dressed in their white robes seemed to be more comfortable with the excessive heat. I made sure Nixon had some water.

I could see the Egyptian government and military were especially happy that Nixon attended the funeral. It was apparent they had pulled out all the stops to make the burial procession a success. At the mosque people were either taking off their shoes or putting on a slip cover over their shoes. Nixon had untied his shoes and was beginning to take them off when McCann interrupted him and pointed to a large pile of shoes. He asked Nixon, "Are you sure you will be able to find them when everything is over?" Nixon retied his shoes and put on a pair of the shoe covers. Inside the mosque Nixon was in the front row for the ceremony. McCann and I stayed closer to him than usual due to the controlled chaos outside. When everything was over and the public had dispersed we departed the area quietly.

Everyone exhaled a sigh of relief when the short visit came to an end. We got some rest before the departure the next morning. Still somewhat exhausted from the heat and walking the day before, we boarded our commercial flight back to New York looking forward to a restful flight home. It was during the flight that I thought about Nixon's presence at the funeral and the security challenge presented to our detail. Our agents did a great job along with the Egyptian Special Forces. McCann and I were happy our guys performed so admirably with such short notice. I thought again how lucky I was to have McCann. By taking control of the planning from the very beginning, he was most responsible for the success of the trip.

I either never knew who President Carter had representing the United States at the funeral or don't remember. But I do know Nixon thought that Carter had let down a strong supporter and good friend of the United States when he would not let the shah live there.

❖ ❖ ❖

Back from the funeral, the hot New York summer was a relief from the scorching heat of Cairo, Egypt. President and Mrs. Nixon drove out to West Hampton on the south side of Long Island to enjoy a day with Tricia and her family at the Cox family summer home on Shinnecock Bay. Tricia's husband, Ed Cox, had grown up around the bay and the ocean and was very comfortable in the water. A handsome man, he was very athletic-looking and a strong swimmer. I remember one cloudy day watching him dive into the bay and swim the half-mile or so to the other side and immediately reverse course and return to their Shinnecock Bay home. When he got out of the water he did not seem to be breathing heavily. I was surprised at the good physical shape he maintained.

❖ ❖ ❖

Shortly after returning to New York, Nixon hired L. Nicholas Ruwe to replace Brennan as his chief of staff to manage his schedule and office in New York. Ruwe, a staunch Republican from Grosse Point, Michigan, first worked for Nixon in the 1960 presidential campaign. He was a knowledgeable political operative and well-known within the leadership of the Republican Party. Ruwe was easy to work with and very supportive of the needs of the Secret Service. He would be in the office and have the coffee made when Nixon arrived shortly after 6 a.m. Ruwe would often remark to Nixon or me about the good old Navy coffee he made. Nixon would complement Ruwe on the coffee periodically.

❖ ❖ ❖

With the presidential campaign in high gear, President Carter was being attacked because of the Misery Index. According to press reports at the time, Robert Barro, an economist from Chicago, is credited with coining the term the "Misery Index" in describing the economy in the 1970s. The index was attained by adding the unemployment rate and the inflation rate together. In the months before the 1980 election the misery index peaked at a high of 21.9 and was still over 19 on Election Day. The Misery Index was constantly cited during the 1980 presidential campaign by Republicans, and voters were reminded every night on both the news and *Nightline* of the frustration with our in inability to get our fifty-two hostages released by Iran.

In the fall of 1980, Nixon told me he would be picking up his son-in-law, Ed Cox, in the mornings on his way to the office. During the ride Nixon briefed Cox on world affairs, national issues, and the

1980 presidential campaign before dropping him off near his law office. Our stretch limousine had a thick movable glass partition between the front and rear compartments of the car. The partition could be operated from either the front or back of the car. Nixon would leave the partition down when he briefed his son-in-law and I could listen. Nixon, who would sometimes put the partition up when he had a guest, was well aware that I could hear him. I felt he was leaving it down for me to close if I chose. The rides became a political science seminar and a world affairs session. The briefings went on for several weeks and were interesting and enlightening to me. They enhanced my thirst for knowledge. All of a sudden I found myself reading the first section of *The New York Times* before the sports section. *The Wall Street Journal* was also now on my daily reading list just before *The New York Post.*

On November 4, 1980, Reagan won the presidential election in a landslide, mostly due to the continuing Iranian hostage situation coupled with high inflation, unemployment, and interest rates. Nixon was delighted to see the conservative former governor of California sworn in as the fortieth president of the United States. In a final affront to President Carter, Iran released the fifty-two American Embassy hostages, who had been held captive since November 4, 1979, on January 20, 1981, at the same time Ronald Reagan was sworn in as the fortieth president of the United States. Nixon said the conservatives finally had a candidate to rally around.

❖ ❖ ❖

It was during the Christmas season in 1980 that President Nixon first mentioned to me that he thought he wanted to move to New Jersey. I sensed he missed the beauty and privacy of Casa Pacifica. Over the first months of 1981, Nixon would routinely go for rides across the George Washington Bridge to Bergen County, New Jersey. During the treks across the Hudson River into Bergen County, Nixon explained that he wanted to find a more relaxed location. He said he would like to have a large yard with his own swimming pool. Nixon told me Mrs. Nixon loved flowers and he looked forward to a place where she could have a flower garden. He finished his comments by telling me a big yard would provide more area for watching and playing with his grandchildren.

Nixon seemed to enjoy reacquainting himself with the northwest corner of Bergen County, Ridgewood, Saddle River, and Alpine, New Jersey, where he had often campaigned going back to the 1952 presidential campaign. He mentioned he had a realtor searching for a home. According to Nixon, Ruwe and his wife were coordinating the house search for him in New Jersey. They would screen the houses for the president and Mrs. Nixon and tell the president which houses he should visit. Sometimes, when we drove around, Nixon would have an address and we would drive by so he could see what the realtor was proposing. There were other times he enjoyed driving through the general area just to look at homes.

During a ride home from the office in March, Nixon told me that before he moved to New Jersey he would like to drive through the Bronx one day and see Fort Apache. I was a little surprised that he knew about the infamous New York City Police Precinct that had been immortalized in the February 1981 movie *Fort Apache* starring Paul Newman and Ed Asner. I told him it would not be a problem, saying, "Just let me know."

About two months later going into his residence for lunch Nixon asked if he could use a smaller off-the-record-car and take a tour of the South Bronx. He said he wanted specifically to visit Fort Apache.

One of the agents working in the New York Field Office, Eddie Ryan, who was familiar with the area, was requested to meet us and drive our armored Lincoln Town Car. When we departed Nixon asked to pick up Tricia to accompany him.

Over the next hour we drove up and down streets through various sections of the Bronx. There were black, Italian, Irish, and other ethnic areas. Some of the Bronx devastation was just unbelievable, some was similar to Harlem, and yet other sections were neat and clean. Nixon was amazed by the destruction, rubble, garbage, and poverty in some areas. He asked questions, most rhetorical, out loud as we drove around the South Bronx. "Why are some neighborhoods all black, Hispanic, or Caucasian on one side of the street and a different race on the other? Do they cross the street?"

Nixon was trying to understand the poverty and devastation he was seeing side by side with neatly maintained areas of middle-class residences. "Can't someone do something about this?"

Tricia, not used to seeing such poverty and destruction, became frustrated with the devastation, piles of rubble, burned-out buildings, and boarded-up apartments. She said she had seen enough and told her father it was time to leave the area. President Nixon, who was not ready to leave, took charge and told her he was not leaving until he saw the police building that was referred to as Fort Apache. When we finally approached the area where the police station was located the devastation and destruction reflected the worst of the South Bronx. There were many burned-out and boarded-up buildings, and piles of rubble that used to be buildings. I remember thinking, "So this is Fort Apache."

It was really difficult to imagine how people survived in some of the areas of the South Bronx. Once he got a good look at the devastated street with the besieged police building, a distraught Nixon, in what was almost a whisper, said, "Let's go home." Tricia was delighted the drive was over. I could see Nixon was deep in thought about what he had just seen. I am sure the deplorable conditions he saw had a powerful impact on him. I think the excursion turned out to be much more than he had expected.

❖ ❖ ❖

In June 1980, President and Mrs. Nixon, joined by the Ablpanalps and Rebozo, took a trip to Europe celebrating the Nixons' forty years of marriage. The trip started in Paris with two nights at the luxurious five-star Hôtel de Crillon located on the Place de la Concorde. Across the street was the Louvre Museum, a twenty-minute walk away the Champs-Élysèes, and nearby, across the Seine River on the Champs de Mars, the Eiffel Tower.

The visit to Paris was relaxing. The party went out to dinner each night and rested during the day. President and Mrs. Nixon enjoyed the luxury of their suite that had a view of the Eiffel Tower. When we departed Paris in our four-car motorcade our group included a car driven by Rainier Kuplien and Georges Guillemot. They worked for Precision Valve's Paris operation. Ablpanalp invited them along to take care of the logistics of the French portion of the trip. They coordinated the meals, wine, housing, and paid all the bills. I usually rode in the lead car with the two of them and sat with them at meals.

Our motorcade took us to Lyon, France, via the Autostrasse where there was not a lot of traffic at the time. Speed limits on the Autostrasse were 120 km/h to 130km/h (75-80 mph), somewhat faster than our 55-60 mph back in the United States at the time. As long as we were on highways that had speed limits I felt comfortable having the motorcade drive at the posted limits. However, when we traveled on motorways that did not have a speed limit I suggested to the drivers we continue at 130km/h in order to keep the motorcade together safely.

We made a sightseeing and luncheon stop in Lyon. From there it was off to the quaint village of Mionnay, France. The well-known Alain Chapel Hotel/Restaurant, with twelve rooms, had a *Michelin Guide* three-star rating, which was their highest rating. According to the *Michelin Guide,* three stars translated to "excellent cuisine and worth the journey."

Our advance agent for the stop in Mionnay was agent Jurge Mattman of our Paris office. He spoke fluent French and did an outstanding job. The entire entourage was delighted with the visit. The ambiance and privacy of the unique hotel, along with the wonderful meals and wines provide by owner/chef Alain Chapel, made the stop especially delightful for President and Mrs. Nixon and the Abplanalps.

After Mionnay, our next motorcade destination was Switzerland, where we had lunch at Girardeau's, a restaurant just outside of Geneva. There were five in President Nixon's party and we had four at our table including Kuplien and Guillemot at the well-known restaurant. Everyone ordered their meals and Kuplien and Guillemot ordered the French wines for the various courses. The meals and wines were exquisite and the bill reflected it. When it was presented to our table for the nine of us it was over $1,500 without the tip. Kuplien was preparing to pay the bill when President Nixon asked if the chef could come to the table. When Chef Girardeau arrived he thanked Nixon for coming to his restaurant, telling him that he was not charging his party for the meal. Nixon thanked him but said that this was not necessary. The chef, however, insisted on not charging for the meal. He seemed surprised but pleased when Nixon asked if he could visit the kitchen and meet the staff.

I accompanied Nixon and chef Girardeau into the kitchen, not realizing we would see twenty young men in clean white chef dress working as apprentices in the back. Nixon received a tour of the facility and met all the staff and the sous chef. Since there was no charge for the meal, Rebozo left a $1,000 tip when we departed. Chef Girardeau mentioned to Rebozo that having a famous person like Nixon dine in his restaurant would get him his third Michelin star. A couple of months later the television program *60 Minutes* did a piece on the most expensive lunch in the world, Giradeau's Restaurant.

The drive through the treed countryside where we could see the snow- covered Alps reminded me of driving to Mount Rainier in Washington State when I grew up there. We arrived at the Beau Rivage Hotel in Geneva, which was located in the middle of town on the main road across the street from Lake Geneva, for an overnight. The Abplanalp son and daughter, John and Marie, arrived in Geneva and joined their mother and father at our hotel for the remainder of the trip. The view of Lake Geneva and the Alps from the hotel was stunning. There was dinner out for the official party and breakfast in their rooms the next morning. For most of the rest of us we were able to get out for an evening on the town. Breakfast at the hotel was served at a secluded garden site with shrubs and flowers all around where you could see the lake. There must have been eight different types of rolls, pastries, and breads. It was nice sitting in the warm morning sun enjoying a cup of coffee and the continental breakfast.

When the stay at the Beau Rivage Hotel was over, we departed on a morning train from the nearby Montreux Railroad Station. Abplanalp had previously arranged through his assistants to rent a private train car to take the party to Interlaken and Zurich for our overnight visits. At the train station McCann and I boarded the private car. The train left the station and Kuplien and Guillemont departed for Paris. Our motorcade cars also left after the train and would bypass the Interlaken stop and meet us at the train station in Zurich.

Boarding the private car I was reminded of the television series, *The Wild Wild West*. The interior of the private car was right out of the 1800s. There were gas lanterns mounted on the walls, a deep red velour covering the walls, and comfortable seats. At the back of the train car a small alcove with very limited seating and a table was available for seating passengers. The private car was placed at the end of the train and was uncoupled when we arrive in Interlaken, Switzerland. Only McCann and I rode in the private car with the official party and the rest of the agents rode on the regular train.

Abplanalp had sent Chef Bruno Bandenberger in advance from Walker's Cay to Interlaken to make sure everything was set. Chef Bandenberger was Swiss and spoke multiple languages and Ablpanalp knew he would be useful to everyone. Also Abplanalp had a big heart and understood that Bandenberger would be admired by his friends and the local community when they saw his role in the visit of President Nixon. When we arrived at the Interlaken train station our motorcade of local vehicles was waiting and took us to the hotel. The first night was a quiet time of dinner, socializing, and reviewing the schedule for the next day.

The name Abplanalp means "from Planalp." This was the village from which Mr. Abplanalp's father had immigrated to the United States. In the morning the official party and any of the agents that wanted to rode a one hundred-year-old small steam train to the quaint Alpine village of Planalp 4,500 feet above Lake Brienz. The train had a number of small, open to the air wooden train cars with bench seats. About three-fourths of the way up the mountain the train entered a tunnel. Partway through the tunnel we came around a curve where the outer wall was missing. The train stopped and the passengers were allowed to leave their cars and approach the opening to look out across the lakes and valley to see the snow-capped French Alps.

The day was clear, the view was spectacular, and cameras were clicking to record this once-in-a-lifetime trip. With my acrophobia (fear of heights) I stayed close to the train, standing safely by the engine where I could see the French Alps. When we reloaded to continue our ride up the mountain, my fear transferred from the altitude to worrying the train would go backwards downhill instead of going forward. As we continued through the tunnel I began to relax. Coming out of the upper end of the tunnel, the view of the snow-covered Alps and the rolling hills was breathtaking.

When our little train arrived at the station a resident of Planalp in native Swiss dress announced the arrival of President Nixon and his party to the village below by blowing into a curved wooden horn, called an alpenhorn. The alpenhorn looked to be at least eight to ten feet long and was traditionally used by herders to call cows to the pasture. It was also used to announce special holidays and events.

Our group took the short ten-minute walk from the station down the path to the waiting villagers, many of whom were also in traditional Swiss folk dress. Halfway to the village I took a fork in the path to the left, up the side of the mountain for about twenty yards, and sat down on the soft green grass to relax and enjoy the warm sunlight. I knew we had more than enough security with Nixon. After soaking in the scenery of the Swiss Alps with the snowy peaks, fields of grass with small yellow, blue, and white flowers, and random patches of snow I laid back, closed my eyes, and took a short nap. When the ceremony and luncheon were over I joined everyone for the train ride back down the mountain.

In the evening after dinner Chef Bandenberger took Mr. Abplanalp, his son and daughter, several agents, and some members of the greeting party to various establishments in Interlaken to enjoy the local ambiance. I had to be up early in the morning and did not join the group. Brandenberger and his party stayed out late drinking more than their fair share. I am sure they did not get much rest.

The next morning when we assembled our party for the motorcade to the train station, Mrs. Abplanalp was wearing a new green alpine hat with numerous pins and other adornments. She said she was making a statement for her husband staying out late the night before. Mrs. Abplanalp joked, saying she had spent considerable money to purchase the hat and bought most of the pins being sold at the hotel souvenir shop. I sensed she was probably a little more upset than she projected.

As the train departed the station with our private car at the end, Mrs. Abplanalp was seated with Mrs. Nixon. Her husband and their two children were ensconced in the small rear alcove. It was surprising that the three of them could get into the alcove at the same time.

During the train ride to Zurich the festive mood of the day before had vanished. Without the participation of Mr. Abplanalp, John, and Marie, it was quiet. My acrophobia did not kick in while riding in the train and I was able to sit back and enjoy the scenery as the train worked its way from the floor of the valley up and over the mountains on the way to Zurich. Each turn through the mountains and along the valleys brought new and exciting scenes. President and Mrs. Nixon were enjoying the train rides and the grandeur of the vistas.

Our vehicles had arrived from Geneva and were waiting at the Zurich train station for us. The motorcade took us to the Dolder Grand Hotel, where we were all staying, while a truck from the hotel transported all the baggage. Everyone relaxed in their room when we got to the hotel. In the evening president and Mrs. Nixon, along with the Abplanalps and Rebozo, went out to dinner. I was off that evening and would be leaving the trip the next day to return to the United States. Several of us went out to dinner and on returning stopped at a hotel a five-minute walk below the Dolder Grand to have a drink.

We were joined by John and Marie Abplanalp and several other agents who had been out to dinner. Everyone was enjoying themselves laughing and telling stories when Mr. Abplanalp walked into the bar. He sat next to me and recognized everyone with his trademark deep voice greeting, "Hello, boys." He enjoyed interacting with his children and with the agents. Mr. Abplanalp placed several $100 bills on the bar and said the drinks were on him. The loud conversations at the bar continued with Mr. Abplanalp joining in on many of them. It was an enjoyable several hours of storytelling and reminiscing about some of our earlier stops, other trips, and visits to Walker's Cay. Mr. Abplanalp and I spent quite a bit of time talking about President Nixon and the White House days.

As people began leaving for the Dolder Grand, Mr. Abplanalp paid the bill and the two of us left. We were lagging behind everyone on the walk up the hill toward the hotel. Abplanalp, who was not inebriated but tired from the night before and the long day, would take a step or two, pause, back up one, and then repeat the process. We were twenty yards up the hill when a taxi passed us with a passenger headed to our hotel. Abplanalp stopped walking and, turning to me, said, "There is my ride."

I continued walking up the hill and got to the entrance of the Dolder Grand before the taxi arrived with Abplanalp aboard. I folded a $10 bill in my right hand. Abplanalp got out of the vehicle and gave the driver a $100 bill. As he headed for the entrance I reached into the taxi and changed the $100 with the $10. Catching up with Abplanalp, I put the $100 into his coat pocket. I knew the large bill meant less to him than the ten to me but I just couldn't see the driver getting $100 for driving Abplanalp a little more than thirty yards.

The next day Nixon and the party were back in their motorcade headed to Germany. They had two stops and would be gone for another four or five days. The Zurich advance agent took me to the airport and I returned to New York.

When they got back to New York, President and Mrs. Nixon told me how much they enjoyed the trip. They said they really enjoyed the visits to Interlaken and to Germany where one day they went sightseeing in Cologne. Mrs. Nixon mentioned visiting the beautiful Gothic Cologne Cathedral built on the banks of the Rhine River.

❖ ❖ ❖

Nixon on occasion enjoyed telling me about how Rebozo and he made some money over the years through real estate investments. Nixon said that several times he had joined Rebozo in some of his land investments. According to Nixon, Rebozo would buy property a little off the beaten track and sell it as the growth reached his property. He also mentioned that once he and Rebozo were part of a group that bought Fisher Island off of Miami. He said they wanted to develop it but things didn't work out. He said when they sold it they still made money.

Heading home up East River Drive to his residence, Nixon mentioned that he, Rebozo, and Abplanalp recently purchased a piece of property previously owned by Rockwell International on Cat Cay in the Bahamas. He said the property had a main house, a swimming pool, and three cabañas. The property extended across the island near the northern end. Nixon mentioned the property had its own little inlet and dock on the side where the house was located.

According to Rebozo the next time I saw him in Key Biscayne, Rockwell International had been using the facilities for seminars and other company meetings before the three of them bought it. Rebozo pointed out to me that Ernest Hemingway used to hang out on Cat Cay, often visiting the Kit Kat Club. Cat Cay is located about eight miles from the island of Bimini, which has regularly scheduled flights from Miami. When Abplanalp was involved in the visits he used his Mallard seaplane or one of the other small Walker's Cay Airlines planes to fly the three of them to Walker's Cay and Bimini. Rebozo would make arrangements for a boat to transport our group to Cat Cay. When Ablpanalp was not involved we would fly commercially into Bimini.

The house at Cat Cay was two-storied, with four bedrooms and a dining room that would seat over twenty. There was a swimming pool out back with three small guest cabañas strategically located around it. A small one-bedroom cabin, once used by the overseer of the facility, was near the back door of the main house. The property was only seventy-five to one hundred yards wide and had beaches on both sides. In the morning you could watch the sun come up from the main house side and in the evening make the short walk to the other side of the island and see the sun set into the crystal clear blue waters.

Nixon liked the small nine-hole, par thirty-three golf course that was named the Windsor Downs Golf Club after the Duke of Windsor, who was the governor of the Bahamas at one time. The course, though available, was rarely used by other guests and Nixon normally played alone. There was no club house or locker room. The course did not have a pro or someone else to support those playing. Generally Nixon and I were alone on the course and occasionally he would play two balls, focusing on the mechanics of his game. Nixon normally would play eighteen holes in the morning starting right after his usual breakfast of dry cereal, toast, milk, and fresh fruit. He liked to get started before it got too warm. After the morning round of golf Nixon would relax, have lunch, take a nap and then go for a swim. In the late afternoon he would play a second round of eighteen holes and then shower and change for dinner.

Food at the dining room at Cat Cay was sometimes inconsistent and Rebozo would on occasion bring in someone to cook at the house or would prepare dinner himself. Rebozo was an excellent chef; his signature dishes were Cuban black beans and rice with fish. Nixon used to say Rebozo's Cuban dishes were better than those he had eaten in restaurants. In fact, he said he would only eat Cuban food prepared by Rebozo.

The unique Kit Kat Club, a cabaña on a concrete slab with open sides, had not been in operation for years. It was, however, one of the more interesting bars I had ever seen. The fairly small structure was built of wood. The poles, beams, tables, and long bar all bore the hand-engraved initials of patrons who had visited the establishment over the years. I can only imagine the Kit Kat Club in its heyday. I am sure that Ernest Hemingway is lucky the walls cannot talk.

Nixon's trips to Florida and the Bahamas were usually for three or four days. Abplanalp would host Nixon and Rebozo on all the trips to Walker's Cay and occasionally joined them on visits to Key Biscayne or Cat Cay. President Nixon would usually depart New York on a commercial flight from LaGuardia Airport either Thursday or Friday afternoon, arriving at Miami International Airport later that day and returning early the next week. Our agents would fly into the Bahamas using Chalks Airlines out of Miami or Walker's Cay Airlines out of Fort Lauderdale depending on which island was being visited. The trips to Florida and the Bahamas were usually very relaxing with boat rides, swimming, and some evenings out for dinner. On occasion Mrs. Nixon would accompany her husband on the trips south.

Rebozo bought a home in the private gated community of Ocean Reef, Florida. The beautiful three-bedroom home was right on the water. It included a game room with a pool table, although I don't remember ever seeing anyone use the pool table. Rebozo told me he enjoyed getting away from the changing and hectic living style taking place in Key Biscayne.

When he first began visiting Florida, Nixon would usually spend the first night at Key Biscayne and then go to Rebozo's Ocean Reef Club residence on Saturday. Ocean Reef, a private, gated community, was very upscale and offered the agents good accommodations, excellent restaurants, swimming pools, and other activities within the complex. Sometimes the agents would choose to drive the twenty minutes to Key Largo for a change of scene to have dinner.

Rebozo sold his Key Biscayne home after purchasing the Ocean Reef house. He began building a new home on the other side of the old Key Biscayne complex, just north of the helicopter pad. It was going to be a spectacular home with a large great room that had huge windows extending up two floors overlooked Biscayne Bay. An indoor waterfall would be at one end of the great room cascading down two stories from the ceiling.

Nixon enjoyed boat rides, car rides, and visits to the many outstanding restaurants when in Florida. He and Rebozo enjoyed the excellent food at the Ocean Reef Club; however, sometimes Nixon talked Rebozo into cooking instead of going out for dinner. Every once in a while Nixon, Rebozo, and Abplanalp, if he were visiting, would drive to Key Largo. The three of them liked to go to dinner at either the Egret Restaurant or Mary and Stan's Restaurant. Of all the restaurants in the Florida Keys, it seemed to me they preferred Mary and Stan's, where they had been going for well over twenty-five years. All three of them told me, "You have to eat the fried yellowtail snapper." They were in agreement that it was the best yellowtail they had ever tasted. Rebozo told me he would love to have the recipe, but the owner, who had passed away, and now his son Don would not give it to him. After that first trip to Mary and Stan's I agreed with them about the yellowtail snapper. It was a firm, sweet, white fish. The fillets were usually around six ounces. I made up my mind that one day I would get the recipe.

On several occasions during trips to Key Biscayne, Nixon and Rebozo asked to take a ride across Interstate 95, sometimes referred to as the Everglades Parkway. Interstate 75, the highway better known as "Alligator Alley" by Floridians, extended from Naples on the west coast to Weston on the east. From the toll booth at the eastern to the one at the western end Alligator Alley was approximately eighty miles. We would leave the Miami area around 11 a.m. so they could have lunch in Naples. Passing through the toll booth at the western end of the highway, we headed for Naples. Nixon said he needed to use the restroom and Rebozo suggested we go to the public pier at the beach. He directed our driver to the long pier where the restrooms were located. We parked in the lot and walked out on the pier to the bathrooms. I waited a few minutes and followed the two of them to use the facilities myself.

As I walked in, Rebozo and Nixon were standing in the area where there were two very small wash basins. Looking around, they seemed a little confused as I walked past them to the back of the restroom and around the concrete wall to the urinals and toilets. When I came out Rebozo met me on the pier and as we walked slowly with Nixon he quietly said, "You S.O.B." I quickly replied "What?" Rebozo then told me they did not know the urinals were in back and had used the wash basins instead. I smiled as I realized he thought I already knew what they had done. I didn't let him know I had no idea about what they did. It made my day.

Later, back in the New York office, Nixon had me get a blank arrest warrant from the Ho-Ho-Kus Police Department. We filled it out together charging Rebozo with unlawful use of a wash basin. We all had a good laugh the next time Bebozo visited New York and Nixon served the warrant on him in front of me.

❖ ❖ ❖

Nixon's routine was to go to Florida or the Bahamas roughly every six to eight weeks. He also liked to take periodic trips overseas to meet with leaders to share views on world affairs and to promote his new books. Without question, Nixon had one of the most recognizable faces in the world. He was constantly approached at airports, hotels, walking the streets, in restaurants, just about every time he was out in the public by people asking for autographs. He made it clear to the agents around him that he wanted to meet and talk to the people who approached seeking an autograph.

Most of the air travel for Nixon was aboard commercial airliners. On his flights he always flew in first class. The working supervisor also flew first class and sat next to him unless his staff assistant was along.

On domestic flights, agents were allowed to carry their issued weapons but on overseas flights we were required to surrender all weapons to the airplane captain prior to departure. We carried special metal suitcases lined with foam to transport our weapons on the overseas flights.

After several commercial flights accompanying Nixon I became fascinated with some of the passenger interaction with the former president. Nixon had made it very clear early on that he was willing to sign autographs and have pictures taken. He asked me to tell the men and women on his detail not to keep any people away. In greeting him on a flight, occasionally someone would tell him they had met him before. Once a woman in her fifties told Nixon she had met him in Iowa when he visited there. Nixon quickly responded, "Was that in '52, '56, '64, '68, or '72?" Before she could reply he asked further, "Was it at the fairgrounds, the airport, or downtown?" Narrowing the visit more, Nixon continued, "Was it raining?" In less than a minute Nixon had received a positive response on the year and the location of the visit.

Another time on a commercial flight a young lady approached Nixon advising him that her grandfather used to work at the Pentagon and attended monthly meetings at the White House with him when he was president. Nixon asked a couple of questions about the branch of service her grandfather was in and his last name. He then replied saying he remembered her grandfather. Using her grandfather's first name, Nixon told her he was a general. This happened quite often and I would listen intently and be amazed each time that he could remember so much.

During the eleven years I was with Nixon there must have been eight to ten times I saw him seemingly pluck a name, date, or place out of the air. He did it so many times when I was around I was trying to understand how he did it.

❖ ❖ ❖

Robert (Bobby) Re, the police chief in Ho-Ho-Kus, New Jersey, where I resided, and I had become friends. He invited me to join the Bergen County Police Chiefs Association in early 1981. Re was very active in the association and was their president the first time I was invited to attend a meeting. Through the Police Chiefs Association I got a chance to meet all the Bergen County chiefs. I made a special point of spending time with police chiefs William Smith of Saddle River, Frank Milliken of Ridgewood, Ted Preusch of Upper Saddle River, and Danny Lupo of Waldwick, all towns that surrounded Saddle River. The four of them plus Re were in charge of very progressive departments and I enjoyed good relations with all of them.

After a year and a half in New York City, Nixon decided to move to the wealthy Republican bedroom community of Saddle River, New Jersey. He had visited a number of Bergen County towns and viewed a number of homes. Nixon made his final choice a Saddle River home designed by well-known architect Eleanor Peterson of Saddle River. She had studied under famous architect Frank Lloyd Wright and had designed several homes in Saddle River. The house Nixon purchased was situated on two treed acres at the entrance of a cul-de-sac that abutted an apple orchard. It was the perfect place to provide the privacy that he and Mrs. Nixon desired.

Hidden by the trees, the house had big windows that brought the outside into the house in a classic Frank Lloyd Wright design. Downstairs was a living room, family room, den/office, formal dining room, and a very large kitchen with an eat-in area. The bedrooms upstairs gave a commanding view of the property. Outside, the swimming pool and tennis court would provide them many hours of enjoyment with their grandchildren.

Nixon was a wine connoisseur and his new home had a wine cellar in the basement that could hold one thousand bottles. The entrance area had a rough surface type of barn wood on the walls with an old wooden table and four primitive wooden chairs. Hanging over the table, only about two feet above it, was an appropriately aged wooden wagon wheel chandelier with a half-dozen candles strategically placed to be lit during tasting. On the left as you entered the narrow opening to the wine racks was a wooden cabinet with a top that held a wine opener, a couple of glasses, a candle, and a rack for decanting a bottle of wine. The area in back where the wine was stored in the racks had very low lighting. Nixon was proud of his wine cellar and I was sure it would not take him long to get a good supply of wine stored there.

Agent Bert Vint was designated the advance agent for the new residence and was selected to get the new security system installed and co-ordinate the move from our office in the World Trade Center to a building at 60 Craig Road, Montvale, New Jersey. Putting in the security alarms and cameras required a lot of digging and laying of cables. We encountered problems after laying the cables, which were buried inside a conduit. Due to the high ground water pressure (hydrostatic pressure) in the area, water got into the conduits and created problems. Much of the system needed to be dug up, sealed, and reinstalled. A security room (command post) used to monitor all cameras and alarms was built in one stall of the three-car garage. Outside in the woods, partially hidden by trees and other growth, a small wooden guard booth was erected overlooking the entrance gate. A gravel path was built, starting at the guard booth and proceeding through the woods. It turned at the property line and headed toward the rear of the yard. Once beyond the back yard it turned again, passing the tennis court and the cabaña and joined the gravel road.

It would take almost four months for renovations and the security equipment to be installed before the Nixons could move into their new residence. However, they did visit their new home occasionally, not only to see the progress on the work but to get out of the oppressive summer heat of New York City. They would be joined by their daughter Tricia, her husband, Ed Cox, and their twelve-year-old son Christopher.

In light of the purchase of the Saddle River, New Jersey, house during the summer of 1981, I spoke to Protective Operations about increasing our detail, adding two more special officers and an operations assistant. Protective Operations agreed and Bill Burch was promoted to fill the new operations position. I was delighted to be reunited with Burch, whom I knew from my days on the vice presidential detail. Burch was a people person and would get along well with our agents. There was no question in my mind he was going to excel in the operations position. I was also delighted that McCann could now relax and focus on working with Nixon.

❖ ❖ ❖

There was some excitement during a summer visit to Saddle River before the Nixons moved into their new home. The Cox family joined the President and Mrs. Nixon to spend a relaxing day at the new home. Some of the family was at the tennis court when the arm used for tightening the net on the tennis court was inadvertently released, hitting Christopher in the mouth. The incident required a quick Sunday trip to Valley Hospital emergency room in nearby Ridgewood, where Christopher was treated. The emergency room doctor expressed some concern that Christopher might lose a tooth and suggested to Tricia and Ed Cox to check with their doctor back in New York City. As you can imagine, it took a little while for everyone to settle down. In the end Christopher did not lose his tooth.

❖ ❖ ❖

One day in early August 1981 on the ride from the office to his Manhattan residence, Nixon mentioned he was planning to take a tour along with Rebozo of the Bordeaux wine region of France. They would also visit Rebozo's friend Eric in Flensburg, Germany. I believe Eric's last name was Heider but have been unable to confirm it.

I was advised arrangements were being made for Nixon, Rebozo, and me to stay at a chateau owned by Nixon's friend Baron Elie Robert Rothschild located in the middle of the Bordeaux region. As I got involved in the planning phase of the trip it turned out the trip would be over two weeks long and would include additional stops in Lausanne, Switzerland, and Vienna, Austria.

The trip started with two nights in Paris and then it was off to the Bordeaux region. Nixon and Rebozo visited the vineyards of Chateau Lafite Rothschild, Chateau Mouton Rothschild, and several others.

I had the good fortune of staying with Nixon at the Rothschild B & G Chateau during the visit to the wine region. The carefully crafted schedule included daily excursions to visit some of France's finest vineyards. Nixon would be taken to the cellar beneath the chateau where the wines were stored in oak barrels the first year before bottling. The vintners would greet Nixon and Rebozo and describe the wine-making process, including the picking, crushing, and squeezing of the grapes. They also explained about the bottling process and presented Nixon and Rebozo an opportunity to sample their wines.

Chateau Mouton was one of the wine operations where the visit to see the wine-making process was unlike any of the others we had seen. We were escorted to a large warehouse operation that was not using big oak vats for fermenting. Instead they were using huge stainless steel fermentation vats. The vintner at Mouton carefully monitored the temperature level and the sugar (specific gravity) content of the must (crushed/mashed grapes). He said if the must (skins, seeds, and juice of the crushed grapes) heated up too fast they could pump the macerated grapes into a stainless steel pipe and move it around the facility to cool it down. After the fermenting process was over, the must was squeezed and the wine was aged in new oak barrels for a year before bottling. We saw one of the crushing processes that used a machine that removed the skin and stems from the grape when they made certain wines.

Chateau Lafitte Rothschild was the most memorable stop in the Bordeaux area. The huge underground cavern beneath the chateau had a series of rooms on one side with wine stored dating back to the early 1700s. The valuable, aged wine was secured by a locked entry gate and cyclone fencing that reached to the ceiling.

Neatly stacked down the middle of the room were new oak barrels filled with the current wine aging. According to the vintner, the Lafitte Rothschild winery decanted the new oak barrels after only six months. Once the barrels were cleaned, six beaten egg whites were put into each barrel before the wine was returned for another six months of aging. The vintner told us the beaten egg whites took any remaining solids out of the wine, helping to give it a silky rich color.

Nixon returned to two of the chateaus for dinner. The kitchens for the chateaus were located about twenty yards or so outside the gated entrance to the chateau. When Nixon had dinner at Chateau Lafitte Rothschild, four of us accompanied him and were invited by the English-speaking chef to sit at a table in the kitchen for a meal. Also with us were two members of the French gendarmerie, who drove the marked police lead car and only spoke French.

When we got settled at the table our police escort immediately asked the chef for some wine. The chef pointed to a case of wine on a small side table. He had obviously placed it there for the security detail. The gendarmerie took out one of the unlabeled bottles, opened it, and sampled it. He then began talking to the chef and a heated argument ensued. I surmised it was about the quality of the wine being offered. Eventually it appeared the chef had a change of heart and gave the two officers a key and pointed to a large outbuilding inside the compound. The officers left and returned fifteen minutes later with two cases of wine and big smiles on their faces.

While they were gone the agitated chef said the men were demanding wine of the highest quality. He said he could not win arguing with the police officers since he did not have time to engage them. He told them where to go to get a case of better wine. During the course of the evening the chef prepared extra food and the six of us had a wonderful meal. One bottle of wine was shared between the four of us while our counterparts enjoyed several bottles. Shortly after dinner the officers took the remaining wine and put it in their marked police car. We could not see them from the kitchen and didn't know if they were drinking, sleeping, or resting.

Later, when Nixon came out to return to our chateau, we checked on the two officers, who were asleep in their car. Since we knew the way back to our chateau we did not bother to wake them.

To have the opportunity to visit some of the top French wineries with a former president was an unimaginable experience. Back in the United States I found myself more interested in wine and paid more attention to the wines I purchased.

We returned to Paris, then visited Versailles and Rheims before working our way to Flensburg. We rode a train through the countryside from France to Lausanne, Switzerland. Staying at the Beau Rivage Hotel on Lake Geneva was a special treat with its view of the lake, swimming pool, and beautiful grounds. Nixon and Rebozo enjoyed the breakfasts at the Beau Rivage Hotel and went out for a light lunch and dinner. Much of Nixon's time was spent in the rooms relaxing, reading, and working on a new book.

The next train ride took us to Vienna, where Nixon stayed at the grand Imperial Hotel. There was a side trip into the countryside one evening to hear the Vienna Philharmonic play at a castle about half an hour or so outside Vienna. The concert was wonderful and afterwards Nixon and Rebozo ate at one of the top restaurants near the Imperial Hotel.

The last night in Vienna led to an interesting story. Nixon and Rebozo ate in the hotel dining room and I went out. Several of us had a leisurely dinner at a small café around the corner recommended by the hotel staff. When I returned to the hotel, the command post reported that Nixon wanted to see me. I knocked on his door and let myself into the suite. Actually it was a very large room with a king-size bed and an elegant chandelier hanging over the foot of the bed. There was a sitting area off to one side with a large desk nearby.

When I came into the room Nixon was preparing to take a shower before going to bed. He greeted me with the statement, "Mike, I can't get the chandelier lights to go off." He advised that the switch on the wall wasn't working. I suggested he take his shower and I would take care of the problem. I spoke to the command post and found out the hotel engineer was home and they were told he would not be available until the next morning. I took out my small Swiss army knife and took the cover off the light switch. Everything looked normal but when I tried to unscrew one of the wires I got a lot of sparks. Not being comfortable with electricity, I put the cover back onto the switch.

I thought for a couple of moments knowing the problem needed to be resolved or Nixon was going to have to try to sleep under the bright chandelier lights. I could hear the shower running in the bathroom as I took off my shoes and moved a chair underneath the chandelier. Slowly with my handkerchief in my hand I methodically twisted all of the bulbs until they went out. There were over twenty light bulbs so it took a while. I had just put the chair back in front of the desk when Nixon came out of the bathroom dressed in the hotel terry cloth robe. Looking at the chandelier with the lights off I am sure he did not realize what I had done. Nixon smiled and thanked me for fixing the problem.

The next morning we boarded the flight to Germany. Shortly after takeoff I realized I had forgotten to tell the front desk how I had solved the chandelier problem. I chuckled as I told Nixon the saga of the chandelier from the night before, wondering how long it would take the electrician to realize the light bulbs needed to be twisted into place. Nixon got a good laugh out of the story.

We arrived in Hamburg, Germany, and drove half an hour to Flensburg, which is on the Abenra Fjord. Rebozo's friend Eric owned a large hotel restaurant complex located outside the north side of Flensburg four or five kilometers from the Danish border. The hotel had a duty-free type store with liquor, chocolates, souvenirs, and other food stuffs. On the German side of the border along the highway halfway between the border and the hotel was a gas station with eight pumps, also owned by Rebozo's friend.

Due to the high taxes in Denmark, bus tours brought people daily to the duty-free store for shopping and lunch in the restaurant. Cars would stream across the border to buy their gas. Eric said the gas pumps were busy all day. I don't remember the numbers, but the hotel had two great border business operations going. Nixon took a ride into Denmark to look at the countryside. The area was mainly farmland. We saw huge plumes of light grey smoke coming from the fields as we crossed the border. Many of the farmers were burning their fields instead of harvesting them, according to Eric, because of the depressed government prices to farmers.

For the agents this was a good stop. We were able to buy things to take back home with us and the hotel, restaurants, and quaint beer *keller* (pub) provided a very relaxing atmosphere. The wooded area around the hotel was nice for walking or jogging. The agents enjoyed not having to leave the grounds and got some rest before returning to the United States.

❀ ❀ ❀

As soon as we got back to New York, President and Mrs. Nixon took a ride to Saddle River and viewed the progress on their new home. Mrs. Nixon had closed on the sale of their townhouse to the Syrian government while we were on the trip to Europe, according to Ruwe. He advised me that the Nixons would move to Saddle River before the first of October.

Nixon was in his new house when President Anwar Sadat of Egypt was assassinated on October 6, 1981, while reviewing their annual 6th of October parade. They were celebrating their victory over Israel during the 1973 war. As Sadat sat in the reviewing stands a number of the ceremonial troops in a truck shot at Sadat and also threw grenades. The leader of the assassins ran into the reviewing stand and shot President Sadat in the head. These troops were not supposed to have ammunition in their weapons.

Nixon got the word on Wednesday afternoon, October 7, that President Reagan was inviting former Presidents Carter, Ford, and Nixon to accompany Secretary of State Alexander Haig to attend the funeral of President Sadat in Egypt on Saturday, October 10. We had less than twenty-four hours to get our agents ready to depart. McCann, who would be traveling commercially, worked with Burch to take care of the logistics. They made arrangements for flights and requested State Department support for the agents traveling without visas. McCann and Burch agreed that all agents traveling should be told it was mandatory for them to wear their bullet-proof vests at the funeral.

As I got ready for the trip the next afternoon, I thought about the shah's funeral in July 1980. I was sure we needed to be ready for the controlled chaos similar to that of the shah's funeral. There was a possibility Nixon would make additional stops, but we did not have any specific information. I selected two lightweight suits to wear on the trip. From information provided during the earlier call from the Andrews AFB operations desk I knew that the each former presidents was flying on a JetStar and would land thirty seconds apart in descending order of seniority, with Nixon arriving last. Newark Airport was only thirty minutes from Saddle River.

When we got to Newark Airport, the limousine was escorted directly to the waiting JetStar. We arrived early and waited for about ten minutes before leaving the ramp area. Sitting on the ramp I thought about the times that just Mrs. Nixon and I flew from Andrews Air Force Base on the JetStar for her visits to New York City. As we waited, Nixon surprised me by saying that after the funeral he thought he was going to make stops in Saudi Arabia, Jordan, Tunisia, and Morocco. He said he would not know for sure for a couple of days.

What followed after our departure from Newark was an amazing program and a feat of logistical genius. Our JetStar was picked up immediately after becoming airborne by the radar center in the Washington, D.C., area. Andrews was monitoring the three JetStars arriving from Colorado, Georgia, and New Jersey. Carter touched down, followed thirty seconds later by Ford, and followed thirty seconds later by Nixon. I watched out of a window as the three planes parked with their wing tips with only a couple of feet between them. The doors were opened about ten seconds apart, and first Carter then Ford and finally Nixon came down the stairs and moved toward the walkway leading to a microphone. The three of them came together simultaneously and walked the last ten yards shoulder to shoulder. Later, according to a press report, Joe Canzeri, my friend when he was special assistant to Vice President Rockefeller, was identified as the person who had choreographed the arrival of the former presidents.

Arriving at the White House, the three presidents were escorted to the Blue Room to meet President Reagan and Secretary Haig. Once we entered the White House, I stayed downstairs and went to the White House detail's family security room. I quickly called Burch, confirming the information of the possibility of additional stops in the Middle East.

Next I called our Foreign Intelligence Branch and passed our tentative new itinerary on to them.

When I was through, I walked up the stairs and stood near the grand staircase leading to the First Family's private residence. Surveying the assembled press, staff, agents, and dignitaries I saw Nancy Reagan, Barbara Bush, and Patricia Haig standing near the Blue Room door. Mrs. Reagan made eye contact with me and smiled. I realized I had not talked to her since 1969. As I watched, she excused herself and walked over to me. The first lady seemed surprised to see me and asked why I was at the White House. I told her I was in charge of Nixon's detail.

Mrs. Reagan said, "Don't go away. I have to finish my conversation with Barbara Bush and I will come and get you." She finished by saying, "Ronnie is going to love to see you."

I waited for her to return to her conversation with Mrs. Bush. Since her back was to me as she spoke to Mrs. Bush, I left and went out to the south grounds and got on the helicopter. I contacted CROWN radio, the White House Communication Center, and told them if the first lady or anyone else was looking for me to tell them I was off the air. I did keep my radio on to monitor in case something I needed to hear was broadcast.

Sitting on the helicopter I thought about Mrs. Reagan. I knew if I had waited she would have said to President Reagan, "Look who is here." It was not that I did not want to see and talk to the president. I understood this was about three presidents going to Egypt for a funeral. It was President Reagan and their day. I did not think it was appropriate for Michael Endicott to be interjected into their day, even if the first lady wanted to do it.

It was early evening when we took off from Andrews aboard SAM 2600, the old Air Force One and now the back-up to Air Force One.

Director Simpson was on the flight along with the heads of the other former presidents' details. In addition, Secretary of State Haig's security detail was on the plane. It was interesting for me to be sitting in the same VIP area as the former presidents. Rosalynn Carter accompanied her husband and was seated next to him in the VIP area. Just before we landed to refuel at Torrejon Air Force Base outside of Madrid, Director Simpson took me aside and told me he was making me his representative to all the former presidents. He said I would be responsible for them and my first assignment was to let them all know he wanted them to wear their armored vests during the Sadat funeral.

Nixon and I were the first to get off the aircraft to take a walk. We were followed by the Carters and Ford and their agents leaders.

I gave Nixon a briefing on the intelligence provided to me for the funeral. Afterwards I passed on Director Simpson's request that he wear his vest. Nixon asked about the others, wanting to know if they were going to wear theirs also. I told him I would be talking to each one of them with the same message from Simpson.

When I spoke to Ford, I introduced myself, briefed him on the intelligence, and made the vest request. I told him I had spoken to Nixon and he had agreed to wear his. Ford told me he would wear the vest if the others were. Looking around the ramp, I saw that President Carter was about fifty yards away. I cut across the ramp and caught up with him and his wife. Introducing myself, I once again went over the intelligence for the funeral and passed on the request from Director Simpson. President and Mrs. Carter both had questions about the intelligence and he seemed reluctant to wear the vest. He would not make the commitment even after I told him Nixon and Ford were going to wear their vests. Finally he told me he would talk with his detail leader first. I thanked him and we headed for the plane where all the other passengers had already re-boarded.

Director Simpson was standing at the top of the stairs. He had been monitoring my progress from his distant perch. When President Carter arrived at the top step Simpson asked him, "Well, how did my salesman do?"

Carter barely paused as he answered Simpson, "Okay, okay, I'll wear it."

Later on the plane I spoke with his detail leader, Bill Hoskyn, and told him about my conversation with President and Mrs. Carter.

There were two armored limousines on the ramp in Cairo, Egypt, on Friday, October 9 as we deplaned. President and Mrs. Carter got in one and Nixon and Ford in the other. Simpson had told me during the final approach that I would ride in the front seat of the limousine shared by Ford and Nixon. As we left the airport for the first time since I had been around Nixon, I heard him called something other than Mr. Nixon or President Nixon. A very relaxed Ford said, "So, Dick, how are you doing?" I put the partition up to give them privacy.

The funeral was scheduled for the next day. I thought it would be a quiet night at the hotel. I was wrong. The American delegation, including the three former presidents, had a dinner at Cairo's El Salam Hotel. Before the dinner I spent time with McCann going over the proposed schedule of our other stops. About all we knew was that Nixon was waiting on word to see if a Saudi aircraft was going to pick him up on Sunday. I was sure Burch would find out before us and take care of the notifications.

The next morning I reminded Nixon to wear his vest. He once again questioned me, "Are the others going to wear theirs?"

"Yes," I replied. I was waiting outside the command post when the day shift leader came out to accompany me to the funeral. I noticed he was not wearing his vest and told him to go put it on for the funeral. He told me he did not bring it. I told him McCann advised everyone that the vest was mandatory for the visit. Frustrated, he snapped back to me that it was his life. Trying to control my emotions I said, "I care about Nixon's life, not yours. I need people who can survive an attack to keep Nixon alive." The shift leader was told to stay at the hotel and run the command post. I directed him to have the agent running the command post to go with me.

We arrive at a staging area near the parade grounds where Sadat was assassinated. There were a number of large tents set up. The procession to the mosque was designed for dignitaries and their delegations to group by continents. The American dignitaries were assembling in their tent and would be notified to join with other delegations for the procession to the interment. There was heightening concern due to the fact that the procession would pass by the exact point where Sadat lost his life. About five minutes before we were to begin the procession, the ID agent told me some ceremonial soldiers had shown up with ammunition in their weapons that were supposed to be empty. He told me to hold the departure of our delegation until a platoon of special operations troops arrived. Word quickly spread about the ceremonial troops, and soon the top leaders of Europe migrated to our tent. Everyone seemed to know we would have a special military group surrounding our delegation. As we departed, the European delegation joined us and the Egyptian special operations unit completely surrounded our enlarged group. We were escorted along the procession route. It was a little nerve-wracking but went well. Fortunately it was a fairly short walk without the general public being allowed access.

The next day a Saudi aircraft flew Nixon and our agents to Riyadh, Saudi Arabia. Nixon had meetings and a dinner there. The next day he was off to meetings, dinner, and an overnight in Amman, Jordan. Our third stop was Tunis, Tunisia, for the next round of meetings, dinner, and an overnight. While Nixon had dinner, we were in a separate room for a dinner hosted by the head of their security. It was a sumptuous dinner with couscous, lamb, and vegetables. The second course, a large, whole, white-flesh fish, fed over twenty people. The fish had been placed in the middle of the table in front of our English-speaking host and McCann. We were relaxing after the fish course waiting for the dishes to be taken away before they served dessert. Our host reached out in front of McCann and plucked the quarter-size eye out of the fish. McCann got an incredulous look on his face as he watched our host put the eye in his mouth and slowly eat it. I thought McCann was going to lose it. For me it was the highlight of the night, no, of the trip.

Our last overnight before leaving for New York was Morocco. Nixon seemed to especially enjoy seeing his friend King Hassan II. With Nixon's whirlwind tour of five countries in eight days over we all looked forward to getting back to New Jersey. At the Rabat Airport the king had made arrangements for Nixon and our agents to fly on a government-owned, regularly scheduled Moroccan commercial aircraft. Moroccan security forces armed with machine guns boarded the Royal Moroccan aircraft first and had everyone in first class move to coach. We were all seated in first class. Needless to say, there were a few unhappy passengers in the coach section.

❖ ❖ ❖

When the move to the home in the borough of Saddle River, New Jersey, finally came in the fall, it gave President Nixon what he wanted a more relaxing location, his own pool, privacy, and a place to walk. The house, the pool with cabaña, and the lighted tennis court were hidden by the trees and could not be seen by sightseers driving by on Charlden Drive. The previous owner had put in a gravel road extension off the circular drive that allowed vehicles access to a small parking area in back for people who came only to use the tennis court or swimming pool. Between the small lot and the swimming pool was a cabaña that also helped protect the privacy of the residence. The heavily treed parcel next door at the end of a cul-de-sac was not developed and adjoined the apple orchard. The lot and orchard gave an additional buffer of privacy to the Nixons.

The residence on the property behind them was on the far side of their two-acre parcel facing Chestnut Ridge Road in Woodcliff Lake, New Jersey. One Saturday afternoon I was in the command post when we were advised by the back post that two men were entering the wooded property belonging to Nixon from the Woodcliff Lake property. I immediately responded by heading in that direction carrying an Uzi machine gun. It turned out it was Mr. Danny Luciano, who owned the property abutting the rear of Nixon's property. Luciano, the athletic director at Northern Valley High School in Old Tapan, New Jersey, was showing a friend Nixon's property, not realizing a Secret Service agent would respond. We had a nice talk and exchanged phone numbers in case we ever needed to contact each other.

At my request, shortly after he moved to Saddle River, Nixon hosted a reception for some members of the Bergen County Chiefs Association. The gathering of approximately twenty people included a couple of associated members of the organization. Nixon met everyone present and spoke to them, thanking them for their service to their communities and reaffirming his support for law enforcement. He had his picture taken with each of the guests and later signed all of them.

Saddle River did not have cable television when Nixon moved into the borough. He had asked me and, I am sure, Burch several times about the cable television situation in Saddle River. He was advised by both of us that unfortunately there was no cable and there was no future date scheduled for the borough to bring in cable television. Nixon was told that most of his neighbors had satellite dishes.

I spoke to operations assistant Burch about the cable situation. He mentioned he had already contacted one of the vice presidents of the cable television provider that served the houses on Chestnut Ridge Road, which bordered the back of the orchard and went past the Lucianos behind Nixon's property. Agent Burch said the cable company was willing to bring the cable to a telephone pole at the apple orchard which was over a quarter of a mile away. Burch said we would have to get the cable from the pole to Nixon's house. He said the cable would be a win-win for both Nixon and the detail, since we would both have cable television. I was delighted to see Burch recognize a need and immediately address the issue. I knew I had my back covered.

Not wanting to complicate the issue, I spoke with Luciano and he agreed to have the cable brought to the telephone pole at the front corner of his property. It would not be any problem to get the cable through the woods to Nixon's house from there. Burch arranged for the cable to be brought to Luciano's property.

Once we had a date for the cable to be brought to the pole, I contacted Al Fasstto, a contractor friend who lived in Saddle River. I had previously spoken with him of our cable television project. He brought two of his construction employees over one Saturday morning and with hand tools they dug a six-to-eight-inch trench to Nixon's property, burying the cable along the way. The television line was buried halfway through the forested area at the rear of Nixon's property and then elevated up one of the trees to about ten feet and strung through the trees to the garage. There the cable was split, going both to the Secret Service command post and to the residence. With the assistance of another contact, we got the cable and cable boxes hooked up to all the televisions in Nixon's house and to the one in the command post. Needless to say, everyone on our detail, along with the Nixons, was delighted to have cable television. Arrangements were made for the bill to be mailed to Chief Re, who had a cable account. He sent it to President Nixon's office for payment.

❖ ❖ ❖

Julie and David Eisenhower followed the President and Mrs. Nixon to the Northeast in 1981. With daughter Jenny and son Alex, the Eisenhower family settled in Berwyn, Pennsylvania. The Nixon families were now all together. You could see how elated both President and Mrs. Nixon were having their children and grandchildren moving so near to them.

Like many grandparents, the Nixons had special names given to them by their grandchildren. President Nixon was fondly called Ba and Mrs. Nixon was referred to as Ma. For the grandparents there were regular weekend trips to Berwyn to relax and enjoy their family. Mrs. Nixon stayed for a number of days with Julie to help with Jenny and Alex when her granddaughter Melanie was born in 1984.

On Nixon trips to Pennsylvania to visit with the Eisenhower family, we would take a limited number of agents and stay in a nearby motel. Our motorcade would normally leave Friday afternoon or Saturday morning and return Sunday afternoon. It was usually a very relaxing time for us since the Nixons stayed at the Eisenhower residence. On rare occasions there were side trips, but normally the weekends were spent entirely at the Eisenhower residence. Agent McCann, who had previously been assigned to the Philadelphia Field Office, introduced me to the renowned Philly steak and cheese hoagie during this time.

❖ ❖ ❖

The move to Saddle River, New Jersey, required a minor adjustment to the day shift schedule. Two members of the day shift and the driver would report along with the supervisor to the Nixon residence by 5:45 a.m. to escort Nixon into his lower Manhattan office. After departing the residence, the limousine would drive five minutes to the paper shop in Ho-Ho-Kus to pick up *The New York Times* and *The Wall Street Journal*. President Nixon would turn on the rear light and read the editorial page and front section of *The New York Times* and the editorial page of *The Wall Street Journal* before arriving at his office approximately fifty minutes after leaving his house. His normal routine was to depart his office at noon for the return to Saddle River.

Once in a while he stopped at the Cox residence for lunch with Tricia. He also used her apartment for special meetings when he wanted a more intimate setting than his office. There were occasions when former Secretary of State Kissinger would come by the apartment for a private meeting. Once, as Nixon got out of the car at the apartment, he said, "Mike, I know you don't normally do this, but you know Kissinger, so would you mind greeting him and escorting him to the apartment? I want to stroke him a little and make him feel comfortable for our meeting." I agreed and did as Nixon requested. Kissinger said hello when I greeted him and seemed appreciative to be escorted to Tricia's apartment for his meeting.

When the meeting was over, Nixon came out ten minutes after Kissinger and thanked me and commented on how much he enjoyed the meeting with Kissinger. From my assignment with Secretary of State Kissinger and conversations with Nixon I believe that the two of them respected each other professionally. I could also see they were very different in their personalities and both understood that fact. I don't believe that either saw the other necessarily as a rival and they both appeared to me to be mission-driven and results-oriented. Nixon had relied heavily on Kissinger during the White House years in developing foreign policy and Kissinger was loyal to Nixon.

Nixon once told me that he interviewed Kissinger twice for the position of national security advisor when he became president. He mentioned that some on his senior staff did not want Kissinger in the position. Nixon said there was concern over the fact that Kissinger was associated with the liberal Rockefeller wing of the Republican Party. Nixon said he knew Kissinger was very bright and a strategic global thinker. He told me there was no question in his mind that he and Kissinger could work well together and felt it would be important to have his help in planning and carrying out foreign policy. Nixon said he needed the world and the press to perceive Kissinger as the power player. I sensed that President Nixon felt that if the press perceived Kissinger as the power player they would be more acceptable of his foreign policy.

After the move to New Jersey, agent Burch entered our detail in a slow pitch softball league in the spring of 1982. The teams were all from the law enforcement community. Paramus PD, Ridgewood PD, Hakensack PD, New Jersey State Police, and Port Authority Police were some of the departments that had teams in this league. We played seven-inning games early on Friday evenings. Our home games were played at the Saddle River Country Day School, less than a mile away from Nixon's residence. The softball field was in a lower recreation area behind the school.

It was a relaxing and fun league. We had a talented group of athletes, led by Special Officer Johnny "Fever" Keirans, agents Fran "Primo" Primavera, Gary Ross, Pat "Sully" Sullivan, Bill Burch, Larry McCann, John Barry, Tom Sloan, Gerry Connolly, Stan Dobrynio, and Doug Ferry, among others. Many of our wives and families often came to the games. President Nixon came to several of our home games and seemed to enjoy watching us play. He took time to talk with the wives and was a magnet drawing all the kids around him. Nixon greeted the opposing players and the umpires. He had his picture taken with the children and after the game joined us in the team picture.

We became acquainted with two of the umpires, Bert Ammerman and Ed Koehler, who umpired some of our games. They both had an opportunity to meet Nixon and became good friends with many of our players. When they umpired our games, Ammerman and Koehler were invited to join our team after our games to celebrate, win or lose. The two of them worked at Northern Valley High School in Old Tapan, where Nixon's neighbor Danny Luciano was the athletic director. I shared the Luciano Uzi machine gun story with them. Koehler was a physical education teacher and Ammerman was in the administrative office. The two of them were sent invitations to our office Christmas party and, along with their families, were invited to our summer Secret Service picnic.

Christmas holidays in Ho-Ho-Kus were a fun time at the detail and especially the Endicott household. There were the usual rounds of parties with friends and associates. President Nixon would have a reception at his house for the staff, agents, and a few friends. Mrs. Nixon did an absolutely wonderful job of decorating her home with fresh wreaths, poinsettias small, medium, and huge, a crèche, and a lighted

Christmas tree with an enviable collection of special balls, bells, and bows. Everyone on the detail looked forward to bringing their wife or significant other to visit at Christmas time. The former first lady looked spectacular and was so graceful in a red or green Christmas dress.

Our Secret Service group would have a get-together for our staff and friends at our office. The party was pot-luck with everyone sharing in providing food, drink, and decorations for the event. At the first Christmas get-together, agent John Rodrigues made the award-winning gingerbread house on the cover of *Family Circle* magazine. He was extremely talented and his decorated house looked exactly like the magazine cover. I envied his artistic talent.

As a courtesy, we invited President Nixon to our office Christmas party. We were somewhat surprised but pleased when he accepted our invitation. In the almost two years I had been with Nixon, I was beginning to understand that he appreciated how important the local community of police, merchants, and friends were to the Secret Service and to him. Nixon was such a complex individual it was often difficult for me to see through the blur of Nixon the person, the politician, and the president. There was no question he seemed to enjoy the interaction with the members of the community. However, I also realized that he saw greeting people as something public figures should do. He commented to me privately on many occasions how few people in our country had the opportunity to meet and speak with a president.

Nixon's relationship with the agents on the detail was very good. He went out of his way to sign books and pictures for the agents and their friends. He made arrangements through his friend Don Kendall, CEO and chairman of the board of Pepsi Cola, to deliver sodas to our command post and his office each month. Nixon often talked with agents about their families and personal lives. He seemed to enjoy the informality of the detail.

On the occasion when Nixon came to our office for the Christmas party, he stood in a receiving line and had his picture taken and shook hands with the guests, agents, and their wives. After the receiving line and pictures were over, Nixon gave a short, upbeat address about the holidays. He remained for a short time chatting with many of the guests. Often I would be near and observe him working the people at the event, wondering did he really enjoy these parties or was it a duty?

During the holidays there were periodic evening drives into the neighborhoods of the surrounding towns in New Jersey and New York to enjoy seeing the elaborately decorated homes. Many homes had lights along the eaves, around the windows and doors, and some had shrubs and trees also wrapped in lights. There were inflatable Santa Clauses big and small, some on the roof, and others in the yard. Painted plywood reindeer and red sleighs full of gifts, often bathed in lights, looked ready to fly. Other lighted, stationary, or mechanical reindeer adorned some yards while crèche scenes would highlight others.

Drives around midtown Manhattan to see the Christmas decorations might follow dinner at the Cox apartment or dinner at home. President and Mrs. Nixon both enjoyed seeing the trees on Park Avenue that were decorated with white lights. Rockefeller Center's decorations, its annual Christmas tree, and the angels of light between the buildings, always drew large crowds.

Horse-drawn carriages, moving slowly with the traffic down Fifth Avenue, were decorated with red ribbons, wreaths made of fresh evergreen boughs, and Christmas lights. The clickity-clacking of the horse's shoes could be heard as the carriages approached and passed some of the slower moving cars. Other holiday favorites of the Nixons included hotels such as the Helmsley, the Plaza, and the Waldorf Astoria, along with the well-known toy store FAO Schwartz with its elaborate Christmas decorations. After the holiday receptions were over, many of the bowl games played, and the New Year's Eve ball dropped in New York's Time Square, it was back to work.

❖ ❖ ❖

Former President Nixon probably had the most recognizable face in the world and was perceived by many in and out of the Secret Service as having the highest threat level of any of the former presidents. Personally I felt the threat level had diminished dramatically since he left the White House and was basically nonexistent. Nixon, however, generated a high interest level, and some people confused interest level with threat level. As the Nixon detail leader, I understood how low his threat level was and I was comfortable using fewer people at the residence and traveling with smaller numbers than any of the other former presidents' details. I was probably the only one in the Secret Service to articulate the difference between threat level and interest level and managed my personnel accordingly. One of the things I enjoyed about working for the Secret Service was that it gave supervisors a lot of latitude in implementing policies. I had become very comfortable using fewer people.

Having a smaller detail was driven by security concepts I developed over the years through exposure to so many different types of Secret Service details and security plans. It also helped that Nixon preferred small numbers. There were times when I knew I could justify taking more people, but I saw our major role as stopping an embarrassing situation, not stopping someone who wanted to harm the former president. In all the time I had been with President and Mrs. Nixon, there were no real threats and I could not bring myself to increase the number of agents in order to address theoretical security threats.

❖ ❖ ❖

President and Mrs. Nixon were invited to use a friend's beach home in Montego Bay, Jamaica, one summer. President Nixon spoke to his friend Rebozo and they decide to take Mrs. Nixon and Rebozo's friend Jane Lucke for a short, quiet vacation to Jamaica. McCann was on vacation and I was scheduled to make the trip. At the last minute I was unable to go so my new assistant Bill Burch replaced me as the working supervisor and made the trip to Jamaica.

Two days before President Nixon was scheduled to return to the United States, Burch called to tell me that someone had stolen a purse out of Lucke's room with several hundred dollars in it. He said the police were investigating the theft and he would brief me when he got back. Burch mentioned that Nixon was very upset over the theft.

When he got back, Burch explained the residence being used by Nixon and Rebozo was inside a walled compound. He said Nixon and the rest of the group went out for dinner one night and Burch said he left one person back, along with the local police, for security at the residence. When the party returned, Lucke discovered her purse with the money in it was missing. According to Burch, she reported it to Rebozo and Nixon. The two of them could not believe the purse with the money was taken out from under the noses of the Secret Service. Nixon reported it to the agents and that got the investigation going, according to Burch.

The room where Lucke was staying was at the back of the compound near the rear wall. The preliminary police investigation led to one of the house staff and a friend as suspects. The police found the purse abandoned on the other side of the back wall near where Lucke was staying, but the money was missing. Burch told me that the investigation had not been completed by the time he left but we would get the final report. He added that Nixon was really upset over the theft and had been in several discussions with Mrs. Nixon and his guest about it. Burch advised that one of the agents had overheard a discussion where Nixon referred to our detail as "twenty-six incompetent assholes."

I told Burch it certainly looked that way since the purse was stolen from a room inside our inner security perimeter. I mentioned that I didn't think either one of us believed Nixon really thought our detail was either incompetent or assholes but I could understand Nixon's frustrations. I asked Burch to speak to the agent who had overheard the comment and make sure Nixon's comments did not become an issue. Everyone on the detail should be aware of the fact we were lucky that only the purse was stolen. Burch and I understood the incident could have been much worse.

When he got back to the office, Burch coordinated the Jamaican police investigation of the purse theft with headquarters. Arrangements were made with our Office of Investigations for a Secret Service polygraph examiner to travel to Jamaica. According to Burch, both the maids and the butler were given polygraph tests. He said one maid failed the polygraph and the other one ratted on her and confirmed she stole the purse. The last Burch heard the maid that stole the purse was taken away by the police. He was not advised as to the punishment that was meted out.

❖ ❖ ❖

Back in Saddle River Nixon enjoyed his daily walks around the neighborhood and on Chestnut Ridge Road. Usually one agent would walk with him and one would trail in one of our cars. The former president, an early riser, normally went out for his walks around five in the morning when it was still dark.

Nixon continued writing books, completing *Leaders* in 1982 and *Real War* in 1984. He made occasional trips domestically, speaking to various foreign policy groups around the country. He also visited Washington periodically for meetings or speeches. Since Reagan became president in 1981, Nixon seemed to be more relaxed and more involved. He traveled overseas to keep up on foreign policy issues and continued to have access to top leaders in the United States and around the world. Some of his travel between 1980 and 1985 was to keep in touch with world leaders, some for research for a new book, or promotion for one of the many books he had already written.

In the summer of 1982 Burch made arrangement for us to have a detail picnic gathering at the Rindlaub Park behind the Borough Hall in Saddle River. The picnic was a big success. All the agents and their families showed up and President Nixon dropped by for a visit. The focal point of the picnic was the children. There were foot races, sack races, a race carrying an egg on a spoon, and a water balloon-catching contest. Everyone brought side dishes and we cooked hot dogs, hamburgers, and baked beans. Nixon arrived in time to mingle with the kids and watch some of the competitions.

I was especially fortunate because my children Michael, Robin, Leslie, and James were staying with Stacy and me for the summer. They had a wonderful time enjoying the activities and the food. Also my mom came out from Prairie Ridge on the plateau above Puyallup, Washington. She helped Stacy take care of David, who was only a year old. My mom, Flora Endicott, enjoyed meeting President Nixon and having her picture taken with him holding David. It turned out to be a perfect day for me and my family.

❖ ❖ ❖

Mrs. Nixon made regular visits to Elizabeth Arden's and occasionally would also go shopping at Saks Fifth Avenue or other small boutiques. Normally when she went out special officer Keirans or O'Grady would drive her. Inasmuch as Mrs. Nixon went out infrequently, the officers were also used to drive the former president and work the command post. On one Wednesday when the maid was off Mrs. Nixon had a hair appointment and one of the agents drove her. I was in New York City and was not at the residence when Mrs. Nixon got back.

The next day Heidi Retter, the maid, called me in the security room and said she needed to talk with me. I met her outside the front door and she told me she had overheard a conversation between Mrs. Nixon and the president. Mrs. Nixon told him that the day before when she was shopping the agent accompanying her spent time shopping and trying on clothes, according to the maid. She told her husband when they arrived back at the house that she mentioned to the agent that she knew agents did not carry bags. She told the agent, however, that the maid was off and could an exception be made for one day. According to the maid, the agent declined to help with the bags. I asked the maid not to repeat this story to anyone else.

I checked the shift report from the previous day to confirm the name of the agent that drove Mrs. Nixon the previous day. The agent was working the four to twelve shift and was in the guard booth on post one later in the afternoon. I told the shift leader I was going out to the guard booth. Entering the booth I said hello to the agent and followed with, "You see everything in black and white, don't you?"

The agent asked, "What do you mean?"

I said, "You don't help with bags or open doors."

The agent told me that was correct. I said, "You are two-faced." I then proceeded to tell the agent, "You accept free sodas, you get free books signed for relatives and friends, you get pictures signed, and you go to the Christmas party and other events sponsored by President Nixon. Everything you get is given to you by the president. Yet you deny a seventy-three-year-old woman's request to help with bags. I have never told anyone to carry a bag or open a door and I never will. You were under an overhang in an area completely protected from public view and you said no to a reasonable request. If you were outside your own home and a seventy-three-year-old woman neighbor was taking packages out of her car to carry into her house you would voluntarily go over and help her. There is something called common courtesy. I am not asking you to carry packages or open doors. I am asking you not to be two-faced. Don't accept things from the Nixons if you can't show them common courtesy. The road needs to run two ways at certain times." I never told anyone about the incident. It was not my intent to embarrass the agent but have the agent look at a broader picture. Later I apologized to Mrs. Nixon and told her I didn't think it would happen again.

❖ ❖ ❖

As the number of Nixon grandchildren increased and they grew big enough to play and swim, President Nixon enjoyed spending more time with them. The tennis court came to be an enjoyable playground for the president and his grandchildren. He and the kids developed their own games using a bat, tennis racket, and balls. During visits by the grandchildren on Saturday and/or Sunday afternoons, the grandchildren could be found playing games on the tennis court with their grandpa. It was apparent the grandchildren loved playing with Ba.

❖ ❖ ❖

In February 1983 McCann was replaced by Bill Wasley to assist as a working supervisor with Nixon. He, like McCann, would also take Nixon out of town domestically and overseas. Once again I hit a home run getting Wasley. He had spent time in PSD and was excellent at dealing with multiple tasks. He came highly recommended by my PSD colleagues Barney Boyett and Bill Bush and I knew he was going to be great with Nixon and the agents.

On one of the overseas trips Nixon went to Paris, France. He got together there with his old friend, retired Ambassador Vernon Walters who spoke six Western European languages plus Chinese and Russian. Walters and Nixon first met during the Eisenhower administration when Walters did translations for President Eisenhower, Vice President Nixon, and other government officials. Walters was in the car with Vice President Nixon in Caracas, Venezuela, in 1958 when demonstrators stoned the limousine. Walters suffered superficial cuts to his face during the attack on Nixon. He and Nixon continued their close relationship when Nixon appointed him to the position of deputy director of the CIA in 1972. Walters was also used by Nixon to support Kissinger's secret negotiations with the North Vietnamese to end the Vietnam War.

Nixon and Walters had lunch together at a restaurant in the center of Paris not far from Walter's Paris apartment. After lunch Walters asked Nixon if he would like to walk to his nearby apartment to see how he lived. It was a warm, beautiful day and Nixon agreed. Walking down the street Nixon was instantly recognized and people began asking for his autograph. Soon there was a large crowd surrounding the two of them and with Nixon signing autographs it had become difficult for us to keep walking. After about ten minutes Walters turned to me and said I needed to get Nixon away from the crowd. Smiling, I kidded Walters, "This was your idea; you get him out of here."

Walters knew I had been kidding and I asked where his apartment was located. He pointed across the street and said the entrance was in a small alcove. I asked him to walk alongside Nixon and I would take care of everything. Talking in a low voice into Nixon's ear, I told him we needed to begin walking. Grasping his belt from the back I said,

"When I tell you to turn I will stop you and we will make a quick exit to our right from the crowd."

As Nixon began walking the people waiting for autographs ran to the front to continue asking for autographs. We were able to pick up a little speed and soon everyone was ahead of us as we were nearing a crosswalk in the middle of the street. Slowing down a little, I watched the light at the crosswalk. I timed it so that when the light at the crosswalk changed from red to green I was next to it. I pulled on Nixon's belt and said into his ear, "Turn." Following my lead, we quickly turned and walked away from the autograph seekers. We were crossing the street before the autograph seekers understood what we were doing. Walking the short distance to his apartment Walters turned to me and said, "That was the neatest move I have ever seen the Secret Service execute." When we got to the apartment building Walters said that they would be upstairs in his apartment for a short time. By the time they came down and said their goodbyes we had our cars in front of the apartment building.

In the fall of 1984 Nixon and I were walking together when he brought up the idea that he was thinking about giving up his Secret Service protection. He said he had been thinking about it since he spoke with agent Ed Pollard (assistant director, Protective Operations) a couple of months earlier. Nixon told me he knew he had the fewest number of agents of the former presidents, and at $3.5 million the cost for operating his detail was the least of the former presidents, according to what Pollard had told him. Nixon spoke to me about the Yankees, Mets, and Giants. He told me how he would go to more games if he had fewer people. Nixon said he believed taking six to eight people to ball games inconvenienced too many people. He also said he didn't think he needed the level of security currently being provided. He was not angry or upset and was not excited. He was telling me what was in his heart. For me, I saw his comments as a trial balloon.

I waited for him to get everything off his chest and told him that the security around him was more to facilitate his daily schedule and prevent embarrassment than to stop someone from harming him. As far as I was concerned, I told him, he owed it to his family and to the country to keep his Secret Service detail. I also mentioned that our detail took care of all the logistical and operational needs for him. Nixon did not respond and the conversation died a natural death.

❊ ❊ ❊

Since his move to the East Coast, Nixon had made a couple of trips to Morocco to see his good friend King Hassan II who ruled Morocco 1961-1999. The trips were relaxing and gave the agents an opportunity to enjoy a luxury hotel, visit the *soukh* to buy some local arts and crafts, and enjoy the culture. On one trip in particular, agent Frank Murphy was standing in front of the hotel dressed in local garb wearing a *dishdaha* (robe), a red fez, and Moroccan shoes with curled toes, plus sunglasses. When Nixon arrived, he shook hands and spoke with Murphy on the way to the front door. President Nixon did not realize it was agent Murphy.

After we got settled, Murphy, McCann, and a couple of agents were outside by the pool and a reporter came over and wanted to know who the person in the Arab garb was. He said he had seen President Nixon speak with him and wanted to know if he was a businessman. The reporter was led to believe Murphy was an oil merchant. They made no representations of involvement between Nixon and the Arab-looking Murphy. Afterwards Murphy changed into his regular cloths for the visit and the media people did not realize he was the one who they were trying to identify.

Later in the visit Murphy awoke in the middle of the night to an acrid odor in his room. He opened his door to the hallway to see if there was a problem and saw President Nixon standing in his doorway. Realizing the odor was coming from the small room where his toilet was located, Murphy opened the door. Someone had placed a recently butchered head of a ram, complete with large curled horns, on top of the toilet. A number of candles were burning but did not cover the foul odor emanating from the ram head. As soon as he opened the door to his restroom, Murphy heard President Nixon close his. Murphy told me later he felt Nixon knew of the scheme and was complicit.

On Nixon's departure from the hotel to return to the United States, Murphy was once again dressed in his Moroccan costume. This time he was standing near the rear door of the limousine. As Nixon approached the car McCann said to him, "I want to introduce you..." but before he could finish the sentence "...to agent Murphy," Nixon grabbed Murphy's hand and started talking and then quickly got into the car. Murphy said to Nixon as he was sitting down, "Mr. President, it is Murph." A confused Nixon looked up as Murphy repeated himself. Nixon became irritated as he finally figured out who the person dressed in the Moroccan costume really was. As the car drove off, agent Murphy was not sure if Nixon was upset or not. When Murphy next saw him in New York everything was okay.

❖ ❖ ❖

The Nixon detail had a very talented group of agents, including Larry McCann, Bill Wasley, Bill Burch, and Joe Gallo, who embraced the concept of reducing the number of agents used to protect Nixon. All of them were people persons and developed excellent rapport with the other agents. They worked aggressively in developing Gary Ross, Bert

Vint, Tom Sloan, Frank Murphy, Doug Ferry, Pat Sullivan, and Karen Toll, among others, as future leaders. The leadership roles developed by our detail agents led to a high number of them being promoted. Of the three former presidents, Nixon, Ford, and Carter, our detail had the fewest number of people assigned to it and received the most promotions. Special officers John Keirans and Jim O'Grady worked closely with the detail agents and the Nixons. They were excellent drivers and could always be counted on to assist in any way they could.

Sloan, Ross, and Vint developed a comprehensive small detail training program. They coordinated most of our training exercises with the Bergen County Police and Fire Academy using both their facility and trainees to assist us. They also coordinated with nearby Ramapo College to use their swimming pool for water safety exercises. Since Nixon spent so much time around the water, Sloan, Ross, and Vint developed one exercise involving a boat overturning and saving a drowning person.

The training exercises were up to four hours long and designed to try to create an emergency-type situation around the normal day-to-day activities of the former president. There was one exercise where the person playing Nixon began choking in a car after stopping to get the newspaper. How long before the agents identified the problem and how did they handle it? Another scenario found two agents walking with Nixon without a car trailing, when one of agents was hit by a vehicle. While the agent at the scene radioed the command post agent for help, it was flooded with inane calls looking for an agent, a telephone number, or asking for information about a shift schedule. One of the goals was to try to disrupt the focus of the command post agent while the agent responded to an emergency needing support to the scene and a vehicle to pick up Nixon. A third exercise had Nixon confronted by a disturbed person while walking into his building. Was the person a threat or just disturbed? How long before the person was recognized and how was the person neutralized? On some occasions an exercise was presented with Nixon walking along a crowd line where he was attacked by a person with a gun. How quickly was the shooter identified and did the person get a shot off before being neutralized?

Someone needed to cover and evacuate the person they were protecting and others needed to neutralize the attack. With a small detail like ours, oftentimes there were only two to four agents with Nixon. One thing about people who were disturbed approaching Nixon, they were usually easy to identify right away. If their dress and/or body language didn't immediately give them away, then their eyes would. Their body actions, walking, and head control were so different from the norm that agents simply should not miss them.

Probably the most interesting and challenging exercise was when an aircraft body was simulated inside the indoor pistol range at the Bergen County Police and Fire Academy. During the three-plus hour exercise, agents had to check in for the flight and deal with everything from an inebriated passenger, a mix-up in seat assignments, passengers asking for a picture and autographs, and a United States senator on the flight, to a media representative wanting an interview. Everyone knew the aircraft was going to be hijacked but they didn't know how or when. We used fifteen people from the local community and an equal number of officers from local police departments and a tactical assault team. The support people played the roles of passenger screeners, stewardesses, pilots, passengers, and hijacker. We tried to lower everyone's anxiety by having normal airline activities such as check-in, boarding, announcements, light food and drink, magazine distribution, pilot instructions, and long periods of time with nothing happening.

Scenarios with people on board trying to interface with Nixon were done quietly in the first class section away from the regular passengers. Some of the police from the Bergen County Anti-Terrorist Tactical Team came dressed in garb to confuse the agent as to who was going to hijack the aircraft. The hijacking took place more than an hour and a half after takeoff. It was timed in such a way as to catch as many agents and other passengers as possible off guard. One of the agents heading up the exercise would tell the pilot to make a particular announcement that would alert the hijacker to begin the takeover of the aircraft when he thought the timing was right. The hijacker had full control of the plane and passengers and could draw out the exercise as long as he wanted.

United States commercial aircraft had experienced a number of hijackings in the late 1970s and early 1980s by persons using flammable liquid in a bottle. At the time, a consensus was developing not to use force since if a gun went off you could very likely create a bigger problem. Also, the downside of trying to take flammable liquid from a hijacker could create a bigger problem. One of our biggest concerns was passenger intervention, turning a very difficult situation into a much more dangerous one. Since Nixon normally boarded the plane last we were well aware that passengers in coach might not know Nixon and up to sixteen armed agents were onboard.

Shortly after the simulated hijacking of the aircraft by a quiet, unassuming passenger using a bottle filled with flammable liquid, the agents had to deal with a myriad of other problems. When a passenger went down with a heart attack the attending agent(s) had to use a resuscitator Annie dummy, complete with graph showing the effectiveness of their performing CPR on the fallen passenger. Intervention by one or more passengers had to be addressed by the agents on board in addition to someone negotiating with the hijacker.

The back of the simulated aircraft was open and the entire exercise in the passenger section of the plane was filmed. The overall training exercises were uniquely designed by agents from our detail for our detail with the emphasis on routine activities of the person we were protecting. I believe these training exercises were beneficial to the detail, our law enforcement support in the area, and our community.

❖ ❖ ❖

In November 1984 I began thinking about retiring in the summer of 1985 when I would complete twenty years of government service. By the Christmas holidays I had prepared two resumes, one emphasizing administrative skills and a second focused on law enforcement and security. Both needed some minor updating and would be ready to send out by the end of January.

The first week of 1985, while accompanying former President Nixon back to his house after a morning in his office, I asked to speak with him. Following him into his den he motioned for me to sit down, waiting for me to tell him what was on my mind. Nervously, I began mentioning the wonderful career I had in the Secret Service, visiting over one hundred countries and every state in the Union. Taking a relaxing breath I mentioned my plans to retire in the summer, which did not seem to surprise him. President Nixon volunteered that I was young and there were many great opportunities in the workplace today.

After some light talk I got to the point of my conversation with him by mentioning I would like to send out some resumes to a few of his friends. He asked, "Like whom?"

I replied, "Bill Simon (former secretary of the Treasury), Bob Abplanalp (owner, Precision Valve Corporation), and Bebe Rebozo."

Nixon nodded and then suggested, "Why don't you just give me a copy of your resume and I'll send it out for you. You have missed a few people."

We reminisced for a little while about my five years with him. There had been the move from San Clemente, the streets of New York, trips around the country, and to the Bahamas, Europe, Africa, the Middle East, Central Europe, and Russia. In addition, we spoke of the serenity and privacy of Saddle River, N.J. Knowing it was his lunch time I excused myself after fifteen minutes.

Driving back to my office I was on "Cloud Nine." It looked like 1985 was going to be a very good year for me. My assistant, Bill Burch, was a little surprised when I spoke with him about my conversation with Nixon. The two of us chatted about the possibility of my retirement. I asked him not to tell anyone about my talk with Nixon. July was a long way off and I needed to get everything organized and find out what opportunities were available first. It was great have to an assistant like Burch that I had full confidence in and could trust.

One week later everything seemed to be running normally when I arrived in my office at 60 Craig Road, Montvale, New Jersey. I knew Nixon was not going into his New York office and I would spend the day in the N.J. office. I was thinking about updating my resume to give to Nixon. The former president was in his Saddle River home and I was having my first cup of coffee when Nixon's chief of staff, John Taylor, walked into my office. I knew it must be something important to bring him to my office. Even though Nixon's home was only a short distance away and Taylor visited there quite often, this was his first visit to my office except for the Christmas party.

Nervously he told me we needed to talk. Closing the door behind him a pale-looking Taylor took a seat across the desk from me. He was animated as he advised that President Nixon told him several days ago he was going to give up his Secret Service protection. Taylor said that Nixon had instructed him to contact John Fugazy, who owned Fugazy Limousine Service in New York. Fugazy was a close friend of New

York Yankees' owner George Steinbrenner, whom Nixon had met at Yankee Stadium on several occasions in Steinbrenner's private box.

Taylor advised that he had spoken with Fugazy as directed about providing a limousine Monday through Friday to take the president back and forth from his residence to his office. Taylor seemed concerned and disturbed by Nixon's request. He told me that more recently Nixon asked him to speak with Fugazy about having an armed driver pick him up. Taylor was fidgety speaking about the Fugazy request. He said he did not believe it was a good idea for Nixon to give up the Secret Service. He understood the broad support provided by the Secret Service and was worried about the negative impact on Nixon and his office with the Secret Service out of the picture. I was sure that Taylor was not anxious to accept responsibility for the logistical support and other things that our detail routinely did for President and Mrs. Nixon.

I was sure Taylor was not aware of my previous conversations in 1984 with Nixon about giving up the Secret Service. He also did not know of my recent retirement talk with the former president before he told him he was going to give up the Secret Service. Instincts and experience told me I needed to try and nip this in the bud. I told Taylor I would go to the residence and speak with President Nixon.

Walking outside to my car for the five-minute drive to Nixon's Charlton Drive residence, my mind was working at warp speed. This was not like last fall when Nixon first approached me about giving up his Secret Service coverage. Then Nixon had said, "Mike, I am thinking about giving up my Secret Service detail."

The return so soon to the subject caught me totally by surprise. Yes, Nixon had commented during the earlier discussion about an "excessive" number of agents assigned to him. In fact, he had mentioned it often before and since the meeting. Nixon usually ended these discussions with a comment that, "...if we didn't have so many agents I would go to more ball games, do different things." During these discussions with Nixon I believed he was probing, throwing up a trial balloon, since he was not speaking with his usual conviction. By outlining the various advantages of keeping his detail, such as our vehicles, cameras, alarms, logistical support, and the buffer zone the agents provided when he was in public, Nixon had backed away from pursuing his dream further.

Now, barely three months later, he was again launching an effort to discontinue his relationship with the Secret Service. Realizing the earlier effort had been a trial balloon, I knew this needed to be addressed at once. Knowing Nixon much better now, I realized he was serious. My projected retirement was an issue that I thought was driving his desire to move to a new stage in his life. I was going to need a used car salesman's spiel to get him to change his mind. But I knew I had to try.

I wanted to be ready when I entered his office and had my mental computer absorbing, analyzing, and storing my thoughts as I arrived at the front gate of his residence. The command post had already responded to my radio call and the gate was open. Entering the driveway, I went around to the right and parked outside the command post. Inside I gave a general hello to everyone and slowly picked up the direct line to Nixon's den knowing now was the time to cool down and think clearly. When Nixon answered I asked if he had a few minutes to speak with me. I did not give him advance warning of the subject. He said, "Sure, come in right now."

As I walked the short distance to his den, the battle plan was forming. He greeted me with a smile and robust, "Good morning," as I entered his office/den. Dressed in a dark blue sports coat, charcoal slacks, and blue tie, Nixon was relaxing in his blue over-stuffed chair with his shoes off and his feet resting on the ottoman. The room exuded a warm masculine aura. Motioning with an open hand to an empty chair, he said, "Sit down."

Over the last four and a half years I had learned from Nixon the importance of listening. I took a deep breath and began mentioning my conversation with Taylor. I calmly asked what he was thinking. With a sheepish grin on his face, President Nixon replied, "Well, Mike, you know how I feel about the number of people assigned to me. I know I have fewer agents than the other former presidents, but..." He paused and again mentioned that he would do more things if he did not have so many agents. He told me that first of all he did not believe he needed protection. I was sure he thought he did not have any threats. I knew he didn't. Nixon spoke to me again about his conversation months earlier with Secret Service Assistant Director Edward Pollard. This time he did not get into the cost and manpower numbers.

The former president calmly said he understood that I could not cut the manpower anymore, so therefore, he was going to give up the detail. As he had done several times before Nixon mentioned sporting events that he would attend if he did not have to bring six to eight agents with him. He mentioned it would save the taxpayers money. Nixon clearly said that the cost of private would be considerably less than government costs and I understood he was correct. Initially, I did not respond. I wanted to wait, hoping he would keep talking, continuing to express his desires, his wishes, and his dream to have a normal life.

After listening patiently, allowing him to get it all out, my response was, "I really do understand what you are saying, Mr. President." Letting my mental computer organize my thoughts, I first reminded him that not only was he a former president of the United States, but had perhaps the most recognizable face in the world. Then I pointed out to him that, unlike most world leaders, he generated a level of interest everywhere he went, and it was important for our country that he not be attacked, injured, or embarrassed. Finishing, I said that his sense of loyalty to his office, his family, and the country required him to take minimal precautions, more precautions than using only an armed limousine driver.

Nixon, I had learned, was the consummate disciplinarian. When he made up his mind to do something, he would fully commit himself to whatever sacrifices were personally needed to succeed. He was not thinking about evenings, weekends, and travel. His wife, children, and grandchildren had not entered into his focus on abandoning government protection. Nixon was not thinking about the impact on his staff and friends, or about emergency situations. The man with a global perspective, Nixon was making a decision using tunnel vision.

I was sure Nixon had no real appreciation of what his life would be like if he did in fact implement the Fugazy plan. Some of the activities he was currently doing with his wife, children, grandchildren, and friends would be taken off the table if he proceeded without his Secret Service detail. I cautioned him that others could be affected negatively by a hastily made decision.

He fixed me with a penetrating stare as he thought about what I had just said. I was sure he was not going to respond to my comments, but I paused for a few moments to let everything settle in. Finally, Nixon simply repeated he would be more comfortable without a big detail. I knew he was disciplined enough to go forward with a more cloistered and limited life.

Relaxing and trying to be as unemotional and detached as I could, I spoke about reducing the number of agents to half of the existing level. I told him that I would not retire and would continue as his detail leader. He immediately began shaking his head in a stubborn refusal to negotiate. Nixon did not want to speak about my proposal and kept saying it would not work and it was not what he wanted to do. He was simply unwilling to see it as sufficient for his goal of getting rid of unneeded taxpayer-funded security. Fortunately for me, Nixon and I had a good professional and personal relationship. We both knew our friendship was not part of the discussion. Our conversation was neither elevated nor emotional. We went back and forth in a thoughtful way.

I was able to jockey with him about a smaller Secret Service detail while keeping the conversation light but serious. At one point he told me he used to drive himself when he lived in New York City. Instead of waiting, I immediately reminded him that this was 1985, and he had not driven since 1968.

His quick reply spoke volumes, "Well, Mike, I drive golf carts all the time." It was important that I not smile, laugh, or chuckle. He was actually serious.

Nixon quickly followed up by suggesting that if I could help him get a driver's license he could drive by himself. Looking him directly in the eye, I responded, "I can make arrangements for you to take the test, privately." The comment took some of the air out of his sails. It was the end of the discussion about golf carts and a driver's license.

Nixon, however, continued to speak about his desire to discontinue his government protection. After another half hour of general discussion and back and forth suggestions, I put a plan on the table for him to consider. I offered that I would present to headquarters a proposed detail with eight agents; a driver and I would take him to his office and other appointments, one security person would be at the residence Monday through Friday 8 a.m. to 4 p.m., and during the evenings and weekends there would be no security. This was a plan I did not believe in, but I needed to find the bottom line he would accept.

As we finished the discussion on my final proposal, it became clear it would not be accepted by him.

He calmly responded, "You can never sell it to the people in Washington."

Knowing what he said was true, I quickly responded, "Let me try." We both sat quietly for a few moments. We both needed more time to digest   the last ninety minutes. Inside my head I was searching for options, for a new plan. It had become abundantly clear that talk about a continued Secret Service presence was not going to be accepted. It was time to put the Secret Service option in the shredder. Taking a slow, deep breath and focusing straight at him I said, "Mr. President, why don't you wait until I can retire in July and hire me privately to provide your security?"

Keeping eye contact with me, I could see Nixon begin mulling over what I had just said. The wheels were moving and I immediately knew the door was opening to my new proposal. We spoke for almost another hour trying to find a common ground for a workable plan. He wanted the security to be only me and I wanted one person at the residence around the clock seven days a week and a driver Monday through Friday. He verbalized what he saw as the outline of what I would do. Finally, as he began to talk about the mechanics of the new assignment, I knew he was taking the bait and that I needed more time. When he mentioned the details should be worked out with his lawyer, William "Bill" Griffin, I knew the hook was set. Nixon suggested that we take a break and I come back in two hours to discuss the proposal in more detail. I was happy to have a chance to review the conversation of the last two hours back in my office. I needed a chance to relax and let my thoughts reorganize and get the new plan ready for the next round. I needed to reel him in.

The challenges facing me were to outline the structure and level of security, and to work with attorney Griffin to finance the project. Back in my office I closed the door and spoke to no one. The enormity of over two hours of conversation had overwhelmed me. Sitting back in my chair, I closed my eyes, cleared my mind, and reviewed the historical meeting that had just taken place. It was important that I go to the next meeting with a positive vision that the former president would accept and we could build on.

I knew before I left my office that I wanted to develop an agreement with Nixon that would allow him security changes allowing him to have the privacy he had been so jealously protecting and at the same time keep me from going down in history as the first person to privately protect a former president and failing.

I knew I was living through an historical event and began wondering again, "Why me?" I found myself asking, "Why am I doing this?" I knew I could walk away, get a good job, and make a lot of money. I finally concluded that Richard Nixon deserved the right to live his dream and I believed I was the only person who could help him do that safely.

Over and over in my head I reviewed what his security detail would entail. Nixon was pushing a very limited presence of security for himself and Mrs. Nixon at his residence. The challenge would be to get at least a temporary security level of twenty-four hours a day seven days a week. It would be necessary to keep the agreement broad with Nixon and refine it with Griffin. It would benefit neither of us if we got bogged down in the details at this time. With my batteries recharged and a plan organized in my head, I told my secretary, Donna Cimonetti, I was going to Nixon's residence.

On my return to the residence, the discussion in the den continued where it had left off. As I suspected, the stumbling block was the level of security. President Nixon did not want around-the-clock coverage at his home. He also felt he did not need someone to drive the car since I would be accompanying him. To him it was simply not necessary. According to his thinking, why would he need someone at the residence when much of the week the maid would be in the house?

He envisioned that Heidi Retter, the maid, could deal with routine guests and visitors. I told Nixon I was concerned that routine property maintenance, house cleaning, and duties, along with guest and visitor control, would impinge on the maid's normal day-to-day activities. Additionally, it was mentioned that the maid left the house on occasion for shopping and other errands. I suggested we begin with twenty-four-hour security, explaining that it would be easier to cut back on security at the appropriate time than have to increase it because of a miscalculation.

Finally Nixon either gave up or saw the wisdom of one person, temporarily, at his residence twenty-four hours a day, plus a driver and me on weekdays. Normal evening activities would be my responsibility. If an evening or weekend driver were needed, I would bring in off-duty police officers. It was agreed that the issue of discontinuing twenty-four-hour security at the residence would be revisited at a later date.

The ultimate goal of former President Nixon to have me as his driver with no security at the residence was abundantly clear. Despite my aversion and dislike of the bottom line proposal, I knew eventually we would arrive close to that point. However, I was determined to make the trip to the bottom line as difficult as possible for Nixon. He knew it was going to be tough getting me to change my mind, but I think he knew eventually we would find a common ground with even more limited security at the residence. With the general outline set, I agreed to meet with Griffin to work out the details of cars, equipment, personnel, and travel expenses.

After over four hours of discussions and negotiations we had an outline of the future. It was now going to be my responsibility to talk to Griffin and put a plan together. Driving out the front gate, I was thinking about what had just taken place.

Nixon had received continuous Secret Service protection since June 1968. During the negotiations never once had I thought how the Nixon family, friends, or Secret Service would react to the end of almost eighteen consecutive years of government-provided protection. In my mind I was trying to do what was right for him and Mrs. Nixon. I never saw this in terms of it being his problem so I could just walk away. There was recognition on my part that I was caught up in a very emotional and historical situation. Trying to give Nixon what he wanted, what I thought he needed, and what the two of us would settle on, meant breaking new ground. It meant me assuming personal responsibility for his life. He had a right to live his life in a way that gave him the best quality possible. Nixon should be able to interact with his family and friends without a group of security agents constantly on alert. However, I did not want to create a situation where he or his family would suffer because of my decisions. I had to be firm and knew that, at least initially, there would be some risk.

Back in my office I sat quietly, thinking about the conversations with the former president. The full implication of shutting down the detail and assuming personal responsibility for one of the most controversial presidents in our history was really beginning to sink in. There was no question this was an historic moment. Nixon was correct in saying he did not need twenty-six men and women to take care of him and he knew I knew it. I was sure Nixon knew that I understood why he was changing his security. Sometimes it was like we could read each other's minds. We were aware this was not a case of personal safety, but an issue of privacy and quality of life. Repeatedly, Nixon had stated he would "...do more with less people." Never once did I question whether I was up for the task. Failure was not in my vocabulary. I was acutely aware that for this venture to be successful, the low level of security we agreed upon would have to be kept from the public and especially from the media. I was going to be testing my theory of threat level versus interest level. I was almost totally drained and I leaned back in my chair, closed my eyes, and thought, "Why me?"

❖ ❖ ❖

At the end of the work day I had a short conversation with my assistant, Bill Burch. A very bright person with common sense, Burch saw core issues very clearly, was mission-driven, and was excellent at operations and logistics. Most importantly, Burch knew both Nixon and me well. I spoke to Burch about my conversation with President Nixon. I told him there was no question Nixon was going to give up the detail. I needed Burch to understand there was no way to negotiate a continuation of the Secret Service presence. He was very supportive, never second-guessing the decision. I was so lucky to have his loyalty and counsel.

As our conversation continued, we spoke about the need to start thinking about a plan to decommission the detail. Having been through this once in San Clemente, I knew Burch could handle it without breaking a sweat. We agreed our conversation would remain confidential until the details of Nixon's plan were worked out with Griffin. Once again I knew how fortunate I was to have Burch as my assistant.

A few days later I drove to Yonkers, New York, for an initial meeting with Nixon's lawyer, William Griffin. He had his own law firm, was the secretary/treasurer and legal consul to Precision Valve, and was very active in Westchester County Democratic Party politics. Our first meeting was limited to relaying my conversation with Nixon and outlining my understanding of the agreement with him. A somber, unemotional person, Griffin listened to me intently, taking notes. He asked very few questions and the meeting ended with him telling me he would talk to Nixon and get back to me.

About a week after my first meeting with Griffin, Nixon invited me into his home to speak further about relinquishing his Secret Service detail. He was remarkably relaxed, projecting a peace and calm within himself that I had never seen before. Nixon said he was drafting a letter for Secretary of Treasury James Baker, declining continuing government protection provided by the Secret Service. Once the letter was finalized and signed, Nixon said he would have me hand carry the letter to Baker's Washington office.

After the meeting I contacted Director John Simpson and made an appointment to speak to him when I brought Nixon's letter to Treasury Secretary Baker. It was important for me to give Simpson a heads-up about the letter to the secretary of the Treasury.

My trip to Washington, D.C., went off smoothly. At Treasury Secretary Baker's office I met with Margaret Tutwiler, his personal assistant. After giving her the letter from Nixon for Secretary Baker, I headed for Secret Service headquarters, three blocks west of the White House. During the short walk to my appointment with Secret Service Director Simpson, the historical significance and the awesome responsibility I had just assumed once again brought thoughts of "Can I do this?" and "Why me?"

Upon entering Simpson's office, I gave him a copy of Nixon's letter to Secretary Baker. We discussed my conversations with Nixon and the type of security Nixon would have. Simpson fully understood that I believed Nixon was not going to change his mind and he was very supportive of the project I was undertaking. He never questioned Nixon's decision, the level of coverage, or my ability to provide a safe environment for him. Simpson spoke about the relationship he envisioned between the Secret Service and me. He explained that Nixon giving up physical protection did not relieve the Secret Service of the responsible for providing up-to-date intelligence information on Nixon.

Simpson advised that I should maintain direct contact with the Secret Service's Intelligence Division and would continued to receive regular threat evaluations and other intelligence support. He brought up his concern about me maintaining my "Top Secret" clearances. With my retirement, the Secret Service would be unable to sponsor those clearances. Director Simpson, however, did say that he would assist in any way he could but suggested I should first speak to Nixon about transferring the responsibility for my security clearances to the National Security Council. He said my need for authorization to carry a handgun could be resolved by being made a deputy U. S. marshal. Director Simpson said he would contact the Justice Department about making me a marshal. I knew the federal marshal status would allow me to carry a weapon at all times. This was especially important for future airline travel.

Leaving the meeting with Simpson, I was pleased with his personal counsel and the official support he was offering on behalf of the Secret Service. His personal intervention and support was especially reassuring. By the time I boarded my return shuttle flight to LaGuardia I was much more relaxed. The pieces were beginning to fall into place.

My meetings with Griffin over the next several months were interesting and intriguing. I knew him from a distance since he periodically visited Nixon at his residence and was around on occasion when Nixon visited Abplanalp's Walker's Cay resort in the Northern

Bahamas. A tall man, Giffin's physical size could be intimidating and disarming. Both respected and feared, Griffin was without a doubt the hardest person to get next to and read that I had ever met. He wasn't just a good lawyer; William Griffin, Esq., was an excellent lawyer. Working with Griffin on this project was going to be the greatest challenge of my life and I was looking forward to it.

In one of the last meetings with Griffin on the structure and reimbursement for the project, I found myself as usual doing most of the talking. It was obvious Nixon had spoken with Griffin, but he continually encouraged me to lay out what Nixon wanted and how it would be provided. I showed him a rough draft proposal of costs and needs. Manpower needs were identified, and it was agreed we would need two vehicles. It was understood that all reimbursement for my security company, Michael A. Endicott Associates, would be through East/West. This was Nixon's company that I understood was funded by revenues generated by his writings.

Griffin indicated he was working on a personal services contract for me that would outline not only the reimbursement procedure but personal issues governing my relationship with Nixon and East/West. Leaving the meeting, I knew most of the components of the new detail had been covered and I was looking forward to a formalized written proposal.

On the forty-five-minute drive back to Saddle River, I reviewed the meeting and once again realized that I had not heard one word from Griffin about what he thought. After the discussions I was no closer to understanding Griffin than when I walked into the first meeting. He was still an enigma.

Griffin and I spoke several times over the spring and early summer to refine the coverage. Griffin continued working on a draft of a personal services contract that would make my role official. We both agreed there would be no formal announcement about Nixon's change to private security. Also, Griffin requested I not conduct any interviews or release information about the level or type of Nixon's new security detail.

I contacted Chrysler through the Secret Service and arrangements were made to lease a small limousine that was currently being used by Chrysler Chairman Lee Iacocca. I was told Iacocca's car would be available by August 1, 1985, when Endicott Associates officially became responsible for the Nixons.

Ho-Ho-Kus Chief of Police Bobby Re was hired as a consultant to recruit and coordinate the manpower for my new company. Re lived in Saddle River a couple of miles from Nixon. Security at the residence would be provided by off-duty police officers and retired law enforcement personnel. Re maintained a log of off-duty police officers and deputy sheriffs interested in working at the Nixon residence. He also developed a list of retired police and other law enforcement officers who were interested in part-time work.

Meanwhile, the decommissioning of my Secret Service detail was keeping Burch and me very busy. As was the case in San Clemente, it was really important to me to make sure our agents got reassigned to one of their top choices. Also, there was the usual government paperwork transferring detail vehicles and equipment to other offices. Through discussions with Secret Service headquarters, it was agreed to leave the electronic security system in place rather than to remove it in the interest of cost efficiency. With the limited number of people that would be working security at the Nixon residence after the Secret Service departed, the alarm system would not enhance the level of protection being provided by me privately.

As if the decommissioning of the Secret Service detail and start-up of my new company were not enough, Nixon advised me in late June he would depart August 6 on an overseas trip. Unfortunately for me, it was not going to be a short trip. There would be no assistance overseas from Secret Service, and as usual Nixon did not want any coordination through the U.S. Department of State. This was going to be my baptism under fire; however, I did get one break. Former Texas Governor John Connally, who had been secretary of the Treasury during the Nixon administration, would be joining Nixon in Hong Kong. Connally would arrive via private corporate aircraft. His corporate Boeing 727 would be used for the remainder of the trip. The flight crew would take care of all clearances at the sites to be visited. But before the trip, there were five weeks of hard work ahead. Between Nixon's staff, John Taylor, and assistant Kathy O'Connor, the plan came together nicely. They supported the changes in security and made the transition much easier.

※ ※ ※

Realizing that Nixon was a person who recognized his place in history and often celebrated significant events, I approached him about having a final get-together with the remaining detail agents. The evening of July 31, 1985, was selected as this would be the last night Nixon would have his Secret Service detail. He asked that Chief Smith of Saddle River and Chief Re of Ho-Ho-Kus also be invited to attend. President Nixon said he would like George Hollendersky, the agent in charge of the Newark office, to be invited. Hollendersky had been the head of Nixon's detail after he left his White House office and returned to San Clemente. I suggested we could have a champagne toast. Nixon said not to worry about the toast, indicating he would find something in his wine cellar to celebrate the evening.

On the evening of July 31, we gathered at 7 p.m. in the family room at Nixon's residence. It was a beautiful room with red lacquer walls and ceiling personally selected by Mrs. Nixon as part of the renovations in 1981. The large elevated fireplace, with a wide bench-like hearth made with beige fieldstone, dominated one side of the room. Much of the floor was covered with a white rug that had small solid brown squares inside larger brown squares. The chairs, lamps, end tables, and coffee table were of Asian motif, complementing the rich, light-colored drapes. A dark, round wooden table was near the sliding glass door leading outside to the huge deck. On the table was a magnum of red wine and glasses. Fourteen glasses in all were on the table, eight on a silver tray and six on the table in front of the tray.

With all the guests standing and chatting, Nixon entered the room dressed in a coat and tie. He walked over to the table, surveyed the assembled group, and then realized there were sixteen people all together. He excused himself for a moment, returning with two additional glasses.

Nixon poured some wine into the glasses for each his guests and then for himself. After handing a glass of wine to each person, Nixon turned to face us. Pausing, he cleared his throat, extended his glass toward the guests, and proceeded to explain that the other day he went downstairs to his wine cellar looking for an appropriate wine to celebrate this historic date. Nixon mentioned he first received Secret Service protection on January 20, 1953, the day President Eisenhower and he were sworn into office. He chronicled his break in Secret Service protection from January 20, 1961 until June 7, 1968.

Nixon was aware that most of his guests knew he had a one-thousand bottle wine cellar in the basement. He continued, "I have a little wine cellar in the basement that is not that good." Pausing, he grinned and finished, "But it is not that bad either." There was a chuckle from the gathered guests. He told us, "I found a Grand Vin, St. Julien, that was laid to rest in 1953, the first year I had Secret Service protection." He went on to explain his fondness for the Secret Service and wished all of us well in the future. Finishing the toast, Nixon raised his glass higher as a spontaneous round of "Hear, hear" rang out.

Everyone took a sip of the Bordeaux and relaxed as Nixon invited his guests to be seated. Knowing there were not enough chairs, Nixon urged people to use the fireplace hearth also. Some found places to sit in chairs, or on the sofa. Others used the hearth, while a few remained standing. President Nixon, seated in a comfortable red chair, turned to Hollendersky and said, "George, what is your favorite Secret Service story?" Hollendersky told a story about former President Nixon staying at former Ambassador to Great Britain Walter Annenberg's residence in Palm Springs, California. This was not long after Nixon had left office. Nixon, according to Hollendersky, made arrangements to sneak out of the Annenberg residence lying on the back floor of one of the staff cars. No one on the detail was aware he had left. When Nixon returned he was confronted by his visibly upset detail leader, according to Hollendersky. Nixon had maintained contact with Hollendersky and was obviously very fond of him.

Nixon proceeded to go around the room giving each agent an opportunity to tell a tale. He smiled, laughed, and enjoyed the stories. I told the story about Kissinger, Stebbins, O'Toole, and the moose head. It was very obvious to me that the people in the room had a special place in Nixon's heart. It was also clear that Nixon was special to his guests.

Some Secret Service details have a close personal relationship with the person they protect. It is a private matter and is generally not made public. Richard Nixon did not necessarily have a public persona as being warm and friendly but we knew differently.

When the evening was finally over, I asked President Nixon to sign the bottle for me. He inscribed, "July 31, 1985 January 20, 1953 Richard Nixon Best wishes to Mike Endicott."

❖ ❖ ❖

Six days later I was loading bags into the car and heading to JFK Airport for our flight to China. I had butterflies in my stomach, even though I knew all the bases were covered. There was this nagging voice asking, "Are you sure?" I knew that the support Nixon would receive from the host countries when he traveled would be on a par to when he had the Secret Service protection. Contacts that had been made over the last five years overseas were more than happy to provide the VIP treatment to the former president.

We drove to the Port Authority Police administrative building where we were going to meet the car that would escort our limousine onto the ramp, expediting our departure. A marked Port Authority police car and a uniformed officer were waiting as we got out of our car. The uniformed officer approached our car and asked Nixon if he would like to ride in his car. Nixon said he would and told me to get into the back seat of the police car.

The officer drove us directly to the departure gate, stopping at the exterior stairs of our commercial flight. The airline representative greeted Nixon and before he escorted us up the exterior stairs to our first class seat, Nixon thanked him for his support and said he would sign autographs or take pictures anytime he was out there. Getting in our seats, Nixon relaxed, but I was wondering how everything would go. As our airplane lifted off, heading for China, Nixon, sensing my anxiety, said, "Well, here we go." We chatted after takeoff as Nixon told me about our itinerary and his friendship with Connally.

We arrived in Chicago and changed planes. Our next flight was capable of flying into China non-stop if the winds were not heavy. We would not know for several hours if we would overnight in Anchorage, Alaska, or make our landing in Beijing, China. We ended up spending the night in Anchorage and leaving the next morning. Nixon was relaxed and took everything in stride.

The normal cadre of Chinese officials met Nixon and took him to his Diaoyutai guest house. The China part of the trip, which was mainly meetings, went well. During the visit Nixon had a luncheon meeting with Deng Xiaoping, the de facto leader of China. The luncheon was held in one of the many rooms in the Great Hall of the People. Nixon took daily walks around the Daioyutai compound and, in fact, once we ventured outside the compound where he was greeted by people walking the street.

Walking through the Great Hall of the People to our luncheon rooms, our party passed a huge tapestry mural of Mao Tse-tung. The tapestry depicted Mao on the 1934 Long March with his Communist Army comrades and local peasants. In a country setting he was walking down a gray road leading his supporters through the green countryside. Nixon slowed down and watched the wall as we passed the mural on our right. Mystically the road slowly moved from the near bottom corner of the tapestry and followed us until it reached the opposite corner of the tapestry as we passed.

Deng Xiaoping was waiting outside the luncheon room and greeted Nixon. Before entering the luncheon, Nixon asked me to step forward and introduced me to Xiaoping. After shaking hands with the Chinese leader, I retired to an adjoining room, where Taylor and I were hosted by the head of the Chinese Secret Service. This was Taylor's first trip to China, but it was my third.

Earlier I had briefed Taylor that there would more than likely be a drinking contest during the luncheon with our Secret Service host. Knowing that Taylor was not a big alcohol drinker, I explained it would not be necessary that he participate. In fact, I told Taylor, as the guest host at our table I would be targeted by the security director and he should drop out of the toasting after a few drinks.

Taylor dropped out after a few drinks as did most of the other guests. Around seven drinks the person to my left asked, "How many can you drink?"

"I don't know. I have never done this before," I replied.

The guest, pointing to our host, volunteered, "He can do thirty-five."

I smiled and casually responded, "Oh!"

As the meal and conversation continued, the toasts started coming more rapidly. By toast ten I was trying to find a face-saving way to put an end to the toasts. I remembered a previous visit when I observed an American guest stand up after dinner to leave only to fall to the floor. This was not what I wanted to experience. At number twelve I raised my glass toasting, "I want to thank the director for taking my gun and assuming full responsibility for the safety of President Nixon when we entered China." Continuing I said, "When the luncheon is over I will go to my room and take a nap but you must go back to the office and work. Gombay."

As everyone sat down I sensed the return toast from the director would be short and his last. After a few minutes the director stood and raised his glass. He thanked us for joining him for lunch and, after offering his toast, the director excused himself to return to work. Nixon and Deng Xiaoping finished their luncheon a short time later and we returned to the guest house. Knowing there were no activities for four hours, I laid down for a short nap. It was necessary for me to keep one foot on the floor to stop the room from spinning. After a two-hour nap and a shower I was once again in first-class shape.

With our visit to Beijing over we flew a government-provided China Airlines private flight to Hong Kong for meetings and an overnight stop. Secretary Connally, who had arrived earlier aboard his corporate Boeing 727, met us at the hotel. Nixon and Connally had dinner together and then returned to the hotel to prepare for the rest of our trip. The next day we departed for stops in Tokyo, Japan, and Seoul, South Korea, for meetings and dinners. After Seoul, our next stops included Singapore, Malaysia, and Thailand. Meetings, dinners, and sightseeing kept Nixon and Connally busy. Between Taylor and O'Connor at Nixon's office, the assistance of our private aircraft crew, and the host government, we had appropriate ground transportation waiting for us at each stop. The host governments all provided assistance through immigration and customs and an escort to our hotels.

After Thailand we departed for Rangoon, Myanmar, which had once been known as Burma. I was looking forward to the stop in Rangoon since it was not one of the normal stops for global travelers. The Myanmar government provided customary special clearance through customs and a police escort to our hotel. During the stay Nixon and Connally had a couple of short meetings and later we took a fifty-mile ride north to Bago. There, our group visited the reclining Buddha statue, Shwe Tha Lyaung. According to our guide, the statue was made by King Miga Depa in A.D. 994. It is the largest of the eleven reclining Buddha statues in Myanmar at 108 feet long and 52.5 feet tall. The statue is made of brick and plaster.

The pot-holed road that we followed out of Rangoon to see the statue was in desperate need of a regular maintenance program. Our guide told us that the drive to Mandalay, which was only about three hundred miles north, often took twenty-four hours due to washed-out portions and one-lane travel along the road. The roads and buildings in the Rangoon area showed a lack of maintenance. The exterior of many of the buildings were stained with mildew because of the tropical environment.

Departing Burma, our corporate jet headed for Pakistan. Shortly after takeoff our pilot advised us he had been denied permission by the Indian government to fly across their country due to diplomatic conflicts with Pakistan. He advised that we would have to fly south around India to Pakistan and our flight would be extended several hours. It did make it more palatable flying in a private Boeing 727.

As we entered Pakistani airspace from the south, we were met by four French Mirage fighter jets. Two of the aircraft moved in close to our wing-tips on either side of our Boeing 727. In fact, they were so close I could see the smile on the pilot's face in the closest aircraft as he acknowledged our waves. I was mesmerized as the two jets bobbed up and down less than twenty-five feet from our plane. The Mirage jets escorted us until just before our captain began to lower the plane's landing gear, when the four jets simultaneously hit their afterburners and roared up and away from our 727.

When we arrived at the Islamabad airport we were met by personnel from the U.S. Embassy and transported to a hotel in downtown Islamabad. We spent the night in the hotel, eating in our rooms. The next morning we were driven by cars to a Peshawar Afghan refugee camp. Nixon was greeted by representatives of the Afghan insurgency and the Pakistani government and escorted to a big tent with carpets on the ground.

Nixon and Connally were invited to sit crossed-legged on the rug with the Mujahideen insurgents. The two of them were briefed on the progress in the insurgency's movement to oust the Soviet Union, which had deployed troops in Afghanistan on Christmas Day 1979. After the briefing there was a short question and answer period and then our party was escorted to waiting helicopters for a ride up the Khyber

Pass to Fort Landi Kotal, home of the Khyber Rifles. During the ride our host pointed out several outposts that were over three thousand feet up the side of the mountain, hidden in caves. According to our host, it took a three-man team four days to climb to their assigned cave. The soldiers backpacked their food and water into their lookout with them. They brought out their trash thirty days later.

We arrived at the west end of the pass at historical Fort Landi Kotal, from which you could see the Pakistan border crossing into Afghanistan. At the fort there was a luncheon for Nixon and his party, hosted by the Foreign Ministry. I was seated at a table next to the main party with the commandant of the illustrious Khyber Rifles. During our lunch, the commandant spoke about the occupation of Afghanistan by Russian troops. He advised that he was actively trying to demoralize the Russian troops. The commandant mentioned that he had a successful program of trading Russian soldiers heroin for their guns. In fact, he said, he had traded heroin several days earlier not only for rifles but for a tank.

After the luncheon our party moved to the patio out back where field glasses were mounted for viewing into Afghanistan. Through them you could see several Soviet tanks and trucks lined up near the entrance to the Afghanistan side of the pass. Russian troops could be observed manning the crossing check point, periodically allowing a vehicle through the security post.

After leaving Fort Landi Kotal we returned to Peshawar and drove to our hotel in Islamabad. Once again we ate in the hotel and then prepared for our departure the next morning. Shortly after our airplane lifted off we were joined by our Mirage escort jets from two days earlier. They flew off our wings until our Boeing 727 departed Pakistani airspace. We flew across the Gulf of Oman and landed in Muscat in the Kingdom of Oman for refueling and then headed for meetings and a leisurely overnight in Turkey before our final stop of the long trip, our overnight in London.

Before leaving New York I had decided not to take my weapon. I knew all the countries we were visiting would provide adequate security except England. The hassle of bringing a weapon into London simply was not worth it. Arriving in London, Scotland Yard was not involved in our visit, as I suspected. Nixon and Connally dined that evening with Nixon's friend Jonathan Aitken, who was a Member of Parliament. The next day we returned to New York and I was pleased with how well the trip went. The foreign governments with the one exception seemed pleased to take responsibility for former President Nixon.

❖ ❖ ❖

Several days after the return from overseas, I drove to Yonkers, New York, to see Griffin. I was agitated about the lack of progress on a contract and delay of payments. For me it had been the same two problems for some time and we didn't seem any closer to resolving the personal services contract and the slow reimbursement for expenses. I didn't have a lot of money and was depending on reimbursement of my expenses in a timely manner to keep going. Initially I thought Griffin was hung up on a clause in the contract restricting book writing and other public disclosures of Nixon's life by me. This time, however, I realized it was the six months in salary severance clause I was asking for that was the problem. Though Griffin seemed to be less than enthusiastic about the new security arrangement, he indicated he would take care of the reimbursement issues in a timelier manner. He said he would try to get the personal services contract completed soon.

❖ ❖ ❖

Operationally, Endicott Associates was going well. There were no problems at the residence or the office, and Chief Re had developed a large list of people willing to work the Nixon residence. Nixon seemed comfortable and relaxed with the new security arrangements and was very friendly and easy-going. At his residence he often interacted with the officers working there. Sometimes he would ask for a ride to the store or assistance with a problem around the house. The group of people Chief Re had working residence security were delighted to assist any way they could. It was a special treat for them to interact with the former president.

Nixon continued with his daily routine of an early morning walk before his departure for the office. I wanted to walk with him or have the midnight shift officer go with him, but Nixon was insistent about walking alone. He enjoyed going out without an agent and car accompanying him. I was nervous about the walk but knew I had to pull back and give him some space. As long as word did not get out about him no longer having Secret Service protection and taking solo walks, I felt there was no need to be concerned about autograph seekers. I must admit I had many anxious moments during the first two months wondering if I were doing the right thing. There were several nights when I would awaken in the middle of the night and be tempted to go up to the command post. However, I knew that Chief Smith of the Saddle River Police Department was having his officers keep a close eye on the property.

I was sure Nixon enjoyed the change in security but, I thought, what if something happened? Though I believed in what we were doing, I still had anxious moments. When I saw how much the former President and Mrs. Nixon liked their new life I said a little prayer that everything would work out okay for all of us.

❖ ❖ ❖

The relationship between Nixon and me had been going very well and was only getting better as the days and weeks went into months. The normal pigeon hole of security agent or body guard I started out in had been jettisoned since the day I began putting Nixon's private security together. Soon I was responsible for the house, property, medical issues, and his private schedule. I was taking care of all problems that cropped up.

❖ ❖ ❖

Once, when we had an extraordinary amount of rain, Nixon's basement took in water. I got a call from him at home the evening of the problem. After Nixon explained how much water was in the downstairs area, I made a call to Chief of Police Frank Milliken of Ridgewood.

I knew Chief Milliken through the Bergen County Police Chiefs Association. Also, my daughter Leslie was an officer for the police department there. Milliken had off-duty officers who were electricians, plumbers, mechanics, and general handymen. They could solve almost any household problem. Soon, two people responded to the Nixon residence with pumps, a vacuum, rags, and other equipment. In several hours the water was gone, having been vacuumed and wiped up. Dryers had been strategically placed in the basement to evaporate the remaining moisture overnight. The next morning when I arrived to take President Nixon to his office, he happily proclaimed everything was back to normal.

Weekdays at 6 a.m., Nixon and I would leave Saddle River for his office in the Jacob K. Javits Federal Building at 26 Federal Plaza in lower Manhattan. I drove, using the leased Chrysler executive limousine. We would stop to get *The New York Times* and *The Wall Street Journal* at the paper shop in Ho-Ho-Kus. Nixon would sit in the back seat, reading the newspapers during the thirty-five to forty-minute drive to the Federal Building. He would sometimes comment about an article he was reading. He would say, "Listen to this, Mike," and read me a paragraph or so and then comment on what he believed really happened. Parking in our assigned spot in the basement at 26 Federal Plaza in lower Manhattan, we would walk to the elevator and take it to his office.

When President Nixon had a doctor's appointment, a lunch engagement at Le Cirque or some other restaurant, or was visiting his daughter, Tricia Cox, or someone in New York City, I would normally take him by myself to his appointment. If there was a parking spot available near the building entrance I would use it. If no parking space were available, I would double-park the car, leaving it locked with the flashers blinking while I escorted Nixon inside. Once I got him settled I would return to the car and find a place where I could park using the NYPD special parking sign assigned to him. At times it could be difficult finding a spot. But the Police Department parking placard gave me a lot of flexibility. I knew if a cop came along, whether I was illegally parked or double-parked, I would not be ticketed. If a police car were nearby, I would make sure to call their attention to Nixon so they knew the car was ours.

❖ ❖ ❖

In the fall of 1985 I prepared a final budget projecting the costs of private security for the first year. With the memo in hand I drove to Griffin's office. I was still upset with Griffin when I arrived at his office. Payment for expenses continued to lag and the personal services contract sticking point continued to be a termination clause, and I was beginning to question the commitment from Griffin to make things work. At his office we talked about the budget and the personal services contract. I didn't seem to be making any headway and my frustration boiled over. I told Griffin the personal services contract needed to include six months' salary in the event of the detail being terminated.

Griffin, as cool as a cucumber, paused, looked at me, and said, "I don't know if you will be here one week from now let alone in thirty days."

My jaw dropped. I was stunned. I had totally misread the support from Griffin, Abplanalp, and Rebozo. Griffin's statement made it crystal clear to me that I had been totally unaware there must have been substantial opposition to President Nixon discontinuing his Secret Service detail. I was flustered and found it impossible to read Griffin. His demeanor made it clear he was not happy that Nixon had given up his Secret Service protection. He did not know me, as I did not know him. In retrospect I believe he and others thought I talked Nixon into giving up the Secret Service protection.

Trying to comprehend everything that was going on, I slowed down to focus on the letter Nixon gave to Treasury. I realized Nixon did everything through me. Oh boy, I could now see it. When I went to Treasury, Griffin, Abplanalp and Rebozo knew nothing about it. Everything must have moved so fast they did not have a chance to try and talk Nixon out of his decision.

"What does he think I am getting out of this?" I asked myself. My salary was the same as when I was with the Secret Service. My budget was less than $400 thousand a year versus $3.5 million with the Secret Service. I could not get personal liability insurance. I was upset with Griffin and I wanted to make sure he knew it.

Standing up, I looked at Griffin, set the budget memo on his desk and said, "You don't know me, I have never failed at anything in my life and I am not going to fail at this."

Not waiting for a response I turned to leave, then stopped to add a final remark, "That is my budget for the next year and it is not negotiable."

I returned to Saddle River with renewed energy. As long as Griffin paid the bills, I was going to take care of the President and Mrs. Nixon, contract or no contract. Griffin and I never again spoke about a contract. I worked almost five and a half years with Nixon without a contract.

After the meeting Griffin seemed to become more supportive. Twice my insurance agent approached underwriters about a personal liability policy. In both cases he was advised that the underwriters felt I could not protect Nixon adequately with the limited number of people I was using and they declined to write a policy. When I advised Griffin of the insurance problem it was suggested to him that he increase the insurance coverage on the leased cars and the residence. He made arrangements for me to meet with his insurance agency and immediately re-work Nixon's coverage. Also, my expense vouchers were handled more expeditiously. When I look back it is interesting that never did a family member, close friend of the family, or anyone else ever engage me about Nixon's protection and the decision to go private.

Nixon enjoyed taking rides into the New Jersey and New York countryside, where he could enjoy the scenery. During the spring, when the foliage was budding, and in the fall, when the trees were changing color, the Palisades Parkway was frequently used when returning to Saddle River from the Manhattan office. Sometimes Nixon and I would go for a ride, other times he would ask me to take him and Mrs. Nixon for a "foliage ride." Depending on the time available, the drives with Mrs. Nixon could be three hours round trip to southern Connecticut (Stamford, Bridgeport) or shorter trips to Harriman State Park, West

Point, or Bear Mountain Park, N.Y., which were less than an hour away.

Nixon liked to take short drives by himself. We would go north on Upper Saddle River Road out of New Jersey to Monsey and Spring Valley, N.Y. Upper Saddle River Road was rural with some homes along the way. There were many sugar maple trees on the road, especially once we passed Elmer's (gas station/coffee shop) at Upper Saddle River Road and Lake Street into New York. The bright red, orange, and yellow leaves that began to show up after the first frost of the fall were just beautiful. Other deciduous trees, though not as spectacular as the sugar maples, were also enjoyable with their orange, yellow, and rust colors.

When visiting Bear Mountain Park in New York State, the drive up the narrow, winding road to the fire tower was an enjoyable side trip. From atop the hill you could see the rolling hills of the Ramapo Mountains and the Hudson Valley. The shades of gold, orange, yellow, rust, and red reminded me of a picture puzzle my family often put together when growing up. Frequently Nixon would suggest we bypass Bear Mountain Park and go ten more minutes north to West Point Military Academy. Taking a drive around the grounds of the academy was one of Nixon's favorite trips. He would ask to get out occasionally by the old cannons and walk to the overlook where he could see the Hudson River below. The river had a gray color as it flowed below the academy toward New York City. You could see the turn in the river where in our early history a chain was strung across the river preventing enemy ships from continuing up the river. It was easy to understand how the men and women cadets, dressed in their gray uniforms, became known as the "Gray Knights of the Hudson."

The year around Nixon loved to take a ride north on Route 17 to Harriman Park Seven Lakes Drive near Sloatsburg, New York, to enjoy the scenery. The seven lakes were man-made back in the CCC (Civilian

Conservation Corps) days, 1933-1942. During the fall drives in October, November, and December it was not be unusual to see deer roaming in some of the fields or running across the road. The white-tail deer would raise their large, fluffy white tails when they ran off. They were so graceful. By mid-January the lakes would often be frozen and the ground covered with snow. Driving past the lakes there were occasions we could see people walking and skating on the ice. A close examination revealed a few avid fishermen with a line through a hole in the ice.

❖ ❖ ❖

Nixon rode through Harlem in New York City a couple of times before moving to New Jersey. After the move he would ask to go through Harlem every once in a while. It seemed he wanted to be reminded what the real world was like. Once I took over Nixon's security detail privately the rides became more frequent. Nixon usually sat in the front seat of the car, returning to Saddle River after lunch or a visit to his daughter Tricia's apartment on the Upper East Side of Manhattan. Nixon would ask me to drive through Central Park and Harlem. Exiting the north end of Central Park onto Seventh Avenue, I continued on Adam Clayton Powell, Jr. Boulevard to One hundred forty-fifth Street, Nixon would oftentimes be recognized in the car. Stopping at red lights along the way, he would draw interesting glances from other drivers and people walking. The first reaction of a pedestrian or passenger in a car to seeing Nixon in the front seat of my beige Chrysler sedan was disbelief. But when Nixon smiled and waved, the person being acknowledged would get excited and return the greeting. Most people did not expect to see a former president in the front seat of a car, let alone in Harlem.

Turning west at One hundred forty-fifth Street to Amsterdam and then north to the entrance to the George Washington Bridge gave Nixon a good view of the diverse living accommodations and conditions in the area, which included boarded-up buildings, old dilapidated apartments, brownstone homes, and some renovated rent-controlled co-ops. Over the years he saw changes that were made to clean up the neighborhoods and rebuild sections.

Nixon sometimes made comments to me about the children playing games in the streets or on the stoops, such as "Give kids a stick and some type of ball and kids everywhere will invent games," and "Everyday, everywhere kids play, they play for the world championship."

People often see our politicians such as Nixon as out of touch and isolated from the people at large. However, during the time I was with Nixon in San Clemente, New York City, and Saddle River, he constantly sought to see how people lived and what their lives were like. It was a side of Richard Nixon that few ever saw. Driving through Harlem was not in and of itself an understanding of the plight of the poor living in the area. But it did provide a picture not seen on Harlem River Drive, East River Drive, Riverside Drive, or in Bergen County, New Jersey. Nixon was genuinely interested enough to ask me to drive through Harlem quite frequently.

Sometimes on rides Nixon liked to tell me about activities he used to engage in before his presidential life, before the Secret Service. He talked about trips to the beaches in California, Florida, and the Bahamas with his family and/or his friend Bebe Rebozo. He reminisced about restaurants, movie theatres, athletic events, and other entertainment activities in which he participated. Nixon also spoke of growing up in California and working in his father's small grocery store. He proudly spoke of going early in the morning to the market with his father to select fruit and vegetables to be sold in the store. Nixon prided himself in his ability to select ripe melons, mangoes, and other fruit when he would go to the Fish, Fruit, Fancy in Waldwick, New Jersey.

❖ ❖ ❖

Trips to Cat Cay began to take on a new dimension for me. Nixon knew I belonged to an Italian Club, Fidalians of America in North Haledon, New Jersey, and cooked there regularly. On one of the trips to Cat Cay, before we left Miami, Rebozo commented to Nixon that the restaurant at the club was not as good as it used to be. Nixon suggested to him they should have me cook. I was aware that Rebozo always brought fresh fish, fruit, and vegetables to Cat Cay. I knew they both liked rice and pasta. Without hesitation I told him, "Yes." This was the beginning of a new depth to our relationship in the Bahamas, Key Biscayne, and eventually Montague, Long Island, New York. I would cook a meal on many trips and when Mrs. Nixon was along I would cook more of the meals. She was not always in the mood to go out to public places, often preferring to eat at home.

❖ ❖ ❖

Just back from a July vacation to the Pacific Northwest in July 1986, I drove to Saddle River and picked up Nixon. It was Monday morning, 6 a.m. as we headed south on Route 17 for the Lincoln Tunnel. We had already stopped at the paper shop in Ho-Ho-Kus, picking up *The New York Times* and *The Wall Street Journal.* In the back seat of his Chrysler mini-limo Nixon was scanning the headlines and lead articles on the front page of *The New York Times.*

Before he got engrossed in any article he asked about my trip to the Seattle/Tacoma area. He quizzed me on the weather and the scenery. He knew that Stacy, the kids, and I had driven from my mother's home up on the plateau east of the Puyallup Valley (less than one hour from Seattle) to the Hood Canal southwest of Seattle and then down the coast highway to San Francisco before flying home. For the next ten minutes Nixon and I engaged in a conversation about my vacation. He wanted to know if I drove Interstate 5 or the coastal highway. He said he loved Route 101 down the Oregon coast. He described perfectly the winding coastal road and scenery. Nixon said he had seen the rugged rocks that dotted the coastline many times. He knew the road carried travelers through the hills along the rocky shoreline. I told him we visited the dunes on the Southern Oregon coast where Daved, Ryan, and I had the opportunity to ride in caged dune buggies. He was interested in the ride through the sand dunes. He said he had never heard of that before and asked if everyone enjoyed the dune buggies. I told him it was a lot of fun.

I confirmed the beauty of the scenic drive along the Oregon and Northern California coastline. Nixon alluded to the drive through Redwood National Park, commenting on the huge Sequoia and redwood trees. He told me he had given five Sequoia trees to the Chinese government during the 1972 opening with China.

Nixon continued grilling me on our vacation. "In San Francisco did you see the Giants play?" he asked. I told him we had not but we took a boat to Sausalito where we had lunch. We also drove around the downtown area, up and down the hills. I mentioned Stacy and I drove by MTV's "Real World: San Francisco House" on Lombard Street. My son Daved, who religiously watched the program, wanted to get a picture of the house. We also visited the wharf area, I reported to Nixon. Keeping with my policy of telling on myself, Nixon laughed when I confessed I locked the keys in the rental car with the engine running. At first I tried to tell my family it wasn't my fault. Of course it was and I knew it. Quickly I corrected my denial. As my family headed out to sightsee I waited for a locksmith to open the car before joining them. As the chitchat ended Nixon returned to reading the *Times.*

❖ ❖ ❖

The former president read select paragraphs from several articles and offered his opinion. Before he got to the sports page he surprised me by his announcement that he was going to Moscow soon. Nixon said that the trip was in response to discussions he had with Kissinger, former National Security Advisor Brent Scowcroft, Archer, Daniels, Midland Chairman Dwayne Andreas, and others. He said people were worried that the STRATEGIC ARMS REDUCTION TREATY, START 1 agreement President Reagan had negotiated with President Mikhail Gorbachev was flawed. Nixon said the agreement was not a good deal for either the United States or the Soviet Union. According to him, his friends had encouraged him to visit Moscow to speak with Gorbachev.

Nixon indicated he had recently been in touch with retired Soviet Ambassador to the United States Anatoly Dobrynin. He said that Dobrynin, who now was head of the Communist Party's Secretariat, had agreed to set up the meeting with Gorbachev. Nixon commented that he did not think the meeting date and time would be set before he left for Moscow. President Nixon said that Andreas was taking care of logistical arrangements for the visit to Moscow. He emphasized that the trip was secret and it was important that it be kept that way. He cautioned that at this time no one in the Reagan administration knew of the trip.

According to Nixon, there were logistical problems in getting rooms and cars in Moscow because the 1986 Goodwill Games were being held there at the same time. He said Andreas was having James

Giffen of Mercator Corporation work out the problems for the trip in Moscow.

I suggested to Nixon that it would be better if he had his staff assistant, John Taylor, take care of the rooms and car problems. It would be easier and ensure privacy. It was pointed out that Taylor could go to Washington, D.C., and visit with the Soviet ambassador. He could give him the dates of the private visit to Moscow, provide our passports to the ambassador, and request visas. It was mentioned that if Taylor asked the ambassador for assistance in getting rooms and cars everything would be resolved.

"As a former president of the United States, the Soviet government will put you in one of the Lenin Hills guest houses and assign a KGB security detail with a limousine to you," I told President Nixon.

I could see Nixon was mulling over the suggestion as he picked up *The Wall Street Journal.* By the time Nixon read the editorial page we were entering the underground parking garage at 26 Federal Plaza. Once in his office complex, I went to the small kitchen and made a pot of coffee. Unlike former Chief of Staff Nick Rue, I only used one pouch of coffee to make a regular pot of coffee instead of his "Navy coffee." After it was brewed, I brought a cup of coffee to Nixon. Then I took my cup to my usual security post at my desk near the entrance to the office.

An hour or so later the staff began arriving. When Taylor arrived he began telling me about the trip to Moscow. He asked if the "Boss" had mentioned it to me. I reported to him briefly of my conversation with the former president about solving the rooms/car problem.

Shortly after the routine morning staff meeting between Nixon and Taylor began, I was invited to join the two of them. Sitting down, President Nixon asked me to explain to Taylor how we could solve the problems of cars and rooms in Moscow. Turning my attention to Taylor, I repeated my earlier suggestion made to Nixon concerning the Soviet ambassador in Washington, D.C. Taylor was advised that security, cars, and living quarters could all be resolved during the meeting. At the end of the Moscow portion of the meeting Nixon announced to Taylor he should go to Washington. I returned to my post at the office entrance.

Later when the staff meeting was finally over, Taylor approached my desk. He advised that President Nixon had suggested to him that I should go to Washington instead of him to coordinate the Moscow visit. We talked for a couple of minutes and I asked that the office schedule a meeting for me the next afternoon with the Soviet ambassador.

When Taylor retired to his office, I made a call to Secret Service Protective Operations telling them of the secret trip to Moscow. A request was made for a meeting with their Foreign Intelligence Branch. The Secret Service understood the confidentially of the trip and agreed not to release any information about it. It was also specifically agreed that the State Department would not be advised.

❖ ❖ ❖

On Tuesday, dressed in my best three-piece suit, I flew into Washington National Airport. During the flight to the nation's capital I developed my plan to keep the trip secret. Taking a taxi to Lafayette Square across the street from the White House, I got out, headed across the park, and up fifteenth Street N.W. The Soviet Embassy was on my right. I knew the FBI, who had the responsibility of monitoring people coming and going from the Soviet Embassy, would be interested in identifying me. It was well-known to me that the FBI was under fire. They had been under a microscope since the Walker spy case. U.S. Naval Warrant Officer John Anthony Walker had walked right in the front door of the Soviet Embassy one day. He soon began selling them top-secret encryption codes. It was almost twenty years before he was caught; in the meantime he not only gave them access codes but he put together a spy ring that included his son. I knew it was essential for them to identify all guests and visitors to the embassy.

Armed with a tan folder containing our passports and a copy of our schedule in one hand and a cream-colored folder with my working papers in the other, I approached the entrance to the Soviet Embassy. Nearing the entry gate I could see a uniformed Secret Service officer standing close to the entrance. Somewhere nearby I knew there would be a team of FBI agents filming and monitoring my activities.

Walking past the Secret Service officer, I proceeded to the corner of the embassy property, where I suspiciously loitered for a few moments. As the uniform officer strolled away from the gate area I quickly walked to the gate and entered. Hustling up the steps to the front door I rang the bell. Shortly, it opened. Announcing my name to the greeter and advising that I was there to meet with the ambassador got me inside. In an ornate sitting room that reminded me of my Kissinger visits to Moscow I awaited the ambassador. When he arrived we exchanged greetings. He mentioned that Ambassador Dobrynin had retired and he was the second secretary. Without disclosing the purpose of the trip I advised the secretary that President Nixon would be traveling to Moscow for a short private visit. He was given the tan folder with our passports and a copy of our arrival and departure dates.

I then raised the subject of hotel rooms and a proper car for Nixon, mentioning that I knew everything was tight due to the fact that the Goodwill Games would be going on during our visit. He announced that President Nixon would stay at one of the Lenin Hills guest houses overlooking Moscow. He also advised that a KGB security detail would meet Nixon upon his arrival at the airport. The ambassador remarked that the KGB detail would provide a security car and Chyka limousine for travel out of the compound. Lastly, I was told our passports and visas would be ready for pickup on Thursday. With all issues on the table I departed with just the white folder under my arm.

Sauntering down Fifteenth Street to the Sheraton Hotel on the corner of Fifteenth and K Street, I was well aware that the FBI would be doing their best to find out who it was that had just left a tan folder in the Soviet Embassy. Needing to call the Secret Service, I entered the Sheraton. As I walked through the hotel lobby to the rear area where the telephones were located, I encountered a construction project. The area was partially closed to the general public. I was able to make my way around the workers and material, and arrived at the small bank of phones in the rear of the lobby. These phones were often used by Secret Service agents during protective assignments in the hotel. After confirming my Secret Service appointment I hung up the phone.

Quickly turning to leave, I noticed a female tourist in shorts listening to a walkman. She was loitering in the congested work area, not seeming to be interested in using a phone. Acting oblivious to her I exited the hotel and headed south back across Lafayette Square toward Pennsylvania Avenue. Going west on Pennsylvania Avenue, I casually walked toward Blair House. My mind was working overtime. I knew I needed to ditch my tail. Walking past the Renwick Art Gallery, I slowed down as I approached the corner of Seventeenth Street N.W. Casually turning to look at the Old Executive Office Building across the street, I was able to sneak a peek behind me. The female I had observed at the Sheraton had been joined by a casually dressed black male, also with a walkman on his head. They caught my attention as they both jumped behind the stairs at the Renwick Art Gallery to hide.

Instinctively I changed my plan. Instead of heading directly to Secret Service headquarters, I crossed Eighteenth Street N.W.

I continued on Pennsylvania for two more blocks then crossed to the other side of the street. Now heading back toward Secret Service headquarters, I had stretched my lead over the FBI team to over a half a block distance.

Turning right on Nineteenth Street, I quickly picked up my pace again. Going one block I turned left on G Street and dashed into Secret Service headquarters before my tail could see me. Rushing into the building I lingered out of sight in the back of the lobby waiting for the surveillance team to walk by the building. In less than a minute I was not disappointed. Across the street, with headphones in place, the FBI couple walked past my location. Clearly they were searching for their prey. They were talking to each other and pointing as I entered the elevator. After the briefing by the Foreign Intelligence Branch, I met with Steve Garmon of the Office of Protective Operations. Garmon and I had been on the White House Detail together from 1969-1971. After bringing him up to date on the Moscow trip, he offered to give me a ride to Washington National Airport.

As the car exited the basement parking garage I noticed there were several other people who had joined the original surveillance team. They were obviously trying to find their lost suspect. Smiling, I enjoyed the fifteen-minute ride to the airport knowing the return trip to the Soviet Embassy on Thursday would generate even more interest.

Returning on Thursday and using the same routine, I left the Soviet Embassy with our passports and visas. Walking across Lafayette Square this time I headed east on Pennsylvania Avenue past the Treasury Department. Walking to the nearby metro station, I got on the last subway car heading for Washington National Airport. Sitting in the last car I could observe everyone getting on my car and the next one. At the Arlington Cemetery stop, just before the metro train doors closed to leave the station, I rushed out the exit looking for anyone tailing me. After a short walk in the cemetery I boarded the next train. At the Pentagon stop I repeated my quick exit and short walk. When I arrived at Washington National Airport, if a tail were still with me, they deserved to find out who I was.

Back in Saddle River I called British Airways to prepare for our Super Sonic Transport (SST) flight out of JFK and our overnight stay in London. I spoke with the British Airways passenger representative supervisor explaining that Nixon, Taylor, and I were making a private visit. I mentioned I would not be carrying a weapon and requested his assistance in getting us three rooms at Heathrow Airport. He agreed to make the reservations at an airport hotel for us in their name. He also agreed to provide the three of us with transportation on our arrival at the airport to the hotel.

Taylor took a taxi ahead of us with our luggage to British Airways at JFK Airport. Nixon and I had stopped by the office in New York City so he could finish up a couple of things. When he was ready to depart for the airport Nixon came out of his office with briefcase in hand and paused. Looking at me he said, "Mike, I can't go without telling President Reagan." With that statement he set his briefcase on the floor and turned, going back into his office. Five minutes later he came out of the office, picked up his briefcase, and said, "Ok, we can go now."

In the car Nixon told me he had spoken with Reagan, advising him that he was making a trip to Moscow. He seemed relieved that he had talked with President Reagan. Nixon was unusually quiet as we drove through traffic to meet our prearranged police escort at the Port Authority Building at JFK. I sensed he was preoccupied with the importance of our trip. On our arrival Nixon got out of the limousine, and the waiting uniformed officer asked, "Would you like to ride in my car?"

Nixon responded, "Yes, but I want to go inside first to meet the staff."

Nixon entered the office area unannounced. It was clear he caught everyone there by surprise. He slowly began greeting everyone and thanking them for assisting on his departures and arrivals over the last six years. Nixon had pictures taken with some of the patrolmen, the administrative staff, and a few of the senior officers who handled our support requests. Nixon also signed autographs before returning to the waiting police car outside.

Approaching the car, Nixon suggested I get into the back seat and that he was going to sit in front. With red lights flashing we made the three-minute drive to our waiting commercial flight. Nixon was met at the outside stairs to our aircraft by the British Airways passenger representative. Just like at the Port Authority Building, Nixon took time to thank him and the others on the ramp for their assistance and support. There was a round of photographs and autographs for everyone in the area. With the greetings over we walked up the steps and boarded the Super Sonic aircraft. One of the stewards led us down the narrow aisle to our seats. Nixon and I could stand straight in the aisle with our heads almost touching the ceiling. The plane had two compartments with a total of twenty-five rows of two seats on each side accommodating one hundred passengers in all.

Taylor was seated across the aisle from Nixon and me. In ten minutes we were buckled up and headed down the runway. As we took off I was thinking about Heathrow and Moscow. It was so important to me that we get into Moscow without the press knowing.